THE POLITICOS GUIDE TO
THE NEW HOUSE OF COMMONS
2017

THE
POLITICOS GUIDE
TO THE NEW
HOUSE OF COMMONS
2017

PROFILES OF THE NEW MPS
AND ANALYSIS OF THE 2017
GENERAL ELECTION RESULTS

EDITED BY
TIM CARR, IAIN DALE
& ROBERT WALLER

Biteback Publishing

First published in Great Britain in 2017 by
Biteback Publishing Ltd
Westminster Tower
3 Albert Embankment
London SE1 7SP
Copyright © Tim Carr, Iain Dale and Robert Waller 2017

ISBN 978-1-78590-275-8

A CIP catalogue record for this book is available from the British Library.

Set in Minion Pro

Contents

Index of new MPs

Introduction

Tim Carr

When Theresa May emerged onto Downing Street on the morning of Tuesday 18 April to announce a 'snap' general election, the country either gasped or groaned. No one, however, doubted what the result would be. It couldn't possibly be anything but a thumping Conservative victory. ComRes gave Theresa May a seemingly unassailable 25-point lead and 50 per cent of support. Ipsos MORI suggested that she was the most popular Prime Minister since polling began, surpassing even Margaret Thatcher and Tony Blair at their peak of popularity. Labour and Jeremy Corbyn's personal ratings languished far back. History suggested that no opposition had ever returned from such a deficit with only weeks to go. It was game-over well before half-time.

Except that by the early hours of the 9 June, the British electorate had, once again, rewritten the script. The early lofty predictions of a three-digit Conservative landslide had already evaporated, and now their anticipated authoritative Commons majority had dissipated as well. A historically high vote of 42 per cent counted for little with Labour at their shoulder with 40 per cent – an astonishing result given their position just weeks earlier. The 2017 election illustrated loud and clear that vote share matters less than seats in the UK's first past the post system. The Tories had achieved their largest vote gain since Thatcher in 1979, but this was cancelled out by Labour achieving its largest vote gain since Attlee in 1956.

Like her predecessor in the 2016 referendum vote, Theresa May had gambled and lost in a political miscalculation of historic proportions. The

Conservatives' small, but workable, majority had gone. Their record of having only had two years as a majority government in the twenty years since 1997 was not to be extended. After a campaign widely condemned as inept and disconnected, among the milder criticisms, May's personal reputation and authority were shredded. The British people may take a plucky loser to heart, but conversely, they dislike a seemingly arrogant loser who had it all but threw their advantage away. She would now be reliant upon the ten-strong band of Ulster Unionists to retain power, and only able to do so at all courtesy of a Ruth Davidson-led Tory revival in Scotland. In power, but without authority.

Although soundly beaten where it matters, Jeremy Corbyn had outperformed all expectations, winning over his Labour detractors and attracting plaudits for conducting an energetic and confident campaign. And so the narrative of the glorious defeat of 2017 was born. With renewed rigour and optimism among its now massive activist base, the battle cry is now 'one more heave'.

The Conservatives thought they could rely upon two givens: the electoral liability of Jeremy Corbyn and what Stephen Bush of the *New Statesman* called the 'purple firewall': UKIP voters returning to the Conservative fold post-referendum. In the end, they were wrong about Corbyn, who turned out to be a forceful electoral asset, but largely correct about the firewall, with only one in five purple voters turning to red, rather than blue. To continue the colour theme, what perhaps had not been expected was that the reds would hoover up the Remain vote from the blues, the yellows of the Liberal Democrats and the greens.

Away from the main contest, serious fissures appeared in the SNP's grip of Scotland, with unionist parties fighting back and swathes of Scotland rejecting a second independence referendum. With suggestions that 'peak SNP' has now passed, this view was symbolised by the defeat of the godfather of the SNP, Alex Salmond. The Liberal Democrats advanced, but not by much, losing their former cheerleader and Deputy Prime Minister, Nick Clegg, at the ballot box and their leader, Tim Farron, shortly afterwards, having failed to attract the centre ground and Remainers with their stall of a second EU referendum. The Tory Welsh assault failed to materialise and Plaid Cymru made a solitary gain. UKIP imploded, failing to finish second in a single seat. Its leader Paul Nuttall, the fourth in the last two years, swiftly exited. The Greens built their stronghold walls even higher around Brighton Pavilion and went backwards everywhere else.

Much of the conventional political wisdom surrounding general elections was ripped up and a new rule book needs to be written. Election campaigns do matter. The two-party system is alive and kicking. Class is no longer the defining feature of party affiliation. An election could be won from the left. Some policies really matter in campaigns. Scots can still vote for the Tories. Campaigning by slogan has serious limitations. The young do vote and the middle classes do revolt. There has been a demise in the influence of the MSM and an increase in the importance of the new online media. And on it goes.

The 2017 campaign had some highs and saw many lows. It plunged to the darkest depths with the Manchester and London Borough Market terrorist attacks, and then within days of polling day, the horror and shame of Grenfell Tower and a further terror attack in London.

For good or ill, the 2017 campaign will linger long in our memories. Strong and Stable. Weak and wobbly. Nothing has changed. Progressive alliance. Forward, together. For the many, not the few. Stronger for Scotland. Defending Wales. Coalition of chaos. Standing up for Britain. In the national interest. The Maybot versus Monsieur Zen. The 'most boring campaign ever' (!). Glumbucket and mugwump. Theresa May not finding anyone home. No magic money tree. An earlier than usual weekend wobble. That poor cameraman's foot. Bloody difficult woman. Diane Abbott's counting and her afro thirty-four years ago. Twitter abuse. Jeremy Corbyn holding a speaker aloft at a rally. David Davis and Philip Hammond not checking the 'Hell for your family' poster behind them. Paul Nuttall calling every woman Natalie. Smell my spaniel. The alt-left media. Ed Miliband mowing a voter's lawn. Ed Miliband calling bingo numbers. Boy jobs and girl jobs. Labour's manifesto leak. Campaigning in near deserted aircraft hangars. The 'threats' from Brussels. Oh, Jeremy Corbyn. A sudden enthusiasm for eating bags of chips. Serial U-turner Sir Nicholas Soames campaigning on horseback. Ransomware cyberattack on the NHS. Facebook ads. Jeremy Corbyn's iPad. Theresa May's no-show. George Osborne's glee. The dementia tax and lunch pincher. Running through wheat fields. Conservative MP Greg Knight's campaign video. The Lib Dem's disco manifesto launch. Project Fear, again. That YouGov prediction. The Lib Dem hovercraft. Big girl's blouse and don't be a pillock. (With thanks and apologies to Matt Chorley of *The Times*.)

We should have known that in uncertain times, nothing is certain. The surprises, for most, of a Conservative majority in 2015, the Brexit vote and the election of Trump and Macron, should have taught us to anticipate future shocks. Will we all learn from recent history? Probably not. The Tories could yet recover and unite around a competent leader. The next election will probably not be the breeze for Labour that some predict, as it juggles with its predicament of Northern Leavers and metropolitan Remainers. Sir Vince Cable might yet turn around the fortunes of his party. The future shape of Brexit is now less certain and voters are divided and volatile. If we can make one prediction, it is that for those of us interested in politics, the future will not be dull.

With so many profound changes afoot in British politics right now, we fully acknowledge that this book, produced so shortly after the election, barely scratches the surface of what happened in 2017 and what might happen in the future. There is a focus on the eighty-seven first-time elected and twelve returning MPs and the characteristics of the new Parliament. Expectations and predictions were again central themes of the 2017 general election and so we are very grateful that Joe Twyman of YouGov, an organisation that played a significant role in the election itself, has contributed his account of the campaign and what it means for polling in the future. With the intriguing ebb and flow of political fortunes across the country, election expert Robert Waller has provided his detailed analysis of regional voting patterns and characteristics of the new Parliament. Theo Usherwood, political editor at LBC, takes a critical look at the party's media campaigns and shares some of his direct experiences. One of Scotland's leading journalists, David Torrance, has cast his experienced eye over the changing political landscape in Scotland. We are indebted to them all for their insightful contributions. We are particularly grateful for the support of Octopus Group for generously sponsoring this book.

At the start of the 2017 campaign, Brenda from Bristol now famously said: 'There's too much politics going on at the moment.' She might have a point. Since 2015, we have had the EU referendum; Scottish, Welsh and Northern Irish devolved government elections; two sets of local government elections; mayoral elections; police and crime commissioner elections; ten parliamentary by-elections; Article 50; two Prime Ministers; two Labour leadership contests and now a general election.

However, for those of us who are fascinated, impassioned, amused and frequently baffled by politics, we are probably already thinking ahead to the next time we have to do it all over again.

The 2017 general election results

- The 2017 general election on 8 June 2017 resulted in no political party winning an overall majority of seats, with the Conservatives winning 318 seats (including the Speaker), falling just short of an absolute majority of 326.

- To retain power and command a majority in the House of Commons for key votes, it was necessary for the Conservatives to agree a 'supply and confidence' agreement with the ten MPs of the Democratic Unionist Party (DUP). A deal was signed on 26 June 2017 over two weeks after the election.

- Excluding the Speaker and three deputies (one Conservative and two Labour) who by convention do not vote, and Sinn Féin's seven MPs who do not sit in Parliament because they oppose the British government's jurisdiction in Northern Ireland, there are 639 active MPs. Excluding the Speaker and the one Conservative deputy Speaker, the Conservatives have 316 active MPs. With the DUP's ten MPs, the Conservatives will broadly have the support of 326 MPs.

- Labour won 262 seats and might generally rely on support from fifty-three other MPs (thirty-five SNP, twelve Lib Dem, four Plaid Cymru, one Green and one Independent), but have two non-voting deputy Speakers, leaving the combined opposition with 313. As a result, the Conservatives have a working majority of thirteen votes.

- The UK Independence Party's leader Paul Nuttall resigned the day after polling day and the Liberal Democrat's Tim Farron resigned a week later on 14 June 2017. Sir Vince Cable was appointed the new Liberal Democrat leader on 20 July 2017.

- Theresa May (60), Jeremy Corbyn (68) and Sir Vince Cable (74) are the oldest party leaders of the UK's three main political parties since April 1955 when Winston Churchill (80), Clement Attlee (72) and Clement Davies (71) were in charge.

- The Scottish National Party (SNP) retained their position as the third-largest party in the House of Commons with thirty-five seats, having lost twenty-one seats.

- Overall, the Conservatives gained thirteen seats, Labour gained thirty seats, the SNP lost twenty-one seats, the Lib Dems gained four, the DUP gained two, Sinn Féin gained three and Plaid Cymru gained one. The one Green MP (Caroline Lucas) retained her seat, as did the one Independent (Lady Sylvia Hermon). In total, sixty-nine seats changed hands.

Seats won and lost

	GE2017 SEATS WON	GE2015 SEATS WON	SEAT GAINS	SEATS LOSSES	SEAT CHANGE (NET)
Conservative	317*	330	+20	-33	-13
Labour	262	232	+36	-6	+30
SNP	35	56	0	-21	-21
Lib Dem	12	8	+8	-4	+4
DUP	10	8	+2	0	+2
Sinn Féin	7	4	+3	0	+3
Plaid Cymru	4	3	+1	0	+1
Green	1	1	0	0	No change
Independent (NI)	1	1	0	0	No change
Speaker	1	1	n/a	n/a	n/a

* Not including the Speaker

- The Conservatives won 49% of seats in 2017, down from 51% in 2015; Labour won 40% of seats, up from 36% in 2015.

- Among the MPs to lose their seats are: former party leader and Deputy Prime Minister, Liberal Democrat Nick Clegg; former SNP First Minister Alex Salmond and Westminster SNP Leader Angus Robertson; Conservative Ministers Nicola Blackwood, Jane Ellison and Ben Gummer; and Labour veterans Sir Alan Meale and David Winnick.

- Despite suffering a net loss of thirteen seats, the Conservatives won their largest vote gain since Margaret Thatcher in 1979, but at the same time Labour achieved their largest vote gain since Attlee in 1956.

- Based solely on those seats where the lowest number of voters needed to change their vote from 2015 to win the seat, Labour won twenty of its top fifty target seats, including thirteen of its top twenty target seats, and a further sixteen seats outside its top fifty targets.

- The Conservatives won three of their top twenty target seats and eight in their top fifty. There were nine seats with Labour majorities of less than 1,000 that the Conservatives failed to win, including the City of Chester (ninety-three majority in 2015) and Ealing Central & Acton (274 in 2015).

- There are now more 'super-marginals' than in the previous two general elections. After 2017, there are now fifty-two constituencies with a percentage majority of 2% or under. By way of comparison, there were thirty-eight after the 2010 general election and only twenty-nine constituencies with a 2% or under majority in 2015.

- By number of votes, there were forty-one majorities of less than 1,000 in votes in 2010, thirty-two in 2015 and there are now fifty-one in 2017.

- After the 2015 general election, the Conservatives had fourteen seats with less than a 1,000 vote majority/less than 1.8% majority). The number of Conservative-held 'super marginals' has increased only slightly – seventeen seats under 1,000 votes or fifteen seats under 1.8% majority.

- After the 2015 general election, Labour had only eleven seats with less than a 1,000 vote majority (2% and under majority). There are now nineteen Labour-held 'super marginals' with less than 1,000 votes or 2% majority.

- Nine of the SNP's thirty-five seats now have a majority of less than 1,000 votes or 1.6%. It would only require a uniform swing of 0.5% to a unionist-supporting party for the SNP to no longer hold the majority of Scottish seats, although its position as the party with the largest number of seats looks secure without a dramatic loss of support.

- Excluding Richmond Park (a by-election seat), fifteen out of the twenty largest majorities to be overturned all previously belonged to the SNP. The largest majority to be overturned was the SNP's Banff & Buchan (14,339 in 2015) gained by the Conservatives.

- In England, the largest overturned majorities were Canterbury (9,798 in 2015), Oxford West and Abingdon (9,582), Battersea (7,938) and Kensington (7,361).

- There were several Labour targets with a Conservative majority under 1,000 which did not change (Morley & Outwood, Thurrock, Telford and Bolton West).

Seat changes by region

REGION	SEAT CHANGES BY REGION	SEATS PER REGION/COUNTRY	SEAT CHANGES BY REGION
Scotland	21	59	35.6%
London	6	73	8.2%
South East	6	84	7.1%
East Midlands	5	45	11.1%
North West	5*	75	6.7%
Northern Ireland	5	18	27.8%
East of England	4	58	6.9%
South West	4	55	7.3%
Wales	4	40	10.0%
Yorkshire and The Humber	4	54	7.4%
West Midlands	3	60	5.0%
North East	2	29	6.7%

* Not including Copeland (a by-election seat held by the Conservatives at dissolution and won again)

- Numerically and as a percentage of the region (country), Scotland had the highest number of seat changes at twenty-one constituencies, comprising 35.6% of all constituencies. Northern Ireland was not too far behind with five out of eighteen seats changing hands (nearly 28%). The remaining seat changes were numerically fairly evenly spread among all other English regions and Wales, ranging from 11% of East Midlands and 10% of Welsh seats changing hands to only 5% of West Midlands seats.

Votes and votes share

	VOTES 2017	VOTE SHARE 2017	PPCS 2017	VOTES 2015	VOTE SHARE 2015	PPCS 2015	VOTES +/-	VOTE SHARE +/-%	PPCS +/-
Conservative*	13,670,989	42.4%	639	11,334,920	36.9%	647	+2,336,069	5.5%	-8
Labour	12,877,869	40.0%	631	9,347,326	30.4%	631	+3,530,543	9.6%	0
Lib Dems	2,371,861	7.4%	629	2,415,888	7.9%	631	-44,027	-0.5%	-2
SNP	977,568	3.0%	59	1,454,436	4.7%	59	-476,868	-1.7%	0
UKIP	594,068	1.8%	378	3,881,129	12.6%	624	-3,287,061	-10.8%	-246
Green	525,665	1.6%	467	1,157,613	3.8%	573	-631,948	-2.2%	-106
DUP	292,316	0.9%	17	184,260	0.6%	16	-108,056	0.3%	1
Sinn Féin	238,915	0.7%	18	176,232	0.6%	18	-62,683	0.1%	0
Plaid Cymru	164,466	0.5%	40	181,694	0.6%	40	-17,228	-0.1%	0
SDLP	95,419	0.3%	18	99,809	0.3%	18	-4,390	0.0%	0
UUP	83,280	0.3%	14	114,935	0.4%	15	-31,655	-0.1%	-1
Alliance	64,553	0.2%	18	61,556	0.2%	18	+2,997	0.0%	0
Ind (NI)	16,148	<0.1%	1	17,689	<0.1%	1	-1,541	0.0%	0
Other parties	95,701	0.3%	189	270,723	0.9%	680	-23,551	-0.1%	-304
Other Independents	151,471	0.5%	187						
	32,204,141	100%	3,304	30,698,210	100%	3,971	n/a	n/a	

PPC: Prospective Parliamentary Candidates

SNP: Scottish National Party

DUP: Democratic Unionist Party

SDLP: Social Democratic & Labour Party

UUP: Ulster Unionist Party

* Including the Speaker

- Turnout in 2017 was 68.8%, up 2.6% from 66.2% in 2015 and the highest since 1997 (2017 – 68.8%, 2015 – 66.2%, 2010 – 65.1%, 2005 – 61.4%, 2001 – 59.4%, 1997 – 71.4%, 1992 – 77.7%).

- The South West had the highest turnout (71.8%), with Northern Ireland having the lowest (65.4%). Turnout increased everywhere throughout the UK, apart from in Scotland where it fell by 4.6%.

- At 42.4% of the vote, the Conservative vote share is higher than the 36.9% achieved in 2015 and the 41.9% in 1992, both victories with small majorities.

- The national swing to Labour of 2% was lower than the swing achieved in 1945, 1964, 1966, October 1974, 1992 and 1997. London, the South East and the South West produced above average swings to Labour, but there were lower swings in the North East, East Midlands, West Midlands and Yorkshire & the Humber, Labour's traditional heartlands.

- The Conservatives increased their vote by 2.3 million to just under 13.7 million, but Labour increased its vote by 3.5 million to 12.9 million. The SNP lost just under half a million: a third of its votes from 2015. UKIP were the biggest losers falling from 3.9 million votes in 2015 to just under 600,000 in 2017.

- Gaining four seats (a 50% increase) on 7.4% of the vote, the Liberal Democrats achieved the seats gains despite falling slightly from its vote share of 7.9% in 2015.

- UKIP's vote crashed from 3.9 million votes in 2015 to 594,068 in 2017 (3.04%), failing to win a seat or to come second anywhere. Having come 2nd in 120 constituencies in 2015, UKIP could only manage coming third place in 134 constituencies. They did, however, only field 378 candidates, down from 624 in 2015.

- In 2015, the Liberal Democrats lost 341 deposits (as a result of securing less than 5% of the votes in a constituency); in 2017 they lost 375 deposits. Neither the Conservatives or Labour lost a deposit in 2017.

- Plaid Cymru took the solitary seat of Ceredigion from the Liberal Democrats, but won fewer votes and a lower vote share than it did in 2015.

- The Green Party's share halved from 3.8% to 1.6%. The Brighton Pavilion stronghold of Caroline Lucas remains the Greens' only realistic prospect (majority 14,689 with 52.3% share of the vote). Their next best performance was in the Isle of Wight where they secured only 17.3% of the vote and finished third.

- The two-party Conservative and Labour vote share (82.4%) was the highest since 1970. Only two years ago, their combined vote share was 67.3%.

- The Conservative Party had its highest share of the vote in the East of England (54.6%).

- Labour had its highest share of the vote in the North East (55.4%), marginally ahead of London (54.5%).

- In 2015 only two constituencies had a majority of over 30,000 votes. After the 2017 general election, there are twenty-five. Similarly, in 2015 only eight of the twenty seats with the highest majorities by votes were Labour. In 2017 the top twenty largest majorities are all Labour.

- Labour increased the size of the majority in every seat it won, with spectacularly large increases in previously safe seats. It would clearly have benefited electorally if it had been able to spread its increase in votes across more constituencies.

- To emphasise the concentration of Labour votes, Labour won a total of thirty-seven seats with a higher vote share than the Conservative's highest vote share seat of South Holland & the Deepings (a respectable 69.9%).

- The far-right British National Party (BNP) won 564,321 votes in 2010. This fell to 1,667 votes in 2015 but rose to 4,580 votes in 2017.

- None of the top twenty seats with the lowest winning share of votes are in England and apart from Ceredigion (Wales) and Belfast South (Northern Ireland), the remainder are all in Scotland, which has a number of possible three-way seats.

- Despite having made progress in Scotland, twelve out of twenty of the Conservatives' lowest vote shares were in Scotland, with four in England and four in Wales. Twelve out of twenty of Labour's lowest vote shares are in England, with eight in Scotland.

- Labour achieved many of its biggest increases in vote share along the south coast of England (six seats) and the South West (six seats).

- Labour only lost vote share in nineteen seats (out of 632, excluding Northern Ireland). Thirteen of the falls – and the seven biggest – were in Scotland.

- The Conservatives increased vote share in Scotland at the expense of the SNP and in seats in Northern England benefiting from a collapse in the UKIP vote or the absence of a UKIP candidate.

- Eighteen (out of twenty) of the largest falls in the Conservative share of the vote, whether they won or came second, were in London.

- The SNP lost vote share in every constituency in Scotland, but such were the winning margins in 2015 that they retained many seats even after losing 16–18% in share of the vote.

- One of the characteristics of the 2017 general election was a reduction in the number of political parties returning an MP to Westminster – a fall from eleven in 2015 to eight (the SDLP, UUP and UKIP failing to win a seat). The low incidence of independents or small parties winning seats in UK elections continued, with only one independent (Lady Sylvia Hermon in North Down) being returned. Only two other independents – Claire Wright in East Devon and Louise Irvine of National Health Action in Health Secretary Jeremy Hunt's South West Surrey seat – polled highly, both finishing second.

- In 2015, seven of the ten highest turnouts were in Scotland, coming only one year after the Scottish independence referendum and at the peak of support for the SNP. In 2017 only one Scottish seat, East Dunbartonshire, features in the top twenty turnouts and it is also the only one in which turnout fell. Across Scotland as a whole, the turnout fell in forty-eight (out of fifty-nine) seats, nationally falling from 71% in 2015 to 66.4% in 2017 – the only region or country in the UK to do so.

- Nineteen of the twenty constituencies with the highest turnout are estimated to have voted for Remain at the EU referendum; ten of them voted over 60% Remain.

- At 65.4%, Northern Ireland may still have had the lowest turnout as a country/region in the UK, but it also rose 6.3%, the highest increase of anywhere. Four out of ten of the lowest turnouts in 2015 were in Northern Ireland, but none featured in 2017.

- Fourteen of the twenty seats with the lowest turnout in 2017 voted to Leave in 2016.

Parliament

- There are 182 newly elected Members of the House of Commons, 28% of the Chamber. When combined with the 232 new MPs in 2010, it means that 414 MPs (63.5%) have been MPs for only five years or less.

- There are now 208 women MPs among the 650 MPs in the House of Commons. At 32% of all MPs, this is the highest ever number of women MPs to have sat in a single Parliament. After the 2015 election, the House of Commons had 191 women or 29% of all MPs. There were 143 in 2010, 128 in 2005, 118 in 2001, 120 in 1997 and only sixty in 1992. Of the ninety-nine new MPs elected who were not sitting at dissolution, thirty-six are women.

- A record number of fifty-two BME MPs (8%) were elected to the House of Commons in 2017, compared to forty-one in the 2015 parliament. Out of the forty-one BME MPs who stood for re-election, forty were returned to Westminster.

- The new record number of forty-five LGBTQ MPs now sit in Parliament, representing 7% of the new House of Commons.

- Early research would suggest that the proportion of MPs in favour of Remain at the time of the EU referendum has increased marginally to 73% versus 23% Leave.

- Only thirty-two MPs stood down in 2017: fifteen Labour (including one deselected), twelve Conservatives, one UKIP (as elected), one Liberal Democrat, one Sinn Féin plus two SNP MPs were deselected.

Undoubtedly because of the proximity of the last election in 2015, this is a much smaller number than usual; normally around ninety MPs stand down at each election.

- Thirty-eight Labour and Co-operative MPs were returned to Parliament – the largest parliamentary group in the party's 100-year history.

Thirty memorable quotes of the 2017 general election

'You're joking. Not another one! Oh for God's sake.'
Brenda from Bristol, reacting to the announcement of the snap election.

'He may be a mutton-headed old mugwump, but he is probably harmless.'
Boris Johnson comments on Jeremy Corbyn.

'Boris Johnson is a caggie-handed, cheese-headed fopdoodle with a talent for slummocking about, who would do less damage to Britain's reputation in the world if Theresa May sacked him as Foreign Secretary and replaced him with a souvenir paperweight.'
Tom Watson fires back at Boris Johnson after the 'mugwump' comment.

'That is bollocks.'
Emily Thornberry tells Michael Fallon what she thinks about Tory comments on foreign policy.

'I'm not Natalie, I'm Leanne.'
Plaid Cymru's Leanne Wood corrects UKIP's Paul Nuttall after he misnames her twice during the ITV leaders' debate.

'Nothing has changed, nothing has changed.'
After a U-turn on social care, Theresa May tries to reassure the electorate.

'I don't mean to be rude but you seem to be a bit of a glumbucket.'

Theresa May is criticised on the campaign trail by Daily Mail *political sketch-writer Quentin Letts.*

'I'll give you the figure in a moment ... It will cost ... it will obviously cost a lot to do so, we accept that ... Can I give you the exact figure in a moment?'

Jeremy Corbyn MP can't remember how much Labour's plan for free childcare is going to cost, during an interview on BBC Radio 4's Woman's Hour.

'During the Conservative Party leadership campaign I was described by one of my colleagues as a "bloody difficult woman" – and I said at the time the next person to find that out will be Jean-Claude Juncker.'

Theresa May asserts herself after a German newspaper reports Mr Juncker describing her as 'deluded' and saying that it was 'more likely than not' that Brexit talks would fail.

'If I was sitting in Brussels and I was looking at you as the person I had to negotiate with, I'd be thinking, "She's a blowhard who collapses at the first sign of gunfire." Isn't that right?'

Jeremy Paxman interrogates Theresa May – provoking shock and applause from the audience.

'Last night showed that Jeremy Corbyn's minders can put him in a smart blue suit for an interview with Jeremy Paxman, but with his position on Brexit he will find himself alone and naked in the negotiating chamber of the EU.'

Theresa May has a go at Jeremy Corbyn over his position on Brexit.

'I never do abuse, I never get angry, I'm Monsieur Zen on these matters – but it does make me slightly irritated when I get lectures about the Lib Dems.'

Jeremy Corbyn, Monsieur Zen.

'I had an afro. It was thirty-four years ago. The hairstyle has gone and some of the views have gone. We have all moved on.'

Diane Abbott MP on changing views.

'Look, there's nothing in there because we're not going to do it.'

Jeremy Corbyn MP explains that abolishing the monarchy is not on his agenda.

'There isn't a magic money tree.'

On BBC Question Time, *Theresa May responds to a nurse who says she hasn't had a pay rise in eight years.*

'With all due respect, Emily is not the shadow Defence Secretary. I am.'
Shadow Defence Secretary Nia Griffiths MP dismisses shadow Foreign Secretary Emily Thornberry's comments on Trident.

'Loads of my mates voted Leave and I don't think they're racist.'
Tim Farron MP gets into a heated discussion with a Leave voter, who accuses him of dismissing Leave voters as racist.

'I have to confess, when me and my friends sort of used to run through the fields of wheat, the farmers weren't too pleased about that.'
Theresa May reveals her naughty side during an interview with ITV News.

'Running through fields of wheat is now officially the second worst thing Theresa May ever did.'
Sam Coates of The Times on Twitter.

'Jeremy Corbyn would have surrendered the Falklands to Australia!'
Paul Nuttall.

'UKIP is finished. But at least Paul Nuttall can go back to his day job as Poet Laureate.'
Sue Perkins takes a dig at Paul Nuttall on Twitter.

'The giant sucking sound that you can hear is the SNP tide receding the length and breadth of Scotland.'
Douglas Alexander MP has some choice words about the performance of the SNP.

'You've not seen the last of my bonnet and me.'
Alex Salmond quotes a Jacobite song in his concession speech after losing his Gordon seat to the Tories.

'I, of course, have encountered this evening something that many people have encountered before tonight, and I suspect many people will encounter after tonight, which is in politics you live by the sword and you die by the sword.'
Nick Clegg, after losing his Sheffield Hallam seat to the Labour Party.

'It was a Rolls-Royce at the beginning and a clapped-out Robin Reliant at the end.'

Tory MP Nigel Evans sums up the Conservative election campaign.

'If the exit poll is even remotely in the right territory, it's a political earthquake.'

Robert Peston, ITV News political editor, comments on the exit poll.

'I think Theresa May has won own goal of the season.'

Gary Lineker on Twitter.

'She said she was "strong and stable". The public saw that she was weak and wobbly.'

Tom Watson MP comments on Theresa May's familiar refrain.

'Theresa May is a dead woman walking.'

George Osborne holds nothing back on The Andrew Marr Show.

'Good evening. I know nothing. We, the media, the pundits, know nothing.'

Jon Snow sums up how wrong journalists and pundits were in their predictions about the election.

Scotland

David Torrance

Two years ago, Conservative Party posters depicted Alex Salmond and Nicola Sturgeon with Ed Miliband in their top pockets. A hung parliament was widely expected, one in which the SNP might credibly hold the balance of power, but instead it produced a surprise Tory majority. The 2017 general election turned this dynamic on its head: an even bigger Conservative majority was widely anticipated, yet it actually gave rise to a hung parliament, one in which the Scottish Conservatives – rather than the SNP – appeared pivotal. Not for the first time in Scottish politics, winners ended up looking like losers, and losers, winners.

Scottish National Party

Commentators had long referred to the 2015 general election as 'peak SNP', the party having won all but three of Scotland's fifty-nine constituencies and nearly 50 per cent of the popular vote, and so it proved. Once in possession of a formidable campaigning machine, the Nationalists appeared caught off guard by the snap 2017 election, their campaign struggling to find a coherent theme or even a memorable sound bite.

It was, wrote Alex Massie after the event, 'a shambles'. 'Was it about independence? Yes, unless it wasn't. And vice versa,' he observed. 'All the SNP offered was a promise to protect Scotland against the hateful Tories that many Scots decided weren't actually all that hateful. There was no positive message, no inspiring vision.' The SNP, which once swore by 'positive campaigning', instead appeared defensive and negative.

The backdrop was, unavoidably, the question of independence and, more specifically, a second independence referendum. A Scottish 'win' in the election, the SNP maintained, would constitute a 'triple-locked' mandate for the latter, building on the 2016 Holyrood result and a subsequent parliamentary vote. But having formally requested a second Section 30 Order from Westminster (granting the Scottish Parliament temporary power to hold another ballot) in early March, not only had Nicola Sturgeon's eloquent plea fallen flat, it was rebuffed by Theresa May ('now is not the time') and helped boost the Scottish Tory vote at local government elections in May.

So, by the time the general election came around, the SNP was trying to find a way of diverting attention away from something that appeared to have become a vote loser. 'The issue at the heart of this election is whether you support independence or oppose independence,' was the First Minister's chosen form of words. 'Surely that decision should be taken by people in Scotland, by the Scottish people and the Scottish Parliament, and not by a Tory government at Westminster.' Sturgeon knew she'd misjudged the mood, moving too far ahead of public opinion, but at the same time she had to roll with it.

Brexit also proved difficult. Privately, the SNP knew that many of its own supporters wanted to 'take back control' from Brussels as well as London, so it tried to triangulate, talking of an independent Scotland seeking 'interim' membership of the European Economic Area rather than immediately rejoining the European Union. But this fudge was reluctantly and only occasionally articulated, meaning its target audience didn't get the message while hardcore Remainers detected backsliding on a longstanding commitment to 'independence in Europe'.

Another problem for the SNP was heightened scrutiny of its record in devolved government, having recently marked ten years since entering (devolved) office in 2007. Although health and education had little to do with a Westminster election, both preoccupied voters and journalists, and whenever Sturgeon appeared on television she appeared to come under attack.

A key moment came during the first Scottish leaders' debate on BBC Scotland, when a nurse called Claire Austin told the First Minister her work was 'demoralising' and that she relied on foodbanks to make ends meet. 'Don't come on your announced visits,' she told the First Minister. 'Come in on the middle of any day into any ward, any A&E department, come in and see what we're up against.'

Newspapers later questioned some of these claims (pictures emerged of Austin holidaying in New York and dining in some style), but a Twitter rumour that she was the wife (or daughter) of a Conservative councillor quickly got the SNP into trouble. Joanna Cherry, the party's Home Affairs spokeswoman and a QC, was even forced to apologise after repeating this peculiarly Scottish smear on television. Later, Sturgeon said Cherry had made an 'honest mistake', which rather implied the attacks would have been justified had the Tory connection been true.

When it came to another key policy responsibility, as Fraser Nelson noted, the SNP leader's tactic was to 'drag any discussion about education into the land of acronyms and statistics'. When Sturgeon tried to play down declining standards in one interview, it took Andrew Marr to remind her that 'literacy and numeracy are kind of important'. 'You are very good at standing and speaking at your little podium in Bute House about independence,' remarked another disgruntled voter on a special edition of *Question Time*, 'but when it actually comes to governing the country and tackling the big issues in Scotland … the SNP and yourself are hopeless at it.'

Amid the usual anti-Tory rhetoric – Sturgeon repeatedly said voting SNP was necessary to prevent an 'out-of-control, unfettered UK government' doing 'whatever it wants to Scotland' – Nationalists followed a familiar strategy of tacking to the left in Westminster elections, promising to 'end' austerity (as in 2015) and restore the 50p rate of income tax across the UK (though, confusingly, it declined to do so in Scotland). Reports from the ground campaign, meanwhile, suggested the First Minister provoked strong reactions on the doorstep, 'that woman' being among the politer epithets. The SNP leader's final tour of Scotland in the branded 'Nicolopter', once a novelty, just made her look aloof and out of touch.

Finally, the SNP simply failed to spot a mini-revival in Labour's fortunes before it was too late. Early in the campaign, Sturgeon appeared to share the Conservatives' disdain for the Labour leader and his electoral chances, playing down the prospect of a 'progressive alliance'. But as the polls shifted, the SNP warmed to the idea of an anti-Tory pact and latterly descended into palpable nonsense on the eve of poll. 'If you like Jeremy Corbyn,' Sturgeon appeared to tell Scottish voters, 'vote SNP.'

Panic at the Labour bounce also helped explain another key moment of the campaign when, in a second and final leaders' debate on STV, the First

Minister suggested Scottish Labour leader Kezia Dugdale had told her, in a phone call following the European referendum, that her party might consider dropping its opposition to another vote on independence. If it was an attempt to dampen support for Labour, it clearly failed, but it also did Sturgeon reputational damage. Once renowned for relative honesty and straight-dealing, she was now divulging the contents of official (and therefore private) government business. No longer did the SNP leader, the undisputed star of the 2015 election, appear to be 'the most dangerous woman in Britain'.

Scottish Conservative and Unionist Party

The Scottish Conservative and Unionist Party entered the general election campaign on something of a roll, a remarkable phenomenon given it had been wiped out in 1997 and had failed to gain more than a single seat at any UK election since. A long-mooted 'revival' had begun to manifest itself in the 2016 Scottish Parliament elections and continued to surface in pre-election polling as well as in May's local government elections, at which the SNP doubled its share of the vote and pushed Labour into third place. Given the proximity of the two elections, the party adopted one catch-all slogan: 'We said No. We meant it.'

This was, of course, a reference to the SNP's plans for a second referendum, opposition to which formed the centrepiece of the Scottish Tory election campaign almost at the expense of everything else. Reports during (and after) the election suggested that leader Ruth Davidson had rejected demands from CCHQ to run with the UK party's 'strong and stable' mantra, realising that the only thing that mattered in Scottish politics was opposition to (or support for) another referendum.

Beyond that, however, Davidson and her party had a rather lacklustre campaign. She spent much of it on the back foot, under attack from the SNP and Scottish Labour about the so-called 'rape clause', the prospect of further austerity and a range of other generally unpopular UK Government policies. In the two televised leaders' debates, meanwhile, the Scottish Tory leader was targeted by the First Minister on the same basis, only really reasserting herself on the referendum issue. Gone too were the eye-catching photo-calls Davidson had previously deployed; given she now led the largest opposition party in the Scottish Parliament, her advisers feared more tank riding would make her look frivolous.

After enjoying the obvious momentum in the first few weeks, by the end of the campaign it appeared to have dissipated, especially as the UK Tory campaign unravelled, leaving Davidson with more unpopular policies – chiefly the 'dementia tax' (even though it wouldn't apply in Scotland) – to defend. Also, as in the 2016 Scottish Parliament elections, the party opted for a policy-lite approach, its manifesto being little more than a tweaked version of the UK party's 'Forward Together' offering. What saved the Scottish Conservatives was its mantra-like rejection of a second independence referendum, as well as an unequivocally pro-Brexit position that played well in farming and fishing communities.

Privately, the party had identified fifteen target seats, although it took care not to confirm that publicly lest it fall victim to mismanaged expectations. Four of these constituencies were considered to be the 'inner' core, i.e. seats in the south of Scotland considered easy pickings. The rest, the 'outer' core, were to be targeted with cash and old-fashioned shoe leather. Some of the latter, like SNP Westminster leader Angus Robertson's Moray constituency, were viewed as glittering prizes, while others, like Gordon (held by former SNP leader Alex Salmond); Banff & Buchan; Stirling; Ayr, Carrick & Cumnock and Ochil & South Perthshire were considered possible but unlikely.

Davidson visited Gordon early in the campaign and, although she was personally sceptical that the former First Minister could be ousted, her foray was designed to indicate that safe Nationalist seats were in Tory sights. Salmond responded by accusing the Tories of making 'vainglorious boasts', warning that Davidson could be brought 'back down to earth with a bump' by voters. Similarly, in Perth & North Perthshire, where the SNP staged its delayed manifesto launch,* Pete Wishart described his constituency as 'a line' the Conservatives would 'not cross'. Only one of them was proved correct.

Scottish Labour Party

An indication of how much the core Tory message resonated with voters was its co-option by the other two 'Unionist' parties, Scottish Labour

---

* Both the SNP manifesto launch and second televised leaders' debate were rescheduled following the Manchester terror attack.

and the Scottish Liberal Democrats, both of whom took to echoing Ruth Davidson's lines about 'sending' Nicola Sturgeon 'a message' and for the Scottish Government to get on with its 'day job' of managing public services in Scotland.

Unlike the Scottish Conservatives, however, Labour entered the campaign demoralised and with (understandably) low expectations given its electoral performance since 2015. Then, it had lost all but one of its MPs, while in 2016 it had slipped behind the Tories at Holyrood, and in May 2017 lost control of Glasgow City Council, Scotland's largest local authority. Commentators believed the party had entered a Scottish Tory-like spiral of decline.

Labour strategists were, therefore, realistic, targeting just three seats: Edinburgh South (held by former shadow Scottish Secretary Ian Murray), East Lothian and East Renfrewshire, the last of which was contested by 'Better Together' veteran Blair McDougall. Beyond that trio, however, the party did not seriously expect to erode several massive SNP majorities in its former West-Central Scotland heartlands.

So, until the final week of the campaign, Scottish Labour leader Kezia Dugdale seemed to be done for, particularly after Nicola Sturgeon's curveball about their private telephone conversation a few days before polling. This and a subsequent *Daily Record* poll that put Labour in second place (in terms of vote share and seats) indicated that something unexpected was happening. A crowd of around 200 people, meanwhile, greeted Jeremy Corbyn as he spoke in Glasgow's Buchanan Street; not a patch on his southern audiences, but nevertheless impressive.

Basically, both Corbyn and his surprisingly well-received manifesto had put left-leaning supporters of independence – who'd deserted Labour for the SNP in 2015 – in a quandary: did they continue to support Scotland-only progressive politics (via the SNP) or help shore them up across the UK by voting Labour? Although much-criticised during the campaign, Corbyn's apparent flip-flopping on the referendum question – sometimes he was relaxed about it, at other points opposed – probably helped lure this sort of voter back into the Labour fold.

And while Dugdale performed solidly enough, her party's Lazarus-like comeback in the last week likely owed more to the UK-wide Corbyn 'bounce' than her own efforts. This meant there were, in effect, two Scottish Labour campaigns: one predicated on opposition to a second independence referendum, and the other on the UK Labour manifesto's promise of major economic reform. The former strategy worked in seats like Edinburgh South but not in East Renfrewshire, while the latter appeared to pay dividends in Glasgow North East. Either way, perhaps the real story of the 2017 general election in Scotland was that Scottish Labour was back in the game.

Scottish Liberal Democrats and Other Parties

The Scottish Liberal Democrats, who'd lost all but one of their MPs back in 2015, also did better than expected. Like Scottish Labour, it focused on a small number of constituencies and blitzed each of them with leaflets and activists. The top priority was holding Orkney & Shetland, where former Scottish Secretary Alistair Carmichael had survived a legal attempt to unseat him following the 'Frenchgate' controversy,* while Edinburgh West, East Dunbartonshire and Fife North East – all held by the Liberal Democrats prior to 2015 – were also in their sights.

Meanwhile, like Labour and the Conservatives, meanwhile, the Liberal Democrats exploited anxieties about a second independence referendum while taking a more tactical approach, i.e. promoting themselves as the most credible 'Unionist' party in its target seats. This was hinted at during friendly exchanges between Scottish Lib Dem leader Willie Rennie and Kezia Dugdale in the second of two televised leaders' debates.

Still, the party remained a shadow of its former self. Between 1997 and 2010 it had never fallen below ten seats at Westminster, while between 1999 and 2007 it had governed Scotland in coalition with Labour. During the campaign, however, the Scottish Liberal Democrats appeared spirited yet irrelevant. In the final week, its campaign manager Alex Cole-Hamilton was even reported to the procurator fiscal following allegations he'd breached the legal spending cap during the 2016 Holyrood election that saw him become a Member of the Scottish Parliament.

The Scottish Green Party, meanwhile, made fools of themselves. Already under fire from opponents and journalists for being little more than 'Santa's little helpers' (a reference to its tendency to support the SNP at Holyrood), it went from attacking STV's 'bizarre' decision not to include it in its televised

---

* This concerned Carmichael having approved the leak of a contested memo alleging that Nicola Sturgeon had told the French ambassador that she'd rather David Cameron become Prime Minister than Labour's then leader Ed Miliband. He initially denied doing so, and was challenged in an Election Court by pro-independence campaigners. He won the case but was heavily criticised by judges.

debate, to admitting that it only planned to field three candidates in the general election, including co-convener Patrick Harvie in Glasgow North.

Harvie called this a 'tightly focused campaign', but it represented quite a drop from the thirty-two it had fielded in 2015. Cynics suggested it was standing aside to prevent too many SNP losses. UKIP in Scotland, however, contested ten constituencies, including that of MEP and Scottish leader David Coburn in Kirkcaldy & Cowdenbeath, although both he and the party – in disarray and decline following Brexit – barely registered beyond lightly-mocking stories on BuzzFeed.

The result

The SNP's loss of twenty-one seats and half a million votes represented a dramatic setback for a party that just a few months earlier had dominated Scottish politics and appeared invincible. A dozen of those constituencies were lost to the Conservatives, who regained predominantly rural seats in the south and north-east of Scotland they'd last held in the 1990s, six to Scottish Labour and three to the Liberal Democrats. Remarkably, in terms of total vote share, the once-hated Tories ended up only 220,000 votes behind the SNP and 40,000 ahead of Labour. For the first time in a quarter of a century, the Scottish Tories had returned more than a single MP at a Westminster election.

More worryingly for the SNP, in several other seats it came within a whisker of defeat: two votes in Fife North East, twenty-one in Perth & North Perthshire and seventy-five in Glasgow East, and if the campaign had lasted another week, it's possible the Nationalists would have lost (at least) another dozen seats. Two of the losses, Westminster leader Angus Robertson in Moray and former First Minister Alex Salmond in Gordon (a 'McPortillo' moment 'on steroids' according to Alex Massie in *The Times*), added insult to injury, brutally illustrating the extent of the party's decline. No longer did its surviving MPs have five-figure majorities, and only a few counted as 'safe' seats.

The SNP remained, however, by far Scotland's largest party, with thirty-five MPs and 37 per cent of the vote – an impressive result in historic terms, considering its previous high point (setting aside 2015) was gaining eleven MPs and 30 per cent of the vote in October 1974. It also remained the third-largest party across the UK, albeit shorn of its group leader and other senior

Commons figures. Another 'hung' parliament, in theory at least, offered the Nationalists opportunities a Tory landslide would have denied them.

For Scottish Labour, the result – seven MPs rather than one – represented a much-needed reprieve after a decade of electoral decline. Significantly, it regained seats in working-class areas lost in 2015 and ended up within touching distance of winning several more, providing it with a useful psychological boost ahead of another UK election or, more likely, Scottish Parliament elections in 2021. On the other hand, this boost had unwelcome origins, since party leader Kezia Dugdale and most of her colleagues had been opposed to Jeremy Corbyn's leadership.

The Scottish Liberal Democrats, having lost ten of its eleven MPs in 2015, also enjoyed a partial reprieve, winning two of its three target seats (and coming tantalisingly close in the other), while also regaining Caithness, Sutherland & Easter Ross from the SNP, where the former MSP Jamie Stone made a political comeback. The three Unionist parties – the Tories, Labour and Lib Dems – reduced to a single MP each two years earlier, now had thirteen, seven and four respectively. The sea of yellow on the 2015 electoral map of Scotland now included swathes of red, orange and blue.

Expectations had proved as important as the results, so while Nicola Sturgeon protested that the SNP had 'won' the election, it still looked like the biggest loser, while the Scottish Conservatives, who most observers expected to gain half a dozen seats, emerged as the biggest 'winners'. It was all relative. By historic standards, Scottish Labour and the Liberal Democrats had still done badly, but not as badly as they might have.

Conclusion

The election result in Scotland turned several long-standing Nationalist orthodoxies on their head: that Scots were inherently anti-Tory, that a left-wing Labour Party couldn't possibly win a UK-wide election and, more surprisingly, that Brexit would increase support for the SNP and therefore independence. Not only that, but the once-successful all-things-to-all-men approach was challenged on the right by the Tories and on the left by Labour. Most significantly, the prospect of 'indyref2' unequivocally emerged as a vote loser, even in parts of Scotland – and among groups of voters – who'd hitherto been sympathetic.

That meant the prospect of a second independence referendum was 'off the table' before 2021, if not for even longer: a reality acknowledged by even the most optimistic Nationalists. After promising to 'reflect' on her losses, however, Nicola Sturgeon announced a strategic 'reset' that wasn't a reset at all, but merely a slight tweak to her preferred timescale. All now hinged upon the outcome of Brexit, the SNP promising to redouble its efforts – in London and Edinburgh – to secure a Scottish seat at the negotiating table. After all, what else was there?

Scottish Conservative leader Ruth Davidson, on the other hand, could credibly claim to have saved Theresa May's political career by finally transforming her party from the embarrassing member of the Tory family to the point at which it made a meaningful contribution to the Conservative ranks at Westminster. But assuming she doesn't quit Holyrood for the Commons any time soon (and she won't, certainly not before 2021), then Davidson still has to prove herself – not only that she's capable of becoming First Minister in a few years' time, but that her party, rather than the SNP, is the party that is most effectively 'standing up for Scotland'. The Tory–DUP deal, which granted £1 billion in additional funding to Northern Ireland but nothing to Scotland, punctured that conceit, though one assumes it'll be put right in the 2017 Budget.

The Liberal Democrats' gains in Scotland also contributed disproportionately to the UK party's modest recovery. One of them, Jo Swinson in East Dunbartonshire, emerged as deputy leader and could, one assumes, be a future leader. Still, in Scotland as well as in the rest of the UK, the party had barely appeared on the political radar since 2015. Scottish Labour leader Kezia Dugdale will fare better – her previously shaky position now undeniably strengthened – while, on a practical level, Jeremy Corbyn's life is made easier by having more of a choice when it comes to appointing Scots members of his shadow ministerial team.

Beyond that, the Scottish political landscape looks more stable than it's been in several years. Ironically, Theresa May and Nicola Sturgeon, once viewed as cautious politicians, both threw caution to the wind – the Prime Minister with a snap election and the First Minister with her push for a second referendum – and both continue to grapple with the consequences of those miscalculations. In a further irony, an election that unexpectedly weakened the Conservative and Unionist Party ended up giving the Union a reprieve.

David Torrance is a freelance journalist and author of Nicola Sturgeon: A Political Life *(Birlinn, 2016).*

The polls at the 2017 general election: what could possibly go wrong?

Joe Twyman

At the global headquarters of YouGov in the Old Street area of London, the working week begins with a meeting of the senior management. Only twice has this meeting been interrupted. Once was for the resignation of Pope Benedict, the other for the death of Margaret Thatcher.

On Tuesday 18 April 2017, just after the Easter Bank Holiday, the meeting was interrupted for a third time with the news that Theresa May was about to make a surprise announcement outside Downing Street.

For everyone in the polling industry, it was not meant to be like this. After 2015, things had changed. The next election was going to be different. While rumours of an early election arose occasionally, the expectation was still that the country would go to the polls in 2020 – as set out by the Fixed Term Parliament Act. The polling industry specifically, along with the public more generally, would have five years to prepare for the next general election.

In the end, five years changed to just over two years.

This shorter period of time meant that, in public opinion terms, the whole context in which this surprise election was taking place was so very different to 2015. Back then the politicians, the parties, but most of all the public had five years to 'look forward' to that general election. Surprising though it was to some commentators, the parliament did actually last the full term, with the final year to eighteen months effectively playing the role of one long, unofficial election campaign.

In 2015, David Cameron had been Prime Minister for five years and at the end of that year would celebrate a decade as leader of his party. Nick Clegg had been Deputy Prime Minister in the coalition government for five years and leader of the Liberal Democrats for nearly seven and a half. Even Ed Miliband, the most recent appointment to the trio of leaders, had been leader of the Labour Party for over four and a half years.

In sharp contrast to this in 2017, Theresa May had been Prime Minister and leader of the Conservative Party for just eighty-four days when she stood at the podium and announced her intentions to go to the polls on Thursday 8 June. Her main opponent, Jeremy Corbyn, had been leader of the Labour Party for eighteen months, during a period of turmoil and change that included him winning two leadership elections. Tim Farron, having led the Liberal Democrats for nearly two years, was effectively the veteran leader this time around.

This difference between 2015 and 2017 is important for public opinion. The average person in the street – and the 50 per cent of people less engaged than the average person in the street – doesn't generally pay much attention to politics. A reader of a guide to the 2017 general election may well have been aware of Theresa May from her time at the Home Office or the years proceeding. They might have known about Jeremy Corbyn from his time as MP for Islington North for over thirty years. Tim Farron's role as Lib Dem voice outside the coalition could have rung a bell. But for the average person – people outside the Westminster bubble, not paying close attention to the day-to-day news from Parliament, largely uninterested in the minutiae of British politics – the 2017 general election had been a very different proposition from 2015.

Rather than a parliament lasting five years, the country now had just over two. Rather than over a year to get to know the leaders and the parties better as they adopted a campaign footing, the average person now had just seven weeks.

This point was crucial for public opinion, but also for the world of political polling. The 2015 general election had been a bad night for the political polling industry. Predictions of a hung parliament and a close result between the Conservatives and Labour were replaced by the reality of a surprise majority for David Cameron and his party – albeit still only a small one.

In the aftermath, these pollsters had to do a gret deal of soul searching and naval gazing after the unexpected happened on elecion night. At the same time, a number of people miraculously emerged out of the woodwork to carefully explain how they had, with wildly varying degrees of credibility, predicted the outcome all along. Members of the political commentariat added their voices, saying that the result, rather than being unexpected, had in fact been crystal clear all along.

Even as the final results of the 2015 election were still being counted, an inquiry was announced by the British Polling Council (BPC) into what had happened. It was led by Patrick Sturgis, Professor of Research Methodology and Director of the National Centre for Research Methods at the University of Southampton. Polling companies submitted data, analyses, findings and thoughts to a panel of nine experts with preliminary findings announced by the inquiry team in January 2016. A final report followed, along with recommendations, at the end of March that year.

Separate to the official inquiry, each company carried out their own internal investigations. In most cases the result of this period of research, analysis and reflection in the days, weeks and months after the 2015 general election produced very similar findings to the official inquiry: the inaccuracy had been due to the samples of people who had taken part in the surveys. In short, too many Labour supporters had been polled, while at the same time, too few Conservative supporters were included in the sample.

At the heart of this issue was a problem faced by the entire industry: how to get people to take part in surveys. In theory, measuring public opinion is straightforward. You just have to ask the right people the right questions at the right time. Of course, actually doing that is far from straightforward, particularly when it comes to finding the 'right people'.

Response rates (i.e. the proportion of people contacted who then take part in a given survey) have been falling for many years. Large scale face-to-face surveys sometimes require visits to households up to fifteen or twenty times over a period of weeks or months to give potential survey participants an opportunity to take part. Response rates of over 50 per cent are considered a success.

Getting people to take part in telephone surveys has become more difficult over the last twenty years as people increasingly use only mobile phones, often using their landline (if they even have one) solely for the purpose of calling their mobile when they cannot find it. Even when mobile users are included in a sample – and they aren't always – their response rate is even lower due to caller ID. As a result, response rates can be as low as under 5 per cent.

To make matters worse, these response rates are averages across the entire sample, meaning that for some hard-to-reach groups in society, the response rate will be significantly lower. This situation has, at least in part, led to the movement towards online surveys in the last decade, with respondents specifically recruited to panels and incentivised to take part in future surveys. Online surveys can never, however, hope to capture the views of those people who do not have internet access.

On top of all of this, and regardless of the method used to conduct surveys and contact respondents, the fact remains that some people are never willing to take part in polls. Even the last National Census in 2011 only achieved a response rate of 94 per cent – with response rates in some areas as low as 82 per cent – and taking part in that is a legal requirement, enforced by the threat of fines and even imprisonment.

This situation had, and continues to have, a significant impact on election polling. In 2015, one of the groups that was found to not be represented sufficiently in samples, for example, were young people who were uninterested in politics. It is these people who generally did not vote and do not vote, but the samples for surveys had too few of them included. At the same time, they had too many young people who were interested in politics saying they were going to vote – and generally for Labour – distorting the end result against the Conservatives.

The damaging effects of such a distortion were significantly pronounced by the specific circumstances of the 2017 election: amplified by an election few predicted was coming, a campaign that lasted only seven weeks, leaders who had not been in the job that long and who the average person did not know at all well. This all leads to what Sir Alex Ferguson once referred to as 'squeaky-bum time'.

With all that in mind, the different organisations polling in the 2017 election attempted to address this issue of sampling in a variety of different ways. Some worked hard to recruit specific types of respondents to their survey panels in greater numbers. YouGov, for example, spent hundreds of thousands of pounds on precisely that. Others made adjustments to their quotas for sampling and statistical weighting to attempt to ensure their raw data was more representative of the electorate as a whole. Most polling companies did both of these things, to a greater or lesser degree. These adjustments to the sampling and weighting were, however, only the first thing on the list for pollsters to consider ahead of 8 June.

When it comes to elections, a huge amount of political polling is conducted, covering everything from leaders to policies to reaction to specific events and experimental testing of hypothetical scenarios. Ultimately, however, the thing that really matters – the thing that pollsters lose sleep over – is 'the horse race' between the two main parties. All polls, no matter how perfect they may be, are subject to the laws of probability and therefore have a margin of error. They are also snapshot measurements of public opinion at that given time rather than predictions of the future, but none of this matters if you get the overall story between the two main parties wrong.

What is really important out in the real world is the question of the winners and the losers: who is going to end up in charge once all the shouting is over and done with? In order to answer this question there are three separate but related elements that pollsters and pundits alike have to consider, particularly as 'squeaky-bum time' draws closer.

The first of these is the question of voting intention: which party respondents support. While that is obviously very important and attracts the lion's share of attention, it is far from all that matters. Also crucial is the second element: whether respondents will vote or not. An individual survey respondent may support a particular party, but unless they actually vote, it does not make any difference. To correctly estimate the state of public opinion, both of these elements must be correctly estimated. Thirdly, the national picture derived from a national poll must then be translated into each of the 650 different, individual constituency contests that will determine the eventual outcome on the night.

Adjustments to the samples for surveys should go some way to help address the issue of turnout, but both the BPC inquiry team and internal analysis from polling companies had identified that yet more still needed to be done. To address this, some pollsters chose to predict how likely it was that certain demographic groups would turn out based on the historical behaviour of such groups in previous elections. Others chose to estimate an individual's likelihood to vote through a question or (more often) a series of questions within the survey. Often such adjustments could be proved to have made the polling for 2015 more accurate, but only time would tell if they would be as advantageous this time around. After all, estimating who won the last election is not much use.

To make matters more complicated, these adjustments still only dealt with the national picture. Addressing how each constituency performs is an even more technically demanding process. In the good old days of Uniform National Swing (UNS), constituencies could generally be relied upon to behave themselves in a predictable manner while Bob McKenzie or Peter Snow jumped around the BBC election studio wielding their swingometer. The rise and subsequent collapse of the Liberal Democrats, the insurgency of UKIP and the takeover of Scotland by the Scottish National Party have led to hugely differing patterns of swing that vary at the individual constituency level.

In an attempt to address this potential for variation, Lord Ashcroft had, back in 2015, financed a large number of polls in 167 key marginal constituencies in the twelve months prior to the election, but that did not prove particularly enlightening. To go further and to conduct representative surveys in each of the 650 parliamentary constituencies would not just be impractical, it would also be close to operationally impossible and almost certainly beyond even the financial resources of Lord Ashcroft – who presumably has much better ways to spend his money.

Recent developments in data science had provided a possible alternative to standalone surveys in individual constituencies, but it was unclear ahead of the election to what extent this would help deliver a more accurate estimate. Such developments, along with the three important elements and the performance of polls in 2015 and 2016 meant that 2017 was inevitably approached as an 'experimental election'. New methods would be tried, new assumptions tested and new techniques rolled out.

Of course, it is worth remembering that at the start of the campaign, in spite of everything, things actually seemed quite straightforward for the pollsters. Yes, various adjustments were needed after 2015, assumptions would need to be made and it was hoped that five years would be available to test and fine-tune everything, but at least this time the overall story was clear. In short, the general feeling was that squeaky bums would be avoided this time around.

The Conservatives started in an extremely strong position in the polls – which is, of course, a major reason why the election was called in the first place. The party had enjoyed a double-digit lead over Labour since

October 2016. At the beginning of the campaign the Conservatives were on 48 per cent – 24 per cent ahead of Labour, who themselves were only on 24 per cent. A lead of this size was enormous by historical standards for any stage of a parliament, let alone during an election campaign.

The underlying data also pointed to a large Conservative win. When asked to choose who would make the best Prime Minister, 54 per cent of people said Theresa May, 39 per cent ahead of Jeremy Corbyn who languished on just 15 per cent. Additionally, the Conservatives were seen as the best party by some distance on the issue of the economy, and also on a host of other issues including immigration and Brexit, the latter most often regarded by the electorate as the most important issue facing the country. Only on housing and health did Labour enjoy a lead – and even then it was not large.

Historical precedent states the party that is ahead on leadership and ahead on the economy will win on polling day. Historical precedent also states that, in recent elections at least, campaigns do not make that much of a difference to public opinion, but as the seven long weeks rolled on, the polls offered a clear indication that this time might just be different in some respects from the electoral battles of recent years.

As the campaign progressed and manifesto launches, TV debates and U-turns came and went, the polls were clear that things were changing and the Conservative lead was shrinking. Support for the Conservatives themselves was not dropping hugely; instead it was the rise of Labour that was causing the gap to close. The degree to which Labour were closing was, however, a point of some debate as polls from different organisations told different stories. This difference was, in the most part, due to the way in which polling organisations approached the issue of turnout. Those using assumptions based on demographic groups showed much larger leads for the Conservatives than those using estimates based on self-reported likelihood to vote.

Despite this variation, however, three things remained consistent in all the published polls during the first few weeks of the campaign: firstly the Conservatives were ahead, secondly the gap was not as large as it had been at the start of the campaign and thirdly the Conservatives would still win a majority if the current polling was replicated on election day.

This situation was maintained until Wednesday 31 May when *The Times* published a front page of that read 'Shock poll predicts Tory losses'. This was the result of seat estimates from a new model produced by YouGov that showed the Conservatives heading for 310 seats at that point in the campaign compared to 257 for Labour.

The YouGov model was primarily developed by Dr Ben Lauderdale at the London School of Economics working in conjunction with Prof Doug Rivers from YouGov. It was based on at least 5,000 survey interviews every day, conducted online and then combined over a seven-day period. This data was then used to estimate the probability of an individual with a certain set of characteristics voting for a particular party. At the same time, data from YouGov, the British Election Study, the Office of National Statistics and previous general elections was used to estimate the proportion of different types of individuals within each parliamentary constituency.

In order to do all of this, YouGov utilised recently developed, cutting-edge data science techniques such as multilevel regression and post-stratification (MRP) and Hamiltonian Monte Carlo analysis combined with machine learning. Each day all the data was fed into the model and, nine hours of cloud-based computing later, estimates were produced for the results in each of the 650 individual constituencies. These results were then aggregated to produce a national estimate for both seats and vote share.

It is fair to say that the first publication of YouGov's MRP model was not met with universal acclaim. *The Times* described it as 'controversial', *The Guardian* labelled it 'brave', while others were far less kind. *Mail on Sunday* journalist Dan Hodges said he was 'genuinely surprised *The Times* published that poll'. Helen Lewis, Deputy Editor of the *New Statesman*, said 'I don't believe this but … it would be funny as hell'. Political commentator Isobel Oakeshott described the estimate of a hung parliament as 'bollocks' while the Conservative Party's American 'data expert' (*sic*) Jim Messina announced how he had 'Spent the day laughing at yet another stupid poll from YouGov'.

One feature of YouGov's MRP model was that it produced estimates for the results in individual constituencies and it was this that arguably provoked the most lively debate. The model estimated, for example, that Conservative-held seats like Canterbury and Kensington could go to Labour. Having previously described the model's findings as 'utter tripe' Iain Dale, the broadcaster and publisher (not least of this very book), said of such predictions that 'if you want a good laugh, click on YouGov's constituency prediction page' adding that 'Canterbury is going Labour LOL!'.

Daily seat estimates continued to be published from the YouGov MRP model throughout the remainder of the campaign, along with individual, standalone surveys from YouGov for *The Times* and the *Sunday Times*, produced using the standard methodology. Only towards the end of the campaign did these two different approaches begin to show different results.

By the eve of polling day, a range of different stories were being told by the different polling organisations when it came to estimates of the final Conservative lead over Labour, with results ranging from a one point lead to a thirteen point lead.

	CON	LAB	L D	UKIP	CON LEAD	LEAD ERROR	AVERAGE ERROR
	%	%	%	%	%	%	%
Final GB Result	**43.5**	**41**	**7.6**	**1.9**	**2.5**	**N/A**	**N/A**
Survation	41	40	8	2	1	1.5	1.1
YouGov MRP	42	38	9	3	4	1.5	1.7
Surveymonkey	42	38	6	4	4	1.5	1.9
Kantar Public	43	38	7	4	5	2.5	1.7
Opinium	43	36	8	5	7	4.5	2.7
YouGov Standalone	42	35	10	5	7	4.5	3.5
Ipsos MORI	44	36	7	4	8	5.5	2.7
Panelbase	44	36	7	5	8	5.5	2.9
ComRes	44	34	9	5	10	7.5	3.9
ICM	46	34	7	5	12	9.5	4.5
BMG	46	33	8	5	13	10.5	4.9

In addition to the polling on vote share, a number of commentators, academics and others produced their own seat estimates for the two main parties. Some of these were based on polling, some based on data such as local election results and others were based simply on assessment of the situation on the ground in individual seats.

Of all these seat estimates, only the YouGov MRP model told the correct story, and it was the one YouGov had been the first to tell back at the end of May: the Conservatives would fail to achieve a majority. In addition, the much derided estimates of Labour victory in Kensington and Canterbury both turned out to be true.

	CON	LAB	CON	CON SEATS	LAB SEATS	CON LEAD	LEAD ERROR	AVERAGE ERROR
	SEATS	SEATS	MAJORITY	%	%	%	%	%
Final Election Result	**317**	**262**	**N/A**	**49**	**40**	**9**	**N/A**	**N/A**
YouGov MRP	302	269	N/A	46	41	5	4	2.0
Election Polling	335	232	20	52	36	16	7	3.5
Kantar	341	232	32	52	36	16	7	3.5
PME Politics	348	224	46	54	34	20	11	5.5

Fisher / Goldenberg	349	223	48	54	34	20	11	5.5
Michael Thrasher	349	215	48	54	33	21	12	6
Principalfish	350	222	50	54	34	20	11	5.5
Britain Elects	356	219	62	55	34	21	12	6
Lord Ashcroft	357	222	64	55	34	21	12	6
Elections Etc	358	214	66	55	33	22	13	6.5
Murr / Stegmaier / Lewis-Beck	361	236	72	56	36	20	11	5.5
Electoral Calculus	361	216	72	56	33	23	14	7
Janta-Lipinski	365	211	80	56	32	24	15	7.5
Hanretty	366	207	82	56	32	24	15	7.5
Forecast UK	370	199	90	57	31	26	17	8.5
Lebo / Norpoth	372	202	94	57	31	26	17	8.5
Singh	374	207	98	58	32	26	17	8.5
Marriot	375	202	100	58	31	27	18	9
Dale	386	178	122	59	27	32	23	11.5
Election Data	387	186	124	60	29	31	22	11

In defence of these estimates, a seat range was also included in some of the original published data, but only the midpoint of the estimate is included in the table. YouGov's MRP model, for example, gave a range of 269 to 334 seats for the Conservatives and between 238 and 302 seats for Labour, based on a 95 per cent confidence interval.

Overall, the story of the polls in the 2017 general election was mixed. The narrative changed from estimates of a large Conservative majority to a range of possible outcomes. In 2015 the pollster's final estimates all showed the same thing. 2017 was very different, but it highlighted that political polling still has problems that cannot be overlooked and, for some at least, clearly still need to be effectively addressed and corrected. More work needs to be done.

And it is not getting any easier. Though YouGov's ground-breaking work with MRP modelling points to a possible solution for the industry more widely, it is far from a magic bullet. There are no laurels on which to be resting. Polls will always have a margin of error and they will always be just a snapshot as the situation continues to evolve, but polling companies need to keep thinking and to keep adapting – particularly when things are close and identifying the overall story becomes more difficult.

With that in mind, perhaps the most interesting piece of number crunching was produced by the analyst Owen Boswarva shortly after the all the results were in. He reported that if eleven Labour voters in Kensington, twelve Labour voters in Dudley North, sixteen Labour voters in Newcastle-Under-Lyme, twenty-five Labour voters in Crewe and Nantwich and eleven SNP voters in Perth & North Perthshire had all switched to vote Conservative instead, that would have given the Tories five more seats. Five more seats would have meant 322 seats for the Conservatives, enough for a working majority once the Speaker and absent Sinn Fein MPs are taken into account.

For Conservatives generally and Theresa May specifically, the answer to 'What could possibly go wrong?' is: seventy-five votes.

Joe Twyman– Head of Political and Social Research at YouGov.

The media

Theo Usherwood

At just after 11 o'clock on the morning of 18 April, Theresa May walked out of No. 10. She strode purposefully across Downing Street towards the lectern, set just to the right of the famous black front door. After steadying herself momentarily, the Conservative Prime Minister then triggered what was to be perhaps the most ill-fated election campaign of modern times. Over the next seven weeks, a revered leader whose authority had seemed unquestionable was reduced to a premier held captive in the highest office of state. Behind that demise was a rudderless media operation, devoid of any discerning strategy, while her most senior advisers made wrong moves at almost every turn. And then there was Jeremy Corbyn: a Labour leader who used the power of social media to build a groundswell of support for left-wing politics never seen before in this country. He didn't win, but he defied the odds and now the Conservative party, which was supposed to be enjoying all the trappings a landslide majority brings, finds itself in a self-induced python-like stranglehold, weak and incapable of running a government. There are many reasons for this turnaround in fortunes, but if there is one lesson for journalists only just catching their breath, it is this: the usual rules no longer apply.

From the outset the Tories were going for the big win – a triple digit House of Commons majority. That meant appealing to Labour voters who had deserted the party because of Jeremy Corbyn and winning back UKIP supporters satisfied with the Brexit result and keen for its full and swift implementation. And this in turn meant ditching the Conservative brand from leaflets and posters, limiting the appearance of Cabinet ministers on airwaves and at every opportunity talking about Theresa May, her leadership and her ability to play hardball with Brussels and negotiate a good deal for Britain outside of the European Union. But before the Prime Minister had told the Queen of her decision to go to the country, her team had to tackle the thorny issue of why a Conservative leader, who had repeatedly insisted there would be no vote before 2020, had now changed her mind on a walking holiday in Snowdonia. The reasoning outlined in the speech of Downing Street was that the other main parties wanted to frustrate Brexit. At best this reasoning sounded disproportionate. At worst, the suggestion was Theresa May was playing politics by capitalising on her party's unprecedented lead in the polls. Of course her speech landed well in some quarters. On 19 April, the *Daily Mail* ran the front-page headline 'Crush the Saboteurs' below a picture of Mrs May looking particularly animated. But the awkward questions had started, and the campaign was not even up and running.

Two years ago the mechanics of the Tory media operation – orchestrated by the Australian election guru Sir Lynton Crosby – were straight-forward. A small number of favoured newspaper journalists would be given the announcement or revelation for the next day, a competent minister would appear on the radio or television to talk about it as the nation ate its cornflakes the following morning, and then there would be a press conference, which would be completed in time for the lunchtime news. The narrative was clear: Ed Miliband – who was in the same government responsible for the 2008 recession – would be propped up by Nicola Sturgeon's SNP. Voters were told that meant more borrowing, higher interest rates and therefore less money in their back pockets. It was simple, it worked and there was no room for deviation. This time around, the involvement of Sir Lynton and his small team was much more limited from day one and the deficiencies became clear early on. Fiona Hill – Theresa May's former joint chief of staff and the Tory campaign's director of communications – was in charge of the press operation, helped by an assortment of former special advisers who had made the cut. Add to that Stephen Gilbert, who was officially in charge of the campaign, and Nick Timothy, the other joint chief of staff, tasked with writing the manifesto, and it soon became clear there were lots of bosses, all with very different, conflicting ideas. The disjointedness of the Tory media operation became clear when I was phoned by the Lynton camp on Friday 12 May. They had done some land registry analysis on Labour's inheritance tax plans, which they said would hit nearly two million home-owners in London. It worked for us, and so we pencilled in Gavin Barwell, the housing minister for the Monday morning. But in the wake of the NHS hacking story, our exclusive was scratched by Fiona Hill's team. Gavin Barwell, I was told, was no longer available as he had lost his voice, although from his Twitter account it clearly had not put a dent in his ability to campaign. Instead, Ben Wallace was LBC's Tory voice for the morning to talk about how his party were improving the NHS' antique computer network. The inheritance tax bombshell sank, never to be seen again.

The failure of the Tories to talk about Labour's tax plans cannot be blamed for Theresa May's inability to secure an overall majority. But one story, which many Conservative candidates did feel cut through on the doorstep, was fox-hunting. The Conservative Party policy under David Cameron had been a free Commons vote on repealing the ban. And so perhaps the story by Jack Blanchard, the *Daily Mirror*'s political editor, that the ban could be repealed if Mrs May secured a majority north of fifty, was inevitable. It was based on Tory peer Lord Mancroft declaring that the Hunting Act of 2004 could be overturned. Overnight, CCHQ briefed that this was just an old school Tory peer in red trousers getting carried away. It was not going to happen. The next morning the topic came up as Theresa May was briefed for her question and answer session with journalists later that day. At this point, the PM was told by one senior adviser: 'Give the answer you want to give.' The PM did exactly that, telling reporters she was personally in favour of fox-hunting and that a free vote would indeed follow. A London Tory candidate texted me with a very short message: 'Aren't these barnacles off the boat?' – a reference to Sir Lynton's mantra that a successful campaign never deviates from a core message. Suffice to say, the politically toxic subject of fox-hunting was not part of the script.

Part of the Conservative's problem when it came to the short campaign was that there was not an abundance of good will with journalists on the ground. The controlling nature of the operation has been well-documented and perhaps best summed up by a journalist working for a Cornish news website who live blogged being locked in a room by Theresa May's aides. Cornwall Live said they were not even allowed to film the building which the Prime Minister was visiting, having been told they would only be allowed a three-minute interview in their designated room at the end of the visit. Meanwhile, at the stump speeches, Mrs May started the campaign by only taking questions from selected journalists. There were accusations many had agreed to submit their questions beforehand so that the Prime Minister's team knew exactly what was coming and could prepare a suitably anodyne answer that included at least three deployments of the catchphrase 'strong and stable', a slogan that shrewder members of Team May had argued should be made into a joke in order to avoid the PM becoming a laughing stock on social media. No matter, it was not long before *The Guardian*'s sketch writer John Crace coined the term the Maybot, which neatly summed up the Prime Minister's automaton-like performances that left journalists, and evidently the public, none the wiser as to what a Conservative Britain would look like in 2022.

If the Conservative media operation is best described as an abject failure, what of Labour's efforts? The first thing to say is that Jeremy Corbyn was underestimated. While Tory MPs are now ruing the fact there was no leadership contest after the referendum, which would have given them the chance to test whether Mrs May was up to the job, Mr Corbyn – and his team – had spent the two previous summers trouncing all those who stood against him. The Labour campaign did not, of course, get off to the best of starts. Diane Abbott's failure on LBC to answer simple questions about the cost of Labour's plan to employ 10,000 extra police officers was a particular low point, and enraged the party's press office who had provided her with a comprehensive brief only to be told it wasn't needed. Other members of Mr Corbyn's top team repeatedly found themselves in tight spots on the airwaves, unable to answer questions on everything from whether the Labour leader would use a nuclear weapon (Jon Ashworth), to exactly how the party would fund social care (Andrew Gwynne). And then there was the electoral-suicide-by-24-hour-news-cycle moment that started with the manifesto 'leak' on Thursday 11 May. Tuition fees scrapped, the railways nationalised, zero-hours contracts banned, 100,000 new council homes to be built every year: it was – the *Daily Telegraph* said – a throwback to the 1970s. At first, it did appear to be a genuine leak. Mr Corbyn was due at 9 o'clock to launch the latest party poster in Waterloo but dropped out and was replaced by an apologetic Ian Lavery, the campaign co-ordinator. It was then across the River Thames for a meeting of Labour's National Executive Committee to approve the manifesto. Shortly before lunchtime, Mr Corbyn was driven in by a police officer who ran over a BBC cameraman's foot. The finishing touch came later that afternoon when Len McCluskey, the general secretary of Unite, slipped as he left the meeting and was pictured on his derriere desperately trying to regain his composure. But while many Labour MPs looked on in anguish from their constituencies, those with sub-8,000 majority fearing the imminent arrival of a P45, the dial of public opinion was beginning to turn. The manifesto 'leak' before the NEC met allowed Corbyn to put his ideas out to the public before the more moderate members of the committee had the chance to water them down. And the imposition of election rules on 3 May by the broadcast regulator Ofcom ensuring the main political parties receive comparable coverage on radio and television meant Labour – and its policies – were starting to gain much needed traction. But the really seismic shift was still a week away with the launch of the Conservative manifesto in Halifax.

It was pitched as a brave decision from a Prime Minister prepared to take the necessary, but perhaps unpopular action to deal with one of the great challenges of our time: how to pay for the care of our elderly. It was the central plank of the Conservative party manifesto. The State would pay for your care in your own home but then once you had died, your children would, if necessary, have to sell the family home and reimburse the Treasury with the proceeds, down to their last £100,000. By lunchtime on 18 May the Dementia Tax had been born: the sacred cow of the Conservative Party – the idea that you should be able to pass your wealth onto your children – had been sacrificed at the hands of Nick Timothy. The day after, I was out with Boris Johnson on the streets of Hounslow. 'Don't worry,' he told the voters as he was questioned about the finer details of the policy, 'as long as you're alive you're alright.' For Labour it was an easy win. You'd have to sell your home to pay for your care in old age. Not true, as it would be your children who would have to sell the family home. But it didn't matter. The damage was done. Conservative candidates faced a wall of vitriol on the doorstep that weekend, and by the Monday, Theresa May had announced a cap – but insisted nothing had changed. Politicians are like the rest of us. They are human and they are fallible. But in order to be Prime Minister, they do need a certain aura, a shine that commands a certain level of respect and separates them from mere mortals. David Cameron had lots of it before the referendum. For Theresa May it was something her team worked hard to create, and had been in large part successful. At the beginning of the campaign, the Prime Minister was the Conservative's most prized asset, while Corbyn was Labour's most dangerous liability. But over that weekend – four weeks out from polling day – the consensus shifted. Theresa May lost that aura and what some journalists had suspected from the very beginning, that the Prime Minister was in fact cut out for mid-management but nothing more, started to ring true. From the Tory perspective, the election campaign now became about damage limitation.

On the morning of 31 May, my phone rang shortly after Jeremy Corbyn had finished a fairly dull press conference in central London. It was CCHQ. 'It's a coalition of chaos,' the voice spluttered down the end of the line. 'They don't even know who they are putting up for tonight's television debate. How can they run the country?' The Tories had, of course, attempted to deal with the thorny issue of the broadcast debates on day one, insisting the PM would not be taking part in any head-to-head debates. That's what PMQs was for, we were told. End of. It made sense. As a political leader, the received wisdom is that you only do television election debates if you need to win. If you're twenty points ahead in the polls, there is no need. In 2005, Tony Blair declined the opportunity and won. In 2015, Cameron pulled off the same trick. Theresa May, meanwhile, had agreed to do a series of long-form interviews and take part in a series of town-hall-style question and answer sessions with the major broadcasters. But when it came to the BBC's seven-way debate in Cambridge that evening, the baton had been handed to the Home Secretary Amber Rudd. She had performed well during the EU referendum, cutting Boris Johnson down to size on more than one occasion, and was viewed as a safe pair of hands. Jeremy Corbyn had said he would only debate the Prime Minister and yet still, nine hours until the start of the BBC's set piece, Labour had yet to decide which member of the shadow Cabinet they were putting up – hence the phone call. By lunchtime, of course, Labour had executed their plan to lull the Tories into a false sense of security. Jeremy Corbyn would be taking part to put forward Labour's manifesto, while the Tories were left flat-footed and red-faced. They had been outsmarted. But this debacle was about more than just bruised egos. It spoke to something much more significant. The Tories had made the election about Theresa May and her qualities when it came to strong leadership compared to those of Jeremy Corbyn. And yet, when given the opportunity to test those qualities – and the Conservative's policies – against the Labour leader, she had shied away, hiding behind excuses and stage-managed events which for many voters at home must have felt as if British democracy itself was being somehow subverted.

Aside from the BBC's seven-way debate, this was not a good election for television: it was a good election for social media, and Facebook in particular. The numbers were staggering for Labour. A short film of young voters at Tranmere Rover's Prenton Park ground chanting Jeremy Corbyn's name to the tune of a popular rock song by the White Stripes, amassed 2.6 million views on Facebook; Mr Corbyn's election-day message, a cool 6.9 million views. And a ninety-second attack advert, criticising Mrs May's record on security as Home Secretary in the wake of the London Bridge terrorist attack, was watched more than three million times. In total, eighteen films were posted on the Labour leader's Facebook page between 18 April and 9 June, which garnered one million views or more. By contrast, only three films on the Conservative's page recorded seven figures, despite the party trying to replicate their 2015 strategy by buying up large amounts of advertising on the social media site. The irony is, of course, that Labour's online strategy was low-tech and relied on ensuring there was a constant stream of pro-Corbyn material that could be shared far and wide by supporters. Labour did not just rely on Facebook but also used WhatsApp, as well as Snapchat filters. What's interesting about looking at both the messages which spread through WhatsApp particularly was that the argument had been won from Labour's point of view. It was not about persuading young people to vote for Mr Corbyn ahead of Theresa May; it was about getting them to actually make it down to the polling station, of making it a point of pride to have actually voted, rather than saying they lost their polling card, or were too hungover to walk out of the front door to their nearest ballot box. It is too simplistic to say that Jeremy Corbyn did better than expected because he managed to persuade young people to vote when they hadn't voted en masse before. But the Labour leader did break the convention that those under twenty-five don't vote in significant numbers. It is also true that there are Tories less worried about the message and whether they need to bring about the end of austerity and scrap tuition fees, and more concerned about how that message is communicated. As one adviser to Jeremy Corbyn put it to me, the Conservative social media campaign was analogue.

Elections are always gruelling. Eighteen-hour days become the norm, while the only variation in our diet depends of what selection of Ginsters sandwiches are stocked at any given service station. But this campaign, fought in large part in the Labour heartlands in northern England and against a backdrop of two terrorist attacks, was particularly tough. There were similarities between this election and last year's referendum – Jeremy Corbyn played the insurgent intent on upsetting the status quo, while Theresa May allowed herself to be portrayed as part of an establishment, a distant figure from the woman who stood on the steps on No. 10 just eleven months earlier and promised to represent those struggling to get by, even if it meant upsetting the status quo enjoyed by the global elites. Indeed, the Tory vote share would have been enough to secure the majority Mrs May craved had Labour's vote stagnated as the polls suggested it was going to do only seven weeks before polling day. But instead there was a surge in support for Jeremy Corbyn many in the media failed to spot. There is a lesson there for our industry. Whether it's learnt by the time of the next election is a separate question entirely.

Theo Usherwood is Political Editor at LBC.

The new election rule book after the 2017 general election

Tim Carr

When the 2017 general election result appears in lists or tables of election results, it may not look that surprising to future generations. A casual observer may wonder what all the fuss was about. A hung parliament had, after all, happened recently, and the government survived successfully for five years of a full-term of parliament.

Of course, the crude electoral numbers do not on their own reveal the complex and surprising background to the result of 2017. The result itself may not be unique, but the circumstances of how we arrived there certainly are, and depending upon the direction of future events, it may represent a distinct and profound turning point in the country's political landscape.

As with all history, to make sense of what is to come, we must understand what has just passed to the best of our abilities. These are still early days and more data, research and study may alter or refine our assessment again. But right now, it does appear that much of the conventional political wisdom on how general elections are fought and how the electorate might respond has been unceremoniously discarded. Many of these unwritten rules, which in many cases overlap and interact with each other, have dominated and

guided election strategy and tactics for decades. Some were already looking frayed and worn, and the 2017 campaign simply hastened their demise.
Others will be more genuinely disconcerting to the political classes, as they
were challenged with little or no warning, and will likely be resisted before
eventually being accepted as part of the new political doctrine.

This chapter is an early, and no doubt flawed, attempt at outlining the
new election rule book.

The young do vote, but the under-45s are more significant

Contrary to many expectations, large numbers of young and first-time
voters did turn out to vote at the 2017 election. Precisely how many young
people turned out to vote though, is still open to a degree of speculation
and should be treated with caution until further data is available. We can
probably dismiss some of the wilder estimates made immediately after
polling day (eg. 72 per cent of 18–24s reported in *The Metro*, 9 June 2017)
as almost certainly being inaccurate. However, early data does indeed suggest that more young people voted than have done so for many years.

Nationally, turnout was up 2.5 percentage points from 2015 to 68.7 per
cent in 2017, the highest since 1997. The youth vote certainly followed and
may have exceeded this trend. Historically, turnout fell among all age groups
between 1992 and 2010, but has been increasing across all age groups, including the 18–24s, since 2010.

Ipsos MORI's 2017 How Britain Voted study suggests a 54 per cent turnout
among 18–24s, 55 per cent for 25–34s and 56 per cent for 35–44s. YouGov
have suggested a 57 per cent turnout figure for 18–19s and 59 per cent
for 20–24s. If confirmed by the British Election Study when it releases its
detailed assessment in the autumn, this would probably represent the most
significant increase in youth voting for decades. If such levels continue in
the future, then youth voters must be considered as important a demographic group as the 25–34 and 35–44 age groups, who turned out to vote
in similar numbers. This could have a profound impact upon the policy
developed and targeted at the youth.

Whatever the final estimated turnout figure, the young voted overwhelmingly for Labour. Jeremy Corbyn, the party and Momentum, were clearly
very successful in mobilising student and youth support, attracted by the
campaign (online campaigning, youth orientated celebrity endorsements),

the leader's personality (authentic, accessible, optimistic) and their policy platform (including the reintroduction of maintenance grants and abolition of university tuition fees, clearly set out in the party's manifesto).

Ipsos MORI estimate that 62 per cent of 18–24-year-olds (73 per cent of women, the highest in any population segment, and 52 per cent of men) voted for Labour versus only 27 per cent for the Conservatives. The next age group, 24–34 similarly voted 56 per cent Labour to 27 per cent Conservative. Lord Ashcroft's post-election survey estimated 67 per cent Labour to 18 per cent Conservative for the 18–24s, and 58 per cent Labour to 22 per cent Conservative for the 25–34s.

It is also clear that the size of the electorate in several constituencies with large student populations rose by more than 10 per cent, including Canterbury (which famously changed hands with 13,000 more Labour votes), Cambridge (an increase of over 10,000 votes for the Labour candidate), Bristol West (a stunning increase in the Labour vote of 24,000 votes) and Leeds Central (a Labour increase of 9,000 votes). In all these seats, the Liberal Democrats and Green Party found themselves squeezed dramatically.

However, while attracting the youth vote obviously helped Labour and was clearly instrumental in some seats, the notion that it was the young who turned the tide in favour of Jeremy Corbyn is probably exaggerated. The young have generally voted definitively for Labour. For instance, in 2015 it was 43 per cent Labour to 27 per cent Conservative for 18–24s).

Probably more significant electorally was the move to Labour by voters in their thirties and forties. These voter groups shifted massively towards Corbyn's Labour in 2017 and will be of greater concern to the Conservatives looking to the future. We do not yet know in detail why these age groups deserted the Conservatives, but consisting of people with children, mortgages, careers and older living parents, they may have viewed the proposed 'dementia tax' and changes to free school lunches particularly negatively.

Evenly split in 2015, according to Ipsos MORI (36 per cent Labour to 33 per cent Conservative and 35 per cent each respectively), both groups moved towards Labour in large numbers in 2017, leading by 56 per cent to 27 per cent among 25–34s – a huge gap of 29 percentage points – and 49 per cent Labour to 33 per cent Conservative among 35–44s – a gap of 16 percentage points. Lord Ashcroft's post-election polling confirmed near identical numbers.

As the academic Professor Matthew Goodwin has pointed out, of the twenty seats where the Labour vote increased most dramatically, on average the dominant group is 30–44-year-olds, not 18–24-year-olds.

Interestingly, when considering that youth turnout first began to decline when the current 35–44-year-olds were 18–24 in the 1990s, the generational dividing line may therefore be between the under-45s versus the over-45s. Whatever the reason, the dividing line in voting behaviour at the age of forty-five is real. How the voting pattern of this age group develops as it ages will be crucial to future electoral success.

The Conservatives only had the lead in age groups over forty-five, and overwhelmingly led among the over sixty-fives, who were, perhaps surprisingly, significantly more supportive of the Conservatives in 2017 than they were in 2015, despite the aborted 'dementia tax' and proposed end of the triple pension lock after 2020.

Class is no longer the defining feature of party affiliation

Age was not the only striking characteristic of how Britain voted. Class politics was turned upside down at the 2017 election. Labour, the party founded to represent the working class, made its greatest gains among the middle classes in London and the south of England. The Conservatives, traditionally the party of the middle class, made its biggest gains in the North, advancing by an average of 8 percentage points, and the Midlands, an increase of eight and half percentage points, in previously Labour-held seats. Major seats gains were made by the Conservatives in a number of traditionally working-class seats – Copeland, North East Derbyshire, Mansfield, Middlesbrough South, Stoke-on-Trent South and Walsall North.

The Conservatives may have maintained a six-point lead among the top socio-economic grouping of ABC1s, but the Labour vote share of this group increased by 12 percentage points from 2015, Labour's best score among ABC1s since 1979. Similarly, while Labour had a four-point lead among C2DEs and increased its vote share, the Conservatives enjoyed a 12 percentage point increase, their best score among C2DEs since 1979. According to Professor John Curtice, this pattern is confirmed by the election results themselves, with constituencies with more manual workers showing an 11 percentage point increase in support for the Conservatives, compared to a slight reduction in seats where fewer people are classified as working class.

Another new defining feature of how people vote is by education. According to YouGov's massive 52,615 participant post-election survey, voters with a low level of education (GCSE or below) were far more likely to vote Conservative (55 per cent, versus 33 per cent for Labour). Those with a 'medium' level of education, presumably A-Levels or equivalents, were more evenly split with 45 per cent voting for the Conservatives and 40 per cent Labour. However, those with a degree or higher level of qualification voted for Labour by 49 per cent to the Conservatives' 32 per cent.

Both Lord Ashcroft's polls and Ipsos-MORI also show that younger Labour voters were far more likely to be female, with the two parties roughly level in the 45–54 age group and then the Conservatives winning substantially among older women.

The Conservatives also fell further behind Labour among BME voters. The indications are that Labour's lead among BME voters increased, and the Conservative vote share among BMEs fell. This was potentially on the back of increased turnout. Turnout among BMEs increased 6 percentage points since 2015.

Ironically, for all the clear failings of the Conservative campaign, it was very successful in winning over the votes of working-class voters, which was one of its key targets. Its problem was that it failed to maintain its 2015 level of support among those in the mid-age ranges and among the professional middle classes. The Conservatives still have a problem with BME voters and, increasingly, a problem with younger women. The challenge for Labour is that its vote is composed of many different and sometimes incoherent groups which may be difficult to hold together at future elections. As the veteran pollster and commentator Peter Kellner has pointed out, constituencies such as Bristol West (biggest rise in Labour vote) and Knowlsey (biggest Labour majority by votes), have very little in common.

For the time being at least, Brexit is the defining feature of British politics

The authoritative British Election Study (BES) has shown that beneath all the politicking of the election campaign, the election really was about Brexit, even though other issues dominated the campaign. Of the 30,000 voters surveyed, one in three chose Brexit or the EU as the most important issue in the election, compared to one in ten for the NHS and one in twenty focused on the economy.

The BES reveals that more than half of UKIP's vote in 2015 switched to the Conservatives, compared to only 18 per cent to Labour and 18 per cent who stayed with UKIP. The Conservatives won over 60 per cent of the Leave vote. Labour picked up Remain voters across the political spectrum with more than half of all Remain voters. Nearly two thirds of the Greens' voters in 2015 switched to Labour and around a quarter of the Liberal Democrats. Perhaps surprisingly, around a quarter of Remain voters voted for the Conservatives, showing once again that voters balance a variety of factors when deciding how to cast their vote.

The BES study suggests that the election was subtler than simply Remain or Leave; the manner and characteristics of how the UK leaves the EU was also important. In broad terms, the Conservatives were the party of hard Brexit and Labour were the party for soft Brexit.

On average, there was a one-point swing to the Conservatives in seats where over 60 per cent of people voted Leave, compared to a 7-percentage-point swing to Labour in seats where more than 55 per cent voted Remain.

Election campaigns do matter

The usual political wisdom has been that perception is more important than policy. Voters have made up their minds about the prospective Prime Ministers on offer long before an election is called, having formulated their opinion over a period of months or years. While opinion polls may how some degree of movement during a campaign, reflecting the parties' relative fortunes, campaigns themselves do not matter that much. They have been more about identifying and getting the vote out on polling day. Another conventional wisdom has been that once a party has established its fundamental messaging, they resolutely stick to it, no matter what comes at them.

The decline in the fortunes of the Conservatives and Theresa May in 2017 has probably put an end to such orthodox thinking. Clearly, the style, messaging, manifesto and policy set out in campaigns can matter very much, fundamentally changing people's voting intentions.

The BES study reveals that 19 per cent of voters switched parties during the course of the campaign, but this is only slightly higher than the 17 per cent of voters who did so during 2015. However, in 2015, both Labour and the Conservatives won about a quarter of late switching voters. In 2017

Labour won 54 per cent of switching voters to the Conservatives' 19 per cent. Also, Labour won more than half of those who had not made up their mind about who to vote before the election campaign started.

According to Lord Ashcroft's polls, 57 per cent of Labour voters finally decided how they were going to vote during the last month before polling day, compared to only 43 per cent of Tory voters. This suggests that large numbers of eventual Labour voters were up for grabs had the Conservative campaign been more effective and persuasive. Similarly, ICM data has suggested that young people's commitment to absolutely vote strengthened in the last week of the campaign, as Labour's positive and energetic campaign developed momentum.

The substantial leads in favourability ratings enjoyed by Theresa May at the start of the campaign plummeted by the crucial last two weeks. Sixty-one per cent of voters believed that she would make the most capable PM in April 2017, making her more popular with voters than any leader since the late 1970s. For a campaign based around the premise that the election was a personal confidence vote on the leadership qualities of Theresa May, this clearly had near disastrous consequences. As the election campaign progressed, the criticisms – that she was too arrogant, wooden, uncaring, distant and prone to changing her mind – intensified and gained widespread traction, not least among the political media. As May faltered, Jeremy Corbyn seemingly grew in stature, viewed increasingly by much of the electorate as honest, authentic, positive, energetic and open, being prepared to participate in TV debates and interacting daily with ordinary people. The old adage that a party rally of the faithful does not translate into votes was proved wrong. The mass rallies held throughout the country really did signify a resurgent Labour Party. In stark contrast to May, Corbyn looked as if he was enjoying the campaign and deployed his campaigning skills with energy and enthusiasm, confounding many of his critics and winning over previous doubters in the electorate.

The Conservative campaign has been much criticised for being overly centralised and too rigid, failing to respond to a faltering strategy as the polls narrowed. Campaigns need to be flexible and adapt to circumstances. The more overtly negative Conservative campaign – some have said it was a continuation of so-called Project Fear, used effectively in the Scottish referendum but unsuccessful during the EU referendum – contrasted with the more positive and upbeat tone of Labour, which was clearly more appealing to some parts of the electorate. The idea that 'all politics is local' was largely rejected in favour of national messages, and there have been reports that local Conservative constituency associations were actively warned not to focus on local issues as they would lose votes. Given that the Tory high command believed that a substantial majority was on the cards right up until seats started to be declared in the early hours of election night, the Conservatives clearly need significantly better data. Since the election, several highly critical insider accounts have been published by key Conservative personnel and these suggest that there were structural and personality issues afflicting the campaign. Placards and posters did change during the campaign, moving from focusing on Theresa May personally, and barely mentioning the Conservatives in the first few weeks, to focusing more on the party, although we do not know yet whether this evolution was planned from the start. The Conservative election campaign even failed to enthuse party members, according to a ConservativeHome survey of party members, which showed that only 11 per cent put the campaign in the top three categories for effectiveness, with 32 per cent placing it in the bottom three.

The electorate want substance, not just slogans

Political parties have always sought consistency about what is said or promised during election campaigns. The opposite tends not to go down too well with the voters. Uniting around a slogan has been a political tool for hundreds of years. In modern times, 'message discipline' has largely come to mean soundbites or sloganeering, a carefully manufactured phrase that has been road-tested by focus groups and is deemed to have resonance. Sloganeering formed a central part of the Conservatives' successful 2015 campaign, with 'long-term economic plan' and the 'chaos' of a Labour and SNP alliance endlessly repeated at every opportunity for several months in the run-up to the general election. Although mocked, it worked, and voter recall of 'long-term economic plan' was high.

Two years later the experience of sloganeering was very different. The electorate appeared weary of the soulless, endless repetition of 'strong and stable leadership' and 'coalition of chaos'. They appeared to increasingly grate with voters, particularly when proffered by a party that sometimes seemed to contradict the former and emulate the latter. Their use was met with audible groans by TV debate audiences, they were ridiculed by political commentators and comedians alike and even Conservative supporters started to wince as they were mechanically trotted out in every interview. Slogans, of course, will not disappear, but their future use is likely to be more measured and they should be adaptable to changing circumstances.

Some policies really matter in campaigns

Few voters may read party manifestos, but some key policies really matter in campaigns, either positively or negatively. The idea that policy does not matter is false. There are the big encompassing issues – privatisation in the 1980s and early 1990s, social change in the late 1990s and early 2000s, the financial crash and the deficit in 2010, coalition government in 2015 and Brexit in 2017 – but there are also more localised issues, pertinent to a particular election campaign, that have resonance or dissonance to voters. Generally, the party that has 'issue ownership' over the most pressing current issues usually holds a significant advantage. Polls showed that the Conservatives had leads on Brexit, immigration and the economy, while Labour had big leads on the NHS and education.

Very few party policies apparently proved memorable to voters in 2017, but they may have contributed to voting patterns, particularly among swing voters. Research by Britain Thinks suggests that the main issues with cut-through were, for the Conservatives, social care/dementia tax (and the subsequent U-turn), fox hunting and free school lunches replaced by breakfasts; for Labour, scrapping tuition fees and four new bank holidays; and for the Liberal Democrats, legalising cannabis.

Polling during the campaign also found that there was significant majority support for some of Labour's policy platforms, considered 'radical' in Westminster – re-nationalisation of the railways, Royal Mail and utilities, scrapping tuition fees and higher tax for those earning more than £80,000 a year.

With the Westminster terrorist attack and two more attacks – Manchester and London Bridge – during the campaign, a national debate about how to tackle extremism and questions in parts of the media about the Labour leadership's attitude towards terrorism, it is perhaps unsurprising that the British Election Study suggested that terrorism and security were important to voters. Nevertheless, it is interesting to note that terrorism and security was marginally considered as the biggest issue by more of those surveyed than the NHS.

Economic competence still matters

It has long been argued that whoever wins the economic argument and record wins the election. In most campaigns, economic competency is the major issue, with voters ultimately voting with their wallets/purses. Historically, Prime Ministers do not choose to fight elections at times when there is a challenging economic environment, and when they have been forced to, they tend to lose.

Yet the economy hardly featured in the campaigns, and only one in twenty polled voters suggested that the economy was the single most important issue facing the country. With the Conservatives enjoying considerable leads in the polls on being the most trusted to run the economy, even when their campaign was faltering, it is perhaps surprising that they did not choose to focus more on the economy. Perhaps they read the numbers correctly that, this time, it was not one of the electorate's key concerns. Or perhaps it was a deliberate strategy given there are several potential economic challenges: historically slow wage rises, an uncertain direction for inflation and the weak post-EU referendum pound. Economic competence may not have been front and centre in the campaign, but it would have been there, beneath the surface. It would undoubtedly be a mistake to diminish the importance of economic competence as an election issue.

Local election results are a poor indicator of general election performance

The performance of parties at the local elections preceding a general election have generally been considered a reasonable indicator of how the parties will perform in a national vote. Putting to one side that every party almost inevitably claims victory on some set of criteria, local voting figures are extrapolated to determine what the equivalent performance might be at a general election. Even taking into account the typical 'mid-term blues' that most governments experience, such as specific local issues and protest votes, they are generally seen as a good indicator of the underlying voting trends towards parties. On this basis, it has been claimed that opposition parties generally do not achieve higher shares of the vote in a general election than they have in the local election before. Perform well and the opposition has a chance. Perform badly and it is not looking good.

The local elections in May 2017 should put paid to this concept. After the strongest local election gains for a governing party for more than forty years, achieving 38 per cent of the votes cast, and Labour's dismal 27 per cent, many observers claimed that the writing was on the wall for the general election only one month away. Labour was fighting for survival and would struggle to achieve a similar vote weeks later.

Yet within a month, Labour added a whopping 13 per cent to its vote, pushing the Conservatives into a minority government and exceeding expectations in achieving 40 per cent of the vote, breaking historical records. 2017 was a rarity in that local elections are typically held on the same day as a general election, as they were in 2015, 2010 and 2005. Not since 1992 have they been held in the same year as a general election, but preceding the general election by weeks. Although unusual, the 2017 result should confirm that general election results can never be assumed on the basis of local election results.

Predictive models are the future, not polls

As is well chartered, most polling companies had another bad election in predicting the outcome. But they were clearly not alone. Most politicians, commentators, academics and poll watchers expected a large Conservative majority. The clear exceptions were YouGov, Survation and, in some respects, Panelbase. This time they cannot be accused of 'herding', tweaking their models to move closer to a central assessment, although they did all generally show a narrowing of the gap between the two major parties as the campaign progressed.

In some respect, the pollsters had a good election. The conclusion of the British Polling Council (BPC), the industry's oversight body, is that the pollsters were very good at predicting the Conservative vote, with an average of the final polls being only 0.2 per cent higher than the actual result. They were also very close to predicting the result for the Liberal Democrats, with the average poll figure only 0.3 per cent different from the result. In Scotland, as early as 18–21 April, Panelbase correctly predicted twelve seat gains to the Conservatives, although they predicted a 33 per cent vote share versus the 29 per cent achieved and 44 per cent to the SNP with only eleven seat losses, versus 37 per cent vote share and a loss of twenty-one seats.

The problem, which will bedevil the sector, was Labour, with an average predicted Labour vote 5.2 per cent below their actual share. They simply did not predict Labour's dramatic surge in support. The pattern more recently has been to overestimate Labour and underestimate Conservative support. As the BPC pointed out, this was only the second election since 1987 when the pollsters have underestimated the Labour share of the vote.

YouGov's now infamous predictive 'MRP' model is discussed in detail elsewhere in these pages by Joe Twyman, but this seat-by-seat analysis, based on 50,000 interviews, was by far the most accurate forecast produced, predicting a hung parliament with twenty Conservatives losses and thirty Labour gains on 31 May 2017.

It has all been said before, of course, but with the voting complexities of the UK's first past the post system, perhaps it really is time to focus on predictive models that analyse large amounts of data and take account of regional and local factors, rather than national polls that typically sample 1,000 individuals.

An election could be won from the left

It has been an adage of modern political thinking that a UK election cannot be won from the left. This idea developed out of the infamous 1983 election campaign in which Michael Foot's Labour Party fought on a strongly left-wing platform and lost heavily to the Conservatives (losing 3 million votes, vote share falling 9 per cent and the loss of fifty-two seats). It was at the core of the modernising movement in the Labour Party that began with Neil Kinnock and culminated with Tony Blair. His New Labour eschewed democratic socialism in favour of a social justice platform that would appeal to the public and make Labour electable again.

In 2017, all of the evidence suggests that the left-wing platform promoted by Jeremy Corbyn and Labour's manifesto policies were an electoral asset, with many 'left-wing' policies supported by a majority of voters. The result was that Labour won its best share of the vote since 2001, beating Tony Blair, Gordon Brown and Ed Miliband in 2005, 2010 and 2015 respectively. It was also the party's largest increase in Labour's vote between elections since Clement Attlee in 1945 – 9.6 per cent to Attlee's 10.4 per cent, with Blair only managing 8.8 per cent between 1992 and 1997.

Jeremy Corbyn defied his critics both externally and within his party, and far exceeded expectations with a very impressive share of the vote, but Labour still clearly lost this election, the third loss in a row. It may have been a moral victory for Labour, but it was certainly not an electoral one. Labour ended up fifty-six seats behind the Conservatives, worse than Gordon Brown in 2010 (forty-eight behind), Harold Wilson in 1970 (forty-two behind) and Clement Attlee in 1951 (twenty-six behind). In terms of Labour MPs, the party now has more MPs (262 in 2017) than it did in 2015 (232) and marginally more than in 2010 (258), but significantly fewer than in 2005 (348) and 2001 (402).

The momentum may well be with Labour. It needs to win around thirty-four seats to become the largest party and sixty-four to have a majority. It has a very large and enthusiastic membership base (600,000+), driven by the highly effective Momentum movement which was able to deliver hundreds of canvassers in target seats. Over two thirds of members have joined since 2015. It has been suggested that half of the new members have voted for the Liberal Democrats or Greens in the past, indicating a broader base than is sometimes credited. There are plans to develop a grassroots Labour cultural programme including social spaces, cinema clubs, food banks, breakfast clubs and health clinics on popular organisation, mobilisation and political assertiveness. This may be possible with such a large and enthused membership.

Jeremy Corbyn is secure as party leader as long as he wishes to stay. The moderate's strategy of stepping back to let him suffer a bruising defeat at the ballot box and wait for his resignation, which may not have been forthcoming, clearly failed. Many have swallowed their pride and have embraced Corbyn now that he has demonstrated his electoral attractiveness. The Corbyn grip on the party will only tighten. The McDonnell amendment to be discussed at the September 2017 Labour Party annual conference will seek to lower the nominations threshold for future leadership contests from the current 15 per cent to only 5 per cent. The real party machinery changes are likely to happen at the 2018 conference in Liverpool when re-selection, or the more benign sounding 'candidate selection and accountability', requiring high levels of local support and a threshold of 66 per cent support among branches and affiliates rather than simple majority are likely to be promoted. There are also likely to be motions to reform the NEC (increasing the number of CLP representatives from six to ten) and introduce elections for the position of General Secretary.

It takes more than optimism to win a general election. The electoral road ahead could be tough and expectations will need to be managed. The Conservatives only need a 0.5 per cent swing to win a majority and, while possible, it is unlikely to conduct as poor a campaign at the next election, whenever that will be, as it did in 2017, and will have the potential benefit of a new leader. Labour achieved a 2.05 per cent swing in 2017, but a similar swing would make them the largest party, not secure a majority. To achieve a majority would require a uniform swing of 3.7 per cent and that has only been achieved previously in 1997 and 1945. Of Labour's sixty-four target seats on paper, eighteen are held by the SNP. While Labour did have a recovery of sorts, the reality is that it only gained 10,000 votes in 2017. To stand any chance of winning a further eighteen seats from the SNP, it would have to perform significantly better. The seats with large numbers of Remain voters, or young voters, or higher educated voters have, to a large degree, already been won.

Labour increased the size of the majority in every seat it won, with spectacularly large increases in previously safe seats. It would clearly have benefited electorally if it had been able to spread its increase in votes across more constituencies. Labour won a total of thirty-seven seats with a higher vote share than in the seat of the Conservatives' highest vote share. The concentration of Labour votes and its struggle to uniformly add votes across a wider range of seats remains a significant electoral challenge.

As set out earlier, Labour has a major problem with attracting working-class voters. Labour MP for Sedgefield Phil Wilson published a brutal assessment of the problem after the election. The higher the percentage of working-class voters in a constituency, the more there was a swing to the Conservatives. There was a swing against Labour in 130 seats, primarily comprised of seats typically classified as solid Labour territory – Northern and Midlands, old coal-mining constituencies. In the North East, the Conservatives achieved their highest vote since 1983. Although having achieved huge gains in middle-class support, the reality is that a Labour victory is only going to possible if it can marry middle-class support with its traditional core working-class support. As Phil Wilson summarised:

> The route to a sustainable Labour victory will not be found by travelling only the middle-class streets of Kensington and the campuses of our university towns; the route must take us through the working-class communities of the North too. To win over the middle classes, but lose the support of the working classes would be the Labour party's gravest folly.

Given the uncertainties in the political landscape and volatile mood of the

British electorate, all options are open. The Conservatives may perform better or Labour could perform worse. The increased number of super-marginal seats means that relatively small shifts in individual seats may impact the electoral picture. Labour's fence-sitting on Brexit, considered masterly by some, unsustainable by others, could yet have a major impact on levels of support. Jeremy Corbyn has, though, revitalised the Labour movement and although the electoral maths remains tricky, Labour may enter the next election cycle as the underdog, rather than the no-hoper.

Scots can still vote for the Tories

The longest-standing joke in Scottish politics is no more. There are now significantly more Tory MPs in Scotland than there are pandas (there are two, apparently, in Edinburgh Zoo). With thirteen MPs after the election, there are now more Conservative MPs than there have been since 1987. There were none in 1997 and only one from 2001 until 2017 (David Mundell since 2005). The Conservative vote share went up 13.7 per cent to 28.6 per cent (adding 320,000 votes).

Scots were attracted back to the Conservatives for the first time in two generations by a combination of the popularity of Ruth Davidson, who has confounded the longstanding belief that the party could never again do well in Scotland, and a focusing of the unionist vote, opposed to a second independence referendum. The Conservatives won a swathe of seats in south and north-east Scotland, defeating the Scottish National Party deputy leader Angus Robertson and the party's former leader Alex Salmond in the process. Without these gains in Scotland, Theresa May would certainly not have been able to stay in power.

The election showed that the Scottish National Party (SNP) is not invincible, with their vote falling 13.1 per cent to 36.9 per cent. It is estimated that around a quarter of SNP voters in 2015 did not bother to vote in 2017, that around one in ten SNP voters in 2015 switched to Labour and that slighter fewer, around 8 per cent, of SNP voters even switched to the Conservatives. Despite falling from fifty-six seats in 2016 to thirty-five seats in 2017 – nearly 40 per cent of their seats – the SNP remains the largest party and won a clear majority of seats and so just about managed to carry off their post-election narrative that they had 'won' the election in Scotland.

Labour was beaten by the Conservatives in Scotland for the first time since 1959, finishing third with 27.1 per cent of the vote, up by 2.8 per cent. Despite having won seven seats, Scottish Labour only increased their vote in the general election by under 10,000. Dismissing the notion of the impact of a 'Corbyn surge' in Scotland, the journalist Alex Massie has pointed out that this equates to 166 voters per constituency.

The prospect of a second independence referendum was probably not the only factor influencing voters, but the sharp decline in support for the SNP and the resurgence of all three unionist parties (the Liberal Democrats gained three seats) means that the prospects of a so-called IndyRef2 have diminished for now. With the SNP running the Scottish Government and as the largest Scottish party in Westminster, the issue has certainly not gone away and is certain to be revisited in the future, probably post-Brexit negotiations and perhaps dependent upon the result of the next Scottish Parliament elections in 2021.

The two-party system is alive and kicking

When the combined vote share of the Conservatives and Labour fell below 70 to 67.6 per cent at the 2005 general election, the two-party system that has dominated British politics since 1945 looked threatened. When it fell further to 65.1 per cent, resulting in a Conservative–Liberal Democrat coalition government, the end of the two-party system was loudly proclaimed. In 2015, the combined vote share remained stubbornly at 67.3 per cent, the SNP won fifty-six of fifty-nine seats and the Liberal Democrats, UK Independence Party and the Greens all achieved respectable vote shares, even if this did not translate to seats under first past the post. The fragmentation of British political parties looked set to remain.

Then in 2017 the Conservatives and Labour won 84.4 per cent of the UK vote, the highest combined vote share since the 1970 general election. Largely seen as an irrelevance post-EU referendum and bereft of Nigel Farage, UKIP's share of the vote plummeted from 12.6 per cent in 2015 to less than 2 per cent The Greens saw their vote halved from the 3.8 per cent it gained in 2015 and the Liberal Democrats slightly increased its share of the vote, rising to 7.9 per cent, but failed to make substantive gains with its central policy of a second EU referendum and fell back in the number of seats it is likely to genuinely contest at the next election.

Of course, Brexit may, at least for the next election or two, continue to polarise the electorate with Leavers largely coalescing around the Conservatives and Remainers with Labour. But with the SNP in retreat in Scotland and no sign currently of the re-emergence of a substantive third force in national British politics, the dominance of the Conservatives and Labour looks set to continue for the time being, unless there is a fundamental realignment of the political landscape and the emergence of a new political force, probably from the centre.

TV and radio matter, but the influence of newspapers continues to decline

The 2017 election campaign provided further evidence that the mainstream media, and particularly the press, has a declining impact on influencing how people vote. If it was ever true, no longer can it be said that 'It's The Sun Wot Won It'.

Large numbers of readers of some broadsheets generally considered influential simply did not vote in 2017. YouGov estimates that 52 per cent of *Sun* readers did not vote in 2017, 35 per cent of *Mirror* readers and 24 per cent of *Daily Mail* readers. Furthermore, despite the obvious political positions taken by some newspapers, large chunks of their readership often defy a paper's editorial stance or simply do not vote. The YouGov post-election survey revealed that 30 per cent of *Sun* readers voted Labour while 19 per cent of *Mirror* readers voted Conservative.

A large proportion of the press conducted a vociferous and personal campaign against Jeremy Corbyn, highlighting his views on the Falklands and reported relationships with the IRA and other terrorist organisations in the 1980s. The result would suggest that 40 per cent of people either did not believe the evidence presented, agreed with his views or simply did not care. Using terminology that would be recognised in financial markets in the City of London, leading Corbynista Matt Zarb-Cousin suggested the reason why voters ignored the anti-Corbyn press: 'By the time the election began a lot of what was thrown at Jeremy had already been priced in by the public. They weren't so concerned by things Jeremy might have said or done in the past, they wanted to know what he would do for them.'

If the 2017 election campaign suggested a further decline in the influence of newspapers, it re-confirmed the impact of television and radio, despite continued accusations of bias from both the left and the right.

The set piece TV debates, interviews and panel discussions proved once again to be a centrepiece of the campaign and highlighted that they cannot be ignored. The genie of the TV debate has been released and there is no going back. Theresa May's decision not to attend the BBC seven-way debate when Jeremy Corbyn had announced his last-minute appearance was clearly disastrous. Her replacement, Amber Rudd, may have performed well, but the impression, rightly or wrongly, was that May was dodging a genuine debate. Corbyn said that she was showing 'weakness' by not attending, while Labour's Angela Rayner said that Mrs May is 'for turning, but not for turning up'. The Conservatives' response that Corbyn should stop 'counting his TV appearances' and 'start thinking about Brexit' failed to stem the tide of criticism.

Only a small proportion of voters may have watched the *Question Time* special a week before polling day, but the programme's reach was substantially larger than the official viewing figures. Polling suggested that 72 per cent of voters had seen or heard something about the debate. There was widespread discussion and distribution on social media and in news clips of the 'no magic money tree' response to an NHS nurse. Radio provided some of the campaign's most compelling and dramatic 'car crash interviews', with Jeremy Corbyn, Diane Abbott, Tim Farron and others all falling prey to unpreparedness or forensic dissection of policy positions. All of them were gleefully shared on social media to a potentially massive audience by opponents.

At first, there appeared to be little discernible pattern to Jeremy Corbyn's constituency visits and rallies, visiting a Conservative-held marginal and then holding a big rally in a very safe Labour seat. The answer appears to be the importance of regional TV news and big local rallies with thousands of enthusiastic supporters looking good on television and seen by voters in marginal constituencies.

The growing importance of the new online media

Although it does have obvious limitations, 2017 confirmed that election campaigns are increasingly fought online. It is the medium through which campaigns are reported, gaffes are highlighted, policies are ridiculed or promoted, and TV and radio appearances are condensed. That is not to say that the campaign on the doorstep and the TV screen are not still crucial, but online provides a lively arena for the battle for votes.

There is a clear generational divide over how voters consume and digest news. Every age group under forty-five identifies online sources for news and opinion ahead of the more traditional sources of television, radio and newspapers. Research by the Reuters Institute at the University of Oxford puts the figure at 88 per cent for 18–19-year-olds, 83 per cent for 20–24s, 59 per cent for 25–29s and 60 per cent for 30–39s. It is not until the age of forty or thereabouts that offline (traditional) media consumption overtakes online, with 40 per cent online for 40–49s, 29 per cent for 50–59s, 21 per cent for 60–69s and 16 per cent for the over-70s.

Nearly half of voters (47 per cent) may still go directly to the websites of broadcasters or newspapers for their news, particularly the BBC, but the news is increasingly sourced from either social media (Facebook, Twitter etc) or search engines (Google etc).

There have long been concerns that social media encourages the formation of echo chambers or filter bubbles, where people only get information from news sources or individuals with whom they already agree, rather than seeking more independent reporting and views, although with a distinctly partisan newspaper industry this problem has arguably long existed in a different form. It is alternatively argued, with some evidence, that syndicated news via search engines might actually increase the number of news sources available to people. This debate will continue long into the future.

There are reports that the Conservative Party spent huge sums on Facebook adverts, exceeding the estimated £1.2 million spent in 2015. The early evidence suggests that they lost the Facebook war. The top ten links shared on Facebook during the campaign were either pro-Labour or anti-Tory, with roughly half a million shares each. Labour dramatically increased its online following on Facebook, Instagram and Twitter, with only small increases by the Conservatives.

A phenomenon that has been developing for some time, certainly since Jeremy Corbyn's leadership victory, has been the growth of a new online, left-leaning media, dubbed the 'alt-left media'. The much-maligned mainstream media (MSM) began to sit up and take notice during the 2017 campaign, although ironically it was a journalist, Jim Waterson, from another online news organisation, BuzzFeed, that brought it to wider attention.

Fuelled by a distrust of overt bias of newspapers (including *The Guardian*, which has for long spells been highly critical of Jeremy Corbyn) and the perceived bias of the BBC and ITV, this 'alt-left media' provides a distinct alternative political view. These outlets – including Novara, Evolve, Skwawkbox, Red Pepper, Another Angry Voice and the Canary – largely eschew Twitter, which they regard as dominated by the MSM, and instead focus on Facebook, delivering and sharing content directly to supporters and like-minded individuals. They are supported by popular viral content produced by a range of political activists/youth culture icons such as Lowkey, Stormzy and JME. Utilising the online guerrilla tactics of viral graphics, tabloid attention-grabbing headlines and deploying instant rebuttal, some figures suggest that their viral content was shared more widely than many news organisations, although the traditional news outlets continue to dominate in direct visits to websites or through mobile apps. The Canary has claimed that its articles regularly receive 500,000 views each and one article on Another Angry Voice attracted 1.5 million views. It is clear that collectively these sites now command a readership in the millions composed of a left-leaning and largely youthful audience. They routinely reject criticism, from the mainstream media, that they are too ideologically driven, lack journalistic integrity and oversight and are responsible themselves for 'fake news'.

These sites have been highly influential internally within the Labour movement, attacking criticism of the Corbyn project and the Labour Party's move to the left. BuzzFeed reported that many Labour MP's felt unable to place stories or comment pieces targeting potential floating voters in *The Sun* or the *Daily Mail*, for fear of online attack pieces accusing them of co-operating with hated media outlets.

All the available data and anecdotal evidence suggests that the Conservatives lost the online communications battle to Labour and this may have had a significant impact on why the under-45s largely voted Labour. The new online and increasingly bi-partisan media is here to stay and its influence is likely to increase.

What this means for the next parliament and election

Beyond the immediate aftermath of the election and the formation of the new, minority Conservative government, the full implications of the 2017 general election have yet to become fully apparent. It is suggested above that many of the unwritten rules around which elections are fought have fundamentally changed. Whether all, or some, of these changes are temporary or permanent remains to be seen; little in British politics can be taken for granted anymore. The next parliament, however long it lasts, will be characterised by the implications of the result: a parliament dominated by Brexit and its various potential shades; policy in flux as both major parties seek to formulate an election-winning policy platform; a controversial Conservative–DUP alliance that could be problematic further down the line; a fiery Conservative leadership contest with no clear heir apparent; a Labour Party that could become divided once again as internal procedural changes threaten moderate Labour MPs; a slender majority, inevitably leading to losses and some rebellions; English votes for English laws saving the government on occasion; an empowered House of Lords that seeks to establish its role under a minority government and resolve the Salisbury Convention dilemma; the scrapping of the proposed 2018 boundary changes; and ending with a highly uncertain next general election with a volatile electorate fought under an evolving mix of campaign rules.

The 2017 election showed a nation that is sharply and almost evenly divided across many fault lines – politically, demographically, regionally and in terms of Brexit. Navigating these complexities at a time of historic constitutional transformation as Brexit is realised will prove a major challenge for all political parties. Whether a single party can rise to the challenge to claim outright victory at the next election will be fascinating to observe.

2017 general election – regional Survey

Robert Waller

East Midlands

This is a regional survey, but it is essential to acknowledge that there were very significant differences within each region of the United Kingdom, as well as between them. What's more, these differences reveal the important factors and trends that explain the outcome of one of the most fascinating, complex and unpredictable general elections for decades.

We start, in alphabetical order, with the East Midlands. This is indeed a region which illustrates several key points that need to be made. Labour gained three seats, but also lost two – of only five altogether. This mixed result was not due to the proud differences between the counties included in the region. Two of the gains were in Derbyshire – Derby North and High Peak. However, so was one of the losses – North East Derbyshire. In neighbouring Nottinghamshire, Labour lost Mansfield and nearly Ashfield too, where the Conservative vote share increased by over 19 per cent, one of their very best performances anywhere outside Scotland, in a seat ranked only No. 94 on their national target list. The 4,600 votes for an 'Ashfield Independent' may even have denied the Tories a remarkable gain, which would have been redolent of the famous 1977 Ashfield by-election.

How can this wide apparent variation even within sub-regions be explained? The first place to look is the relation of the 2017 results to voting in the 2016 European Union referendum. In general, Labour did better in the more strongly 'Remain' areas, and worse in those that heavily preferred 'Brexit'. Derby North was their No. 1 target in the East Midlands, and indeed their No. 2 anywhere, having lost it by only forty-one votes in 2015. However, it also only voted for Brexit by 53.7 per cent, well under the average for an English seat. High Peak was a much more unlikely gain, ninth in the region and forty-fourth overall – but it registered close to 50–50 in the referendum. Labour was able to mobilise almost all of that Remain support in High Peak, especially as the Liberal Democrats polled less than 5 per cent in June 2017.

By contrast, in North East Derbyshire, where Labour were ousted, the Brexit vote reached over 62 per cent. Their other loss, Mansfield, was one of the dozen most strongly Brexit seats in the UK – 70.9 per cent. There is clearly something in the argument heard after the June general election that it constituted the 'revenge of the remainers'. The strategy of those around Theresa May was to appeal to Tory Europhobes and UKIPpers by emphasising that 'Brexit means Brexit' and that her negotiating position would be tough – for example, without concessions being made to secure full access to the single market. This inevitably led to a weaker performance in constituencies where substantial numbers of voters either had preferred EU membership or favoured a softer landing.

This analysis applies to other regions in England and Wales, of course. It is related too, to another key point: what happened to the UKIP vote? The Conservative campaign aimed to gather in the vast majority of ex-UKIP voters as that party appeared to crumble, having achieved its main goal and suffering from changes in leadership. In Mansfield, UKIP had a 25 per cent share in 2015 and this went down to 5 per cent – while the Conservatives added fully 18 per cent. Next door in Ashfield, UKIP went down from 21 per cent to 4 per cent. However in High Peak, UKIP had only polled 11 per cent in 2015, well below their average in England. This may also help to explain Labour's third gain in the East Midlands region, Lincoln – not only the most Remain place in a strongly Brexit county, but a constituency where UKIP managed a mere 12 per cent two years ago.

We can delve deeper still when explaining the variations within the East Midlands. Attitudes towards Europe relate to more fundamental characteristics of British voters. For example, it is fair to describe Mansfield and

Ashfield as predominantly 'white working class' seats, both being situated on the former Nottinghamshire coalfield. Even though the miners of that county were noted as opponents of Arthur Scargill's strike in 1984–85, all pits in the county have now been closed, the last to go being Thoresby Colliery in July 2015. Like other ex-mining areas in Yorkshire and County Durham, these sub-regions, perhaps feeling left out and searching for a role, proved fertile ground for UKIP in 2015 – and largely swung to the Conservatives in 2017. Formerly strongholds of the Labour Party, such places have not responded well to its apparent switch to support for minority groups, and the metropolitan leadership of Miliband and now Corbyn.

It might be noted here that North East Derbyshire is also situated on an old coalfield, and perhaps most striking of all was the result in Bolsover. There could hardly be a better example of an ex-mining seat with its archetypal veteran 'beast' of an MP, Dennis Skinner, eighty-five years of age, a miner from 1949 to 1970 and seemingly a permanent growling denizen of the Commons since then. In 2017, the Conservative share in Bolsover increased by 16 per cent (the same as the UKIP fall) and Skinner's majority was reduced to just 5,000. The electoral geography is changing rapidly.

To continue with this theme relating to social characteristics, Labour did very well in the urban seats of Nottingham and Leicester, both with high levels of black and ethnic minority residents and high numbers of students. Labour's share in the Nottingham seats, home to its two universities, East and South, went up by 16 per cent and 15 per cent respectively. In white working-class Nottingham North, which has one of the lowest levels of educational achievement in the UK, it improved by only 5 per cent and there was a swing to the Tories. In Leicester South, where there is a university as well as very populous Asian communities, Labour's frontbench spokesman Jon Ashworth increased his majority to over 26,000.

The Conservatives won easily in most of the rural and small town, white, Brexit-supporting seats in the counties of Leicestershire, Lincolnshire, Nottinghamshire and Derbyshire. In fact, they obtained their highest vote share in the UK, 69.92 per cent, in one of these: South Holland & the Deepings in the low 'fenland' deep south of Lincolnshire on the East Anglian border. The whole region is weak territory for the Liberal Democrats and Greens, with no viable targets before the 2017 election and no good performances in it. However, to return to the third party that is significant in the region, UKIP counted its best target anywhere as being Boston & Skegness on the Lincolnshire coast, so this was the seat that their newest leader, Paul Nuttall, chose to fight. The outcome? UKIP dropped from 34 per cent to 8 per cent, a poor third place, and Nuttall resigned the next day. His party now has no feasible target in any region.

Many people think that Jeremy Corbyn is a kind of 21st-century Robin Hood, the legendary or mythical Nottinghamshire outlaw who redistributed from the wealthy to the poor. Yet in reality, the area around Sherwood Forest saw Labour's weakest performances in the 2017 election. The East Midlands did see some very strong Labour showings, though not among traditional working-class communities, but rather among those representing the present and future of the country: black and minority ethnic groups, young people – especially students, and those more positive about modern developments like strong links with the EU. The region's varied results reflect the divisions and cleavages among British society.

East of England

The East of England saw some of the best Conservative performances in the 2017 election, yet they still lost three seats to Labour. We define the region as containing the counties of Bedfordshire, Cambridgeshire, Essex, Hertfordshire, Norfolk and Suffolk, so it is somewhat more extensive than just 'East Anglia'. The overall pattern of vote share was similar to that of England as a whole. The Conservatives increased by 5.6 per cent, and Labour by 10.7 per cent. The Liberal Democrats fell back a little (0.4 per cent) and UKIP a lot (13.7 per cent). It would be incorrect to assume that Labour took more of the UKIP votes, as turnout went up by 2.6 per cent overall, and the new voters seem to have been disproportionately enthused by Jeremy Corbyn. There would also have been some switching directly from Conservative to Labour. Finally, the evidence is that some former UKIP voters stayed at home – for example, the biggest drop in turnout was at Castle Point (based on Canvey Island), where their share collapsed.

Seat analysis tells us that the Conservatives actually did in best areas of previous great UKIP strength – predominantly coastal areas with elderly populations and low Lib Dem support, such as Waveney, Great Yarmouth, Castle Point and, of course, Clacton – where they made a gain with a 24.6 per cent increase in share and a majority of nearly 16,000. Douglas Carswell had retained Clacton as UKIP's only seat in 2015 despite the 4 million votes the party polled nationally, but he had quit the party to sit as an independent in March 2017 and chose to leave the Commons in June. Technically, though, Clacton counts as a Tory gain from UKIP compared with the previous general election. Castle Point, also in Essex, is another illustration of the point being made, unclouded by the 'Carswell factor'. Between 2015 and 2017, UKIP's share dropped from 31 per cent to 5 per cent. Rebecca Harris's share for the Conservatives went up by 16 per cent, Labour's by only 11 per cent. In this group of seats, mostly very strongly pro-Brexit in the referendum, probably only Waveney (the area round Lowestoft) was a realistic target for Labour. However, Peter Aldous increased his majority from 2,508 to 9,218, a swing against the tide of 6.4 per cent, probably strengthened even further as Labour's candidate was no longer the former MP Bob Blizzard.

The Conservatives also still hold many of the constituencies in this region with massive majorities. Three of their ten highest shares of the vote anywhere in the UK lie in a tight-knit corner of Essex: Maldon, Castle Point, Rayleigh & Wickford, all over two-thirds of total votes cast. Brentwood & Ongar is in their top ten as well. In Norfolk and Suffolk there are seven Conservative MPs with majorities over 16,000. The swing to Labour across Essex, Suffolk and Norfolk was well below the average for England. It must not be forgotten that the Tory vote increased markedly almost everywhere. In general, the further east in the East of England, the better they did. Across the region they now have a clear majority of the votes – 54.6 per cent compared with 49.0 per cent in 2015. Yet even here they must count the decision to hold an election as a mistake.

Labour increased their vote even more than their rivals. They gained three of their five main targets from the Tories: Bedford, Peterborough and Ipswich. They only missed Waveney, as discussed above, and Thurrock, a wholly aberrant seat that will be analysed below. Previously vulnerable Labour seats now look very safe: their vote increased by 21.7 per cent in Norwich South where both the Liberal Democrat and the Green challenges collapsed, by 18.2 per cent in Luton South, and by 15.9 per cent in Cambridge where many had thought Julian Huppert could regain his former seat for the Lib Dems. Turnout increased most of all in Cambridge (by 9.6 per cent), followed by the two Luton constituencies. The seats where Labour did very well are mostly urban, young, 'studenty' and with above average (for the region) ethnic minority populations. They did well, too, in constituencies where the EU referendum result had been close to the national average – that is, more 'Remain' than the region as a whole. Labour's share declined in only three of the fifty seats in the region. These were Waveney and two others where Labour supporters clearly cast tactical votes for the Liberal Democrats: North Norfolk and St Albans. In fact, in every other seat but these three, Labour's share increased by over 6 per cent. They did significantly less well than average in a cluster of constituencies in South Essex, in Hertsmere with its high Jewish population and in those with a very high Brexit percentage.

The Liberal Democrats trod water, in both their vote share and their number of seats. Assisted by Labour tactical voting, Norman Lamb held on to Norfolk North with around the same 4,000 majority as before, and in their best performance they advanced by 13.9 per cent into a strong second place in St Albans. However, their former MP failed to regain Cambridge by over 12,000 votes, and their share imploded in Watford and Colchester as well as Norwich South – despite former MPs also contesting the latter two seats.

For UKIP, the election was, of course, a disaster, as they held their deposit (5 per cent of the vote required) in only five of the thirty-seven seats they contested in one of their strongest regions. We do, however, need to mention Thurrock. One of their strongest candidates, Tim Aker MEP, achieved far and away their best result anywhere: a 20 per cent share and 10,000 votes. This was still only good enough for third place, though, as yet again Jackie Doyle-Price narrowly held on against Labour, winning her third successive election here – each of these by majorities well under 1,000. Hugging the north bank of the Thames around Grays and the historic port of Tilbury, Thurrock is still a working-class constituency. Over 70 per cent voted for Brexit, and even after the triggering of Article 50, UKIP's staunchly patriotic (or English nationalist) appeal still has considerable traction here. But Jackie Doyle-Price does apparently have the 'heart and stomach' for a desperate battle, and so far has emerged as triumphant as the lady who is said to have made that renowned speech at Tilbury in 1588.

The East of England has often seemed at the forefront of the defence of Britain against a threat emanating from Europe. It is increasingly looking like it is the only region that will ever have elected a UKIP Member of Parliament in a general election. Yet although there was some evidence of a response to Mrs May's appeal to strengthen her hand in the Brexit negotiations, it is well-nigh impossible to force the British public to vote along narrow one-issue lines in a general election, and Labour's broader campaign struck enough chords to move the results in their direction in the region as a whole.

London

The nation's capital was always expected to be Labour's best region, even when those expectations encompassed the idea that they would lose seats overall in the face of the predicted Tory landslide. Their two leading figures, John McDonnell and Jeremy Corbyn, are both London MPs, and the latter's constituency, Islington North, is often (rather crudely) characterised as the epitome of 'urban metropolitan left wingery'. No region is as multi-cultural, multi-ethnic and open to change. Sadiq Khan had wrested the London mayoralty from the Conservatives just over a year before. Even more recently, Greater London had run strongly against the Brexit trend in June 2016, 59.9 per cent favouring Remain, a preference expressed by all but five of the thirty-two boroughs. At a constituency level, twelve of the twenty with the highest Remain votes were in London, headed by Streatham and followed by, yes, Diane Abbott's Hackney North and Corbyn's Islington North.

Thus, it came as less of a surprise when, in 2017, Labour retained their seats that had been ultra-marginal in 2015. What was a shock was the majorities. In Ealing Central & Acton, the first of these to be declared, Rupa Huq's lead went up from 274 to 13,807. In Brentford & Isleworth in the borough of Hounslow, there was a re-run of the 2015 contest between Ruth Cadbury and the former Tory MP Mary Macleod. This time Labour won by over 12,000 compared with 465. Cadbury was ahead in every single ward, including those in Chiswick held by the Tories at borough council level. In Hampstead & Kilburn, Tulip Siddiq's share went up by over 15 per cent and her lead increased from 1,138 to 15,560. All the existing MPs greatly strengthened their position, with many now enjoying huge majorities. Jeremy Corbyn himself achieved a majority of over 33,000, and Diane Abbott, despite her difficulties during the campaign, reached over 35,000. Lyn Brown (West Ham), who temporarily replaced Diane Abbott at the end of the Labour campaign won a majority of 36,754. The highest of all was that of Stephen Timms, the MP who had once been attacked by a kitchen knife wielding assailant, whose margin in East Ham reached 39,883. It is true that some of these seats have grown due to the time elapsed since the last boundary review, but also turnout in London was universally stronger than in 2015. The electorate was enthused – and not by the campaign focused on Mrs May. Overall, Labour achieved 54.5 per cent of the vote in Greater London, which represented an increase of no less than 10.8 per cent from 2015, and a positive swing of 6.3 per cent from the Conservatives.

The outstanding Labour performance did, of course, also bring gains. The most vulnerable Conservative was Gavin Barwell in Croydon Central, who, despite being much liked personally, was dispatched to pastures new as the wounded Prime Minister's new and more emollient Chief of Staff. The other changes were less expected. Wandsworth had long been seen as a model Conservative borough with its relatively low council tax regime, but Battersea was convincingly taken by the disability campaigner (who is registered as blind) Marsha de Cordova. Rather symbolically, Enfield Southgate, site of the 'Portillo moment' in 1997, was regained by Labour. Everyone had to wait till Friday evening for the final and most dramatic gain of all: Kensington, which, at 122nd on their national target list, was the safest Conservative seat won by Labour in the 2017 contest. It was the last to declare in the whole nation by a very wide margin, but, at twenty votes, not quite the narrowest majority.

Overall, Labour performed best of all in areas of inner London and mainly in constituencies which had previously been seen as marginally Labour, and also in one or two safe Conservative areas that were heavily Remain voting. They did outstandingly well where there were large numbers of young voters. Swings where there are significant ethnic minorities were not generally high by London standards – those with the highest numbers such as East Ham were already so safe for Labour that a swing of this magnitude wouldn't have been possible.

The Conservative disaster may have ended chronologically with Kensington, but it does not end there in our survey. Unlike in every other region in Britain, the Conservatives actually lost 1.7 per cent of their share of the vote, dropping from 34.8 to 33.1 per cent. This puts them 21.4 per cent behind Labour if all the votes across the capital are added up. They suffered their worst declines in share in an entirely contiguous area surrounding Central London and in the most heavily Remain voting areas of the country, from Battersea (-10.8 per cent) through Chelsea & Fulham (-10.3 per cent) through Kensington (-10.1 per cent) to seats such as Westminster North and Hampstead & Kilburn.

They also lost two seats to the Liberal Democrats. Both were regains by former MPs whose seniority is reflected in their knighthoods: Sir Ed Davey in Kingston & Surbiton and Sir Vince Cable in Twickenham. Both were convincing victories, too, with Cable securing the largest Lib Dem majority anywhere – 9,762 – this being bolstered by the fact that Twickenham recorded the highest turnout of any of the 650 seats, at 79.5 per cent. Just as impressive for the Liberal Democrats and disappointing for the Tories was Carshalton & Wallington, where Tom Brake held on again, despite it being one of the few 'Leave' seats in London and despite the Labour share increasing rather than being squeezed.

For good-ish news for the Conservatives, one can only look to a few places. There was a parliamentary contest in Richmond Park for the third time in two years. Zac Goldsmith managed to book-end his defeat as an Independent in the by-election he had occasioned in December 2016 on the issue of a third runway at Heathrow, by recapturing it from the Liberal Democrat Sarah Olney. This was hardly an unalloyed triumph though. His majority in 2015 had been over 23,000 – in 2017, it was just forty-five. The Tories also strengthened their grip on Sutton & Cheam, yet another 2015 gain from the Lib Dems, as Paul Burstow did not stand this time and the Labour share increased in third place.

There were some Conservative seats that did not fall to Labour despite the city-wide swing. This may have something to do with their demographic characteristics. Hendon and Finchley & Golders Green are the two constituencies with the highest Jewish population in the United Kingdom, and Harrow East is also in the top ten on this ranking scale. The Labour Party, particularly since Jeremy Corbyn and his allies took over, has been accused of entertaining elements who have slipped over the line from legitimate anti-Zionism to anti-Semitism, which led to a 2016 inquiry chaired by Baroness Chakrabarti. The inquiry findings stated that although anti-Semitism and other types of racism were not endemic within Labour, there was an 'occasionally toxic atmosphere'. Nevertheless, it should also be reported that nationally Labour won fifteen of the thirty seats identified by the Institute for Jewish Policy Research as having the highest Jewish populations.

The Conservatives also did secure a couple of positive swings against Labour on the outermost fringes of London towards Essex, in working-class Dagenham & Rainham and more middle-class Hornchurch & Upminster – both places where they had substantial UKIP votes to squeeze, unlike most of London. This only tends to confirm the suggestion, though, that the 'more London' a seat is, the more inclined to Labour in 2017; the Borough of Barking & Dagenham, which includes the Dagenham & Rainham seat, voted Leave by over 62 per cent in 2016, and Havering, which contains Hornchurch & Upminster, by 69.7 per cent. Havering in particular behaves electorally more like Essex, where the 2017 results followed an entirely different pattern. Havering does not really behave as if it is part of London, and indeed many of its residents consider it not to be.

The heart of the capital, on the other hand, became in many ways the heart of Labour. However it did deviate significantly from national preferences in 2017, as it had in the vital referendum the year before. Labour did not actually win this general election, though the reaction to it in some quarters may sound like they did. They will have to do as well in many other regions before they can form another government at Westminster.

North East England

As our smallest English region, covering just twenty-nine constituencies, the North East may seem to be relatively uninteresting. After all, there was no net change of strength between the two major parties who shared all the seats between them again. Yet, below this pacific surface appearance, there was a lot going on. What's more, there is always significance in what does *not* happen – the dogs that do not bark in the night.

Even the flat net outcome disguises the fact that two seats did change hands. Labour gained Stockton South from the Conservatives, which was a considerable surprise. The reverse happened in Middlesbrough South & East Cleveland, which was not. A clue to the way the wind was blowing in the latter seat lay in the retirement (at the age of thirty-six) of its Labour MP, Tom Blenkinsop. He announced that he was to stand down because he could not campaign for Labour while Jeremy Corbyn is party leader. Many others expected at that stage that Corbyn would prove a massive electoral liability. As a result, some apparently very unlikely Conservative gains were bruited in this region, so long a Labour Party fortress. Bishop Auckland, Labour since 1935, was frequently mentioned. It was assumed that the more regularly marginal Darlington was a shoo-in for the Tories this time. Peter Mandelson's old seat, Hartlepool, was expected to fall to the Conservatives or even UKIP. Yet only Blenkinsop's former constituency was lost in the end, and perhaps with his incumbency vote, Labour (even though led by Corbyn) may have held it too.

It is true that the North East proved a *relatively* weak area for Labour. It was one of the few that registered a swing to the Conservatives, though this was a paltry 0.5 per cent. Because the first seats in the country to declare are always in this region (in 2017 Newcastle Central just pipped the perennially speedy Sunderland to the post) there was a momentary wobble in faith in the superb BBC/ITN/Sky exit poll conducted by Ipsos MORI. The three Sunderland seats showed a higher increase for the Tories than for Labour as the UKIP share collapsed. The swing to the Tories was higher in seats with low mean incomes. Yet Helen Goodman did hang on in Bishop Auckland by 502 votes, and in Hartlepool Labour actually more than doubled their majority to over 7,000, even with a new candidate. It might be noted that Hartlepool was still UKIP's second best performance in the country (10 per cent) – the only one in double figures apart from Thurrock. Most significantly of all, there was effectively no swing in Darlington. As the first Labour marginal to declare on the night, Darlington was the seat that most clearly suggested that Theresa May's gamble was going to fail.

As with the national results, there appears to be a correlation between high numbers of young voters and a poorer swing to the Tories. Labour's best performance of all in the region was in Newcastle East, which includes Jesmond, a popular area for students, where their Chief Whip Nick Brown's share increased by 18 per cent. Interestingly, no apparent correlation may be detected by analysing between the Leave vote and the Labour and Tory votes in 2017. That said, there was a correlation with Remain voting and a greater Lib Dem share.

Taking all the demographic and political variables into account, the Labour gain in Stockton South seems inexplicable. It might be to do with incumbency. The Conservatives did relatively badly in all their existing seats (save Berwick-upon-Tweed, where the Liberal Democrats had been the challengers) and perhaps James Wharton suffered from a 'rewind' after himself achieving a high 'sophomore surge' in his first re-election campaign in 2015. This phenomenon, known as 'double incumbency', is both provable and explicable. The argument runs as follows. In 2010 James Wharton managed to beat an incumbent MP (Dari Taylor). At that point, she had a personal vote, and he did not. In 2015 Wharton had built up five years of service and name recognition, while Labour no longer had Dari Taylor's. In these circumstances, MPs seeking a second term measurably do better than their party average. By 2017, however, this relative advantage no longer applied, and the challenging party could recover.

One thing about which there is no doubt: the Lib Dems seem down and out in the region. They achieved thirty-seven second finishes altogether in Britain – but none here, not even in Berwick, which they held for over four decades to 2015. They declined in all but three seats, and these increases were all less than half a per cent. With UKIP's even more vertiginous decline, the North East remains a two-party struggle. It also remains a two-party battle dominated by Labour, radical leadership and all.

North West England

Although Labour's positive results in London attracted much attention, in some ways they did as well in the North West of England, traditionally a marginal-rich cockpit that has decided the outcome of British general elections. Certainly they outperformed expectations more than in London, as Jeremy Corbyn's appeal had been recognised as likely to be greater in the metropolitan culture and cosmopolitan diversity of the capital. Labour made four gains in the North West, just as they did in Greater London. They successfully defended all their vulnerable seats. What's more, Labour's share increased in a wide variety of constituency types within the region, which was not the case in, for example, the Midlands.

Labour's gains included one in Greater Manchester, Bury North, two in Cheshire (Weaver Vale and Crewe & Nantwich) and one in a unitary authority covering historical segments of both Lancashire and Cheshire (Warrington South). Their successful defences ranged from the City of Chester, where Chris Matheson's majority rose from just 93 to 9,176 votes, to perhaps an even more unlikely success in Barrow & Furness, where the arch-critic of his own leadership, John Woodcock, held on in a town whose economy is heavily dependent on the manufacture of a new generation of nuclear submarines. They also vastly increased their wafer-thin lead in Wirral West, in the orbit of Liverpool, and on the Lancashire coast in Lancaster & Fleetwood. The Tories did not make progress in their targets in Bolton North East, Chorley or Hyndburn. Trudy Harrison did retain her recent by-election gain in Copeland, though with a reduced majority, but Labour held the neighbouring west Cumbrian constituency of Workington.

Any consolation for the Conservatives came purely at the expense of the Liberal Democrats. They gained Southport, which lies on the coast between Liverpool and Blackpool. They had been given more encouragement here when the veteran MP John Pugh announced that he was not standing again, but as late as the previous year the Liberal Democrats had performed very strongly in Sefton council elections in the Southport wards. In the event, not only did the Lib Dems lose the seat, but they slipped to third place, behind Labour as well (who increased their share by 13.6 per cent). What this may mean is that at the next general election, the new Conservative MP Damien Moore will find himself vulnerable not to a Liberal Democrat recovery but to Labour – which sounds very dangerous in a seat technically in the Merseyside sub-region.

The Liberal Democrats nearly suffered a much bigger disaster. New party leaders usually benefit from a personal surge in their vote, but in Westmorland & Lonsdale Tim Farron's majority fell from 8,949 to 777. As in the case of Southport, there was no hint of this in the recent local elections, as the Lib Dems have continued to dominate South Lakeland council, which they have controlled since 2006, and did well in the Westmorland divisions of Cumbria county council in May 2017. Perhaps Tim Farron's national role in the campaign did not go down well locally, although apparently the Conservatives launched an energetic 'decapitation strategy' here as well, perhaps wrongly assuming that neighbouring Barrow was in the bag. Farron remains as the sole representative of his party in the region, and it looks as if they have no other viable chances.

Unlike in other traditional citadels of Labour strength like the Yorkshire and Durham coalfields, the North West region (like London) saw large increases in the party share even in their safest seats. This has resulted in some enormous majorities and monolithic vote shares. In fact, Labour's safest seats anywhere are again found in the North West, particularly in Merseyside. In Bootle, Peter Dowd now enjoys a majority of over 36,000 with 84 per cent of the vote. In Knowsley, George Howarth's lead was over 42,000, the highest anywhere, not only in this election but since 1970, and his share was 85 per cent. But the safest of all was, again, Liverpool Walton, where Steve Rotheram vacated the seat to become the directly elected Mayor of the Liverpool City Region. He was replaced by a young Corbyn (and Unite) loyalist, Dan Carden. The Labour share now? Nearly 86 per cent. Labour's majority across the four seats in Liverpool is 130,000, and if the Garston & Halewood constituency is included, it's over 160,000. These massive majorities are not confined to Merseyside. In Manchester Central, Lucy Powell's lead rose from 21,000 to 31,000. The by-election scheduled in Manchester Gorton by the death of the Father of the House of Commons, Sir Gerald Kaufman, was cancelled by Mrs May's snap decision. On 8 June, Labour's Afzal Khan held Gorton with a lead approaching 32,000 – though George Galloway, standing as an Independent, did just manage to reach the 5 per cent threshold to save his deposit in his attempt to represent his fourth different constituency.

These huge percentages and numerical majorities are impressive, but they do have an implication that is decidedly not favourable to Labour. For several recent elections Labour distributed their vote more efficiently than their main rivals, so that on an equal Labour–Conservative split, Labour would have won many more seats. Now the situation has reversed. In 2017, Labour finished 2 per cent behind the Conservatives across the UK but secured 56 fewer MPs. Contrary to popular belief, the relationship between vote share and representation between the two largest parties is much more influenced by how effectively the votes are distributed than by constituency boundaries. Nevertheless, if the planned 2018 boundary review (which also reduces the number of MPs to 600) were to go through, it would make it even harder for Labour actually to win a general election, even with a lead in votes cast. However the DUP would also suffer from the Boundary Commission's proposals, so it may well be that the Ulster party might demand the cancellation of the boundary changes, given their enhanced role in maintaining the Conservatives in government.

Northern Ireland

There has been a tendency in some quarters to discount the results in Northern Ireland in Westminster elections: none of the main British parties have been able in recent times to win seats in the province, so 'let's just put them down as 18 Others'. That this is a foolish as well as an unfair view was brought home decisively by the outcome of the 2017 general election, as the hung parliament result led to frantic googling of the Northern Irish parties, especially the one that emerged with the most seats – the DUP. Suddenly and unexpectedly, the detailed results in Northern Ireland mattered very much.

They should matter in any case. The politics of this unique corner and quarter of the United Kingdom have undergone rapid development recently in the context of their unique issues and also as a result of the particularly strong potential impact of the 2016 Brexit decision on the only part of the country with a direct border with the EU. Mrs May's sudden decision to go to the polls came at an inconvenient time for the governance (or lack of governance) of Northern Ireland, which had not had a working Executive since the breakdown of power-sharing in January 2017. The Sinn Féin Deputy First Minister Martin McGuinness resigned, citing concerns about the

Democratic Unionist Party's 'arrogance' at how they had handled allegations of a financial scandal. The party's leader, Northern Ireland First Minister Arlene Foster, is implicated in a government scheme which was badly handled under her tenure. The Renewable Heat Incentive scheme, which was set up in 2012, was designed to encourage local businesses to use renewable heat sources, however it appears to have been seriously flawed in its implementation and instead paid businesses money to pointlessly burn fuel. It is estimated that the affair has cost the taxpayer more than £490 million.

Under the terms of the Good Friday Agreement of 1998, this meant that the Executive could no longer function. Talks about the return of Sinn Féin to the Executive proved fruitless, and when Mrs May made her surprise announcement on 18 April, the prospect was looming ever larger of a return to direct rule of Northern Ireland from Westminster for the first time since 2007. It can be regarded as quite certain that she did not expect that just two months later she would be fairly desperately trying to make an arrangement with one of the Northern Irish parties to secure her very future as Prime Minister.

This all makes the specific outcome of the eighteen constituencies even more critical. In some ways the situation was simplified. Two of Northern Ireland's most historically successful political parties were completely eliminated from representation at Westminster: the Ulster Unionists and the SDLP (Social Democratic and Labour Party). Apart from the Independent Lady Sylvia Hermon, whose majority at North Down was greatly reduced, all the seats were won by the two now dominant parties: the Democratic Unionists (DUP) and Sinn Féin.

This represents a further polarisation of Northern Irish politics, as the DUP are generally regarded as the more trenchant face of 'loyalty to the United Kingdom', while Sinn Féin are republicans, traditionally linked to the Provisional IRA, and do not take their seats in the Commons on principle. This apparent move towards the extremes could be expected for two reasons: firstly, the circumstances of the timing of the 2017 Westminster election during the standoff precipitated in January; and secondly, because it has become a long-term trend. This can be seen in the rather fruitless Stormont assembly election that was held in March 2017, when Sinn Féin advanced relative to the other parties and were just 0.2 per cent behind the DUP in total vote and won twenty-seven seats compared to their twenty-eight. However, the Single Transferable Vote system of proportional representation used in all internal Northern Irish elections somewhat masked the decline in the smaller parties, which became all too apparent on 8 June.

The Ulster Unionist Party, the linear descendant of the dominant force within the province from its inception in 1921 until the first imposition of direct rule in 1972, lost both its Westminster MPs. Its share dropped from 16.1 per cent in 2015 to just 10.3 per cent. In Antrim South, which has been toggling between the UUP and the DUP in recent elections, Danny Kinahan's two year stewardship was reversed as the DUP's Paul Girvan took over on a 5 per cent swing. In Fermanagh & South Tyrone there was yet another close result, but Sinn Féin's Michelle Gildernew regained the seat she had won by just four votes in 2010 and ousted Tom Elliot by the comparatively massive margin of 876. This was despite the UUP's Elliot again benefiting from a unionist pact in which the DUP withdrew in the constituency which is the most balanced of any between the two communities or 'traditions'.

The SDLP fared even worse, as they had previously held three seats, all now lost in one of the surprises of the 2017 contests. In Belfast South, a constituency that has been regarded as a multi-party marginal and which in 2015 was won by Alasdair McDonnell with a mere 24.5 per cent share (the lowest winning percentage anywhere), Emma Little-Pengelly increased the DUP vote by nearly 5,000 and 8.2 per cent to win by nearly 2,000. Meanwhile, the two seats in predominantly nationalist areas fell to Sinn Féin. Margaret Ritchie, the MP for South Down (once held by Enoch Powell) since 2010 suffered a swing of 9.3 per cent to Chris Hazzard. Even more of a blow, the former SDLP leader Mark Durkan was beaten in Foyle (based on the city of Derry) after holding it for twelve years after he replaced John Hume. Foyle had been in SDLP hands since its creation in 1983. Durkan was defeated by Elisha McCallion of Sinn Féin by the painfully close margin of 169 votes after another huge swing, 8.4 per cent.

Sinn Féin's share went up by nearly 5 per cent to 29.4 per cent, and they now have seven MPs. None will take the oath of loyalty to the crown and none will sit or vote at Westminster. This policy of abstentionism was known beforehand and is what the republican party always campaigns on. They do point out that it would be hypocritical to seek to influence affairs in a United Kingdom they do not believe the six counties should be part of; after all, they do not believe that Westminster should determine the affairs of any part of Ireland. Their success does, of course, mean that the number of seats needed to control the Commons is in effect reduced.

That still did not give Theresa May an overall working majority, though, and to shore up her position, negotiations soon commenced with the triumphant DUP, which now has ten of the eighteen Northern Irish MPs – an absolute majority for the first time. Founded in 1971 by Ian Paisley as a successor to his Protestant Unionist party (and closely associated with his own Free Presbyterian Church of Ulster), the DUP has come a long way. During Paisley's thirty-seven years as leader, it overtook the Ulster Unionists as the most popular party in the unionist tradition and tasted power, providing three First Ministers of the Executive since 2007. In 2017 the DUP's share rose by no less than 10.3 per cent to its highest ever by far, at 36.0 per cent – and Northern Ireland's turnout as a whole rose by the largest of any of the constituent parts of the UK, by 7.3 per cent. Now it seemed that the DUP would enter centre stage in the power politics of the United Kingdom as well, and the Conservatives were warned that they would find them tough bargainers. If an agreement of some kind is attained, whether this will take the form mainly of demands for money to help the infrastructure and services of Northern Ireland, or whether the DUP's hard-line unionism and social conservatism will influence government policy remains to be seen. In either case, it is a salutary reminder that the electoral outcome in every region of the United Kingdom will remain well worthy of study.

Scotland

Breaking alphabetical order, we started the regional survey in the Politico's guide to the 2015 House of Commons with Scotland, because in a unique development, more than half of the seats north of the border changed hands, with the Scottish National Party winning fifty-six of the fifty-nine constituencies, leaving the three 'main' parties that operate across the whole of Britain with just one MP each. This changed the face of Westminster politics, and left Labour in particular with a much harder task ever to form a government again; the Conservatives, on the other hand, were long used to failure in Scotland, not having had more than one member elected there since 1992. This time, although the story was not quite so dramatic, Scotland again produced the highest proportion of changes of hand – and also the highest proportion of close results, so the record of exciting developments is likely to continue in the next Westminster general election – whenever it may be.

After the unprecedented surge to the SNP in the 2015 election, the main story this year in Scotland is the marked decline in the SNP's vote. With 36.9 per cent of Scottish voters favouring the nationalists, they are still decidedly Scotland's largest party – as their leader, First Minister Nicola Sturgeon, was quick to point out. However, their vote share dropped by 13.1 per cent from 2015 and 9.6 per cent from last year's Holyrood elections based on the constituency vote. In June 2017, the SNP lost twenty-one seats, leaving thirty-five MPs. This represents a major setback, though it still places the SNP far ahead of their position in 2010 of just six seats and allows them to comfortably retain their new role as the third largest party in the House of Commons. Ironically, the outcome of the election will probably result in them having more influence in a hung parliament than they had when they had 95 per cent of the Scottish MPs.

Two major faces will be departing from the SNP's benches as a result. Alex Salmond, the former First Minister of Scotland, lost his seat in Gordon to a 29 per cent increase in the Conservative vote and, to show that it was not just a matter of reversals of 2015 gains, the SNP's Westminster Leader Angus Robertson lost neighbouring Moray, also to the Conservatives, who advanced by 16.5 per cent. It could have been much worse for the SNP however, as the party retained a number of seats by tiny margins. Closest of all was North East Fife, which saw the SNP beat the Liberal Democrats by just two votes: 13,743 to 13,741. Several others were nearly as close, or fortunate: Glasgow East returned a Nationalist by a margin of only seventy-five votes and Glasgow South West by sixty, both over Labour. In Perth & North Perthshire, Pete Wishart, an MP since 2001, held on by just twenty-one votes over the Conservatives. Altogether the SNP won nine seats by fewer than 1,000 votes and fifteen by under 2,000. Having enjoyed very large majorities in almost all their seats in 2015, their highest now are two just over 6,000 – Dundee East and Kilmarnock & Loudoun.

Voters deserting the SNP mainly seem to have favoured the Conservatives at this election. Under their highly regarded young leader, Ruth Davidson, the Tories have largely managed to 'detoxify the brand' in Scotland. Thus the Tories have taken a leading position among unionists in the majority of Scots who voted No in the 2014 referendum, and also recaptured their ancestral support, particularly in the north eastern quadrant of Scotland.

The Conservatives achieved a vote share of 28.6 per cent, an increase of 13.7 per cent from 2015 and 6.6 per cent from their strong performance in last year's Scottish Parliament election. After years of possessing just one seat north of the border, the Conservatives won thirteen seats, a gain of twelve, giving them multiple Scottish seats for the first time since John Major's victory in 1992. Their gains were mainly in the more rural areas, but not universally: now firmly established as the main opposition to the

SNP, the Conservative gains from the SNP also included urban Aberdeen South on a 15 per cent swing and suburban East Renfrewshire (Jim Murphy's former seat), both being seats where they leapfrogged Labour to win from third place. Even in seats they did not win, the Tories achieved a marked improvement on 2015, for example more than doubling their vote share to 32 per cent in Lanark & Hamilton East, which became the closest three-way marginal result anywhere in Britain, with three parties polling between 16,000 and 16,500 votes.

Labour enjoyed more modest progress. After a long history as Scotland's largest party, Labour dropped forty seats to just the one Scottish MP in 2015. This time round, Labour advanced by six seats to a total of seven, which is still, apart from 2015, their lowest since 1931, and they now rank only as Scotland's third party. At 27.1 per cent of the vote, Labour showed a slight improvement of 2.8 per cent on 2015 and 4.5 per cent on their constituency vote in the 2016 Holyrood elections. They gained seats such as Coatbridge, Chryston & Bellshill with a 1,536 vote majority, and East Lothian, which saw Labour beat the SNP by a 36.1 per cent to 30.6 per cent margin. Labour supporters were also pleased to see Gordon Brown's former seat return to the fold as the party took Kirkcaldy & Cowdenbeath from the SNP by 259 votes. Another narrow (265 vote) Labour victory occurred in Rutherglen & Hamilton West. The pattern in these Labour gains was more that the huge switch from SNP to the Conservatives let them in, as their own share did not improve much. In fact, the only double figure increase (16 per cent) in Labour share occurred in the one seat they already held, Edinburgh South, where Ian Murray clearly benefited again from tactical 'unionist' voting – the Conservatives went up by 2 per cent, by far their lowest improvement on the Scottish mainland. Edinburgh South and its MP have gone from having the smallest majority in Scotland in 2010 to the largest (15,514) in 2017. It is, however, the number of really close contests in 2017 that give Labour a sound platform for further advance at the next Westminster election: they came within 500 votes of making six more gains from the SNP.

The Liberal Democrats also made some progress at this election. In common with the Tories and Labour, they lost all but one of their Scottish seats in 2015. This time, the Lib Dems gained three seats for a total of four. The party achieved a vote share of 6.8 per cent, a small drop of 0.8 per cent from 2015 and a 1 per cent drop from their constituency score in the 2016 devolved election, but they effectively focused their efforts on regaining a handful of key targets where they had been beaten two years before. A highlight of the night for the Lib Dems was the re-election of the still youthful former minister Jo Swinson, who lost her seat in 2015, in East Dunbartonshire with 40.6 per cent of the vote, their highest in Scotland. Caithness, Sutherland & Easter Ross also returned to the Lib Dems after a 17 per cent drop in SNP support in the constituency. Results for the Lib Dems were variable, however, with little progress in seats like Glasgow East, where they doubled their vote but just to 1.6 per cent, and even collapsed in some places such as Inverness, Nairn, Badenoch & Strathspey which saw a 19 per cent decline in Lib Dem support after the former 'Quad' coalition member Danny Alexander did not seek a return to Westminster.

After seeing a trebling of their seats in last year's Holyrood elections, it was surprising to see so few Green candidates in Scotland this year. As a result, the Greens scored just 0.2 per cent of the vote share, a drop of 1.1 per cent on 2015 and 0.4 per cent on their 2016 constituency performance. The Greens could however celebrate a strong performance in Glasgow North with 9.7 per cent of the vote, a 3.5 per cent improvement on 2015.

One striking feature of the 2017 general election in Scotland was the turnout, which dropped sharply against the trend in every other region. Turnout was down almost across the board in Scotland, from 71.1 per cent in 2015 to 66.4 per cent in 2017. This was almost certainly connected with the dramatic decline in SNP support, as some electors, enthused in 2015 by the 2014 independence referendum, had felt their fervour ebb away two years later. Turnout only increased in three constituencies – Glasgow Central, Glasgow North and Orkney & Shetland. The biggest drop was in West Dunbartonshire, where turnout fell by 8.7 percentage points. Glasgow North East registered the smallest turnout in the country, at 53 per cent. This supports the theory that it was differentially erstwhile SNP supporters who were abstaining, as North East was the only seat in Glasgow regained by Labour.

While the European Union is an issue that has had a huge impact on this year's general election, in Scotland the issue seems to have been more about the nation's future in the United Kingdom. A division between the SNP on the one hand and the unionist parties on the other has seen an increasing polarisation of Scottish politics with some signs of tactical voting for whichever unionist party can deliver in a given seat. It would seem that many Scottish voters were alarmed at the prospect of another independence referendum and decided to fire a shot across Nicola Sturgeon's bows. Although these elections have seen the SNP remain dominant in Scottish politics, the three unionist parties have enjoyed a significant recovery and it would seem that the brief era of a virtual one party state for the nationalists is over.

South East England

The South East of England (outside London) is our largest defined region, with over eighty constituencies, but usually one of the least electorally interesting and fluid. To put it bluntly, it is a Conservative stronghold with relatively few marginals. In 2015, only five seats broke the monolithic pattern of true blue: in order, from relative safety, Oxford East (Labour), Brighton Pavilion (the sole Green seat), Slough, Southampton Test and Hove (all Labour, the last two by very little). Predominantly middle class, prosperous, relatively elderly, lacking large cities and many significant concentrations of ethnic minorities, the South East seemed poised overwhelmingly to reject a Labour Party flirting with socialism for the first time for over three decades. In general, it could be said that that proved to be the case – but in most places there was a substantial increase in the Labour share, and there are now more than twice as many non-Tory seats as there were.

Labour achieved four gains, scattered around the region and around the order in their target list. The easiest was Brighton Kemptown, which contains the east end of the renowned Sussex resort and some much more Tory coastal communities such as Saltdean and Peacehaven. The Labour hurricane proved overwhelming in Kemptown, and the MP Simon Kirby was blown away by nearly 10,000 votes. Then there was Reading East, fifth on their list and a much more surprising change of hands. To explain it we need to consider two things: the presence of Reading University and the 2016 referendum vote – 62 per cent voted for Remain (while Reading West voted Leave). Then, becoming progressively more adventurous, we need to move down to Labour's tenth target before the election: Portsmouth South. This really was off most people's radar, as Labour were only third as recently as two years ago when the Conservatives picked up the seat from the Liberal Democrats. In 2017 Labour's share increased by a massive 21.5 per cent. This was due to the end of tactical voting now that the Lib Dems had lost the seat, and the presence, once again, of a university combined with an increased student and youth turnout. The defeated Conservative MP Flick Drummond actually increased both her share and her total vote. Finally (and for many the greatest shock in the whole election, never mind the South East) there was Canterbury – their fourteenth target in the region and 104th overall.

Canterbury deserves a paragraph to itself. When the pollsters YouGov produced an index suggesting constituency outcomes based on aggregation of their polling, their allocation of Canterbury as a possible Labour gain elicited almost universal disbelief and even contempt. After all, the small city in Kent that is best known for the cathedral and the prime archbishop of the Church of England had not elected any party other than Conservative since 1868. Labour needed a swing of over 9 per cent. Rosie Duffield achieved a 20.48 per cent increase in her share and Sir Julian Brazier was out. What on earth happened? For a start, the city of Canterbury itself has two universities: Kent and Christ Church. It has been said that this is the greatest proportion of students to townspeople of anywhere in England. The constituency does include other areas such as Whitstable, but students have residences there too, and in any case that port has always had a Labour element. Overall, Canterbury is in the list of the top twenty constituencies for students, and none of them elected a Tory in 2017 – with Portsmouth South also being a gain. Secondly, in 2016 this seat voted nearly 55 per cent to Remain in the EU. Its ex-MP, Julian Brazier, is a Brexiteer. Thirdly, the YouGov polling was given wide publicity locally and would have assisted campaigning energy, turnout and tactical voting: there had been 10,000 Liberal Democrat and Green votes in 2015, and this was nearly halved. So YouGov may have contributed to their own vindication – at least as far as this aspect of their work was concerned.

Why was Labour's advance as patchy as we have seen it to be? They failed in their second easiest target to oust Royston Smith in Southampton Itchen by a mere thirty-one votes, and as a first-term MP he did benefit from the incumbency effect. Their third target was indeed a major one – the Home Secretary herself, Amber Rudd, in Hastings & Rye. She only survived after two recounts, the news of which formed one of the main indications during the night of just how well Labour was doing. No such progress was made in Dover, next in line – or indeed in any other Kent seat apart from Canterbury. Most of Kent was actually aberrant in the 2017 election in that, apart from Scotland, it was a rare area in which turnout tended to go down; and perhaps strongly related to this, Labour's swing from the Conservatives was the lowest of any county in the South East, at just 2.2 per cent. That Kent was also the strongest county for Brexit suggests that Leavers tended to stay at home, while Remainers flooded to the polls in 2017. Crawley in Sussex required a bigger swing than Dover, but came nearer to falling – perhaps because of discontent with the Southern Rail service. Finally, Labour will be disappointed not quite to have taken either of the Milton Keynes seats in north Buckinghamshire, both close to 50–50 in the referendum.

Labour did advance substantially in some very safe Conservative seats, as in Worthing (Greater Brighton, perhaps because property prices are a little more reasonable along the coast to the west). There are still plenty of places where the Tories dominate, though. Overall, the Conservatives achieved 54.6 per cent of the vote in the South East, an increase of 2.9 per cent from 2015. The whole of Surrey remains very safely in their hands, although mention may be made of the National Health Action Party's second place with 20 per cent of the vote in Jeremy Hunt's South West Surrey. The highest majority recorded by any Conservative MP again belongs to Ranil Jayawardena of North East Hampshire (27,772). Two other seats in the region are also in the top ten of the list if arranged by percentage of the Tory vote: New Forest West and Maidenhead, where Theresa May's huge win was dampened by the obvious disappointment in her manner during her acceptance speech.

Two other of the Prime Minister's colleagues lost their seats in the South East as a result of her ill-judged decision to hold an early election. In Eastbourne, Caroline Ansell had to give way after just two years to the man she ousted in 2015, the Liberal Democrat Stephen Lloyd (one of twelve 'retreads' in all returning to the Commons). In Oxford West & Abingdon, the 'Remain' and 'university' factors struck again for a new Lib Dem candidate, Leyla Moran, to oust Nicola Blackwood – probably more the former, in this case, as the bulk of the university is in the now massively Labour Oxford East.

So, overall, there is more variety in the representation of this populous quadrant of England. Just as in the UK as a whole, the Conservatives still won more seats than anyone else, though the circumstances of the calling of the election and direction of its results means it does not feel like this is the case – both regionally and nationally.

South West England

The election in the South West of England was thought to be one where, outside of a few pockets of (often declining) Labour support, the battle for seats would be between the Conservatives and Liberal Democrats. As with so much commentary concerning this election, this proved to be fairly off the mark. From the formerly Hampshire redoubt of Bournemouth, up through Bristol and Gloucestershire and down to the mineral mining village of Constantine in Cornwall, the beginnings of a Labour revival not seen since the 1960s is the story of June 2017. Labour are now second in thirty-two constituencies, with Independent candidate Claire Wright second in East Devon. It is hard to believe that the Liberal Democrats have had MPs in eighteen seats here.

There are fifty-five constituencies covering the traditional counties of Cornwall, Devon, Somerset, Dorset (plus Bournemouth and Christchurch), Wiltshire and Gloucestershire. Before the election, there were fifty-one Conservative MPs and four Labour MPs, the Liberal Democrats having lost all eleven of their seats at the 2015 general election. If there was to be a revival of fortunes for Mr Farron's party, this was thought to be the place where it would be strongest.

In the event, they managed to regain only one seat, that of Bath, from the Conservatives. Labour held its four seats and gained three (Stroud, Plymouth Sutton & Devonport and Bristol North West), while the Conservatives continued to hold the vast majority of seats with forty-seven MPs, losing the four aforementioned seats.

So far, so simple – but not really, as Labour did not only hold their seats, two of which (Bristol West and East) were at some point during the election campaign seen as at risk, but they piled on the votes to significantly increase their majorities. Their vote share in Bristol West went up a stunning 30.3 per cent for Thangam Debbonaire, to 65.9 per cent, and an extraordinary 47,213 votes (37,336 majority) on a 22.15 per cent swing from Green to Labour, where the Green Party candidate's challenge saw them fall to third place. The former Lib Dem MP, Stephen Williams, saw his vote fall into fourth place, from 18.9 per cent to 7.3 per cent. The Conservatives' Annabel Tall grabbed the runner-up slot on the basis of her vote share falling the least. This constituency had seen a 12 per cent increase in voter registration since December of 2016, the sixth highest in the UK.

Bristol North West was Labour's gain in the city, and a serious disappointment for the Tories who will have hoped that the fact that most of their local councillors are from this constituency and that former MP (2010–17) Charlotte Leslie had built up a healthy share of the vote in 2015, made this a shoo-in against an apparently unpopular Labour Party. Not so, with a swing of 9.15 per cent to Labour's Darren Jones, the losing candidate in 2015, giving him a 4,761 majority. Ms Leslie has a higher share of the vote than when she was first elected in 2010, and must have assumed that the UKIP vote from 2015 was there for the taking but, as we see again and again, this was not to the advantage of the Conservatives, and her share of the vote fell by 2.1 per cent. In Gloucestershire, Labour will be delighted and surprised with their regain of Stroud which, after a seven-year hiatus (otherwise known as the Conservative MP, Neil Carmichael) sees the return of David Drew, who had previously announced his retirement from politics having failed to regain the seat in 2015. In Plymouth Sutton & Devonport, Labour's Luke Pollard took the seat from Conservative incumbent Oliver Colvile, who had held the seat since gaining it from former Labour MP Linda Gilroy in 2010. When the result was first announced, the council's returning officer hadn't included all wards, adding to a nightmare to do with not registering votes in time for the election. The UKIP votes, unlike in their northern neighbour Plymouth Moor View, swung heavily behind Mr Pollard, eventuating in a swing of 7.2 per cent to Labour and a 6,807 majority.

Elsewhere, Labour did very well, but in a way not well enough. In Wiltshire, North Swindon and South Swindon are seats Labour need to gain if they are to be in government and, again in this part of the South West, they failed to advance enough. They came close in South, with a swing of 3.45 per cent putting them within 2,464 votes of regaining the seat they lost to Solicitor General Robert Buckland in 2010. Among the 'slap your face with your hand' results of the general election, were those in the two Bournemouth divisions, where Labour managed to achieve their highest ever vote shares of 35.6 per cent (East) and 36.2 per cent (West). However, Labour are unlikely actually to win seats in Bournemouth any time soon. In Plymouth Moor View, the UKIP vote fell by 17.4 per cent and swung heavily to the Conservative defending MP, Johnny Mercer, whose vote increased to 51.9 per cent (+14.3 per cent). In second place, Labour will be disappointed to have failed to retake the seat they only lost in 2015 by 1,026. Sue Dann managed to take the Labour vote up to 40.8 per cent (+5.6 per cent), but it appears that former military man Mr Mercer has gained from incumbency and the fact that the former MP, Alison Seabeck, did not stand this time.

The only bright light for the Liberal Democrats in the whole of the South West was their regain of Bath from the Conservatives' Ben Howlett, only two years years after losing the seat. It was a remarkable victory for former Rochdale Conservative councillor (later Rochdale Liberal Democrat leader), German-born Wera Hobhouse, with a swing of 9.8 per cent from the Conservatives and 47.3 per cent of the vote, up 17.6 per cent on 2015. She was only selected at the beginning of May after the former candidate, Jay Risbridger, stood down due to family and work commitments. This is a city that was unhappy with the vote to leave the EU and saw a 9 per cent increase in voter registration, the tenth highest in the UK. If Brexit had an effect, this is one of the seats where it was most pronounced, against the government.

Elsewhere in the South West, it was a tale of disappointment for the Liberal Democrats in what is historically their strongest region of England. In Cheltenham, they put in a lot of effort and achieved one of their rare large vote increases, up 8.2 per cent on 2015, giving former MP Martin Horwood 42.2 per cent of the vote, but it was not enough to catch the defending Conservative, Alex Chalk. In Wells in Somerset, former Liberal Democrat MP Tessa Munt was widely believed to be in with a fair chance of regaining the seat she held from 2010–15, having taken it from long-term Conservative MP and former minister David Heathcoat-Amory. In the event, and despite increasing the party's share of the vote to 37.6 per cent (+4.9 per cent), she managed only a 0.45 per cent swing from the Conservatives' Major James Heappey, who held the seat with a majority of 7,582, only three votes less than in 2015. In North Devon, former Armed Forces Minister Sir Nick Harvey's hopes were dashed of regaining the seat he held for the Liberal Democrats for twenty-three years, but lost in 2015, despite a closer result than in many former Liberal Democrat seats in the South West. He saw his share of the vote go up to 38 per cent (+8.6 per cent), but failed to close the gap of the re-elected Conservative, Peter Heaton-Jones, who managed to take 45.8 per cent (+3.1 per cent).

There is one more seat of great interest before we 'leave England and go to Cornwall'. Devon East, to the east of Exeter and with a shoreline on the Jurassic Coast, which includes the towns of Exmouth, Budleigh Salterton, Sidmouth, Cranbrook and Ottery St Mary, had one of the most fascinating contests of the 2017 general election, with former minister Sir Hugo Swire, the local Conservative MP since 2001, facing a real challenge from Independent local councillor Claire Wright, who received a lot of publicity and backing. Councillor Wright took 24 per cent of the vote from nowhere in 2015, and was seen as the one person who might dislodge the incumbent knight. She made a good fist of it, increasing her vote to 21,270 (up by 8,130) and taking 35.2 per cent of the vote (+11.2 per cent). The UKIP vote seems to have solidly swung behind the anti-establishment figure of Claire Wright. Sir Hugo managed to hold on by increasing his share of the vote to 48.5 per cent (+2.1 per cent), but his majority was cut to just over 8,000.

Cornwall was a fascinating election story, with the Duchy returning six Conservative MPs again, but with Labour becoming the main challengers in four of the seats (up from one in 2015). It is hard to believe that the Liberal Democrats recently dominated Westminster politics here (all of the constituencies in 2005) as Labour saw massive increases in the Labour share of the vote in Truro & Falmouth (up 22.5 per cent to 37.7 per cent), St Austell & Newquay (up 18.8 per cent to 29 per cent), Camborne & Redruth (up 19.3 per cent to 44.2 per cent) and South East Cornwall (up 13.3 per cent to 22.6 per cent). The Liberal Democrats only remain contenders in North Cornwall and St Ives. In North Cornwall, former MP Daniel Rogerson (2005–2015) increased the share to 36.6 per cent (+5.3 per cent), but still lost to Scott Mann who took 50.7 per cent (+5.8 per cent) and has a majority of 7,200. In St Ives, Andrew George, Liberal Democrat MP for eighteen years, came within 312 votes of retaking the seat from Derek Thomas, with a swing of 2.3 per cent. Christopher Drew, the Labour candidate, took 14.2 per cent (+4.9 per cent). Labour's vote in Penzance has become very strong and it seems to have cost Mr George his chance to retake the seat.

It has been a conundrum for a long time as to why an area of relative deprivation such as Cornwall has not been more successful for Labour. Well, that may now have changed for future elections, when they will be looking to squeeze the Liberal Democrats further to overcome the 1,577 Conservative majority of George Eustice in Camborne & Redruth (where the Liberal Democrats fell by 6.3 per cent to 6.1 per cent) and the 3,792 majority of Sarah Newton in Truro & Falmouth (which witnessed a Lib Dem drop of 1.9 per cent to 14.9 per cent). In the latter, the local press reported that tactical voting to keep out the Tories should go to the Lib Dem's Rob Nolan. Maybe this cost Labour a famous victory. One anecdote from Cornwall, where Labour's membership increased dramatically in the last two years, which has had a galvanising effect in some areas, is that on the day of the election it was tweeted: 'the main roads in Penryn are full of Labour posters'. If you know Penryn, you'll know that was a major sign of political times a'changing. The highest increase of Labour share of the vote in any region was in the South West, where it rose by 11.46 per cent to over 29 per cent. In 2015 Labour were roughly at parity with the Liberal Democrats across the region. In 2017 they polled nearly twice as many votes. The South West is still the best region for the Liberal Democrats, but they actually slipped just under 15 per cent this time. With the collapse of UKIP, the opposition to the Conservatives in this rather independent and even awkward part of the world now seems firmly in Labour's hands.

Wales

For almost the whole of the 2017 general election campaign, the Conservatives were expecting to make highly significant gains in Wales. The first two opinion polls of the campaign suggested the Conservatives were the most popular party in the principality, a lead that defied all modern election results – indeed, for well over a hundred years, the Liberals then Labour have dominated Welsh elections. Even the initially much doubted but overall highly accurate TV exit poll projected that the Tories would make some gains from Labour in Wales. The reverse of all these expectations proved to be the case.

In the end, Labour achieved a 49 per cent share across Wales as a whole, 12 per cent more than in 2015 and their strongest performance since their 1997 landslide. The Conservatives were 15 per cent behind on 34 per cent, a more modest increase of 7 per cent. By the rules of calculating electoral 'swing', this represents a net 2.5 per cent movement from Conservative to Labour. That inevitably generated changes in hands among marginal seats, and it was Labour who gained three – Gower, Vale of Clwyd and Cardiff North. One could ask who might have lost votes if Labour and Conservative went up by 19 per cent between them; the answer is predominantly UKIP, down 12 per cent, but also the Greens (3 per cent) and the Liberal Democrats (2 per cent). One must be very wary of assuming that the UKIP vote 'broke' more to Labour, though. The turnout in Wales increased by 3 per cent to 69 per cent, and it is likely that this was mainly down to young voters who voted heavily for Labour. Indeed some disillusioned former UKIP voters may not have voted at all this time. Voters always 'churn' around more than the overall net figures suggest.

While there is no doubt about the scale of Labour's triumph in Wales, the reasons for it have been questioned. There have been suggestions that a role was played by the emphasis placed on the popular leadership of the First Minister at Cardiff Bay, Carwyn Jones, rather than Jeremy Corbyn's national leadership. However it looks more as if Labour's advance was due to the same reasons as in England. Overall, Wales voted in 2016 to leave the EU, but the three gains were all in seats that were more in favour of remaining: 61 per cent in Cardiff North, 50 per cent in Gower, 44 per cent in Vale of Clwyd. Cardiff North, where the greatest swing was needed, has a high proportion of public sector workers, students and graduates. The changes in electoral pattern in Wales were demographically similar to those in England, and the overall swing was also similar. So it would seem that the centrally led campaign does deserve most of the credit.

Similarly, the failure of the Conservatives to make any gains at all may be the responsibility of their general campaign. After all, only four weeks previously, the May local election results had suggested that seats such as Wrexham in North Wales and Bridgend in the south should certainly fall. That they did advance to their highest share in Wales since 1935 is scant compensation for actually losing seats in an election called in order to achieve a comfortable increase in the party's overall majority.

For the Liberal Democrats, historically strong (as the Liberal party) in this particular 'Celtic fringe', the results were a disaster of a different kind. With the loss of Ceredigion (Cardiganshire in English) to Plaid Cymru, they now have no seats at all in Wales for the first time since the modern party system emerged in the 1850s. Local expertise suggests that this shock result was because an informal anti-Plaid coalition collapsed. The evidence for this theory is that in 2017 there was the highest Labour vote in Ceredigion since 1997, and the highest Conservative vote since 2001. Both Labour and Conservatives campaigned more actively than previously, for example putting up posters. A higher turnout among students at the university in Aberystwyth has also been noted as contributing to Labour's share more than doubling. All this enabled Plaid Cymru's 24-year old candidate Ben Lake to win even though their share went up by only 1.6 per cent.

The Liberal Democrats also went sharply backwards in the other seats in which they have recently been competitive. Their only three genuine targets were Cardiff Central and Brecon & Radnorshire, both of which they had held until 2015, and Montgomeryshire, which they had won all but once in the elections between 1880 and 2010, when their most recent MP, Lembit Öpik, was defeated. They suffered another 5 per cent plus swing to the Tories in Montgomeryshire, and now have less than half the vote share of their main rival. The Conservatives increased their grip on Brecon & Radnorshire too, and now have a lead of over 8,000, their highest in Wales. Finally, the urban Cardiff Central proved a catastrophe for the Liberal Democrats. Their share was more than halved, Labour's increased by 22 per cent to give Jo Stevens a majority of over 17,000 and the Tories overtook them for second place.

Plaid Cymru, the Welsh nationalists (or, as they like to call themselves in English, the Party of Wales) had mixed results. They did increase from three seats to four, gaining Ceredigion as explained above. But their vote share went down overall from 12 per cent to 10 per cent. They only just held on to Arfon by ninety-two votes over Labour after a recount, and at the other end of the alphabet, though just across the Menai Strait, not only did their former leader Ieuan Wyn Jones fail to win Ynys Môn (Anglesey) from Labour, but fell back to third place. Plaid came nowhere near making any breakthrough in the southern ex-mining valleys, where their threat is always trumpeted but never seems to materialise. Their strength remains focused on Welsh speaking parts of west Wales and it is clear they will not make an SNP style breakthrough any time soon.

Wales very much illustrates the main story of the 2017 UK general election: the difference between expectations at the beginning of the campaign and the eventual result. It was said by many that Labour's days of hegemony would come to an end, and that maybe even they would become the second party behind the Conservatives. Now that really would have been a story to report, in a part of Britain with a strong nonconformist (and Nonconformist) tradition that has marginalised the Tory party for far longer than living memory. In the end Labour have emerged even stronger than before, and Mrs May's hopes were dashed – just as they were on an even wider stage.

West Midlands

Rather like its counterpart the East Midlands, this region displayed a kind of Janus face in 2017. Some types of constituency swung heavily to Labour, and Jeremy Corbyn's party achieved one of its most unlikely gains, but on the other hand the Tories did take two traditionally Labour seats and very nearly a third. Again, this is because there are several types of West Midland marginals – and several types of West Midlander.

Some of these West Midlanders reflect demographic and cultural change. As is the case in the giant London conurbation, Britain's second city, Birmingham, is now extremely ethnically diverse. Four of its constituencies have a substantial BME majority. Immigration has been shaping the politics of the whole West Midlands metropolitan area for many decades now, going back to Peter Griffiths's highly controversial 1964 election victory in Smethwick (now part of Sandwell borough and Warley constituency) and to the career of the Wolverhampton MP Enoch Powell. Residents of Sikh, Hindu, and Afro-Caribbean background form a vital and vibrant part of the collective life of Birmingham and the Black Country, and the largest ethnic group in many areas is Muslim, with Hodge Hill being the most heavily Muslim constituency in Britain.

BME voters have usually supported the Labour Party in the West Midlands, and this proved more true than ever before in 2017. In Hodge Hill, Liam Byrne's majority rose to over 31,000. Higher turnout also contributed to massive leads, as in Birmingham Ladywood (28,714) and, highest of all, Hall Green (33,944). However, the Labour increase in share was a city-wide phenomenon ranging from 9 per cent to 18 per cent, with no noticeable difference in majority white seats like Northfield and Yardley. In Birmingham, there was no clear correlation between the results of the 2017 election and the EU referendum in 2016. All this was much less noticed at the time, but the second city backed Corbyn's Labour as strongly as London did.

Ethnic voters probably helped Labour to defend some of its other targets successfully, for example, Wolverhampton South West, which Labour managed to defend even though its popular MP Rob Marris had retired. However, there were parts of the urban West Midlands, further away from the centre of the massive built-up area, where the Conservatives did advance. David Winnick, aged eighty-three, lost Walsall North after thirty-eight years. In Dudley North it took more than one recount before Ian Austin held on by twenty-two votes, suffering a 5.4 per cent negative swing. A number of other such marginal seats on the outer fringes of the conurbation also swung to the Conservatives, such as Stourbridge and Halesowen & Rowley Regis. However, it was Walsall North that was the epitome. A couple of pieces of statistical information help to explain what was going on. Walsall North had the second highest proportion voting for Leave of all the 650 UK constituencies in the 2016 referendum – a mighty 74.2 per cent. It also figures in the lists of seats with the fewest in professional and managerial employment, and it has the second lowest number of people with degrees. The preferences fit with the demographics. Walsall North is an archetypal white working-class constituency. Dudley North is also on the list of the ten most strongly Brexit seats, the second most Eurosceptic in this region.

It should therefore come as no surprise that the third most strongly anti-EU constituency in the West Midlands also happens to be the other seat that the Tories gained in 2017: Stoke-on-Trent South. There were only five Conservative gains from Labour anywhere, so it takes a combination of circumstances to explain them. The city of Stoke has for many years endured a series of political upheavals, often involving splits and defections in the local Labour Party. It was among the most fertile ground for UKIP in 2015. The whole of the Staffordshire Potteries swung away from Labour this time, and it was probably Paul Farrelly's reputation as an active and likeable local man, along with the help of Keele University students, that enabled him to hold on to Newcastle-Under-Lyme by a mere thirty votes well after dawn had broken on 9 June. The defeated Conservative still increased the party share by 11 per cent to 48.1 per cent, the highest of any beaten candidate anywhere in 2017.

Other white, working-class, pro-Brexit parts of the region also saw strong Conservative performances in the 2017 general election. Gains achieved in 2010 in semi-rural, ex-coal mining areas like Cannock Chase and North Warwickshire were consolidated with increases in majority for Amanda Milling and Craig Tracey. Labour made little or no impact in most of their other potential targets, such as Nuneaton, usually an early declaring bellwether, Worcester, Redditch, Stafford... or even their No.1 target in the West Midlands, the New Town of Telford, where Lucy Allan's majority was cut just from 730 to 720. Every one of these seats could well have fallen if they had been situated in London – or the city of Birmingham.

There was, however, one seat, lying eighth on the list of targets, that Labour did gain. That was Warwick & Leamington, where the swing was of Birmingham proportions, but not for Birmingham reasons. A swing of over 7.5 per cent removed Chris White's 6,606 majority. Such an unusual performance for the region outside its inner urban core can be explained by two main facts. Its Remain vote was 59 per cent, by far the highest of any Conservative-held seat in the region. It is also the opposite of Walsall North in another sense: it has a highly educated electorate, not far from a prominent university.

Although the 2017 election generally marked a revival of two-party politics, with over 80 per cent of the national vote going to Labour and Conservative for the first time since 1970, the Liberal Democrats did have hopes of regaining a couple of seats they had lost just two years before – Birmingham Yardley to Labour, and Solihull to the Conservatives. One of the ousted MPs, John Hemming of Yardley, was the candidate once again. However, the outcome was very disappointing. In both cases not only did the Lib Dem share fall much further, but they were relegated to third place. In fact, they did not come second anywhere in the region, and nor did UKIP. With the final disappearance of Wyre Forest's Independent Community and Health Concern challenge, this leaves the West Midlands as the most 'major-party' dominated of all regions in the United Kingdom.

Yorkshire and Humberside

Overall, Labour is the only party that can take real satisfaction from the 2017 results in Yorkshire and Humberside. They gained four seats overall, their equal most of any English region, and lost none. Two of these were from the Conservatives, and two were from the Liberal Democrats, including the 'decapitation' of their former leader, Nick Clegg, that they had so longed for in 2015. Yet there were also parts of this region where Labour's share declined. These were principally strongly pro-Brexit areas where UKIP used to do well: predominantly white, working-class and often formerly heavily involved in coal mining – in other words, places that for generations have been regarded as Labour heartlands. Labour did best in the big cities, particularly the sectors dominated by universities, and some, but not all, of the ex-textile manufacturing valleys of West Yorkshire. As with so many other regions, we must break down our analysis into the sub-regions of England's largest county.

The place to start must be Sheffield. The biggest story in Yorkshire and the Humber was Clegg losing Sheffield Hallam. Hallam is not only the leafy 'west end' of Sheffield, but one of the most middle class and highly educated constituencies in the whole of Britain. Labour have never won the seat before, so this is the first time every single South Yorkshire MP has been from Labour. Why did they finally capture it? At 77.8 per cent, turnout here was the highest since 1951. The Conservative vote was up 10.2 per cent, the first increase since 1979, suggesting that tactical voting had helped to save Clegg in 2015. Momentum have claimed credit for the gain, having said that it wasn't a target seat for the Labour Party as a whole. The new MP Jared O'Mara has praised their contribution. O'Mara has cerebral palsy and is a disability campaigner.

Sheffield Central saw the highest turnout since 1987, and Paul Blomfield increased his majority to 58.0 per cent and vote share to 70.9 per cent, both records for the seat. The Lib Dems just held their deposit, taking 5.1 per cent, despite having been only 165 votes behind Blomfield in 2010. This was one of very few constituencies where the Greens took second in 2015, and former Green leader Natalie Bennett stood, but fell to third and saw the party's vote share fall from 15.8 per cent to 8.0 per cent. Although the Conservatives only took 13.0 per cent, this was their best performance here since 1992. Sheffield South East, Sheffield Heeley and Sheffield Brightside & Hillsborough are all safe Labour seats and remain so, the Conservatives replacing UKIP as the main challengers in each. In Heeley, the Conservatives had their best vote share since 1983.

Elsewhere in the 'people's republic of South Yorkshire', though, Labour did not perform so well. Penistone & Stocksbridge has been a Conservative target for some time, and they ran Labour close, coming only 2.6 per cent behind – it now seems to be the most marginal seat in South Yorkshire. Dan Jarvis's Barnsley Central and Barnsley East are both safe Labour seats, held with slightly increased majorities and the Conservatives replacing UKIP as the main opposition (though UKIP held their deposits in both). It was the same story in Rotherham, where the Yorkshire Party took 3.8 per cent, their strongest performance yet in a Parliamentary election. Moving from the towns to the former coalfield, in Rother Valley the Conservatives reduced the Labour majority to 7.8 per cent, the closest anyone has ever come to Labour since the seat was created in 1918, and Caroline Flint's majority was reduced from nearly 9,000 to just over 5,000 in Don Valley. In Wentworth & Dearne, UKIP took 24.9 per cent last time, but didn't even stand this time round; the Conservative share increased by over 16 per cent, and Labour's by 8 per cent.

Moving to West Yorkshire, or by tradition the West Riding, again we may start with the 'big city', Leeds. Again, Labour were the winners here in every sense. Leeds North West saw a similar result to Sheffield Hallam, as Greg Mulholland lost his seat after twelve years – a seat even more influenced by students and a university than Nick Clegg's. The Lib Dems now have no MPs in the region, and Labour won the only two seats nationally where they were second to the Lib Dems in 2015. But, surprisingly, turnout here was slightly down on 2015, so the Leeds North West result was not just due to young voters 'coming to the party'. Leeds North East and Leeds Central were other seats where Labour took their highest ever vote share; in Leeds North East, it was also their highest ever majority.

Not far outside the Leeds city boundaries, the Conservatives took 45 per cent in their target seat of Wakefield – not enough to win it, but their best performance since a 1932 by-election. They increased their majority, stymying Labour's attempt to regain Ed Balls's Morley & Outwood, another seat with only three candidates (and 97.4 per cent of the vote going to the top two parties). While ex-mining Hemsworth remains a safe Labour seat, the Conservatives' 33.9 per cent was their highest since 1918.

Bradford East saw the Lib Dem vote plummet from 29.5 per cent to 1.8 per cent, and the party fell from second to fifth (doubtless partly because former MP David Ward was removed as a candidate and instead stood as an independent, saving his deposit with 7.8 per cent and third place). Bradford West also had a high-profile independent, Salma Yaqoob, former leader of Respect, and she managed 13.9 per cent and a close third place. Pudsey was a Labour target, and they reduced the Conservative majority to just 331. Labour did gain Keighley on a swing of 3.3 per cent, while in Shipley, Philip Davies's majority was almost halved, to 9.1 per cent, though the Women's Equality Party leader Sophie Walker had little impact, taking just 1.9 per cent.

In the western valleys, where textile mills had been founded to take advantage of the rivers flowing down from the Pennines, Labour increased their majority from 1.0 per cent to 11.1 per cent, despite Halifax being a prominent Conservative target. Labour similarly held Dewsbury with an increased majority, although the Conservative's 45.1 per cent is their best ever share in the seat since its creation in 1885, including several occasions on which they have held it. Colne Valley was a somewhat surprising Labour gain, but the party fell short by 1.0 per cent in Calder Valley, though it ranked as an easier target. This may be explained by the 2016 referendum vote: a majority in Calder Valley preferred to Leave, while Colne Valley voted (narrowly) to Remain. This in turn is probably due to Colne Valley including some affluent western wards of Huddersfield. Finally, Batley & Spen was rumoured as a Conservative target, but ultimately Labour won a 16.7 per cent majority. Excluding the by-election occasioned by the tragic murder of Jo Cox, this is their largest majority in the seat since its creation in 1983.

In North Yorkshire, despite York Central being regarded by some as a marginal, Rachael Maskell's vote went up 22.8 per cent to 65.2 per cent, the highest share Labour have ever taken in York (including City of York, the very similar former constituency). This was one of the seats where the Greens withdrew in Labour's favour, having taken 10.0 per cent in 2015 (their best performance in any seat where they stood down this time). Nearby Skipton & Ripon was one of only three mainland seats where the Lib Dems didn't stand. They agreed a local Progressive Alliance with the Greens, who stood aside in Harrogate & Knaresborough. This had a limited effect: the Green vote share went up 0.7 per cent in Skipton & Ripon, one of the handful of ten seats in the UK where they did better than when they stood in 2015, but the Labour share went up 10.9 per cent. Similarly, the Lib Dem vote share went up 1.4 per cent in Harrogate & Knaresborough, but the Conservatives actually increased their majority, and Labour moved into a close third.

Finally, our tour of this vast region ends in Humberside – or, as many on both sides of that river prefer, the East Riding of Yorkshire and North Lincolnshire. Indeed, the Conservative preference did hold up well here. No seat changed hands, but in this strongly Brexit-favouring sub-region, the Tories improved by over 15 per cent in Great Grimsby to take close order behind Labour, and maintained the strength of their challenge in their other target, Scunthorpe. The largest city, Hull saw a swing from Labour to Conservative, and Labour fell further back in their own target of Cleethorpes, now facing a 10,400 majority in a seat that they held until 2010. Rather fittingly, Haltemprice & Howden lies in this neck of the woods – the seat of David Davis, still entrusted after the election with the front line of the Brexit negotiations.

Robert Waller wishes to thank the following for their vital input into this Regional Review: Pete Whitehead, Andrew Stidwill, Joe Ridout (North East), Peter Lucas (Scotland), Ged Barry (South West), Harry Hayfield (Wales), Mickey Conn (Yorkshire and Humberside) and Roger Mortimore of Ipsos MORI and Anthony Wells of YouGov.

Regional Shares of Vote and Swings, 2017

ENGLISH REGIONS, 2017 %	CON	LAB	LD	UKIP	GREEN	OTHERS
Eastern	54.64	32.72	7.89	2.51	1.90	0.34
East Midlands	50.73	40.49	4.31	2.39	1.46	0.62
Greater London	33.14	54.50	8.80	1.29	1.76	0.51
North East	34.42	55.45	4.56	3.86	1.26	0.46
North West	36.20	54.86	5.37	1.87	1.15	0.55
South East	53.83	28.61	10.51	2.22	3.10	1.73
South West	51.36	29.15	14.94	1.10	2.26	1.17
West Midlands	49.03	42.48	4.42	1.81	1.68	0.57
Yorkshire & the Humber	40.47	49.03	4.98	2.60	1.25	1.67

% CHANGES, 2017/2015	CON	LAB	LD	UKIP	GREEN	OTHERS	SWING, CON TO LAB
Eastern	5.60	10.70	-0.36	-13.71	-2.05	-0.18	2.55
East Midlands	7.27	8.85	-1.25	-13.38	-1.51	0.02	0.79
Greater London	-1.74	10.81	1.09	-6.83	-3.09	-0.24	6.27
North East	9.10	8.56	-1.93	-12.88	-2.37	-0.48	-0.27

North West	4.98	10.21	-1.17	-11.77	-2.06	-0.19	2.61
South East	2.98	10.30	1.10	-12.50	-2.08	0.22	3.66
South West	4.82	11.46	-0.18	-12.45	-3.66	0.01	3.32
West Midlands	7.26	9.57	-1.10	-13.89	-1.57	-0.27	1.15
Yorkshire & the Humber	7.87	9.88	-2.14	-13.43	-2.28	0.11	1.00

SCOTLAND		
SNP	36.9	-13.1
Con	28.6	+13.7
Lab	27.1	+2.8
LD	6.8	-0.8
Green	0.2	-0.2
UKIP	0.2	-1.4
Others	0.3	+0.2

NORTHERN IRELAND		
DUP	36.0	+10.3
Sinn Fein	29.4	+4.9
SDLP	11.7	-2.2
UUP	10.3	-5.8
Alliance	7.0	-0.6
Green (NI)	0.9	-0.0
Others	3.7	-3.7

WALES		
Lab	48.9	+12.1
Con	33.6	+6.3
Plaid Cymru	10.4	-1.7
LD	4.5	-2.0
Green	0.3	-2.2
UKIP	2.0	-11.6
Others	0.2	-0.1

2017 general election statistics

Compiled by Tim Carr

TOP 100 MARGINAL SEATS: ALL PARTIES BY % MAJORITY

	% MAJ	VOTES	CONSTITUENCY	PARTY
=1	0.0%	2	North East Fife	SNP
=1	0.0%	20	Kensington	Lab
=1	0.0%	21	Perth & North Perthshire	SNP
=1	0.0%	45	Richmond Park	Con
=1	0.0%	31	Southampton Itchen	Con
=6	0.1%	48	Crewe & Nantwich	Lab
=6	0.1%	22	Dudley North	Lab
=6	0.1%	30	Newcastle-under-Lyme	Lab
=9	0.2%	60	Glasgow South West	SNP
=9	0.2%	104	Ceredigion	PC
=9	0.2%	75	Glasgow East	SNP
=12	0.3%	92	Arfon	PC
=12	0.3%	187	Canterbury	Lab
=12	0.3%	148	Stirling	Con
15	0.4%	169	Foyle	SF
=16	0.5%	195	Airdrie & Shotts	SNP
=16	0.5%	209	Barrow & Furness	Lab
=16	0.5%	239	Keighley	Lab

=16	0.5%	259	Kirkcaldy & Cowdenbeath	Lab
=16	0.5%	266	Lanark & Hamilton East	SNP
=16	0.5%	265	Rutherglen & Hamilton West	Lab
=22	0.6%	353	Chipping Barnet	Con
=22	0.6%	312	St Ives	Con
=24	0.7%	346	Hastings & Rye	Con
=24	0.7%	331	Pudsey	Con
=24	0.7%	242	Glasgow North East	Lab
=24	0.7%	318	Motherwell & Wishaw	SNP
=24	0.7%	345	Thurrock	Con
29	0.8%	314	Preseli Pembrokeshire	Con
30	0.9%	441	Ashfield	Lab
=31	1.0%	609	Calder Valley	Con
=31	1.0%	384	Inverclyde	SNP
=33	1.1%	507	Norwich North	Con
=33	1.1%	687	Stroud	Lab
35	1.2%	502	Bishop Auckland	Lab
=36	1.3%	607	Peterborough	Lab
=36	1.3%	816	Oxford West & Abingdon	Lib Dem
=38	1.5%	915	Colne Valley	Lab
=38	1.5%	863	Broxtowe	Con
=38	1.5%	777	Westmorland & Lonsdale	Lib Dem
=41	1.6%	844	Dunfermline & West Fife	SNP
=41	1.6%	789	Bedford	Lab
=41	1.6%	663	Stoke-on-Trent South	Con
=41	1.6%	720	Telford	Con
=45	1.7%	875	Fermanagh & South Tyrone	SF
=45	1.7%	836	Ipswich	Lab
=45	1.7%	888	Stockton South	Lab
48	1.8%	936	Bolton West	Con
=49	2.0%	1,072	Hendon	Con
=49	2.0%	807	Northampton North	Con
=49	2.0%	635	Aberconwy	Con
=49	2.0%	885	Midlothian	Lab
=53	2.1%	1,057	Mansfield	Con
=53	2.1%	1,020	Middlesbrough South & East Cleveland	Con
55	2.2%	1,097	Edinburgh South West	SNP
56	2.3%	1,206	Warwick & Leamington	Lab
=57	2.6%	1,725	Milton Keynes South	Con
=57	2.6%	1,322	Penistone & Stocksbridge	Lab
59	2.7%	1,369	Carshalton & Wallington	Lib Dem

=60	2.8%	1,328	Argyll & Bute	SNP
=60	2.8%	1,609	Eastbourne	Lib Dem
=60	2.8%	1,279	Pendle	Con
=60	2.8%	1,267	Central Ayrshire	SNP
=60	2.8%	1,625	Edinburgh North & Leith	SNP
65	2.9%	1,159	Northampton South	Con
66	3.0%	1,915	Milton Keynes North	Con
=67	3.1%	1,399	Morecambe & Lunesdale	Con
=67	3.1%	1,208	North Down	Independent
=67	3.1%	1,060	Glasgow North	SNP
=70	3.2%	1,657	Finchley & Golders Green	Con
=70	3.2%	1,538	Lincoln	Lab
=72	3.3%	1,577	Camborne & Redruth	Con
=72	3.3%	1,554	Putney	Con
=74	3.4%	1,757	Harrow East	Con
=74	3.4%	1,554	Portsmouth South	Lab
76	3.5%	1,586	Coatbridge, Chryston & Bellshill	Lab
77	3.6%	2,092	Watford	Con
78	3.8%	2,125	Sheffield Hallam	Lab
=79	4.0%	1,695	Copeland	Con
=79	4.0%	2,104	Morley & Outwood	Con
=81	4.1%	2,015	Derby North	Lab
=81	4.1%	2,190	Vale of Glamorgan	Con
=81	4.1%	2,549	Warrington South	Lab
84	4.3%	2,322	High Peak	Lab
85	4.4%	2,416	Battersea	Lab
=86	4.5%	1,996	Belfast South	DUP
=86	4.5%	2,690	Corby	Con
=86	4.5%	2,027	Glasgow South	SNP
=86	4.5%	2,081	Belfast North	DUP
=86	4.5%	2,569	Cheltenham	Con
91	4.7%	2,176	Wakefield	Lab
=92	4.8%	2,607	Gordon	Con
=92	4.8%	2,464	South Swindon	Con
=92	4.8%	2,446	South Down	SF
=95	4.9%	2,023	Blackpool North & Cleveleys	Con
=95	4.9%	2,457	Crawley	Con
=95	4.9%	2,508	Worcester	Con
=98	5.2%	2,438	Chingford & Woodford Green	Con
=98	5.2%	2,919	Linlithgow & East Falkirk	SNP
=98	5.2%	2,288	West Dunbartonshire	SNP

There are now more 'super-marginals' than in the previous two general elections. After 2017, there are now fifty-two constituencies with a percentage majority of 2% or under. By way of comparison, there were thirty-eight after the 2010 general election and only twenty-nine constituencies with a 2% or under majority in 2015.

By number of votes, there were forty-one majorities of less than 1,000 in votes in 2010, thirty-two in 2015 and there are now fifty-one in 2017.

TOP 50 SEATS: CONSERVATIVE MARGINALS BY % MAJORITY

	% MAJ	VOTES	CONSTITUENCY	2ND PARTY
=1	0.0%	45	Richmond Park	Lib Dem
=1	0.0%	31	Southampton Itchen	Lab
3	0.3%	148	Stirling	SNP
=4	0.6%	353	Chipping Barnet	Lab
=4	0.6%	312	St Ives	Lib Dem
=6	0.7%	346	Hastings & Rye	Lab
=6	0.7%	331	Pudsey	Lab
=6	0.7%	345	Thurrock	Lab
9	0.8%	314	Preseli Pembrokeshire	Lab
10	1.0%	609	Calder Valley	Lab
11	1.1%	507	Norwich North	Lab
12	1.5%	863	Broxtowe	Lab
=13	1.6%	663	Stoke-on-Trent South	Lab
=13	1.6%	720	Telford	Lab
15	1.8%	936	Bolton West	Lab
=16	2.0%	1,072	Hendon	Lab
=16	2.0%	807	Northampton North	Lab
=16	2.0%	635	Aberconwy	Lab
=19	2.1%	1,057	Mansfield	Lab
=19	2.1%	1,020	Middlesbrough South & East Cleveland	Lab
21	2.6%	1,725	Milton Keynes South	Lab
22	2.8%	1,279	Pendle	Lab
23	2.9%	1,159	Northampton South	Lab
24	3.0%	1,915	Milton Keynes North	Lab
25	3.1%	1,399	Morecambe & Lunesdale	Lab
26	3.2%	1,657	Finchley & Golders Green	Lab
=27	3.3%	1,577	Camborne & Redruth	Lab
=27	3.3%	1,554	Putney	Lab
29	3.4%	1,757	Harrow East	Lab
30	3.6%	2,092	Watford	Lab

=31	4.0%	1,695	Copeland	Lab
=31	4.0%	2,104	Morley & Outwood	Lab
33	4.1%	2,190	Vale of Glamorgan	Lab
=34	4.5%	2,690	Corby	Lab
=34	4.5%	2,569	Cheltenham	Lib Dem
=36	4.8%	2,607	Gordon	SNP
=36	4.8%	2,464	South Swindon	Lab
=38	4.9%	2,023	Blackpool North & Cleveleys	Lab
=38	4.9%	2,457	Crawley	Lab
=38	4.9%	2,508	Worcester	Lab
41	5.2%	2,438	Chingford & Woodford Green	Lab
42	5.6%	2,876	Reading West	Lab
43	5.7%	2,860	North East Derbyshire	Lab
44	6.0%	2,774	Ayr, Carrick & Cumnock	SNP
=45	6.1%	2,599	Carlisle	Lab
=45	6.1%	2,914	Southport	Lab
47	6.2%	3,359	Ochil & South Perthshire	SNP
48	6.4%	3,216	Rossendale & Darwen	Lab
49	6.6%	2,645	Angus	SNP
50	6.7%	3,792	Truro & Falmouth	Lab

After the 2015 general election, the Conservatives had fourteen seats with less than a 1,000 vote majority (less than 1.8% majority). As the table above shows, the number of Conservative-held 'super marginals' increased only slightly.

TOP 50 SEATS: LABOUR MARGINALS BY % MAJORITY

	% MAJ	VOTES	CONSTITUENCY	2ND PARTY
1	0.0%	20	Kensington	Con
=2	0.1%	48	Crewe & Nantwich	Con
=2	0.1%	22	Dudley North	Con
=2	0.1%	30	Newcastle-under-Lyme	Con
5	0.3%	187	Canterbury	Con
=6	0.5%	209	Barrow & Furness	Con
=6	0.5%	239	Keighley	Con
=6	0.5%	259	Kirkcaldy & Cowdenbeath	SNP
=6	0.5%	265	Rutherglen & Hamilton West	SNP
10	0.7%	242	Glasgow North East	SNP
11	0.9%	441	Ashfield	Con
12	1.1%	687	Stroud	Con
13	1.2%	502	Bishop Auckland	Con
14	1.3%	607	Peterborough	Con

15	1.5%	915	Colne Valley	Con
16	1.6%	789	Bedford	Con
=17	1.7%	836	Ipswich	Con
=17	1.7%	888	Stockton South	Con
19	2.0%	885	Midlothian	SNP
20	2.3%	1,206	Warwick & Leamington	Con
21	2.6%	1,322	Penistone & Stocksbridge	Con
22	3.2%	1,538	Lincoln	Con
23	3.4%	1,554	Portsmouth South	Con
24	3.5%	1,586	Coatbridge, Chryston & Bellshill	SNP
25	3.8%	2,125	Sheffield Hallam	Lib Dem
=26	4.1%	2,015	Derby North	Con
=26	4.1%	2,549	Warrington South	Con
28	4.3%	2,322	High Peak	Con
29	4.4%	2,416	Battersea	Con
30	4.7%	2,176	Wakefield	Con
=31	5.2%	2,185	Wolverhampton South West	Con
=31	5.2%	1,832	Wrexham	Con
33	5.5%	3,083	East Lothian	SNP
34	5.6%	2,359	Stoke-on-Trent North	Con
35	5.9%	3,321	Dewsbury	Con
36	6.1%	2,379	Vale of Clwyd	Con
37	6.7%	3,749	Reading East	Con
=38	7.2%	2,523	Blackpool South	Con
=38	7.2%	3,269	Gower	Con
=38	7.2%	2,565	Great Grimsby	Con
41	7.3%	3,280	Darlington	Con
=42	7.8%	3,882	Rother Valley	Con
=42	7.8%	3,928	Weaver Vale	Con
44	8.0%	4,174	Cardiff North	Con
45	8.4%	3,797	Bolton North East	Con
46	8.5%	3,431	Scunthorpe	Con
47	8.9%	4,761	Bristol North West	Con
48	9.0%	4,355	Enfield Southgate	Con
=49	9.1%	4,375	Bury North	Con
=49	9.1%	4,694	Gedling	Con

Note: the swing required is half of the % majority

After the 2015 general election, Labour had only eleven seats with less than a 1,000-vote majority (2% and under majority). As the table above shows there are now nineteen Labour-held 'super marginals' with less than 1,000 votes or 2% majority.

SCOTTISH NATIONAL PARTY SEATS BY % MAJORITY

	% MAJ	VOTES	CONSTITUENCY	2ND PARTY
=1	0.0%	2	North East Fife	Lib Dem
=1	0.0%	21	Perth & North Perthshire	Con
=3	0.2%	60	Glasgow South West	Lab
=3	0.2%	75	Glasgow East	Lab
=5	0.5%	195	Airdrie & Shotts	Lab
=5	0.5%	266	Lanark & Hamilton East	Con
7	0.7%	318	Motherwell & Wishaw	Lab
8	1.0%	384	Inverclyde	Lab
9	1.6%	844	Dunfermline & West Fife	Lab
10	2.2%	1,097	Edinburgh South West	Con
=11	2.8%	1,328	Argyll & Bute	Con
=11	2.8%	1,267	Central Ayrshire	Con
=11	2.8%	1,625	Edinburgh North & Leith	Lab
14	3.1%	1,060	Glasgow North	Lab
15	4.5%	2,027	Glasgow South	Lab
=16	5.2%	2,919	Linlithgow & East Falkirk	Lab
=16	5.2%	2,288	West Dunbartonshire	Lab
18	5.6%	2,613	Paisley & Renfrewshire North	Lab
19	6.1%	2,541	Paisley & Renfrewshire South	Lab
20	6.3%	2,267	Glasgow Central	Lab
21	6.6%	2,561	Glasgow North West	Lab
22	6.8%	1,007	Na h-Eileanan an Iar	Lab
23	7.2%	3,866	East Kilbride, Strathaven & Lesmahagow	Lab
24	7.4%	3,878	Livingston	Lab
25	7.7%	3,633	North Ayrshire & Arran	Con
26	7.8%	3,425	Edinburgh East	Lab
27	8.1%	3,267	Glenrothes	Lab
28	9.1%	4,923	Falkirk	Lab
29	9.4%	4,924	Inverness, Nairn, Badenoch & Strathspey	Con
30	9.7%	4,264	Cumbernauld, Kilsyth & Kirkintilloch East	Lab
31	11.3%	4,139	Aberdeen North	Lab
32	13.4%	6,269	Kilmarnock & Loudoun	Lab
33	13.6%	5,262	Dundee West	Lab
=34	15.4%	6,645	Dundee East	Con
=34	15.4%	5,919	Ross, Skye & Lochaber	Con

Nine of the SNP's thirty-five seats now have a majority of less than 1,000 votes or 1.6%. It would only require a uniform swing of 0.5% to a unionist-supporting party for the SNP to no longer hold the majority of Scottish seats, although its position as the party with the largest number of seats looks secure without a dramatic loss of support.

TOP 20 SEATS: HIGHEST SCOTTISH NATIONAL PARTY VOTE SHARE BY % VOTE

	% VOTE	% VOTE +/-	VOTES	CONSTITUENCY	POSITION/WINNER
1	46.7%	-15.3%	18,045	Dundee West	1st
2	44.7%	-7.8%	16,096	Glasgow Central	1st
3	43.6%	-16.3%	19,122	Cumbernauld, Kilsyth & Kirkintilloch East	1st
4	42.9%	-16.2%	18,890	West Dunbartonshire	1st
=5	42.8%	-16.9%	18,391	Dundee East	1st
=5	42.8%	-17.0%	17,291	Glenrothes	1st
=7	42.5%	-6.7%	18,509	Edinburgh East	1st
=7	42.5%	-12.0%	16,508	Glasgow North West	1st
=9	42.3%	-13.3%	19,690	Kilmarnock & Loudoun	1st
=9	42.3%	-8.2%	21,804	Perth & North Perthshire	1st
11	42.2%	-15.9%	13,395	Glasgow North East	2nd / Lab
12	41.3%	-15.2%	15,170	Aberdeen North	1st
13	41.1%	-13.8%	18,312	Glasgow South	1st
=14	40.7%	-16.5%	14,386	Glasgow South West	1st
=14	40.7%	-10.3%	16,964	Paisley & Renfrewshire South	1st
16	40.6%	-13.8%	6,013	Na h-Eileanan an Iar	1st
17	40.3%	-7.9%	15,480	Ross, Skye & Lochaber	1st
18	40.1%	-16.8%	21,036	Livingston	1st
19	39.9%	-10.2%	21,042	Inverness, Nairn, Badenoch & Strathspey	1st
20	39.1%	-21.1%	16,283	Banff & Buchan	2nd / Con

LIBERAL DEMOCRAT SEATS BY % MAJORITY

	% MAJ	VOTES	CONSTITUENCY	2ND PARTY
1	1.3%	816	Oxford West & Abingdon	Con
2	1.5%	777	Westmorland & Lonsdale	Con
3	2.7%	1,369	Carshalton & Wallington	Con
4	2.8%	1,609	Eastbourne	Con
5	5.7%	2,988	Edinburgh West	SNP
=6	6.6%	2,044	Caithness, Sutherland & Easter Ross	SNP
=6	6.6%	4,124	Kingston & Surbiton	Con
8	6.7%	3,512	North Norfolk	Con
9	10.3%	5,339	East Dunbartonshire	SNP
10	11.5%	5,694	Bath	Con
11	14.8%	9,762	Twickenham	Con
12	19.6%	4,563	Orkney & Shetland	SNP

In 2015 the Liberal Democrats lost 341 deposits (securing less than 5% of the votes in a constituency); in 2017 they lost 375 deposits. Despite increasing their number of seats from eight to twelve, the Liberal Democrat share of the vote fell by 0.5%.

TOP 20 SEATS: HIGHEST LIB DEM VOTE SHARE BY % VOTE

	% VOTE	% VOTE +/-	VOTES	CONSTITUENCY	POSITION/WINNER
1	52.8%	14.7%	34,969	Twickenham	1st
2	48.6%	7.2%	11,312	Orkney & Shetland	1st
3	48.4%	9.3%	25,260	North Norfolk	1st
4	47.3%	17.6%	23,436	Bath	1st
5	46.9%	8.7%	26,924	Eastbourne	1st
6	45.8%	-5.7%	23,686	Westmorland & Lonsdale	1st
7	45.1%	25.8%	28,543	Richmond Park	2nd / Con
8	44.7%	10.3%	27,810	Kingston & Surbiton	1st
9	43.7%	14.8%	26,256	Oxford West & Abingdon	1st
10	42.6%	9.4%	21,808	St Ives	2nd / Con
11	42.2%	8.2%	24,046	Cheltenham	2nd / Con
12	41.0%	6.1%	20,819	Carshalton & Wallington	1st
13	40.6%	4.3%	21,023	East Dunbartonshire	1st
14	39.3%	3.5%	21,312	Lewes	2nd / Con
15	38.0%	8.6%	21,185	North Devon	2nd / Con
16	37.6%	4.9%	22,906	Wells	2nd / Con
17	36.6%	5.3%	18,635	North Cornwall	2nd / Con
18	36.3%	5.4%	19,824	Cheadle	2nd / Con
19	35.8%	0.7%	11,061	Caithness, Sutherland & Easter Ross	1st
20	34.3%	1.2%	18,108	Edinburgh West	1st

HIGHEST UKIP VOTE SHARE BY % VOTE

	% VOTE	% VOTE +/-	VOTES	CONSTITUENCY	POSITION
1	20.1%	-11.6%	10,112	Thurrock	3rd
2	11.5%	-16.5%	4,801	Hartlepool	3rd
3	8.7%	-21.4%	3,316	Rotherham	3rd
4	8.5%	-13.2%	3,339	Barnsley Central	3rd
5	8.0%	-15.5%	3,247	Barnsley East	3rd
6	7.9%	-13.8%	4,168	Buckingham	3rd
7	7.7%	-26.1%	3,308	Boston & Skegness	3rd
8	7.6%	-36.8%	3,357	Clacton	3rd
9	7.5%	-20.6%	3,704	Rother Valley	3rd
10	7.4%	-14.6%	3,006	South Shields	3rd

UKIP failed to finish second in any seats, having finished second in 120 seats at the 2015 general election. UKIP finished in third place in 132 seats but lost vote share in every one of these seats. The party only gained vote share in every fourth-place finish (156) but, apart from Buckingham (the Speaker's constituency where the top three parties did not stand), they attracted less than 3,000 votes in each.

HIGHEST GREEN PARTY VOTE SHARE BY % VOTE

	% VOTE	% VOTE +/-	VOTES	CONSTITUENCY	POSITION
1	52.3%	+10.4%	30,149	Brighton Pavilion	1st
2	17.3%	+4.0%	12,915	Isle of Wight	3rd
3	16.3%	+2.5%	8,574	Buckingham	2nd
4	12.9%	-14.0%	9,216	Bristol West	3rd
5	9.7%	+3.5%	3,251	Glasgow North	4th
6	8.0%	-7.8%	3,848	Sheffield Central	3rd
7	6.5%	+1.1%	2,549	North Down	4th
8	6.4%	+0.7%	3,734	Skipton & Ripon	3rd
9	5.5%	-1.4%	2,771	North Herefordshire	4th
10	5.3%	0.0%	2,965	North East Hertfordshire	4th

The Brighton Pavilion stronghold of Caroline Lucas remains the Greens only realistic prospect at the moment.

HIGHEST PLAID CYMRU VOTE SHARE BY % VOTE

	% VOTE	% VOTE +/-	VOTES	CONSTITUENCY	POSITION
1	45.1%	4.3%	13,687	Dwyfor Meirionnydd	1st
2	40.8%	-3.1%	11,519	Arfon	1st
3	39.3%	0.9%	16,127	Carmarthen East & Dinefwr	1st
4	29.2%	1.6%	11,623	Ceredigion	1st
5	27.4%	-3.1%	10,237	Ynys Môn	3rd
6	22.3%	-4.7%	7,350	Rhondda	2nd
7	21.2%	12.3%	6,880	Blaenau Gwent	2nd
8	18.2%	-4.7%	7,351	Llanelli	3rd
9	14.4%	-0.2%	5,962	Caerphilly	3rd
10	13.9%	-4.2%	5,339	Neath	3rd

TOP 20 SEATS: MPS WITH HIGHEST MAJORITIES BY VOTES

1	42,214	George Howarth	Knowsley	Lab
2	39,883	Stephen Timms	East Ham	Lab

3	37,931	Meg Hillier	Hackney South & Shoreditch	Lab
4	37,336	Thangam Debbonaire	Bristol West	Lab
5	37,316	Harriet Harman	Camberwell & Peckham	Lab
6	36,754	Lyn Brown	West Ham	Lab
7	36,200	Peter Dowd	Bootle	Lab
8	35,947	Louise Ellman	Liverpool Riverside	Lab
9	35,393	Rushanara Ali	Bethnal Green & Bow	Lab
10	35,139	Diane Abbott	Hackney North & Stoke Newington	Lab
11	34,899	Vicky Foxcroft	Lewisham Deptford	Lab
12	34,584	David Lammy	Tottenham	Lab
13	33,944	Roger Godsiff	Birmingham Hall Green	Lab
14	33,215	Jeremy Corbyn	Islington North	Lab
15	32,908	Stephen Twigg	Liverpool West Derby	Lab
16	32,551	Dan Carden	Liverpool Walton	Lab
17	32,365	Steve Reed	Croydon North	Lab
18	32,149	Maria Eagle	Garston & Halewood	Lab
19	32,017	Stella Creasy	Walthamstow	Lab
20	31,730	Afzal Khan	Manchester Gorton	Lab

In 2015 only two constituencies had a majority of over 30,000 votes. After the 2017 general election, there are twenty-five. Similarly, in 2015 only eight of the twenty seats with the highest majorities by votes were Labour. In 2017 the top 20 largest majorities are all Labour.

TOP 20 SEATS: HIGHEST LABOUR VOTE SHARE BY % VOTE

	% VOTE	CONSTITUENCY	ELECTED MP
1	85.7%	Liverpool Walton	Dan Carden
2	85.3%	Knowsley	George Howarth
3	84.5%	Liverpool Riverside	Louise Ellman
4	84.0%	Bootle	Peter Dowd
5	83.2%	East Ham	Stephen Timms
=6	82.7%	Birmingham Ladywood	Shabana Mahmood
=6	82.7%	Liverpool West Derby	Stephen Twigg
8	81.6%	Tottenham	David Lammy
9	81.1%	Birmingham Hodge Hill	Liam Byrne
10	80.6%	Walthamstow	Stella Creasy
11	79.6%	Liverpool Wavertree	Luciana Berger
12	79.4%	Hackney South & Shoreditch	Meg Hillier
13	77.8%	Camberwell & Peckham	Harriet Harman
14	77.7%	Garston & Halewood	Maria Eagle
15	77.6%	Birmingham Hall Green	Roger Godsiff

16	77.4%	Manchester Central	Lucy Powell
17	77.0%	Lewisham Deptford	Vicky Foxcroft
18	76.9%	Birkenhead	Frank Field
19	76.7%	West Ham	Lyn Brown
20	76.3%	Manchester Gorton	Afzal Khan

Labour increased the size of the majority in every seat it won, with spectacularly large increases in previously safe seats. It would clearly have benefited electorally if it had been able to spread its increase in votes across more constituencies.

TOP 20 SEATS: HIGHEST CONSERVATIVE VOTE SHARE BY % VOTE

	% VOTE	CONSTITUENCY	ELECTED MP
1	69.9%	South Holland & The Deepings	John Hayes
2	69.8%	South Staffordshire	Gavin Williamson
3	69.6%	Christchurch	Christopher Chope
4	67.9%	Maldon	John Whittingdale
5	67.3%	Castle Point	Rebecca Harris
6	66.8%	New Forest West	Sir Desmond Swayne
7	66.7%	Rayleigh & Wickford	Mark Francois
8	65.8%	Brentwood & Ongar	Dr Alex Burghart
9	65.7%	Meon Valley	George Hollingbery
10	65.5%	North East Hampshire	Ranil Jayawardena
11	65.4%	Aldridge-Brownhills	Wendy Morton
=12	65.3%	Beaconsfield	Dominic Grieve
=12	65.3%	Mid Worcestershire	Nigel Huddleston
14	65.0%	Fareham	Suella Fernandes
15	64.9%	North Dorset	Simon Hoare
16	64.8%	Maidenhead	Theresa May
=17	64.4%	North East Cambridgeshire	Stephen Barclay
=17	64.4%	Windsor	Adam Afriyie
19	64.3%	Witham	Priti Patel
20	62.2%	Sleaford & North Hykeham	Dr Caroline Johnson

As if to emphasise the concentration of Labour votes, Labour won a total of thirty-seven seats with a higher vote share than the Conservative's highest vote share seat of South Holland & the Deepings with a respectable 69.9%.

TOP 20 SEATS: LOWEST WINNING VOTE SHARE BY % VOTE

	% VOTE	CONSTITUENCY	WINNING PARTY	2ND % VOTE	2ND PARTY
1	29.2%	Ceredigion	PC	29.0%	Lib Dem
2	30.4%	Belfast South	DUP	25.9%	SDLP

3	32.6%	Lanark & Hamilton East	SNP	32.1%	Con
4	32.9%	North East Fife	SNP	32.9%	Lib Dem
5	34.0%	Edinburgh North & Leith	SNP	31.2%	Lab
6	34.3%	Edinburgh West	Lib Dem	28.6%	SNP
7	35.5%	Dunfermline & West Fife	SNP	33.9%	Lab
8	35.6%	Edinburgh South West	SNP	33.4%	Con
9	35.8%	Caithness, Sutherland & Easter Ross	Lib Dem	29.2%	SNP
10	36.0%	Argyll & Bute	SNP	33.2%	Con
11	36.1%	East Lothian	Lab	30.6%	SNP
12	36.3%	Linlithgow & East Falkirk	SNP	31.1%	Lab
13	36.4%	Midlothian	Lab	34.4%	SNP
14	36.8%	Kirkcaldy & Cowdenbeath	Lab	36.3%	SNP
15	37.1%	Stirling	Con	36.8%	SNP
16	37.2%	Central Ayrshire	SNP	34.4%	Con
17	37.4%	Paisley & Renfrewshire North	SNP	31.8%	Lab
18	37.5%	Rutherglen & Hamilton West	Lab	37.0%	SNP
=19	37.6%	Airdrie & Shotts	SNP	37.1%	Lab
=19	37.6%	Glasgow North	SNP	34.5%	Lab

It is noticeable that none of the top 20 seats with the lowest winning share of votes are in England and apart from Ceredigion (Wales) and Belfast South (Northern Ireland), the remainder are all in Scotland which has a number of possible three-way seats.

TOP 20 SEATS: LOWEST CONSERVATIVE VOTE SHARE BY % VOTE

	% VOTE	CONSTITUENCY	POSITION
1	8.7%	Orkney & Shetland	4th
2	10.1%	Rhondda	3rd
3	10.3%	Manchester Withington	3rd
4	12.9%	Glasgow North East	3rd
5	13.0%	Bermondsey & Old Southwark	3rd
6	13.9%	Glasgow Central	3rd
7	14.6%	East Dunbartonshire	3rd
8	14.7%	Glasgow North	3rd
=9	14.8%	Hornsey & Wood Green	3rd
=9	14.8%	Blaenau Gwent	3rd
11	15.6%	Glasgow South West	3rd
=12	16.2%	Dundee West	3rd
=12	16.2%	Coatbridge, Chryston & Bellshill	3rd
14	16.3%	Cambridge	3rd
15	16.4%	Arfon	3rd

16	16.5%	Na h-Eileanan an Iar	3rd
17	17.2%	West Dunbartonshire	3rd
18	18.0%	Glasgow North West	3rd
19	18.3%	Cumbernauld, Kilsyth & Kirkintilloch East	3rd
20	18.4%	Ceredigion	4th

Excluding the eighteen seats of Northern Ireland

Despite having made progress in Scotland, twelve out of twenty of the Conservative's lowest vote shares were in Scotland, with four in England and four in Wales.

TOP 20 SEATS: LOWEST LABOUR VOTE SHARE BY % VOTE

	% VOTE	CONSTITUENCY	POSITION
1	8.1%	Eastbourne	3rd
2	8.6%	Berwickshire, Roxburgh & Selkirk	3rd
3	9.1%	Richmond Park	3rd
4	9.2%	Twickenham	3rd
5	9.3%	Westmorland & Lonsdale	3rd
=6	9.5%	Cheltenham	3rd
=6	9.5%	Banff & Buchan	3rd
8	9.6%	North East Fife	4th
9	9.9%	North Norfolk	3rd
10	10.4%	Perth & North Perthshire	3rd
11	10.9%	Moray	3rd
12	11.1%	West Aberdeenshire & Kincardine	3rd
13	11.2%	Lewes	3rd
=14	11.4%	East Devon	3rd
=14	11.4%	Orkney & Shetland	3rd
=16	11.7%	Wells	3rd
=16	11.7%	Winchester	3rd
18	11.8%	Gordon	3rd
=19	12.1%	North Cornwall	3rd
=19	12.1%	Thornbury & Yate	3rd

Twelve out of twenty of Labour's lowest vote shares are in England, with eight in Scotland.

TOP 20 SEATS: BIGGEST RISES IN LABOUR VOTE SHARE BY % VOTE

	PARTY SHARE	CONSTITUENCY	POSITION
1	+30.3%	Bristol West	1st

2	+22.8%	York Central	1st
3	+22.5%	Truro & Falmouth	2nd
4	+22.4%	Cardiff Central	1st
5	+21.8%	Hove	1st
=6	+21.7%	Bristol South	1st
=6	+21.7%	Norwich South	1st
=8	+21.5%	Bristol East	1st
=8	+21.5%	Portsmouth South	1st
10	+20.5%	Canterbury	1st
11	+19.8%	East Worthing & Shoreham	2nd
12	+19.3%	Camborne & Redruth	2nd
=13	+19.2%	Aberavon	1st
=13	+19.2%	Brighton, Kemptown	1st
15	+19.1%	Colchester	2nd
16	+18.9%	Bournemouth East	2nd
17	+18.8%	St Austell & Newquay	2nd
18	+18.7%	Bradford East	1st
19	+18.5%	Bournemouth West	2nd
20	+18.2%	Luton South	1st

Labour achieved many of its biggest increases in vote share along the south coast of England (six seats) and the South West (six seats).

BIGGEST FALLS IN LABOUR VOTE SHARE BY % VOTE

	PARTY SHARE	CONSTITUENCY	POSITION
1	-8.4%	Ochil & South Perthshire	3rd
2	-7.3%	East Renfrewshire	3rd
3	-6.2%	Aberdeen South	3rd
4	-4.1%	Paisley & Renfrewshire South	2nd
5	-3.8%	Dumfries & Galloway	3rd
=6	-3.4%	Ayr, Carrick & Cumnock	3rd
=6	-3.4%	Stirling	3rd
8	-3.2%	Richmond Park	3rd
9	-2.3%	Twickenham	3rd
10	-1.5%	Kilmarnock & Loudoun	2nd
11	-0.9%	Paisley & Renfrewshire North	3rd
=12	-0.5%	North Ayrshire & Arran	3rd
=12	-0.5%	Brighton Pavilion	2nd
14	-0.4%	Edinburgh South West	3rd
=15	-0.3%	Central Ayrshire	3rd

	PARTY SHARE		CONSTITUENCY	POSITION
=15	-0.3%		North Norfolk	3rd
17	-0.2%		St Albans	3rd
=18	-0.1%		Edinburgh North & Leith	2nd
=18	-0.1%		Oxford West & Abingdon	3rd

Labour only lost vote share in nineteen seats (out of 632, excluding Northern Ireland). Thirteen – and the seven biggest – of the falls were in Scotland.

TOP 20 SEATS: BIGGEST RISES IN CONSERVATIVE VOTE SHARE BY % VOTE

	PARTY SHARE	CONSTITUENCY	POSITION
1	+29.0%	Gordon	1st
=2	+24.6%	Clacton	1st
=2	+24.6%	Inverness, Nairn, Badenoch & Strathspey	2nd
4	+20.8%	Ochil & South Perthshire	1st
5	+20.3%	Ayr, Carrick & Cumnock	1st
6	+19.8%	Boston & Skegness	1st
=7	+19.3%	Aberdeen South	1st
=7	+19.3%	Ashfield	2nd
9	+19.2%	Banff & Buchan	1st
10	+19.0%	West Aberdeenshire & Kincardine	1st
11	+18.9%	Heywood & Middleton	2nd
12	+18.6%	Ross, Skye & Lochaber	2nd
13	+18.5%	Mansfield	1st
14	+18.3%	Argyll & Bute	2nd
15	+18.0%	East Renfrewshire	1st
=16	+17.9%	Berwickshire, Roxburgh & Selkirk	1st
=16	+17.9%	Stoke-on-Trent North	2nd
18	+17.5%	Burnley	2nd
19	+17.2%	Stoke-on-Trent Central	2nd
20	+17.1%	Linlithgow & East Falkirk	3rd

The Conservatives increased vote share in Scotland at the expense of the SNP and in seats in Northern England benefiting from a collapse in the UKIP vote or the absence of a UKIP candidate.

BIGGEST FALLS IN CONSERVATIVE VOTE SHARE BY % VOTE

	PARTY SHARE	CONSTITUENCY	POSITION
1	-13.1%	Richmond Park	1st
2	-10.8%	Battersea	2nd

3	-10.3%	Chelsea & Fulham	1st
4	-10.1%	Kensington	2nd
5	-10.0%	Hampstead & Kilburn	2nd
6	-9.7%	Putney	1st
7	-8.8%	Tooting	2nd
8	-8.5%	Westminster North	2nd
9	-8.4%	Hove	2nd
10	-8.2%	Hammersmith	2nd
11	-7.9%	Ealing Central & Acton	2nd
12	-7.8%	Harrow West	2nd
13	-7.5%	Cities of London & Westminster	1st
14	-6.7%	Enfield Southgate	2nd
15	-5.6%	Wimbledon	1st
=16	-5.3%	Brentford & Isleworth	2nd
=16	-5.3%	Poplar & Limehouse	2nd
18	-5.0%	Ilford South	2nd
=19	-4.7%	Islington North	2nd
=19	-4.7%	Witney	1st

Eighteen (out of twenty) of the largest falls in the Conservative share of the vote, whether they won or came second, were in London.

TOP 20 SEATS: BIGGEST FALLS IN SCOTTISH NATIONAL PARTY VOTE SHARE BY % VOTE

	PARTY SHARE	CONSTITUENCY	POSITION
1	-21.1%	Banff & Buchan	2nd
2	-18.8%	Falkirk	1st
3	-18.1%	Glasgow East	1st
4	-18.0%	Motherwell & Wishaw	1st
5	-17.5%	Coatbridge, Chryston & Bellshall	2nd
6	-17.1%	Caithness, Sutherland & Easter Ross	2nd
7	-17.0%	Glenrothes	1st
8	-16.9%	Dundee East	1st
=9	-16.8%	Livingston	1st
=9	-16.8%	East Kilbride, Strathaven & Lesmahagow	1st
11	-16.6%	Inverclyde	1st
12	-16.5%	Glasgow South West	1st
=13	-16.3%	Airdrie & Shotts	1st
=13	-16.3%	Cumbernauld, Kilsyth & Kirkintilloch East	1st
=15	-16.2%	West Dunbartonshire	1st

=15	-16.2%	Lanark & Hamilton East	1st
=15	-16.2%	Midlothian	2nd
=18	-16.0%	Central Ayrshire	1st
=18	-16.0%	Kirkcaldy & Cowdenbeath	2nd
20	-15.9%	Glasgow North East	2nd

The SNP lost vote share in every constituency in Scotland, but such were the winning margins in 2015 that they retained many seats even after losing 16–18% in share of the vote.

TOP 20 SEATS: HIGHEST INDEPENDENT/SMALL PARTY VOTE SHARE BY % VOTE

	PARTY SHARE	INDEPENDENT/SMALL PARTY	CONSTITUENCY	POSITION
1	35.2%	Independent	East Devon	2nd
2	20.0%	National Health Action	South West Surrey	2nd
3	13.9%	Independent	Bradford West	3rd
4	11.0%	Independent	Hereford & South Herefordshire	3rd
5	10.7%	Independent	Buckingham	3rd
6	10.2%	People Before Profit	Belfast West	3rd
7	9.2%	Independent	Ashfield	3rd
8	7.8%	Independent	Bradford East	3rd
9	6.8%	Traditionalist Unionist Voice	North Antrim	4th
=10	6.5%	Independent	Bethnal Green & Bow	3rd
=10	6.5%	North East Party	Easington	3rd
12	6.3%	Independent	North Somerset	4th
13	6.2%	Independent	Rochford & Southend East	3rd
=14	5.7%	Independent	Makerfield	3rd
=15	5.7%	Independent	Manchester Gorton	3rd
16	5.5%	Independent	Kingston upon Hull West & Hessle	4th
=17	5.0%	National Health Action	Redditch	3rd
=17	5.0%	Independent	East Surrey	4th
19	4.2%	Independent	Sittingbourne & Sheppey	3rd
20	4.1%	Independent	Bognor Regis & Littlehampton	4th

One of the characteristics of the 2017 general election was a reduction in the number of political parties returning an MP to Westminster – a fall from eleven in 2015 to eight (the SDLP, UUP and UKIP failing to win a seat). The low incidence of independents or small parties winning seats in UK elections continued, with only one independent (Lady Sylvia Hermon in North Down) being returned. Only two other independents – Claire Wright in East Devon and Louise Irvine of National Health Action in Health Secretary Jeremy Hunt's South West Surrey seat – polled highly, both finishing second.

TOP 20 SEATS: HIGHEST TURNOUT %

	TURNOUT 2017	TURNOUT 2015	CONSTITUENCY	PARTY
1	79.5% ↑	77.3%	Twickenham	Lib Dem
2	79.1% ↑	76.5%	Richmond Park	Con
3	78.8% ↑	74.6%	Winchester	Con
4	78.8% ↓	81.9%	East Dunbartonshire	Lib Dem
5	78.5% ↑	75.6%	Wirral West	Lab
6	78.4% ↑	73.5%	Wirral South	Lab
7	78.3% ↑	75.1%	St Albans	Con
8	78.0% ↑	75.3%	Rushcliffe	Con
9	77.9% ↑	72.9%	Hornsey & Wood Green	Lab
10	77.9% ↑	74.3%	Westmorland & Lonsdale	Lib Dem
11	77.8% ↑	74.9%	Central Devon	Con
12	77.8% ↑	75.3%	Sheffield Hallam	Lab
13	77.6% ↑	71.0%	Hove	Lab
14	77.4% ↑	74.8%	Kenilworth & Southam	Con
15	77.4% ↑	74.1%	South West Surrey	Con
16	77.4% ↑	76.1%	Cardiff North	Lab
17	77.4% ↑	74.0%	Hitchin & Harpenden	Con
18	77.4% ↑	70.8%	City of Chester	Lab
19	77.2% ↑	73.5%	Wimbledon	Con
20	77.1% ↑	71.8%	Chesham & Amersham	Con

In 2015, seven of the ten highest turnouts were in Scotland, coming only one year after the Scottish independence referendum and at the peak of support for the SNP. In 2017 only one Scottish seat, East Dunbartonshire, features in the top twenty turnouts and it is also the only one in which turnout fell. Across Scotland as a whole, the turnout fell in forty-eight (out of fifty-nine) seats, nationally falling from 71% in 2015 to 66.4% in 2017 – the only region or country in the UK to do so.

The impact of constituency demographics on turnout is discussed elsewhere, but it is worth noting that nineteen of the twenty constituencies with the highest turnout are estimated to have voted for Remain at the EU referendum; ten of them voted over 60% Remain.

TOP 20 SEATS: LOWEST TURNOUT %

	TURNOUT 2017	TURNOUT 2015	CONSTITUENCY	PARTY
1	53.0% ↓	56.8%	Glasgow North East	Lab
2	53.2% ↓	55.1%	Leeds Central	Lab
3	54.6% ↓	60.3%	Glasgow East	SNP

4	54.7% ↑	53.4%	West Bromwich West	Lab
5	55.1% ↑	52.7%	Manchester Central	Lab
6	55.5% ↑	53.6%	Kingston upon Hull East	Lab
7	55.9% ↑	55.4%	Glasgow Central	SNP
8	56.0% ↑	51.6%	Blackley & Broughton	Lab
9	56.2% ↓	61.8%	Glasgow South West	SNP
10	57.2% ↑	53.3%	Birmingham Erdington	Lab
11	57.3% ↑	53.6%	Nottingham North	Lab
12	57.3% ↑	55.0%	Walsall North	Con
13	57.4% ↑	55.5%	Kingston upon Hull North	Lab
14	57.4% ↑	53.9%	Kingston upon Hull West & Hessle	Lab
15	57.5% ↓	57.7%	Great Grimsby	Lab
16	57.7% ↑	53.2%	Stoke-on-Trent North	Lab
17	57.9% ↑	54.6%	Leicester West	Lab
18	58.2% ↑	49.9%	Stoke-on-Trent Central	Lab
19	58.3% ↑	52.9%	Middlesbrough	Lab
20	58.3% ↑	56.1%	Easington	Lab

At 65.4%, Northern Ireland may still have had the lowest turnout as a country/region in the UK, but it also rose 6.3%, the highest increase of anywhere. Four out of ten of the lowest turnouts in 2015 were in Northern Ireland, but none featured in 2017.

Fourteen of the twenty seats with the lowest turnout in 2017 voted Leave in 2016.

The demographics of the new House of Commons

Compiled by Robert Waller

Oldest MPs

CONSERVATIVE

Sir Bill Cash	May 1940
Kenneth Clarke	Jul 1940
Sir Roger Gale	Aug 1943
Glyn Davies	Feb 1944
Sir Peter Bottomley	Jul 1944
Sir Paul Beresford	Apr 1946
Christopher Chope	May 1947
Gordon Henderson	Jan 1948
Sir Nicholas Soames	Feb 1948
Pauline Latham	Feb 1948
David Davis	Dec 1948
Keith Simpson	Mar 1949
Sir Greg Knight	Apr 1949
David Evennett	Jun 1949
Bob Stewart	Jul 1949
Keith Simpson	Mar 1949

Sir Greg Knight	Apr 1949
David Evennett	Jun 1949
Bob Stewart	Jul 1949

LABOUR

Dennis Skinner	Feb 1932
Paul Flynn	Feb 1935
Ann Clwy	Mar 1937
Geoffrey Robinson	May 1938
Barry Sheerman	Aug 1940
Jim Cunningham	Feb 1941
Kelvin Hopkins	Aug 1941
Frank Field	Jul 1942
Dame Margaret Beckett	Jan 1943
Ronnie Campbell	Aug 1943
Dame Margaret Hodge	Sep 1944
Louise Ellman	Nov 1945
Adrian Bailey	Dec 1945
Roger Godsiff	Jun 1946
Kate Hoey	Jun 1946
David Crausby	Jun 1946
Ann Coffey	Aug 1946
Sir Kevin Barron	Oct 1946
Virendra Sharma	Apr 1947
Marie Rimmer	Apr 1947
John Spellar	Aug 1947
Stephen Pound	Jul 1948
Jack Dromey	Sep 1948
Jeremy Corbyn	May 1949
George Howarth	Jun 1949
Jack Dromey	Sep 1948
Jeremy Corbyn	May 1949
George Howarth	Jun 1949

OTHERS

Sir Vince Cable (LD)	May 1943
Marion Fellows (SNP)	May 1949

Longest-serving MPs

Kenneth Clarke	Con	1970
Dennis Skinner	Lab	1970
Sir Peter Bottomley	Con	1975
Geoffrey Robinson	Lab	1976
Barry Sheerman	Lab	1979
Frank Field	Lab	1979
Harriet Harman	Lab	1982
Dame Margaret Beckett	Lab	1983
Sir Edward Leigh	Con	1983
Jeremy Corbyn	Lab	1983
Nick Brown	Lab	1983
Sir Kevin Barron	Lab	1983
Sir David Amess	Con	1983
Sir Nicholas Soames	Con	1983
Sir Roger Gale	Con	1983
Ann Clwyd	Lab	1984 May
Sir Bill Cash	Con	1984 May
Sir Patrick McLoughlin	Con	1986 May
George Howarth	Lab	1986 Nov
John Redwood	Con	1987
Ronald Campbell	Lab	1987
David Tredinnick	Con	1987
Keith Vaz	Lab	1987
Paul Flynn	Lab	1987
Diane Abbott	Lab	1987
Kate Hoey	Lab	1989

Youngest MPs

Mhairi Black	SNP	12 September 1994
Ben Lake	PC	February 1993
Jack Brereton	Con	13 May 1991
David Linden	Lab	14 May 1990
Danielle Rowley	Lab	25 February 1990
Ben Bradley	Con	December 1989
Paul Sweeney	Lab	16 January 1989
Kirstene Hair	Con	1989

| Tom Pursglove | Con | 5 November 1988 |
| Laura Pidcock | Lab | 18 June 1988 |

Twenty constituencies with highest proportion of voters over 65

		%	PARTY HOLDING SEAT
1	Christchurch	36.0	Con
2	Clacton	35.0	Con gain from UKIP
3	North Norfolk	34.1	LD
4	New Forest West	33.9	Con
5	East Devon	31.7	Con
6	Bexhill & Battle	31.3	Con
7	West Dorset	31.1	Con
8	Totnes	30.9	Con
9	Louth & Horncastle	30.5	Con
10	Worthing West	30.1	Con
11	Dwyfor Meirionnydd	30.0	Plaid Cymru
12	Suffolk Coastal	29.7	Con
13	Tiverton & Honiton	29.2	Con
14	Chichester	28.9	Con
15	Westmorland & Lonsdale	28.8	LD
16	Lewes	28.6	Con
17	West Worcestershire	28.5	Con
18	Aberconwy	28.4	Con
19	Arundel & South Downs	28.3	Con
20	Brecon & Radnorshire	28.2	Con

- The YouGov post-election analysis suggests that the Conservatives did by far their best among voters aged over 60, gaining a 58% share among the 60–69-year-olds and no less than 69% (compared with Labour's 19%) among the over-70 group.

- Not surprisingly, therefore, the party holds almost all of the constituencies with a high proportion of more elderly residents. The Liberal Democrats won a couple in 2017, though their leader Tim Farron faced one of the Tories' best performances anywhere as they cut his majority in Westmorland and Lonsdale from nearly 9,000 to just 777.

- Older voters did also tend to favour exit from the EU in 2016, another indicator of Labour not doing so well in 2017. However, Labour could still make strong advances in some of the seats in the list, such as Worthing West, where their share advanced by 17.5%, so any correlation is not strong or universal.

Twenty constituencies with lowest proportion of voters over 65

		%	PARTY HOLDING SEAT
1	Poplar & Limehouse	6.9	Lab
2	Bermondsey & Old Southwark	8.2	Lab
3	Bethnal Green & Bow	8.3	Lab
4	East Ham	8.4	Lab
5	Vauxhall	8.4	Lab
6	Bristol West	8.5	Lab
7	West Ham	8.6	Lab
8	Hackney North & Stoke Newington	8.6	Lab
9	Lewisham Deptford	8.9	Lab
10	Battersea	9.1	Lab gain from Con

- Labour did outstandingly well among young voters in 2017, and correspondingly poorly among those over sixty. According to the post-election analysis supplied by Ipsos MORI, all the swing to Labour was among under-44s (and highest of all among 25–34s), while there was a swing to the Conservatives among over-55s. This is the biggest age gap MORI had seen in their analysis of all elections going back to the 1979.

- It is therefore unsurprising that Labour won all ten seats on this list, including making a gain in Battersea. However, it might also be noticed that other factors are at work in their success, with all the seats being urban and nine of them being located in Labour's Greater London stronghold.

Twenty constituencies with highest proportion of black residents

		%	PARTY HOLDING SEAT
1	Camberwell & Peckham	37.4	Lab

2	Croydon North	31.5	Lab
3	Lewisham Deptford	28.9	Lab
4	Edmonton	27.3	Lab
5	Hackney South & Shoreditch	26.9	Lab
6	Tottenham	26.7	Lab
7	Lewisham East	25.8	Lab
8	Erith & Thamesmead	25.7	Lab
9	Brent Central	25.5	Lab
10	Dulwich & West Norwood	25.0	Lab
11	Vauxhall	24.7	Lab
12	Streatham	24.3	Lab
13	West Ham	23.1	Lab
14	Birmingham Ladywood	22.6	Lab
15	Lewisham West & Penge	22.4	Lab
16	Barking	20.2	Lab
17	Bermondsey & Old Southwark	20.1	Lab
18	Greenwich & Woolwich	20.1	Lab
19	Hackney North & Stoke Newington	19.6	Lab
20	Walthamstow	18.9	Lab

Some interesting features:

- All these top twenty seats we very safely held by Labour in 2017, having gained two from the Liberal Democrats in 2015 after Sarah Teather's retirement in Brent Central and the defeat of Simon Hughes in Bermondsey.

- Nineteen of the twenty seats are within the boundaries of Greater London – the only exception being Birmingham Ladywood.

- There are no constituencies with a black majority, whereas there are six with an Asian majority.

- There are no Conservative seats in the top twenty; the highest in the list is Harrow East (8.4%) at number 59.

- Only four of the top twenty have black MPs at present: Tottenham (David Lammy), Streatham (Chuka Umunna), Hackney North (Diane Abbott) and Edmonton (Kate Osamor).

Twenty constituencies with highest proportion of Asian residents

		%	PARTY HOLDING SEAT
1	Leicester East	58.1	Lab
2	Ilford South	57.2	Lab
3	Bradford West	54.5	Lab
4	East Ham	53.8	Lab
5	Brent North	52.4	Lab
6	Ealing Southall	50.7	Lab
7	Birmingham Hodge Hill	49.8	Lab
8	Birmingham Hall Green	49.5	Lab
9	Harrow East	45.7	Con
10	Harrow West	42.9	Lab
11	Poplar & Limehouse	42.2	Lab
12	Feltham & Heston	40.8	Lab
13	Birmingham Ladywood	40.5	Lab
14	Slough	40.3	Lab
15	Bethnal Green & Bow	40.0	Lab
16	Bradford East	39.3	Lab
17	Birmingham Perry Barr	38.8	Lab
18	Blackburn	37.5	Lab
19	Leicester South	37.4	Lab
20	Hayes & Harlington	36.4	Lab

Some interesting features:

- The number of the top twenty Asian seats with an MP of Asian origin is still only nine. In 2017 it went up by just two when Fiona Mactaggart (Slough) retired and was replaced as Labour candidate by Tan Dhesi. Labour still holds nineteen of the twenty with the only exception being the Conservative Bob Blackman's Harrow East.

- The British Asian population is much more spread out than the Afro-Caribbean population, with just half of the twenty seats above being located in Greater London.

Twenty constituencies with lowest proportion of white residents

		%	PARTY HOLDING SEAT
1	Leicester East	58.1	Lab
2	Ilford South	57.2	Lab
3	Bradford West	54.5	Lab
4	East Ham	53.8	Lab
5	Brent North	52.4	Lab
6	Ealing Southall	50.7	Lab
7	Birmingham Hodge Hill	49.8	Lab
8	Birmingham Hall Green	49.5	Lab
9	Harrow East	45.7	Con
10	Harrow West	42.9	Lab
11	Poplar & Limehouse	42.2	Lab
12	Feltham & Heston	40.8	Lab
13	Birmingham Ladywood	40.5	Lab
14	Slough	40.3	Lab
15	Bethnal Green & Bow	40.0	Lab
16	Bradford East	39.3	Lab
17	Birmingham Perry Barr	38.8	Lab
18	Blackburn	37.5	Lab
19	Leicester South	37.4	Lab
20	Hayes & Harlington	36.4	Lab

Some interesting features:

- The number of the top twenty Asian seats with an MP of Asian origin is still only nine. In 2017 it went up by just two when Fiona Mactaggart (Slough) retired and was replaced as Labour candidate by Tan Dhesi. Labour still holds nineteen of the twenty with the only exception being the Conservative Bob Blackman's Harrow East.

- The British Asian population is much more spread out than the Afro-Caribbean population, with just half of the twenty seats above being located in Greater London.

Twenty constituencies with highest proportion of Muslim residents

		%	PARTY HOLDING SEAT
1	Birmingham Hodge Hill	52.1	Lab
2	Bradford West	51.3	Lab
3	Birmingham Hall Green	46.6	Lab
4	East Ham	37.4	Lab
5	Bradford East	36.9	Lab
6	Blackburn	36.3	Lab
7	Bethnal Green & Bow	35.4	Lab
8	Birmingham Ladywood	35.2	Lab
9	Ilford South	34.9	Lab
10	Poplar & Limehouse	33.6	Lab
11	Manchester Gorton	28.8	Lab
12	Leicester South	27.8	Lab
13	West Ham	26.8	Lab
14	Walthamstow	25.4	Lab
15	Luton South	25.3	Lab
16	Oldham West & Royton	24.6	Lab
17	Edmonton	24.5	Lab
18	Slough	23.8	Lab
19	Rochdale	23.6	Lab
20	Birmingham Perry Barr	22.7	Lab

- After the 2017 election, all twenty seats still have a Labour MP. Muslims appear to have much reduced their support in Bradford West for Respect since George Galloway's dramatic 2012 by-election victory, and this time the former Respect leader Salma Yaqoob, standing as an Independent, came in third after the Conservatives. In Bradford East, they appear to have ended their dalliance with the Liberal Democrats and returned to their previous solid pattern of Labour support. However, most of these twenty seats did not produce the above average swings to Labour that they had in 2015, perhaps because many have already reached 'saturation levels' in terms of massive Labour percentages. There were, however, some large increases in turnout, reflecting the younger age patterns in strongly Muslim seats. For example, Ilford South recorded the highest turnout increase in Greater London – 12.9%.

- Only six of the top twenty in the list currently have Muslim MPs, and has increased by just one after the 2017 election, with the late Sir Gerald Kaufman being replaced by Afzal Khan as Labour candidate in Manchester Gorton, where a scheduled by-election was countermanded by Theresa May's decision to call a snap general election.

- The 2011 census revealed for the first time that there are now two seats with a majority of Muslim residents (though not necessarily voters, due to the younger age profile among this group). After 2001, there were only three seats over 30% Muslim compared with ten now, and nine over 20% compared with twenty-six ten years later.

Ten constituencies with highest proportion born in Poland

	%	PARTY HOLDING SEAT
Ealing North	8.5	Lab
Ealing Central & Acton	6.5	Lab
Slough	6.0	Lab
Luton South	5.5	Lab
Tottenham	5.4	Lab
Southampton Test	5.0*	Lab
Mitcham & Morden	4.9	Lab
Brentford & Isleworth	4.5	Lab
Brent Central	4.4	Lab
Peterborough	4.1	Lab gain from Con

Though EU citizens, people born in Poland (and Romania, below) may well not be eligible to vote in general elections unless they have UK nationality, but where there is such a concentration it may of course impact the choices of those who do have a vote – and there are several key marginals in the list above. In 2017, Ealing Central/Acton was a prime Conservative target, with a Labour majority of just 274 in 2015, and Southampton Test and Luton South somewhat more outside chances. However, Labour greatly strengthened their position in all three in 2017, and they gained Peterborough from the Tories. This all suggests that despite arguments that European immigration was a main cause of the Brexit vote in 2016, a substantial East European presence if anything correlated with Labour success the next year. Community cohesion may be warmer than some allege.

Five constituencies with highest proportion born in Romania

	%	PARTY HOLDING SEAT
Harrow East	3.3	Con
Brent North	2.9	Lab
Hendon	2.4	Con
Leyton & Wanstead	1.9	Lab
Walthamstow	1.8	Lab

It should be remembered that these figures are from the 2011 Census, before immigration restrictions on Romanians were eased, but it is likely that any influx would be most concentrated where existing communities are located, such as in north and east London boroughs as above.

Both Harrow East and Hendon are key Labour targets that they must gain to become the largest party nationally, never mind win an overall majority – but they did not fall in 2017 despite Labour's generally very strong performance in Greater London. This may, however, be due to other considerations, such as the high concentration of Jewish voters in the north west sector of the capital, after recent well-publicised allegations of anti-Semitism within sections of the Labour party.

Twenty constituencies with highest proportion of voters with degrees

		%	PARTY HOLDING SEAT
1	Battersea	57.4	Lab gain from Con
2	Richmond Park	55.2	Con
3	Cities of London & Westminster	54.5	Con
4	Wimbledon	54.4	Con
5	Hampstead & Kilburn	54.0	Lab
6	Chelsea & Fulham	53.7	Con
7	Kensington	52.2	Lab gain from Con
8	Hornsey & Wood Green	52.0	Lab
9	Putney	51.6	Con
10	Tooting	51.4	Lab
11	Twickenham	49.5	LD gain from Con
12	Islington North	48.8	Lab
13	Vauxhall	48.7	Lab

14	Ealing Central & Acton	48.5	Lab
15	Dulwich & West Norwood	47.6	Lab
16	Hammersmith	47.5	Lab
17	Islington South & Finsbury	47.4	Lab
18	Westminster North	47.3	Lab
19	Bristol West	47.2	Lab
20	Edinburgh South	46.9	Lab

- After the 2017 election, only five of the top twenty in this list of 'highly educated' seats are in the hands of the governing Conservative Party.

- They lost three of these seats in the 2017 election, a much higher proportion of losses than the Conservatives faced in the election as a whole.

- This is not coincidental, as the Tories did worse in seats that voted remain in the 2016 referendum and the majority in every one of these seats voted to stay in the EU.

- It might also be noted that eighteen of the twenty seats are situated in Greater London, where the Conservatives did particularly poorly.

Twenty constituencies with highest proportion of full-time students

		%	PARTY HOLDING SEAT
1	Sheffield Central	38.1	Lab gain from LD
2	Nottingham South	34.5	Lab
3	Cardiff Central	33.9	Lab
4	Newcastle upon Tyne East	31.4	Lab
5	Liverpool Riverside	30.9	Lab
6	Manchester Central	29.1	Lab
7	Leeds North West	28.6	Lab gain from LD
8	Oxford East	27.7	Lab
9	Cambridge	27.5	Lab
10	Manchester Gorton	26.3	Lab
11	Glasgow Central	25.2	SNP
12	Glasgow North	25.0	SNP
13	Leeds Central	24.9	Lab

14	Leicester South	24.8	Lab
15	Swansea West	24.7	Lab
16	Bristol West	24.3	Lab
17	Portsmouth South	24.2	Lab gain from Con
18	Coventry South	24.2	Lab
19	Canterbury	24.0	Lab gain from Con
20	Birmingham Ladywood	23.3	Lab

Some interesting features:

- Canterbury was perhaps the most surprising gain of the whole election, having been Conservative since 1832. Although the seat includes other areas, Canterbury itself, which has two universities (Kent and Christ Church) has the highest proportion of students compared with permanent residents of any town or city in the United Kingdom.

- Following Nick Clegg's perceived change of position on student fee increases, it was often said that the Liberal Democrats, who have done well in recent elections in constituencies influenced by universities, would suffer greatly at the 2015 election. Four of the five seats on this list that the Lib Dems won in 2010 did indeed fall in 2015; but Clegg himself held on in a seat outside the top twenty but still influenced by the Sheffield universities. Greg Mulholland also held on for the Lib Dems in a top twenty student seat in 2015. However, it seems to have been only a matter of postponing 'the chickens coming home to roost', as both Clegg and Mulholland were defeated in 2017. There are now no Liberal Democrat held constituencies in this top twenty list. One minor compensation was they did gain Oxford West & Abingdon (not really the 'student' seat in Oxford) from the Conservatives.

- The Green party vote in seats with many students fell off dramatically in 2017. In 2015 the Greens did finish a strong second in Bristol West with 17,237 votes (26.8%, their second best share after Caroline Lucas's Brighton Pavilion), and a distant second in Sheffield Central (15.8%), but in 2017 their vote was more than halved in Bristol West and they dropped back into third place – a fate that also befell the former Green leader Natalie Bennett in Sheffield Central.

- As was very much noticed, Labour also performed at their strongest among the 18–24 age group, with 69% of their preferences – and the turnout rose from a very poor 43% in 2015 (compared with over 66% across the country as a whole) to 53% (compared with 69%) according to YouGov's massive post-election poll.

Twenty constituencies with lowest proportion of voters with degrees

		%	PARTY HOLDING SEAT
1	Birmingham Hodge Hill	12.1	Lab
2	Walsall North	12.2	Con gain from Lab
3	Hull East	12.7	Lab
4	Glasgow East	12.7	SNP
5	West Bromwich West	13.1	Lab
6	Nottingham North	13.3	Lab
7	Liverpool Walton	13.3	Lab
8	Clacton	13.4	Con gain from UKIP
9	Stoke on Trent North	13.7	Lab
10	Wolverhampton South East	13.9	Lab
11	Rhondda	14.0	Lab
12	Great Yarmouth	14.2	Con
13	Knowsley	14.3	Lab
14	Rotherham	14.3	Lab
15	Doncaster North	14.3	Lab
16	Boston & Skegness	14.6	Con
17	Great Grimsby	14.6	Lab
18	Blackpool South	14.6	Lab
19	Castle Point	14.6	Con
20	Ashfield	14.6	Lab

- It should be noted that not all of these seats, by any means, are Labour strongholds. Indeed Walsall North, which has the second lowest proportion of voters with degrees, was one of only six Conservative gains from Labour in the 2017 election.

- There is a strong correlation with former UKIP support, as indicated by the presence in the top ten of the only seat they have ever won in a general election, Douglas Carswell's Clacton. Boston & Skegness in Lincolnshire was also regarded as important enough a UKIP target in 2017 that their leader (at the time), Paul Nuttall, chose to contest it, though he finished a poor third.

- Not surprisingly, in the English seats at least, there is also a relationship between this table and a high share for Brexit in the 2016 referendum.

- According to Ipsos MORI, the Conservatives had a large seventeen-point lead among those with no qualifications, and a smaller seven-point lead among those educated to below degree level. Among graduates, though, Labour had a fifteen-point lead.

Twenty constituencies with highest proportion of single parents

		%	PARTY HOLDING SEAT
1	Belfast West	19.1	SF
2	Edmonton	15.3	Lab
3	Barking	14.6	Lab
4	Foyle	14.5	SF gain from SDL
5	Croydon North	14.5	Lab
6	Nottingham North	14.2	Lab
7	Belfast North	13.8	DUP
8	Tottenham	13.6	Lab
9	Liverpool Walton	13.0	Lab
10	Enfield North	12.8	Lab
11	Erith & Thamesmead	12.7	Lab
12	Knowsley	12.7	Lab
13	Birmingham Hodge Hill	12.6	Lab
14	Glasgow East	12.5	SNP
15	Croydon Central	12.2	Lab gain from Con
16	Birmingham Erdington	12.2	Lab
17	Liverpool West Derby	12.2	Lab
18	Camberwell & Peckham	12.1	Lab
19	Dagenham & Rainham	12.1	Lab
20	Birkenhead	12.0	Lab

- An interesting mixture of types of seat: predominantly white working-class areas, such as those in Nottingham and Merseyside; those with a substantial Afro-Caribbean population, such as Edmonton, Tottenham and Erith & Thamesmead; and seats in Northern Ireland and Scotland.

- The two Conservative marginals on this list that fell to Labour in either 2015 or 2017, Enfield North and Croydon Central, moved up the rank order significantly between the 2001 and 2011 censuses, suggesting that long-term demographic change is working to the Tories' disadvantage in Outer London.

Twenty constituencies with highest proportion of social rented housing

		%	PARTY HOLDING SEAT
1	Camberwell & Peckham	50.6	Lab
2	Hackney South & Shoreditch	50.1	Lab
3	Glasgow North East	49.0	Lab gain from SNP
4	Islington South & Finsbury	43.7	Lab
5	Bermondsey & Old Southwark	43.5	Lab
6	Glasgow East	43.3	SNP
7	Bethnal Green & Bow	42.7	Lab
8	Holborn & St Pancras	41.8	Lab
9	Vauxhall	41.2	Lab
10	Glasgow South West	39.8	SNP
11	Greenwich & Woolwich	39.3	Lab
12	Birmingham Ladywood	38.2	Lab
13	Motherwell & Wishaw	37.6	SNP
14	Sheffield Brightside & Hillsborough	37.5	Lab
15	Hackney North & Stoke Newington	37.3	Lab
16	Blackley & Broughton	37.3	Lab
17	West Dunbartonshire	37.3	SNP
18	Glasgow North West	36.9	SNP
19	Nottingham North	36.8	Lab
20	Poplar & Limehouse	36.8	Lab

- In the 2017 general election, according to Ipsos MORI, who jointly produced the very accurate exit poll on 8 June, there was hardly any swing among voters living in the social rented housing sector (Labour up seven points to 57%, Conservative up eight to 26%. UKIP slumped dramatically from an 18% share in 2015 – actually level with the Conservatives – to just 4%, while the Liberal Democrats also languished with 4%, well below their national average).

- With a 31% lead, it is no surprise that all of the constituencies on this list in England were won by the Labour Party. However, council housing has for many decades been generally more prevalent in Scotland, and the SNP held five of the six Scottish seats on the list, although their majorities in all of these were dramatically reduced – with Labour in second place in each case, even though it was the Conservatives who generally advanced the most in Scotland.

- According to the Ipsos MORI figures, at 60%, those living in the social rented sector were 9% less likely to turn out than the national average.

Twenty constituencies with highest proportion of owner-occupied housing

		%	PARTY HOLDING SEAT
1	East Dunbartonshire	85.8	LD gain from SNP
2	Sefton Central	85.5	Lab
3	Rayleigh & Wickford	84.5	Con
4	Cheadle	83.7	Con
5	Wyre & Preston North	83.5	Con
6	Castle Point	82.6	Con
7	Haltemprice & Howden	82.4	Con
8	East Renfrewshire	82.0	Con gain from SNP
9	Charnwood	81.6	Con
10	York Outer	81.5	Con
11	Mid Derbyshire	80.7	Con
12	Fareham	79.9	Con
13	Old Bexley & Sidcup	79.8	Con
14	Orpington	79.7	Con
15	Staffordshire Moorlands	79.7	Con
16	Solihull	79.6	Con
17	South Leicestershire	79.6	Con
18	Bromsgrove	79.5	Con
19	Sutton Coldfield	79.4	Con
20	Thornbury & Yate	79.4	Con

Some interesting features:

- While high owner occupation is usually a positive feature for Conservatism (remember Mrs Thatcher's sale of council housing), the table shows that this is not universally so. The numbers one and two in this category elected other parties. The point is that these are both in regions where the Conservative party has become unpopular – Merseyside and Scotland. Region can trump housing tenure as a determinant of political preference.

- Only two of the seats above are in Greater London – Old Bexley & Sidcup, the linear descendant of the constituency held by Edward Heath from 1950 to 2001, and Orpington, famously won by the Liberals in a by-election in the 1960s. The Liberal Democrats lost all four of their seats in this category in 2015, even though they had sitting MPs, but Jo Swinson regained East Dunbartonshire from the SNP in 2017.

- According to the Ipsos MORI data released after the election, there was a slight, 1% swing from Labour to Conservative among owner-occupiers, but their turnout declined slightly against the national trend. This was because the rise in turnout was concentrated in the private rented sector – because young people have increasingly found it hard to buy their own property. There was a 6% swing among private renters as the Labour share shot up by 15%, and turnout by 8%.

Twenty constituencies with highest proportion of privately rented housing

		%	PARTY HOLDING SEAT
1	Cities of London & Westminster	42.1	Con
2	Bristol West	40.1	Lab
3	Westminster North	36.8	Lab
4	Liverpool Riverside	36.5	Lab
5	Cardiff Central	36.3	Lab
6	Hampstead & Kilburn	36.1	Lab
7	Sheffield Central	36.0	Lab
8	Kensington	35.6	Lab gain from Con
9	East Ham	34.9	Lab

10	Manchester Central	34.6	Lab
11	Poplar & Limehouse	34.4	Lab
12	Ealing Central & Acton	34.4	Lab
13	Chelsea & Fulham	33.4	Con
14	West Ham	33.4	Lab
15	Tooting	32.8	Lab
16	Manchester Gorton	32.8	Lab
17	Portsmouth South	32.7	Lab gain from Con
18	Brighton Pavilion	32.7	Green
19	Hackney North & Stoke Newington	32.5	Lab
20	Brent Central	32.4	Lab

- This set of constituencies swung more heavily than average to Labour in 2017. Among the exceptionally high increases in Labour vote share are Bristol West (no less than 30.3%), Cardiff Central (22.4%), Portsmouth South (21.5%), Ealing Central & Acton (16.5%) and Hampstead & Kilburn (14.6%).

- This would be because they include a high proportion of young people, for example those who have been unable to gain a foothold on the housing ladder due to unaffordable property prices.

- There is also a high correlation with large numbers of students, especially in the seats here with the highest Labour increases of all, such as Bristol West and Cardiff Central.

Ten constituencies with highest proportion in same-sex civil partnerships

		%	PARTY HOLDING SEAT
1	Bermondsey & Old Southwark	3.2	Lab
2	Brighton Kemptown	3.2	Lab gain from Con
3	Cities of London & Westminster	3.0	Con
4	Brighton Pavilion	2.9	Green
5	Islington South & Finsbury	2.7	Lab
6	Holborn & St Pancras	2.6	Lab
7	Lewisham Deptford	2.6	Lab
8	Camberwell & Peckham	2.6	Lab
9	Hove	2.4	Lab
10	Dulwich & West Norwood	2.4	Lab

- These figures are from reported returns from the 2011 Census, so pre-date the institution of same-sex marriage.

- They also should not be taken as an indicator of 'percentage gay/lesbian', which would include many not in same sex civil partnerships or not reporting to the official government census.

- However the list does still have political interest, as it probably includes the greatest variety of constituency patterns of contest of any of our lists. It inclues the only Green seat (where Caroline Lucas again greatly increased her majority, to nearly 15,000 in Brighton Pavilion); two Conservative seats vulnerable to Labour – one gained in 2017 with a swing of over 10%, Brighton Kemptown, and one retained with an even more massive movement, Hove); a safe Tory stronghold (the Cities of London & Westminster); several safe Labour constituencies in London; and finally the former seat of the Liberal Democrat, Simon Hughes who was also the only gay MP for any of the top 10 seats in this category before the 2015 election but lost to Labour again in 2017. However there is still one – Peter Kyle, the Labour victor in Hove, who increased his majority from just over 1,000 to nearly 19,000.

- The seats with the lowest percentage of civil partnerships recorded in England and Wales are at 0.4%: Castle Point in Essex, which includes Canvey island (now safe Conservative, formerly with a strong UKIP presence in second place); Harrow East (a Conservative seat where they held off a Labour challenge); and Thornbury & Yate in Gloucestershire, which the Liberal Democrats again lost to the Conservatives.

Twenty constituencies with highest proportion of higher professional and managerial workers

		%	PARTY HOLDING SEAT
1	Wimbledon	24.0	Con
2	Cities of London & Westminster	23.8	Con
3	Battersea	23.4	Lab gain from Con
4	Richmond Park	23.3	Con
5	Chelsea & Fulham	22.6	Con
6	Hampstead & Kilburn	21.2	Lab

7	Kensington	20.7	Lab gain from Con
8	Wokingham	20.5	Con
9	Putney	20.4	Con
10	Twickenham	20.2	LD gain from Con
11	South Cambridgeshire	19.9	Con
12	St Albans	19.8	Con
13	Hitchin & Harpenden	19.8	Con
14	Esher & Walton	19.8	Con
15	North East Hampshire	19.5	Con
16	Sheffield Hallam	19.2	Lab Gain from LD
17	Islington South & Finsbury	19.1	Lab
18	Maidenhead	19.1	Con
19	Westminster North	18.9	Lab
20	Altrincham & Sale West	18.8	Con

- Socio-economic class has for many decades been regarded as the strongest single predictor of voting patterns, but the 2017 election marked a significant departure from this rule. Post election surveys such as that by the pollster Ipsos MORI suggested that the age of voters clearly replaced their class as the strongest correlator with preference between Conservative and Labour. According to Ipsos MORI's analysis, the middle classes swung to Labour, while working classes swung to the Conservatives – each party achieving record scores. Although the Conservatives maintained a six-point lead among ABC1s, Labour increased its vote share among this group by twelve points since 2015. Similarly, while Labour had a four-point lead among C2DEs, and increased its vote share among this group, this was eclipsed by the twelve-point increase for the Conservatives. This is simultaneously Labour's best score among ABC1s going back to 1979, and the Conservatives' best score among C2DEs since then.

- This is also supported by the presence in the above list of three Labour gains – and by the fact that Wimbledon, Putney and St Albans were all won by Labour in 1997 and 2001.

- The Liberal Democrats also regained Vince Cable's Twickenham and they only lost Richmond Park by forty-five votes in 2017. So it can be said that having a very high percentage of senior managers and professionals is no longer necessarily a sign of strong Conservatism.

- One of the main reasons for the change is that the seats in this list tended strongly to vote Remain in the 2016 EU referendum: North East Hampshire had the lowest Remain share, at 54.1%.

Twenty constituencies with lowest proportion of higher professional and managerial workers

		%	PARTY HOLDING SEAT
1	Birmingham Hodge Hill	2.9	Lab
2	Liverpool Walton	3.6	Lab
3	Glasgow East	3.8	SNP
4	Rhondda	3.8	Lab
5	Belfast West	3.9	SF
6	Nottingham North	4.0	Lab
7	Blaenau Gwent	4.0	Lab
8	Middlesbrough	4.1	Lab
9	Hull East	4.1	Lab
10	Great Grimsby	4.1	Lab
11	Wolverhampton South East	4.2	Lab
12	Glasgow North East	4.3	Lab gain from SNP
13	West Bromwich West	4.3	Lab
14	Walsall North	4.3	Con gain from Lab
15	Glenrothes	4.4	SNP
16	Wolverhampton North East	4.4	Lab
17	Glasgow South West	4.4	SNP
18	Blackpool South	4.5	Lab
19	Merthyr Tydfil & Rhymney	4.5	Lab
20	Knowsley	4.5	Lab

- The list of seats with the lowest proportion of senior managers and professionals in Britain has in general been strongly correlated with great Labour strength, but in 2015 they lost the four in Scotland with even higher than average swings to the SNP, who recorded among their five highest shares of the vote anywhere in Glasgow North East and Glenrothes. In 2017 Labour only recovered one of these four, and also lost Walsall North in the West Midlands to the Conservatives – apparently an aberrant result against the general swing in England, but it should be borne in mind that the seat voted by 74.2 % to leave the EU in the

2016 referendum. This was the second highest of any constituency in the United Kingdom.

- Generally the constituencies are in the category of 'white working class', as those with more recent patterns of immigration tend also to have more aspirational characteristics, with more educational qualifications and often situated in large cities which themselves host more profession- als and managers. However, right at the top of this list, as of others, is Birmingham Hodge Hill, which has a Muslim and Asian majority, and very high unemployment as well as other indices of social and economic deprivation.

The new MPs and parliament of 2017

Tim Carr

For the third election in a row, the 2017 general election has resulted in the most diverse Parliament in history, with a record number of women MPs, BME MPs, LGBTQ MPs and near parity between MPs educated at comprehensive schools versus private, independent schools.

Whether parity with the wider society that the House of Commons represents will ever be achieved in all areas is debatable (e.g. representative of the 10 million disabled people in the UK), but the progress that has been made will certainly be attributed as a success for pro-active policies such as Labour's All-Women Shortlists and organisations that have encouraged political participation such as the Conservative's Women2Win and LGBT Labour/LGBT+ Conservatives.

Women MPs still only comprise 32% of MPs and 29% of candidates. MPs from a BME background now comprise 8% of MPs, compared to 13% of the UK population. At least 7% of MPs are now LGBTQ, but they do not represent the broad diversity of the UK's LGBTQ community; all are white, none are transgender and only nine are women. There were only three MPs with disabilities. In terms of background, a high proportion of MPs continue to come from the 'political class' and the number of MPs that would traditionally be labelled as 'working class' continues to decline.

There were ninety-nine MPs elected in 2017 who were not sitting at dissolution (including Zac Goldsmith), eighty-seven of whom were elected for the first time. Twelve former MPs returned to Parliament. Seventy former MPs who fought the election lost their seat.

ALL MPS/NEW MPS

	ALL MPS	NEW MPS#	% OF NEW PARLIAMENTARY PARTY
Conservative*	318	32	10%
Labour	262	51	19.5%
SNP	35	1	2.9%
Lib Dems	12	8	66%
DUP	10	2	20%
Sinn Féin	7	4	57%
Plaid Cymru	4	1	25%
Green	1	0	0%
Ind (NI)	1	0	0%
	650	99	

SNP: Scottish National Party

DUP: Democratic Unionist Party

SDLP: Social Democratic & Labour Party

UUP: Ulster Unionist Party

* Including the Speaker

Including the 12 returning/retread MPs (inc. Zac Goldsmith)

Gender

There are now 208 women MPs among the 650 MPs in the House of Commons. At 32% of all MPs, this is the highest ever number of women MPs to have ever sat in a single Parliament. After the 2015 election, the House of Commons had 191 women, or 29% of all MPs. In total, there have only ever been 489 women MPs elected to the Commons since 1918.

Of the ninety-nine new MPs elected who were not sitting at dissolution, thirty-six are women. Alternatively, of the eighty-seven new members elected for the first time in 2017, thirty-three were women.

Of the three largest parties, Labour has the highest number (119, up twenty from 2015) and the largest proportion – 45% – of women MPs, the

Conservatives have 21% (sixty-seven women MPs, one fewer than in 2015) and the Scottish National Party have 34% (twelve women MPs in 2017, down from twenty in 2015). Four of the twelve Liberal Democrat MPs are women, up from zero in 2015. Seventeen of the seventy defeated MPs were women.

WOMEN IN THE NEW PARLIAMENT/NEW MPS

PARTY	ALL MPS	NEW MPS#	ALL MPS (WOMEN)	NEW MPS (WOMEN)	ALL MPS	NEW MPS	ALL MPS (WOMEN)	NEW MPS (WOMEN)
		GE2017				GE2015		
Conservative*	318	32	67 (21.0%)	7 (21.9%)	331	74	68 (20.5%)	27 (36.5%)
Labour	262	51	119 (45.0%)	22 (43.1%)	232	53	99 (42.7%)	34 (64.0%)
SNP	35	1	12 (34.0%)	0 (0.0%)	56	50	20 (35.7%)	19 (38.0%)
Lib Dem	12	8	4 (33.3%)	4 (50.0%)	8	0	0 (0.0%)	n/a
Sinn Féin	7	4	2 (28.6%)	2 (50.0%)	4	1	0 (0.0%)	0 (0.0%)
DUP	10	2	1 (10.0%)	1 (50.0%)	8	1	0 (0.0%)	0 (0.0%)
Plaid Cymru	4	1	1 (25.0%)	0 (0.0%)	3	1	1 (33.0%)	1 (100.0%)
SDLP	0	n/a	n/a	n/a	3	0	1 (33.0%)	n/a
UUP	0	n/a	n/a	n/a	2	2	0 (0.0%)	0 (0.0%)
UKIP	0	n/a	n/a	n/a	1	1	0 (0.0%)	0 (0.0%)
Green	1	0	1 (100%)	n/a	1	0	1 (100.0%)	n/a
Independent	1	0	1 (100%)	n/a	1	0	1 (100.0%)	n/a
	650	99	208	36	650	182	191	81

* Including the Speaker

Including the 12 returning/retread MPs (inc. Zac Goldsmith)

Overall in the 2017 general election, 29.5% of candidates were women (up from 26% in 2015), although the actual number of women candidates fell from 1,033 to 974 (the total number of candidates also fell). Although there were on average 5.1 candidates per constituency, there were only 1.5 female candidates for every constituency.

There were 105 constituencies without a single female candidate (16% of all constituencies). There was just one constituency (Glasgow Central) with no male candidates.

There were 182 Conservative women candidates (out of 639 prospective parliamentary candidates or 28%), 256 Labour (out of 631 or 41%), 184 Lib Dems (out of 629 or 29%), 168 Green (out of 468 or 36%), fifty-one UKIP (out of 378 or 13%), twenty SNP (out of fifty-nine or 34%) and eleven Plaid Cymru (out of forty candidates or 28%).

According to analysis from the House of Commons Library, Labour had a significantly higher proportion of women candidates in safer seats (70% of Labour PPCs who won by a margin of 20–30% in 2015 were women). The Conservatives only had 26% of women candidates in similarly defined safe seats. This suggests that not only did Labour select more women candidates, but they also selected more women candidates in either safe or winnable seats.

Age

The average age of the new House of Commons remains at fifty-one years old – the average age has remained consistently at around fifty years since 1918. Women MPs are slightly younger at 49–50.

The average age of the ninety-nine new MPs is 43–44. If the twelve retread MPs are excluded, this drops slightly to around the age of forty-two. The new Conservative MPs average around 40–41 years of age, slightly younger than the new Labour MPs who average forty-two years of age.

This trend is continued in the whole Commons with Labour MPs averaging around fifty-two years of age, Conservative MPs average around fifty years and SNP MPs younger at 46–47 years.

The youngest new MP elected in 2017 is Ben Lake, Plaid Cymru's youngest ever MP, at twenty-four. The youngest Conservative MP is Jack Brereton, new Conservative MP for Stoke-on-Trent South, who is twenty-six, having been born in May 1991, and Labour's youngest new MP is David Linden born in May 1990.

In the Commons as a whole, the SNP's Mhairi Black remains the youngest MP at twenty-two when re-elected. Born in February 1932, Dennis Skinner is the oldest serving MP, and the oldest Conservative MP is Sir Bill Cash, who was born in May 1940. The Father of the House is the Conservative Ken Clarke, closely followed by Dennis Skinner, both having been elected in 1970.

Two younger candidates were unsuccessful: Labour's Solomon Curtis, aged twenty, stood in Brighton Pavilion (he stood in Wealden in 2015 when only eighteen); and the Liberal Democrat Anton Georgiou, aged twenty-two, stood in Brent Central.

Ethnicity

A record number of fifty-two BME MPs (8%) were elected to the House of Commons in 2017, compared to forty-one in the 2015 Parliament. Out of the forty-one BME MPs who stood for re-election, forty were returned to Westminster, with only Tasmina Ahmed-Sheikh losing her seat in Ochil & South Perthshire, which saw Scotland losing its only minority MP in the process.

With the Office for National Statistics (ONS) Annual Population Survey 2015 indicating that 13% of the UK population are from an ethnic minority background, MPs from a BME background are still substantially under-represented in Parliament. Progress may be slow, but it is worth remembering that only thirty years ago, prior to the 1987 general election, there was not a single MP who was not white. Four BME MPs were then elected in 1987: Dianne Abbott, Paul Boateng, Bernie Grant and Keith Vaz.

Of the fifty-two BME MPs, thirty-two are Labour out of a total of 261 Labour MPs (12%), nineteen are Conservatives out of 315 (6%) and the Liberal Democrats have one MP from a BME background out of twelve MPs (8%).

There were some notable firsts:

- Tan Dhesi, Labour's new MP for Slough, is the UK's first turban-wearing Sikh MP; There have been a total of five Sikh MPs since 2002, but none have been 'visible identity' Sikhs.

- Labour's Preet Gill in Birmingham Edgbaston is the first elected female British Sikh MP.

- Bambos Charalambous, Labour's new MP for Enfield Southgate, is only the second MP of Cypriot heritage, and the first where both parents are Cypriot.

- Layla Moran, Liberal Democrat MP for Oxford West & Abingdon, is the first MP of Palestinian descent and the first female Lib Dem MP from an ethnic minority background.

- Eleanor Smith, Labour MP for Wolverhampton South West, became the Midlands' first black MP.

The twelve BME MPs elected for the first time in 2017 are:

- Bim Afolami (Conservative, Hitchin & Harpenden)

- Kemi Badenoch (Conservative, Saffron Walden)

- Bambos Charalambous (Labour, Enfield Southgate)

- Marsha De Cordova (Labour, Battersea)

- Tan Dehsi (Labour, Slough)

- Preet Gill (Labour, Birmingham Edgbaston)

- Afzal Khan (Labour, Manchester Gorton)

- Layla Moran (Liberal Democrat, Oxford West & Abingdon)

- Fiona Onasanya (Labour, Peterborough)

- Faisal Rashid (Labour, Warrington South)

- Eleanor Smith (Labour, Wolverhampton South West)

- Mohammad Yasin (Labour, Bedford)

According to *Muslim News*, a total of seventy-nine Muslims stood as PPCs in 2017, including ten constituencies where at least two PPCs were Muslims, three in Ilford South and four in Bradford West. This was a reduction on the record ninety-four Muslim PPCs who stood in 2015, although the total candidates fell by approximately 10% between the two elections. There are now fifteen Muslim MPs, including three newly elected in 2017.

Disability

Despite there being around 10 million people in the UK suffering from some form of disability, there have only ever been a handful of disabled

MPs. The number of disabled MPs fell in 2015 with the retirement of Labour's David Blunkett and Anne McGuire and the defeat of Liberal Democrat Stephen Lloyd and Labour's Dame Anne Begg. This left only the Conservative MPs Paul Maynard and Robert Halfon.

The more positive news is that at least three new MPs were elected with known disabilities, potentially bringing the total to five:

- Marsha De Cordova (Labour, Battersea) is registered blind.

- Stephen Lloyd (Liberal Democrat, Eastbourne) is hearing-impaired (re-elected after losing in 2015).

- Jared O'Mara (Labour, Sheffield Hallam) was born with cerebral palsy.

LGBTQ

The House of Commons reputation as one of the leading legislatures in the world for LGBTQ representation continued in 2017. In 2010 there were at least twenty-six LGBTQ MPs, the highest number in the world. This increased to thirty-two openly gay, lesbian or bisexual in 2015, a further record number.

In 2017, the UK elected a new record number of forty-five LGBTQ MPs to Parliament, representing 7% of the new House of Commons. This was composed of eight new LGBTQ MPs: all men, five Labour and three Conservative. Two incumbent LGBTQ MPs were defeated. The rest of the gains are accounted for by existing MPs in the last Parliament publicly declaring their sexuality for the first time.

Before the 2017 election, the Scottish Parliament was marginally considered the legislature with the highest representation in the world (7.7% with ten out of 129 MSPs declared), but this may have changed with at least one publicly declared LGBTQ MSP having resigned on his election as an MP to Westminster.

At dissolution on 3 May 2017, the thirty-nine LGBTQ MPs consisted of seventeen Conservative, fourteen Labour and eight SNP MPs. After the 2017 general election, the forty-five MPs consist of nineteen Conservative, nineteen Labour and seven SNP MPs.

The forty-five MPs do not, however, reflect the broad diversity of the

UK's LGBTQ community – there are thirty-six men, only nine women, all are white and none are transgender.

According to Professor Andrew Reynolds and Gabriele Magni of the University of North Carolina at Chapel Hill, a total of 154 of the 3,304 candidates that stood in the 2017 general election were LGBTQ, equating to roughly 4.5%. 17% of SNP candidates, 7% of Conservative, 7% of Labour, 5% of Liberal Democrat, 5% of Plaid Cymru, 4% of Green and 2% of UKIP were LGBTQ. Out of 154 candidates, twenty-three were women, four were transgender and only three were from a BME background.

Education

More than half of MPs have now been educated in the comprehensive system for the first time following the 2017 general election. 51% of MPs attended comprehensive schools, up from 49% in 2015 and just 43% in 2010, according to the education and social mobility charity, the Sutton Trust.

The number of privately educated MPs has dropped correspondingly. Since 2010, the percentage of Conservatives educated privately has dropped from 54 to 45%, while Labour has fallen from 15 to 14%. Across all parties, less than a third (29%) of MPs attended fee-paying schools, down by 7% since 2010. This proportion remains significantly higher than the 7% of the general population that are privately educated.

The proportion of newly elected MPs educated at a comprehensive is slightly down on 2015, falling from 64% in 2015 to 62.5% in 2017. Around 29% of new Conservative MPs were privately educated, compared to 12% of new Labour MPs. The proportion of MPs who went to grammar schools dropped slightly from 19% to 18% in 2017.

From the available data, the Sutton Trust estimates that around 86% of MPs attended university, with 11% also completing post-graduate qualifications. Around 23% of these went to Oxford or Cambridge, 29% went to other 'elite' Russell Group universities, while the remaining 33% went to other universities or higher educational institutions. In the 2015 parliament, around 26% attended an Oxbridge university. Broken down by political party, 31% of Conservative MPs attended Oxbridge for their undergraduate degree, compared to 20% for Labour and 17% for the Liberal Democrats. It is not believed that any of SNP MPs attended Oxbridge. 31% of Labour MPs attended Russell

Group universities, compared to 29% of Conservative, 42% of Liberal Democrat and 20% of SNP MPs.

The figures for the new parliament and the new 2017 intake of MPs broadly suggests a slow continuation of recent trends: a reduction in the percentage of MPs attending fee-paying schools and corresponding increase in the numbers who attended comprehensives, and a reduction in attendance at Oxbridge, while an increase in broader university education. In the 1951 parliament, 229 of 338 MPs from the three main parties (Conservatives, Labour and Liberals) who had attended university went to either Oxford or Cambridge. Similarly, in 1951, 75% of Conservative MPs had been privately educated and 20% of Labour MPs, reaching a high of 22% in 1955.

According to historian Byron Criddle, the percentage of Old Etonian Conservative MPs has also fallen from 24% in 1951 to 6.3% in 2017. In the 2017 House of Commons there are twenty Old Etonians, all Conservatives. Winchester College in Hampshire and Millfield School in Somerset each educated five MPs.

Work and occupation

With many people now having several distinct careers as they voluntarily or involuntarily leave former jobs, retrain or spot an opportunity, the new MPs are no exception. Many of the 2017 intake of new MPs have had one, two or more distinct careers, with politics usually being one of them. While some new MPs, particularly professionals in the public sector, have had one identifiable occupation in their lives prior to being elected, for many others, focusing analysis on identifying one 'main' profession or occupation is potentially subjective and risks missing observing new trends. This is why the following section refers to 'experience' in a particular area of work or background.

In terms of broad sector experience, forty of the new MPs have experience of earning a living in the public sector (including thirty Labour, or 59%, and four Conservatives). This includes seventeen, including twelve new Labour MPs, who have worked in education either as a primary or secondary teacher or teaching assistant or a higher education lecturer. Seven of the new MPs, all Labour, have worked in primary healthcare or mental health, including the nurses Karen Lee and Eleanor Smith and the NHS GP Dr Paul Williams. The new Tory MP for Ayr, Carrick & Cumnock, Bill Grant, is a former firefighter with thirty-one years of service. Matt Roda, the new Labour MP for Reading East, has been a civil servant in the Department for Education and No.10/Cabinet Office, led projects in the No.10 Strategic Communications Unit and was David Blunkett's ghost writer when he was Education Secretary. There are four former members of the Armed Forces: Andrew Bowie (Conservative), Leo Docherty (Conservative), Bob Seely (Conservative) and Paul Sweeney (Labour).

There may no longer be anything like the number of barristers that have sat in the Commons in the past (16% in 1959), but there are nine new lawyers or barristers – Bambos Charalambous (Labour), Simon Clarke (Conservative), Darren Jones (Labour), Afzal Khan (Labour), John Lamont (Conservative), Emma Little-Pengelly (DUP), Paul Masterson (Conservative), Fiona Onasanya (Labour) and Ellie Reeves (Labour).

Manual workers have long been a small and dwindling band in the Commons, with only 4% in 2010 according to the House of Commons Library. In 1951, 18% of MPs from the three main parties were formerly manual workers. It is hard to find many in the 2017 intake. Labour's Hugh Gaffney has been a postman for all his life and Mohammad Yasin was a taxi driver – at least when he entered local government. Others have moved on to more professional careers. For instance, Labour's Afzal Khan was a labourer in a cotton mill and a bus driver (and a Greater Manchester Police constable) before he became a lawyer. Conservative Ben Bradley was a landscape gardener early in his working life.

Almost exactly half of the new MPs (forty-eight of the intake) have worked at some point in the private sector, including, unsurprisingly, twenty-two of the thirty-two Conservatives (69%). As one Cabinet minister said in defence of the Conservative selections: 'They're Tory candidates! Of course there are lots of lawyers, lobbyists and professionals in there. What did everyone expect? Astronauts?'

The new intake includes farmers and landowners (Conservatives Colin Clark, Alister Jack and Douglas Ross) and oil and gas workers (Conservative David Duguid and the Liberal Democrat Jamie Stone). Labour's Vicky Ford worked for JP Morgan and Bear Stearns before becoming a member of the European Parliament. Faisal Rashid and Ross Thomson were high-street bankers.

There are several successful entrepreneurs among the new intake, including Conservatives Alister Jack and Gillian Keegan, and Labour's Gerard Killen (who started his own construction business), Lesley Laird and Rachel Maclean.

The 35% (eighteen) of the new Labour intake with experience of the private sector is a noticeably dramatic fall from the 57% in 2015.

Below are some of the more quirky and unusual biographical details from the new intake:

- As one historian leaves, another one enters. Tristram Hunt might have moved on to the Victoria and Albert Museum in London, but Alex Burghart has arrived to take his place. He is better known as a special adviser, but is also a respected historian who taught at King's College London and who has written extensively about early medieval England.

- Excluding Jeremy Corbyn, who made a speech, Labour's new MP for Bury North, James Frith, is almost certainly the only MP to have ever performed in a band at the Glastonbury festival.

- The Commons now has two new triathletes in the Conservative John Lamont and Labour's Dr Paul Williams.

- 65-year old former fireman Bill Grant is a motorbike enthusiast and rides a 650cc Yamaha motorbike as a hobby.

- Conservative Douglas Ross is a part-time assistant football referee who has refereed a Scottish Cup Final, Europa League and Champions League matches.

- Labour's victor in Canterbury, Rosie Duffield, was working on a political satire project when she was elected.

- It appears that every recent new intake has to have an 'action' man. Rory Stewart was elected in 2010 and Tom Tugendhat in 2015. In 2017 there is Leo Docherty, suitably the new MP for Aldershot, the home of the British Army. Having served in Iraq and Afghanistan, he spent six months travelling from Turkey to Afghanistan on horseback, foot and bicycle.

- For those old enough to have watched television in the late 1980s, actor-turned-politician Giles Watling is best known as the vicar in forty-nine episodes of Carla Lane's TV sitcom Bread, between 1988 and 1991.

- Labour's Matt Rodda survived the Ladbroke Grove rail crash in October 1999, an event that inspired him to make a more active contribution to his community.

- The Isle of Wight's Bob Seely is a former foreign correspondent, MTV executive and Army veteran with four tours of Afghanistan. He is also an expert in Russian hybrid warfare, asymmetric warfare, information warfare, non-conventional conflict and the Middle East.

The political class

High levels of direct political engagement prior to beginning a career as an MP have become the norm. In 2015, 45% of the new intake had a job working directly in politics, either as an elected political representative in another institution (the European Parliament, the Scottish Parliament, the Welsh National Assembly, the NI Assembly or the London Assembly), as a party worker, a full-time trade union official, full-time councillor or as a researcher/adviser to an MP, MEP, Peer or devolved assembly member.

Of the ninety-nine new MPs in 2017, including the twelve retread MPs, fifty, or 50.5%, fit into this category of active political involvement, a slight increase of 1.5%. When those who have been politically active, either as a part-time councillor, an active member of a political party or those who have previously stood for election to Westminster or another institution, are added, the figure rises to 92% (ninety-one out of the ninety-nine new MPs). All sixteen new Lib Dem, SNP, DUP and Plaid Cymru MPs have previous political experience.

Forty-three (43.4%) of the 2017 intake have previously stood for election to Parliament, while a further four have stood for election to another institution only. In 2015, the figure was only 30%.

Only eight of the new MPs (six Labour and two Conservatives) appear to be relatively new to frontline politics and have not held prominent political positions or stood for election previously.

POLITICAL EXPERIENCE

	NEW MPS	DIRECT POLITICAL JOBS[1]		POLITICAL EXPERIENCE[2]		NEW TO POLITICS?	
All	99	50	50.5%	91	91.9%	8	8.1%
Conservative	32	16	50.0%	31	96.8%	1	3.2%
Labour	51	20	39.2%	44	86.3%	7	13.7%
Others	16	14	87.5%	16	100.0%	0	0.0%

1. Elected political representative, party worker, political researcher/adviser, public policy think-tank, trade union official

2. Includes those from category 1 (direct political jobs) but adds part-time councillors and those who previously stood for election to Parliament, a devolved assembly/Parliament or as a police & crime commissioner

Forty-eight (48.5%) have followed the local government route to the Commons, having been elected as a councillor (fifteen or 47% of the Conservatives, twenty-nine or 56.9% of Labour). While a number have been group leaders or deputy leaders, only two have been a council leader (Andrew Lewer for Derbyshire County Council and Chris Williamson for Derby City Council).

Excluding the twelve former MPs returned to Westminster, only thirty-one of the eighty-seven first-time elected MPs (36%) have previously fought a seat in a UK parliamentary election, although a further four have contested a Scottish parliamentary seat.

Nine of the new Labour MPs have been full-time trade union officials or held senior positions (Dan Carden, Hugh Gaffney, Ruth George, Mike Hill, Alex Norris, Stephanie Peacock, Laura Pidcock, Eleanor Smith – former president of Unison – and Liz Twist).

Five of the new MPs (two Conservative, one Lib Dem and one DUP) have served as special advisers in either Westminster, Stormont or Cardiff Bay:

- Alex Burghart (Conservative, Brentwood & Ongar) – Special adviser on social justice in the PM's policy unit

- Christine Jardine (Liberal Democrat, Edinburgh West) – Media adviser to Michael Moore MP, as Secretary of State for Scotland

- Emma Little-Pengelly (DUP, Belfast South) – Special adviser to Dr Ian Paisley and Peter Robinson, former First Ministers in the Northern Ireland Executive

- Anna McMorrin (Labour, Cardiff North) – Environment and sustainability adviser to Welsh government ministers

- Neil O'Brien (Conservative, Harborough) – Special adviser to George Osborne, former Chancellor of the Exchequer, and to Theresa May in the PM's policy unit, with responsibility for industrial strategy and the Northern Powerhouse

A number of Conservative special advisers were unsuccessful: Simon Burton (Hull East), Jennifer Donnellan (Airdrie & Shotts), David Goss (Blackley & Broughton), Paul Holmes (Southampton Test), Henry Newman (North Tyneside), Meg Powell Chandler (Birmingham Northfield) and James Wild (North Norfolk).

Sixteen of the new MPs (including nine Labour and five Conservatives) have previously worked as a researcher for an MP either in constituencies or Westminster.

There are twelve former MPs returning to Westminster – five Labour, four Lib Dem, two Conservative and one Sinn Féin:

- Sir Vince Cable (Liberal Democrat, Twickenham)

- Sir Ed Davey (Liberal Democrat, Kingston & Surbiton)

- David Drew (Labour, Stroud)

- Michelle Gildernew (Sinn Féin, Fermanagh & South Tyrone)

- Zac Goldsmith (Conservative, Richmond Park)

- John Grogan (Labour, Keighley) – previously MP for Selby

- Stephen Lloyd (Eastbourne, Liberal Democrat)

- Tony Lloyd (Labour, Rochdale) – previously MP for Manchester Central

- Esther McVey (Conservative, Tatton) – previously MP for Wirral West

- Chris Ruane (Labour, Vale of Clwyd)

- Jo Swinson (Liberal Democrat, East Dunbartonshire)

- Chris Williamson (Labour, Derby North)

Most of the returning MPs have been re-elected to their former constituencies, apart from Labour's John Grogan (from Selby to Keighley) and Tony Lloyd (Manchester Central to Rochdale), and the Conservative's Esther McVey (Wirral West to Tatton). Tony Lloyd and Esther McVey were both elected to seats where former MPs had stood down.

With the field quickly whittling down following the resignation of Tim Farron, Sir Vince Cable looks as if he is returning to Westminster to take over the leadership of the Liberal Democrats. David Drew, Tony Lloyd, Chris Ruane and Chris Williamson have all already found themselves appointed to Labour's frontbench team. First-time elected Lesley Laird has done even better, having been appointed shadow Secretary of State for Scotland a day before she even formally took her seat in Parliament. It is unlikely to be long before Esther McVey returns to the ministerial fold.

Nine of the former MPs lost their seat only two years ago at the 2015 general election, which almost certainly explains the relatively high number of returning MPs (there were only five retreads in 2015). In total, forty-three former MPs who had not been MPs during the 2015–2017 parliament stood in the election.

There were four MEPs elected – two Conservative and two Labour:

- Anneliese Dodds (Labour, Oxford East) – MEP for South East England

- Vicky Ford (Conservative, Chelmsford) – MEP for East of England

- Afzal Khan (Labour, Manchester Gorton) – MEP for North West England

- Andrew Lewer (Conservative, Northampton South) – MEP for East Midlands

There were four MSPs elected – three Conservative and one Liberal Democrat:

- John Lamont (Conservative, Berwickshire, Roxburgh & Selkirk) – Ettrick, Roxburgh and Berwickshire

- Douglas Ross (Conservative, Moray) – Highlands & Islands

- Jamie Stone (Liberal Democrat, Caithness, Sutherland & Easter Ross) – Caithness, Sutherland and Easter Ross

- Ross Thomson (Conservative, Aberdeen South) – North East Scotland

There was also one London Assembly Member elected:

- Kemi Badenoch (Conservative, Saffron Walden)

A small number of the new intake has family political connections to national or international parliamentarians:

- Alex Burghart (Conservative, Brentwood & Ongar) – father-in-law is former Tory MP, Sir Reginald Eyre

- Gillian Keegan (Conservative, Chichester) – father-in-law is former Tory MP, Denis Keegan

- Anna McMorrin (Labour, Cardiff North) – partner of Alun Davies AM, the current Welsh Minister for Lifelong Learning and the Welsh Language

- Stephanie Peacock (Labour, Barnsley East) – reported partner of Tom Watson MP, deputy Labour leader

- Ellie Reeves (Labour, Lewisham West & Penge) – married to John Cryer MP, chair of the parliamentary Labour Party, and sister of Rachel Reeves MP

- Danielle Rowley (Labour, Midlothian) – his father is Alex Rowley MSP, deputy leader of the Scottish Labour Party

Brexit

With most MPs having publicly declared their position towards membership of the EU ahead of the referendum on 23 June 2016, it was known that the last parliament was overwhelmingly in favour of Remain – 463 MPs in favour of Remain and 156 MPs in favour of Leave (71% to 24%), with the position of thirty-one MPs not publicly declared.

From analysis of statements and interviews from the new intake of ninety-nine MPs in 2017, it would appear that little has changed, with those in favour of Remain increasing marginally (73% Remain to 23% Leave) with higher numbers of Remain-supporting Labour MPs replacing Leave-supporting Conservatives. 474 MPs are potentially in favour of Remain, although statements from fourteen of the new MPs suggest a Remain position, but are ambiguous. A number of new Labour MPs in strong Brexit-supporting constituencies were understandably nervous about declaring their support for Remain. There would appear to be 150 MPs in the new parliament in favour of Leave, with some doubts over the position of three of the new MPs. The position of twenty-six MPs remain unknown.

Unsurprisingly, the newly elected Conservative MPs appear to be divided on the issue, but by significantly different proportions than the rest of the parliamentary party. There is a clear divide between the twelve Scottish Conservative MPs who were overwhelmingly in favour of Remain (eleven to one) and the twenty new English Conservative MPs who were in favour of Leave by eleven to seven, with the position of two unknown.

Apart from both new Democratic Unionist Party MPs who were in favour of Leave, new MPs from all other parties were in favour of Remain.

MPS AND THE EU REFERENDUM

	ALL MPS			NEW MPS		
	REMAIN	LEAVE	UNKNOWN	REMAIN	LEAVE	UNKNOWN
All MPs	474	150	26	81	15	3
Conservative*	175	136	6	18	12	2
Labour	243	9	10	49	1	1
Others	56	5	10	14	2	0

* Excluding the Speaker

With Brexit looming on the horizon, it is perhaps surprising that more than four current UK MEPs were not elected in 2017, although it is known that Sajjad Karim, Conservative MEP for the North West, and Syed Kamall, leader of the Conservatives in the European Parliament, both sought selection for a seat, and David Campbell-Bannerman and Daniel Hannan were both reportedly blocked from standing.

Three of the newly elected MPs are particularly noteworthy in relation to Brexit. Anneliese Dodds, the Labour MEP and already a member of Labour's Treasury frontbench team, co-authored a Fabian Society paper on how a new deal for financial services can be reached after Brexit, and is likely to give Labour some much needed expertise on European issues. For the Tories, Vicky Ford, the new MP for Chelmsford and former chair of the European Parliament's influential Internal Market and Consumer Affairs Committee when she was an MEP, will also provide depths of much needed experience. Lastly, Luke Graham, the new MP for Ochil & South Perthshire, was finance director of Britain Stronger In Europe during the EU referendum campaign and will likely join the grouping of Conservative Remainers in Parliament.

Ones to watch

Making any predictions in 2017 may appear foolish given the propensity for surprises in the world of politics, but there are always some new MPs that have the look and feel of 'rising stars'. On past experience, some apparent stars will dim and remain largely unknown outside of Westminster and their constituency. Others, however, will inevitably rise rapidly, making a name for themselves both inside and outside Parliament either from the backbenches or in a ministerial/frontbench capacity. Indeed, several of the new intake have already been appointed to Labour's frontbench team.

The 2010 intake of new MPs included Sajid Javid, Liz Kendall, Caroline Lucas, Priti Patel, Jacob Rees-Mogg, Amber Rudd, Liz Truss and Chuka Umunna. The 2015 general election brought us Mhairi Black, Richard Burgon, Boris Johnson (again), Stephen Kinnock, Jess Phillips and Sir Keir Starmer.

Only time will tell, but below are some of the Class of 2017 to watch out for as their political careers develop:

- Bim Afolami   Conservative   Hitchin & Harpenden

- Kemi Badenoch   Conservative   Saffron Walden

- Dr Alex Burghart   Conservative   Brentwood & Ongar

- Dan Carden   Labour   Liverpool Walton

- Leo Docherty   Conservative   Aldershot

- Anneliese Dodds   Labour   Oxford East

- Vicky Ford   Conservative   Chelmsford

- Gillian Keegan   Conservative   Chichester

- Lesley Laird   Labour   Kirkcaldy & Cowdenbeath

- Rachel Maclean   Conservative   Redditch

- Neil O'Brien   Conservative   Harborough

- Fiona Onasanya   Labour   Peterborough

- Laura Pidcock   Labour   North West Durham

- Luke Pollard   Labour   Plymouth Sutton & Devonport

- Ellie Reeves   Labour   Lewisham West & Penge

- Bob Seely   Conservative   Isle of Wight

- Dr Paul Williams   Labour   Stockton South

Index of new MPs

Vicky Ford	Con	Chelmsford
James Frith	Lab	Bury North
Hugh Gaffney	Lab	Coatbridge, Chryston & Bellshill
Ruth George	Lab	High Peak
Michelle Gildernew	SF	Fermanagh & South Tyrone
Preet Gill	Lab	Birmingham Edgbaston
Paul Girvan	DUP	South Antrim
Zac Goldsmith	Con	Richmond Park
Luke Graham	Con	Ochil & South Perthshire
Bill Grant	Con	Ayr, Carrick & Cumnock
John Grogan	Lab	Keighley
Kirstene Hair	Con	Angus
Emma Hardy	Lab	Kingston upon Hull West & Hessle
Chris Hazzard	SF	South Down
Mike Hill	Lab	Hartlepool
Wera Hobhouse	LD	Bath
Eddie Hughes	Con	Walsall North
Alister Jack	Con	Dumfries & Galloway
Christine Jardine	LD	Edinburgh West
Darren Jones	Lab	Bristol North West
Sarah Jones	Lab	Croydon Central
Gillian Keegan	Con	Chichester
Stephen Kerr	Con	Stirling
Afzal Khan CBE	Lab	Manchester Gorton
Gerard Killen	Lab	Rutherglen & Hamilton West
Lesley Laird	Lab	Kirkcaldy & Cowdenbeath
Ben Lake	PC	Ceredigion
John Lamont	Con	Berwickshire, Roxburgh & Selkirk
Karen Lee	Lab	Lincoln
Andrew Lewer MBE	Con	Northampton South
David Linden	SNP	Glasgow East
Emma Little-Pengelly	DUP	Belfast South
Stephen Lloyd	LD	Eastbourne
Tony Lloyd	Lab	Rochdale
Rachel Maclean	Con	Redditch
Sandy Martin	Lab	Ipswich
Paul Masterton	Con	East Renfrewshire
Elisha McCallion	SF	Foyle

Barry McElduff	SF	West Tyrone
Anna McMorrin	Lab	Cardiff North
Esther McVey	Con	Tatton
Damien Moore	Con	Southport
Layla Moran	LD	Oxford West & Abingdon
Stephen Morgan	Lab	Portsmouth South
Alex Norris	Lab	Nottingham North
Neil O'Brien	Con	Harborough
Jared O'Mara	Lab	Sheffield Hallam
Fiona Onasanya	Lab	Peterborough
Stephanie Peacock	Lab	Barnsley East
Laura Pidcock	Lab	North West Durham
Jo Platt	Lab	Leigh
Luke Pollard	Lab	Plymouth Sutton & Devonport
Faisal Rashid	Lab	Warrington South
Ellie Reeves	Lab	Lewisham West & Penge
Matt Rodda	Lab	Reading East
Douglas Ross	Con	Moray
Danielle Rowley	Lab	Midlothian
Lee Rowley	Con	North East Derbyshire
Chris Ruane	Lab	Vale of Clwyd
Lloyd Russell-Moyle	Lab	Brighton, Kemptown
Bob Seely	Con	Isle of Wight
Eleanor Smith	Lab	Wolverhampton South West
Laura Smith	Lab	Crewe & Nantwich
Alex Sobel	Lab	Leeds North West
Jamie Stone	LD	Caithness, Sutherland & Easter Ross
Paul Sweeney	Lab	Glasgow North East
Jo Swinson	LD	East Dunbartonshire
Ross Thomson	Con	Aberdeen South
Liz Twist	Lab	Blaydon
Thelma Walker	Lab	Colne Valley
Giles Watling	Con	Clacton
Matt Western	Lab	Warwick & Leamington
Martin Whitfield	Lab	East Lothian
Dr Paul Williams	Lab	Stockton South
Chris Williamson	Lab	Derby North
Mohammad Yasin	Lab	Bedford

Abbreviations:

Con: Conservative

DUP: Democratic Unionist Party

Lab: Labour

LD: Liberal Democrat

PC: Plaid Cymru

SF: Sinn Féin

SNP: Scottish National Party

Index of new MPs by party

Labour (51)

Mike Amesbury	Weaver Vale
Tonia Antoniazzi	Gower
Dan Carden	Liverpool Walton
Bambos Charalambous	Enfield Southgate
Emma Dent Coad	Kensington
Marsha De Cordova	Battersea
Tan Dhesi	Slough
Anneliese Dodds	Oxford East
Dr David Drew	Stroud
Rosie Duffield	Canterbury
James Frith	Bury North
Hugh Gaffney	Coatbridge, Chryston & Bellshill
Ruth George	High Peak
Preet Gill	Birmingham Edgbaston
John Grogan	Keighley
Emma Hardy	Kingston upon Hull West & Hessle
Mike Hill	Hartlepool
Darren Jones	Bristol North West
Sarah Jones	Croydon Central
Afzal Khan CBE	Manchester Gorton
Gerard Killen	Rutherglen & Hamilton West
Lesley Laird	Kirkcaldy & Cowdenbeath
Karen Lee	Lincoln

Tony Lloyd	Rochdale
Sandy Martin	Ipswich
Anna McMorrin	Cardiff North
Stephen Morgan	Portsmouth South
Alex Norris	Nottingham North
Jared O'Mara	Sheffield Hallam
Fiona Onasanya	Peterborough
Stephanie Peacock	Barnsley East
Laura Pidcock	North West Durham
Jo Platt	Leigh
Luke Pollard	Plymouth Sutton & Devonport
Faisal Rashid	Warrington South
Ellie Reeves	Lewisham West & Penge
Matt Rodda	Reading East
Danielle Rowley	Midlothian
Chris Ruane	Vale of Clwyd
Lloyd Russell-Moyle	Brighton, Kemptown
Eleanor Smith	Wolverhampton South West
Laura Smith	Crewe & Nantwich
Alex Sobel	Leeds North West
Paul Sweeney	Glasgow North East
Liz Twist	Blaydon
Thelma Walker	Colne Valley
Matt Western	Warwick & Leamington
Martin Whitfield	East Lothian
Dr Paul Williams	Stockton South
Chris Williamson	Derby North
Mohammad Yasin	Bedford

Conservative (32)

Bim Afolami	Hitchin & Harpenden
Kemi Badenoch	Saffron Walden
Andrew C Bowie	West Aberdeenshire & Kincardine
Ben Bradley	Mansfield
Jack Brereton	Stoke-on-Trent South
Dr Alex Burghart	Brentwood & Ongar
Colin Clark	Gordon

Simon Clarke	Middlesbrough South & East Cleveland
Leo Docherty	Aldershot
Julia Dockerill	Hornchurch & Upminster
David Duguid	Banff & Buchan
Vicky Ford	Chelmsford
Zac Goldsmith	Richmond Park
Luke Graham	Ochil & South Perthshire
Bill Grant	Ayr, Carrick & Cumnock
Kirstene Hair	Angus
Eddie Hughes	Walsall North
Alister Jack	Dumfries & Galloway
Gillian Keegan	Chichester
Stephen Kerr	Stirling
John Lamont	Berwickshire, Roxburgh & Selkirk
Andrew Lewer MBE	Northampton South
Rachel Maclean	Redditch
Paul Masterton	East Renfrewshire
Esther McVey	Tatton
Damien Moore	Southport
Neil O'Brien	Harborough
Douglas Ross	Moray
Lee Rowley	North East Derbyshire
Bob Seely MBE	Isle of Wight
Ross Thomson	Aberdeen South
Giles Watling	Clacton

Liberal Democrats (8)

Sir Vince Cable	Twickenham
Sir Ed Davey	Kingston & Surbiton
Wera Hobhouse	Bath
Christine Jardine	Edinburgh West
Stephen Lloyd	Eastbourne
Layla Moran	Oxford West & Abingdon
Jamie Stone	Caithness, Sutherland & Easter Ross
Jo Swinson	East Dunbartonshire

Sinn Féin (4)

Michelle Gildernew	Fermanagh & South Tyrone
Chris Hazzard	South Down
Elisha McCallion	Foyle
Barry McElduff	West Tyrone

Democratic Unionist Party (2)

Paul Girvan MP	South Antrim
Emma Little-Pengelly MP	Belfast South

Plaid Cymru (1)

Ben Lake	Ceredigion

Scottish National Party (1)

David Linden	Glasgow East

Index of new MPs by constituency

Constituency	Name	Party
Aberdeen South	Ross Thomson	Con
Aldershot	Leo Docherty	Con
Angus	Kirstene Hair	Con
Ayr, Carrick & Cumnock	Bill Grant	Con
Banff & Buchan	David Duguid	Con
Barnsley East	Stephanie Peacock	Lab
Bath	Wera Hobhouse	LD
Battersea	Marsha De Cordova	Lab
Bedford	Mohammad Yasin	Lab
Belfast South	Emma Little-Pengelly	DUP
Berwickshire, Roxburgh & Selkirk	John Lamont	Con
Birmingham Edgbaston	Preet Gill	Lab
Blaydon	Liz Twist	Lab

Brentwood & Ongar	Dr Alex Burghart	Con
Brighton, Kemptown	Lloyd Russell-Moyle	Lab
Bristol North West	Darren Jones	Lab
Bury North	James Frith	Lab
Caithness, Sutherland & Easter Ross	Jamie Stone	LD
Canterbury	Rosie Duffield	Lab
Cardiff North	Anna McMorrin	Lab
Ceredigion	Ben Lake	PC
Chelmsford	Vicky Ford	Con
Chichester	Gillian Keegan	Con
Clacton	Giles Watling	Con
Coatbridge, Chryston & Bellshill	Hugh Gaffney	Lab
Colne Valley	Thelma Walker	Lab
Crewe & Nantwich	Laura Smith	Lab
Croydon Central	Sarah Jones	Lab
Derby North	Chris Williamson	Lab
Dumfries & Galloway	Alister Jack	Con
East Dunbartonshire	Jo Swinson	LD
East Lothian	Martin Whitfield	Lab
East Renfrewshire	Paul Masterton	Con
Eastbourne	Stephen Lloyd	LD
Edinburgh West	Christine Jardine	LD
Enfield Southgate	Bambos Charalambous	Lab
Fermanagh & South Tyrone	Michelle Gildernew	SF
Foyle	Elisha McCallion	SF
Glasgow East	David Linden	SNP
Glasgow North East	Paul Sweeney	Lab
Gordon	Colin Clark	Con
Gower	Tonia Antoniazzi	Lab
Harborough	Neil O'Brien	Con
Hartlepool	Mike Hill	Lab
High Peak	Ruth George	Lab
Hitchin & Harpenden	Bim Afolami	Con
Hornchurch & Upminster	Julia Dockerill	Con
Ipswich	Sandy Martin	Lab
Isle of Wight	Bob Seely MBE	Con
Keighley	John Grogan	Lab
Kensington	Emma Dent Coad	Lab

Kingston & Surbiton	Sir Ed Davey	LD
Kingston upon Hull West & Hessle	Emma Hardy	Lab
Kirkcaldy & Cowdenbeath	Lesley Laird	Lab
Leeds North West	Alex Sobel	Lab
Leigh	Jo Platt	Lab
Lewisham West & Penge	Ellie Reeves	Lab
Lincoln	Karen Lee	Lab
Liverpool Walton	Dan Carden	Lab
Manchester Gorton	Afzal Khan CBE	Lab
Mansfield	Ben Bradley	Con
Middlesbrough South & East Cleveland	Simon Clarke	Con
Midlothian	Danielle Rowley	Lab
Moray	Douglas Ross	Con
North East Derbyshire	Lee Rowley	Con
North West Durham	Laura Pidcock	Lab
Northampton South	Andrew Lewer MBE	Con
Nottingham North	Alex Norris	Lab
Ochil & South Perthshire	Luke Graham	Con
Oxford East	Anneliese Dodds	Lab
Oxford West & Abingdon	Layla Moran	LD
Peterborough	Fiona Onasanya	Lab
Plymouth Sutton & Devonport	Luke Pollard	Lab
Portsmouth South	Stephen Morgan	Lab
Reading East	Matt Rodda	Lab
Redditch	Rachel Maclean	Con
Richmond Park	Zac Goldsmith	Con
Rochdale	Tony Lloyd	Lab
Rutherglen & Hamilton West	Gerard Killen	Lab
Saffron Walden	Kemi Badenoch	Con
Sheffield Hallam	Jared O'Mara	Lab
Slough	Tan Dhesi	Lab
South Antrim	Paul Girvan	DUP
South Down	Chris Hazzard	SF
Southport	Damien Moore	Con
Stirling	Stephen Kerr	Con
Stockton South	Dr Paul Williams	Lab
Stoke-on-Trent South	Jack Brereton	Con
Stroud	Dr David Drew	Lab

Tatton	Esther McVey	Con
Twickenham	Sir Vince Cable	LD
Vale of Clwyd	Chris Ruane	Lab
Walsall North	Eddie Hughes	Con
Warrington South	Faisal Rashid	Lab
Warwick & Leamington	Matt Western	Lab
Weaver Vale	Mike Amesbury	Lab
West Aberdeenshire & Kincardine	Andrew C Bowie	Con
West Tyrone	Barry McElduff	SF
Wolverhampton South West	Eleanor Smith	Lab

Abbreviations:

Con: Conservative

DUP: Democratic Unionist Party

Lab: Labour

LD: Liberal Democrat

PC: Plaid Cymru

SF: Sinn Féin

SNP: Scottish National Party

Index of new MPs by region

East Midlands (8)

Derby North	Chris Williamson	Lab
Harborough	Neil O'Brien	Con
High Peak	Ruth George	Lab
Lincoln	Karen Lee	Lab
Mansfield	Ben Bradley	Con
North East Derbyshire	Lee Rowley	Con
Northampton South	Andrew Lewer MBE	Con
Nottingham North	Alex Norris	Lab

East of England (8)

Bedford	Mohammad Yasin	Lab
Brentwood & Ongar	Dr Alex Burghart	Con
Chelmsford	Vicky Ford	Con
Clacton	Giles Watling	Con
Hitchin & Harpenden	Bim Afolami	Con
Ipswich	Sandy Martin	Lab
Peterborough	Fiona Onasanya	Lab
Saffron Walden	Kemi Badenoch	Con

London (9)

Battersea	Marsha De Cordova	Lab
Croydon Central	Sarah Jones	Lab
Enfield Southgate	Bambos Charalambous	Lab
Hornchurch & Upminster	Julia Dockerill	Con
Kensington	Emma Dent Coad	Lab
Kingston & Surbiton	Sir Ed Davey	LD
Lewisham West & Penge	Ellie Reeves	Lab
Richmond Park	Zac Goldsmith	Con
Twickenham	Sir Vince Cable	LD

North East (5)

Blaydon	Liz Twist	Lab
Hartlepool	Mike Hill	Lab
Middlesbrough South & East Cleveland	Simon Clarke	Con
North West Durham	Laura Pidcock	Lab
Stockton South	Dr Paul Williams	Lab

North West (10)

Bury North	James Frith	Lab
Crewe & Nantwich	Laura Smith	Lab
Leigh	Jo Platt	Lab
Liverpool Walton	Dan Carden	Lab
Manchester Gorton	Afzal Khan CBE	Lab
Rochdale	Tony Lloyd	Lab

Southport	Damien Moore	Con
Tatton	Esther McVey	Con
Warrington South	Faisal Rashid	Lab
Weaver Vale	Mike Amesbury	Lab

Northern Ireland (6)

Belfast South	Emma Little-Pengelly	DUP
Fermanagh & South Tyrone	Michelle Gildernew	SF
Foyle	Elisha McCallion	SF
South Antrim	Paul Girvan	DUP
South Down	Chris Hazzard	SF
West Tyrone	Barry McElduff	SF

Scotland (22)

Aberdeen South	Ross Thomson	Con
Angus	Kirstene Hair	Con
Ayr, Carrick & Cumnock	Bill Grant	Con
Banff & Buchan	David Duguid	Con
Berwickshire, Roxburgh & Selkirk	John Lamont	Con
Caithness, Sutherland & Easter Ross	Jamie Stone	LD
Coatbridge, Chryston & Bellshill	Hugh Gaffney	Lab
Dumfries & Galloway	Alister Jack	Con
East Dunbartonshire	Jo Swinson	LD
East Lothian	Martin Whitfield	Lab
East Renfrewshire	Paul Masterton	Con
Edinburgh West	Christine Jardine	LD
Glasgow East	David Linden	SNP
Glasgow North East	Paul Sweeney	Lab
Gordon	Colin Clark	Con
Kirkcaldy & Cowdenbeath	Lesley Laird	Lab
Midlothian	Danielle Rowley	Lab
Moray	Douglas Ross	Con
Ochil & South Perthshire	Luke Graham	Con
Rutherglen & Hamilton West	Gerard Killen	Lab
Stirling	Stephen Kerr	Con
West Aberdeenshire & Kincardine	Andrew C Bowie	Con

South East (11)

Aldershot	Leo Docherty	Con
Brighton, Kemptown	Lloyd Russell-Moyle	Lab
Canterbury	Rosie Duffield	Lab
Chichester	Gillian Keegan	Con
Eastbourne	Stephen Lloyd	LD
Isle of Wight	Bob Seely MBE	Con
Oxford East	Anneliese Dodds	Lab
Oxford West & Abingdon	Layla Moran	LD
Portsmouth South	Stephen Morgan	Lab
Reading East	Matt Rodda	Lab
Slough	Tan Dhesi	Lab

South West (4)

Bath	Wera Hobhouse	LD
Bristol North West	Darren Jones	Lab
Plymouth Sutton & Devonport	Luke Pollard	Lab
Stroud	Dr David Drew	Lab

Wales (4)

Cardiff North	Anna McMorrin	Lab
Ceredigion	Ben Lake	PC
Gower	Tonia Antoniazzi	Lab
Vale of Clwyd	Chris Ruane	Lab

West Midlands (6)

Birmingham Edgbaston	Preet Gill	Lab
Redditch	Rachel Maclean	Con
Stoke-on-Trent South	Jack Brereton	Con
Walsall North	Eddie Hughes	Con
Warwick & Leamington	Matt Western	Lab
Wolverhampton South West	Eleanor Smith	Lab

Yorkshire and the Humber (6)

Barnsley East	Stephanie Peacock	Lab
Colne Valley	Thelma Walker	Lab
Keighley	John Grogan	Lab
Kingston upon Hull West & Hessle	Emma Hardy	Lab
Leeds North West	Alex Sobel	Lab
Sheffield Hallam	Jared O'Mara	Lab

Abbreviations:

Con: Conservative

DUP: Democratic Unionist Party

Lab: Labour

LD: Liberal Democrat

PC: Plaid Cymru

SF: Sinn Féin

SNP: Scottish National Party

New women MPs (36) by party

Labour (22)

Tonia Antoniazzi	Gower
Emma Dent Coad	Kensington
Marsha De Cordova	Battersea
Anneliese Dodds	Oxford East
Rosie Duffield	Canterbury
Ruth George	High Peak
Preet Gill	Birmingham Edgbaston
Emma Hardy	Kingston upon Hull West & Hessle
Sarah Jones	Croydon Central
Lesley Laird	Kirkcaldy & Cowdenbeath
Karen Lee	Lincoln
Anna McMorrin	Cardiff North
Fiona Onasanya	Peterborough
Stephanie Peacock	Barnsley East
Laura Pidcock	North West Durham
Jo Platt	Leigh
Ellie Reeves	Lewisham West & Penge
Danielle Rowley	Midlothian
Eleanor Smith	Wolverhampton South West
Laura Smith	Crewe & Nantwich
Liz Twist	Blaydon
Thelma Walker	Colne Valley

Conservative (7)

Kemi Badenoch	Saffron Walden
Julia Dockerill	Hornchurch & Upminster
Vicky Ford	Chelmsford
Kirstene Hair	Angus
Gillian Keegan	Chichester
Rachel Maclean	Redditch
Esther McVey	Tatton

Liberal Democrats (4)

Wera Hobhouse	Bath
Christine Jardine	Edinburgh West
Layla Moran	Oxford West & Abingdon
Jo Swinson	East Dunbartonshire

Sinn Féin (2)

Michelle Gildernew	Fermanagh & South Tyrone
Elisha McCallion	Foyle

Democratic Unionist Party (1)

Emma Little-Pengelly	Belfast South

New BME
MPs (12) by party

Labour (9)

Bambos Charalambous	Enfield Southgate
Marsha De Cordova	Battersea
Tan Dhesi	Slough
Preet Gill MP	Birmingham Edgbaston
Afzal Khan CBE	Manchester Gorton
Fiona Onasanya	Peterborough
Faisal Rashid	Warrington South
Eleanor Smith	Wolverhampton South West
Mohammad Yasin	Bedford

Conservative (2)

Bim Afolami	Hitchin & Harpenden
Kemi Badenoch	Saffron Walden

Liberal Democrat (1)

Layla Moran	Oxford West & Abingdon

Defeated MPs (66) by party

Conservative (33)

Caroline Ansell	Eastbourne
Gavin Barwell	Croydon Central
James Berry	Kingston & Surbiton
Andrew Bingham	High Peak
Nicola Blackwood	Oxford West & Abingdon
Victoria Borwick	Kensington
Sir Julian Brazier	Canterbury
David Burrowes	Enfield Southgate
Neil Carmichael	Stroud
Oliver Colvile	Plymouth Sutton & Devonport
Bryon Davies	Gower
James Davies	Vale of Clwyd
Flick Drummond	Portsmouth South
Jane Ellison	Battersea
Graham Evans	Weaver Vale
Richard Fuller	Bedford
Ben Gummer	Ipswich
Kris Hopkins	Keighley
Ben Howlett	Bath
Stewart Jackson	Peterborough
Simon Kirby	Brighton, Kemptown
Charlotte Leslie	Bristol North West
Dr Tania Mathias	Twickenham

Jason McCartney	Colne Valley
Karl McCartney	Lincoln
David Mowat	Warrington South
David Nuttall	Bury North
Amanda Solloway	Derby North
Edward Timpson	Crewe & Nantwich
James Wharton	Stockton South
Chris White	Warwick & Leamington
Craig Williams	Cardiff North
Rob Wilson	Reading East

Scottish National Party (20)

Tasmina Ahmed-Sheikh	Ochil & South Perthshire
Richard Arkless	Dumfries & Galloway
Phil Boswell	Coatbridge, Chryston & Bellshill
Stuart Blair Donaldson	West Aberdeenshire & Kincardine
Margaret Ferrier	Rutherglen & Hamilton West
George Kerevan	East Lothian
Calum Kerr	Berwickshire, Roxburgh & Selkirk
Callum McCaig	Aberdeen South
Anne McLaughlin	Glasgow North East
Dr Paul Monaghan	Caithness, Sutherland & Easter Ross
Roger Mullin	Kirkcaldy & Cowdenbeath
John Nicolson	East Dunbartonshire
Kirsten Oswald	East Renfrewshire
Steven Paterson	Stirling
Angus Robertson	Moray
Alex Salmond	Gordon
Owen Thompson	Midlothian
Mike Weir	Angus
Dr Eilidh Whiteford	Banff & Buchan
Corri Wilson	Ayr, Carrick & Cumnock

Labour (4)

| Natascha Engel | North East Derbyshire |
| Rob Flello | Stoke-on-Trent South |

| Sir Alan Meale | Mansfield |
| David Winnick | Walsall North |

Liberal Democrats (4)

Nick Clegg	Sheffield Hallam
Greg Mulholland	Leeds North West
Sarah Olney	Richmond Park
Mark Williams	Ceredigion

Social Democratic & Labour Party (3)

Mark Durkan	Foyle
Dr Alasdair McDonnell	Belfast South
Margaret Ritchie	South Down

Ulster Unionist Party (2)

| Tom Elliott | Fermanagh & South Tyrone |
| Danny Kinahan | South Antrim |

Retired or deselected MPs (32) by party

Labour (15)

Graham Allen	Nottingham North
Dave Anderson	Blaydon
Tom Blenkinsop	Middlesbrough South & East Cleveland
Andy Burnham	Leigh
Simon Danczuk*	Rochdale
Jim Dowd	Lewisham West & Penge
Michael Dugher	Barnsley East
Pat Glass	North West Durham
Alan Johnson	Kingston upon Hull West & Hessle
Fiona Mactaggart	Slough
Rob Marris	Wolverhampton South West
Steve Rotheram	Liverpool Walton
Andrew Smith	Oxford East
Gisela	Birmingham Edgbaston
Iain Wright	Hartlepool

*Deselected

Conservative (12)

Simon Burns	Chelmsford
Sir Edward Garnier	Harborough
Sir Alan Haselhurst	Saffron Walden

Gerald Howarth	Aldershot
Peter Lilley	Hitchin & Harpenden
Karen Lumley	Redditch
David Mackintosh	Northampton South
George Osborne	Tatton
Sir Eric Pickles	Brentwood & Ongar
Andrew Turner	Isle of Wight
Andrew	Chichester
Dame Angela Watkinson	Hornchurch & Upminster

Independent/Scottish National Party (2)

| Natalie McGarry* | Glasgow East |
| Michelle Thomson* | Edinburgh West |

*Deselected

Liberal Democrat (1)

| John Pugh | Southport |

Independent/UK Independence Party (1)

| Douglas Carswell | Clacton |

Sinn Féin (1)

| Pat Doherty | West Tyrone |

The class of 2017

Bim Afolami

CONSERVATIVE MP FOR HITCHIN & HARPENDEN

FORMER MP:	Peter Lilley, Conservative, stood down
MAJORITY:	12,031 (20.5%)
VOTE SHARE:	53.1%
CHANGE:	-3.8%
2ND PLACE:	Lab
EU REFERENDUM:	Remain

www.bimafolami.co.uk   @BimAfolami

BIM (ABIMBOLA) AFOLAMI was born in Berkshire in February 1986 but grew up in London, the son of a Nigerian anaesthesia consultant in the NHS and a pharmacist. He was educated at Bishopsgate Preparatory School, Eton College and University College, Oxford, where he studied Modern History and was vice-president of the Oxford Union Society. Embarking upon a corporate legal career, he was an Associate with Freshfields Bruckhaus Deringer in 2011 and worked for Simpson Thacher & Bartlett by 2013, focusing on mergers and acquisitions. Ahead of his election, he was a senior executive for Group Corporate Structuring at HSBC.

He has said that he planned to vote Labour in 2005, but was critical of its policy on selective education and, after David Cameron became party leader in the aftermath, he joined the Conservative Party. A self-proclaimed Cameron moderniser, he worked for George Osborne and Howard Flight in Parliament and is a former treasurer of the Bow Group. He contested the Lewisham Deptford seat in 2015.

Married to Hetti, he is the father of Zachary and Sam. He is a primary school governor, a fellow of the Royal Society of Arts and a member of the Programme (advisory) Committee of the Ditchley Foundation. He is a keen sportsman and supports Northampton Saints and Arsenal FC. ■

Mike Amesbury

LABOUR MP FOR WEAVER VALE

FORMER MP:	Graham Evans, Conservative, defeated
MAJORITY:	3,928 (7.8%)
VOTE SHARE:	51.5%
CHANGE:	+10.1%
2ND PLACE:	Con
EU REFERENDUM:	Remain

www.mikeamesbury.org @MikeAmesbury

Born in May 1969 in Manchester, Mike Amesbury left school at sixteen with few qualifications and prospects, and experienced periods of unemployment. He later returned to full-time education, becoming the first in his family to gain a university degree: a BA in Social Science from the University of Bradford. He also studied careers guidance and education as a postgraduate at the University of West England. A careers adviser focused on young people, he has been a committed member of the Unison and GMB trade unions for thirty years, a Unison shop steward and convenor for Manchester, Trafford, Tameside and Salford Careers services.

A Manchester City councillor representing Fallowfield from 2006, he is a former Cabinet member for Culture and Leisure. As a councillor, he served as a director of the Hallé, the Millennium Quarter Trust board, Manchester Concert Halls Limited, the Library Theatre board, the Manchester Sport and Leisure Trust, the Velodrome Trust and the Manchester International Festival. He has worked for Angela Rayner MP in her role as shadow Education Secretary and was active on Andy Burnham's successful Manchester mayoral campaign. He is a member of the Labour Party's Work and Prosperity Commission. Locally he has actively campaigned against fracking.

He is married to Amanda, who comes from Runcorn, and has a young son named Ted. ∎

Tonia Antoniazzi

LABOUR MP FOR GOWER

FORMER MP:	Byron Davies, Conservative, defeated
MAJORITY:	3,269 (7.2%)
VOTE SHARE:	49.9%
CHANGE:	+12.8%
2ND PLACE:	Con
EU REFERENDUM:	Remain?

www.toniaantoniazzi.co.uk   @ToniaAntoniazzi

TONIA ANTONIAZZI WAS born and raised in Llanelli by a Welsh mother and a Welsh Italian father. She went to St John Lloyd Catholic Comprehensive School and Gorseinon College, now Gower College, before studying French and Italian at Exeter University and a Postgraduate Certificate in Education (PGCE) from Cardiff University. A language teacher, she has been head of Modern Foreign Languages at Ysgol Bryngwyn School, a secondary school in Llanelli, and latterly was seconded to a regional group (Education through Regional Working) working across schools in six participating council areas.

After a century of Labour domination, Gower was won by the Conservatives' Byron Davies in 2015 with a majority of twenty-seven, making it the most marginal seat at the 2017 general election. Having succeeded in winning back the seat for Labour, she is the first woman to represent Gower.

She is a single mother with one son and has played international rugby representing Wales. ∎

Kemi Badenoch

CONSERVATIVE MP FOR SAFFRON WALDEN

FORMER MP:	Sir Alan Haselhurst, Conservative, stood down
MAJORITY:	24,966 (41.0%)
VOTE SHARE:	61.8%
CHANGE:	+4.6%
2ND PLACE:	Lab
EU REFERENDUM:	Leave

www.kemibadenoch.org.uk   @KemiBadenoch

BORN IN 1980 in Wimbledon, Kemi Badenoch, née Adegoke, spent ten years of her childhood living in Lagos, Nigeria, and the US, before studying computer systems engineering at the University of Sussex. She worked for Logica, the Royal Bank of Scotland and was an associate director/vice-president at Coutts & Co between 2008 and 2015, working on a range of regulatory and digital strategic projects. She then spent a year as head of digital at *The Spectator* and *Apollo* magazines. Between 2005 and 2009 she studied law at Birkbeck, University of London, so that she was better qualified to 'become a legislator'.

Joining the Conservatives in 2005, she stood against Tessa Jowell in Dulwich & West Norwood in 2010, finishing third. As an unsuccessful London-wide list candidate for the 2012 London Assembly elections, she was declared a member in 2015 following the resignation of Victoria Borwick. She served as deputy leader of the Conservative Group.

Her husband, Hamish, is chief operating officer for Global Markets UK at Deutsche Bank and a Merton councillor, who stood for Foyle in 2015. The couple have a daughter and a son. She has been a governor of two schools in Southwark and Lambeth, a director of a housing association and has been a TedX speaker on addressing poverty of ambition for ethnic minorities. ■

Andrew Bowie

CONSERVATIVE MP FOR WEST ABERDEENSHIRE & KINCARDINE

FORMER MP:	Stuart Blair Donaldson, Scottish National Party (SNP), defeated
MAJORITY:	7,950 (15.4%)
VOTE SHARE:	47.9%
CHANGE:	19.0%
2ND PLACE:	SNP
EU REFERENDUM:	Remain

@abowie4WAK

ANDREW BOWIE HAD a short military career before pursuing his political career that has led to his successful election to Westminster. He was educated at Inverurie Academy and then served three years in the Royal Navy between 2007 and 2010. After attending the Britannia Royal Naval College, he served as a Junior Warfare Officer operating in the Gulf region and in London as part of the ceremonial events management team. He returned to full-time education in 2010, attending the University of Aberdeen to study History and Politics, where he was president of the university's Conservative Association.

After six months working as a military projects co-ordinator at Divex, a diving equipment manufacturer, he became the Conservatives' North Scotland campaign manager in 2014, campaigning in the 2014 European Election and Scottish Independence referendum. He then spent nearly a year as the parliamentary assistant and rural affairs policy adviser to Conservative MEP Dr Ian Duncan in the European Parliament. Returning to Scotland and Holyrood in 2016, he was head of office to Liam Kerr, MSP for North East Scotland, prior to his election.

Away from politics, he is an enthusiastic fiddler and is Assistant Conductor with the Garioch Fiddlers Strathspey and Reel Society. ▪

Ben Bradley

CONSERVATIVE MP FOR MANSFIELD

FORMER MP:	Sir Alan Meale, Labour, defeated
MAJORITY:	1,057 (2.1%)
VOTE SHARE:	46.6%
CHANGE:	+18.5%
2ND PLACE:	Lab
EU REFERENDUM:	Remain

www.benbradleyformansfield.com

BEN BRADLEY IS the first ever Tory member for Mansfield since its creation in 1885; it was held by Labour since 1923 and by his predecessor, Sir Alan Meale, for the past thirty years. He was born in December 1989 in Ripley, and after attending several schools, he initially studied Sports at the University of Bath, but dropped out and worked as a landscape gardener. He later returned to education, graduating from Nottingham Trent University in 2013 with a first in Politics. He has had a variety of jobs including with De Vere Hotels, Aldi Supermarkets, as an administrator at the Open University and with recruitment firm Hays.

More recently, he has worked in the Sherwood and Grantham & Stamford constituency offices of Mark Spencer MP and Nick Boles MP respectively. He has been an Ashfield District councillor, representing Hucknall North, since 2015 and served as leader of the Conservative Group. Describing himself as a 'reluctant Remainer' in a *Politics Home* interview, he has nevertheless campaigned for delivering a Brexit without freedom of movement in a strongly Leave constituency.

His is married to Shanade, who works as a manager for Aldi Supermarkets, and they have two young sons, Harley and Taylor. He is a school governor at the Holgate Academy and a keen hockey player (goalkeeper), coaching several hockey clubs in the East Midlands. ▪

Jack Brereton

CONSERVATIVE MP FOR STOKE-ON-TRENT SOUTH

FORMER MP:	Rob Flello, Labour, defeated
MAJORITY:	663 (1.6%)
VOTE SHARE:	49.1%
CHANGE:	+16.4%
2ND PLACE:	Lab
EU REFERENDUM:	Remain

www.jackbrereton.co.uk

JACK BRERETON IS the first Conservative to represent Stoke-on-Trent South since the seat was created in 1950. Born in Stoke-on-Trent in May 1991, he is also the youngest Conservative MP in the new Parliament. Educated at St Thomas More Academy and having graduated from Keele University in 2012 with a degree in Politics and International Relations, he has since worked as a sales associate for OER. He later studied at University College London.

At the age of nineteen, in 2011, he became one of the party's youngest councillors in the country, elected to Stoke-on-Trent City Council to represent the Baddeley Green, Milton & Norton ward. Before his election to Parliament he was deputy leader of the Conservative Group and cabinet member for Regeneration, Transport & Heritage. He first stood for Parliament in the Stoke-on-Trent Central by-election earlier in 2017, finishing third behind Labour's Gareth Snell and UKIP's Paul Nuttall.

He married his wife Laura in 2016. He has been a school governor at Hillside Primary since 2011. ■

Alex Burghart

CONSERVATIVE MP FOR BRENTWOOD & ONGAR

FORMER MP:	Sir Eric Pickles, Conservative, stood down
MAJORITY:	24,002 (45.4%)
VOTE SHARE:	65.8%
CHANGE:	+7.0%
2ND PLACE:	Lab
EU REFERENDUM:	Unknown

@alexburghart

ALEX BURGHART WAS born in 1977 in Dorset, the son of two state school teachers. He gained a scholarship to Millfield School in Somerset and went on to read History at Oxford University. He taught at Warwick School, before taking his doctorate at King's College London where he taught and lectured. He has written extensively about early medieval England.

In 2008 he became a policy adviser to Tim Loughton MP, then shadow Minister for Children and Young People. Having worked for the Department for Education on the Munro Review of Child Protection, he worked briefly for Barnardo's, before becoming director of policy at the Centre for Social Justice. In 2016 he was appointed director of strategy and advocacy for the Children's Commissioner for England and latterly was a special adviser on social justice in the Prime Minister's Policy Unit. He stood against Jeremy Corbyn in Islington North in 2015, managing to increase the Conservative share of the vote by 21 per cent.

In 2012 he married Hermione Eyre, a journalist and novelist, whose father is Sir Reginald Eyre, former Tory MP for Birmingham Hall Green and a lawyer. The couple have two young children. He has sat on the board of the Yarlington Housing Group and is vice-chair of Governors at Queensmill School for children with autism. ∎

Rt Hon Sir Vince Cable

LIBERAL DEMOCRAT MP FOR TWICKENHAM

FORMER MP:	Dr Tania Mathias, Conservative, defeated
MAJORITY:	9,762 (14.7%)
VOTE SHARE:	52.8%
CHANGE:	+14.7%
2ND PLACE:	Con
EU REFERENDUM:	Remain

www.vincecable.org   @VinceCable

AFTER AN ABSENCE of two years, Sir Vince Cable has returned to frontline politics, almost certainly to lead his party (again) following the resignation of Tim Farron after the election. Born in May 1943 in York, he studied economics at the University of Cambridge and University of Glasgow (PhD). He worked for the Kenyan Government in the late 1960s, the UK's Foreign and Commonwealth Office and the Commonwealth Secretary-General in the 1970s and 1980s and was chief economist for Royal Dutch Shell from 1995 to 1997.

A former member of the SDP, he first became the MP for Twickenham in 1997. As party deputy leader, he became acting leader for two months in 2007 ahead of the election of Nick Clegg, famously describing PM Gordon Brown as having gone 'from Stalin to Mr Bean'. His predictions of the impending global financial crisis of 2007 to 2010 cemented his reputation as a highly influential figure in Westminster. He served as Business Secretary under the coalition government between 2010 and 2015.

Since he lost his seat he has been a visiting professor at the London School of Economics and has worked as the patron of several charities, including a children's hospice and a day respite care centre. He is married to Rachel and has three children from his first wife, Olympia, who died in 2001. ∎

Dan Carden

LABOUR MP FOR LIVERPOOL WALTON

FORMER MP:	Steve Rotheram, Labour, stood down
MAJORITY:	32,551 (77.1%)
VOTE SHARE:	85.7%
CHANGE:	+4.4%
2ND PLACE:	Con
EU REFERENDUM:	Remain

www.dancarden4walton.org   @DanCardenMP (old account deleted)

DAN CARDEN IS a 'proud Scouser', born and raised in Liverpool, the son of a union shop steward who was fired for refusing to cross a picket line during the Liverpool Dockers' strike of 1995. His mother has worked in the NHS for over forty years. Born in 1987, he was educated at St Edward's College in West Derby, where he was head boy, and studied at the London School of Economics.

Joining the Labour Party while still at school, he has worked in Parliament for former Easington MP John Cummings and successor Grahame Morris MP and as an aide to Len McCluskey, Unite's General Secretary, since 2013.

Following the resignation of former MP Steve Rotherham after his election as Liverpool Mayor in May 2017, Dan was selected for one of the safest seats in the country, but only after an acrimonious contest in which he defeated the former Liverpool City Mayor Joe Anderson, having been imposed on the constituency party by Labour's National Executive Committee. After being elected with the largest vote share in Parliament (85.7 per cent), he and supporters were initially banned for life from a Liverpool city centre pub after his allegedly raucous victory celebrations, a decision reversed a day later after he apologised for any wrongdoing. He is one of the most committed left-wingers and Corbyn supporters in the 2017 intake of Labour MPs. ∎

Bambos Charalambous

LABOUR MP FOR ENFIELD SOUTHGATE

FORMER MP:	David Burrowes, Conservative, defeated
MAJORITY:	4,355 (9.0%)
VOTE SHARE:	51.7%
CHANGE:	+12.7%
2ND PLACE:	Con
EU REFERENDUM:	Remain

www.bambos4enfieldsouthgate.co.uk   @BambosMP

BORN IN DECEMBER 1967 in London, Bambos Charalambous is only the second MP of Cypriot ancestry, and the first where both parents are Cypriot. Raised in Bowes Park, Enfield, he has lived in the constituency since the age of three. He attended Chace Boys Comprehensive School, Tottenham College and Liverpool Polytechnic, where he studied law and was elected as vice-president of the Students' Union in 1990.

He trained as a solicitor at Saunders & Co, further studied law at the University of North London, and was a housing caseworker at Hodge Jones & Allen before joining Hackney Council's housing litigation team in 1998. He is one of nine new lawyers elected to the Commons in 2017.

He joined Labour at the age of sixteen and first stood as a Labour candidate in nearby Epping Forest in 2005, subsequently contesting the Enfield Southgate seat in 2010 and 2015. He has been a councillor for Palmers Green on Enfield Council since 1994, winning five local elections, deputy leader of Enfield Labour Group, cabinet member for Leisure and Culture from 2010 until 2014, and associate cabinet member for Enfield West since 2014.

A member of the Unison and GMB unions, he is trustee of the charity Positive Women, was a founder member of Enfield Law Centre and is a former director of the London Arts board. He is a governor of his old junior school, St Michael at Bowes. ∎

Colin Clark

CONSERVATIVE MP FOR GORDON

FORMER MP:	Alex Salmond, Scottish National Party, defeated
MAJORITY:	2,607 (4.8%)
VOTE SHARE:	40.7%
CHANGE:	+29.0%
2ND PLACE:	SNP
EU REFERENDUM:	Remain

www.colinclark.org.uk

COLIN CLARK WAS one of the giant-slayers at the election, defeating Alex Salmond, the former SNP leader and First Minister, making it the first time since 1987 that Salmond has not been in an elected position in either Westminster or Holyrood. Born in February 1968, Clark was brought up on a farm in the North East, attending Turriff Academy and Heriot-Watt University, graduating in 1990.

He is a businessman and farmer. When he was twenty-four he bought into an M&S supplier of fresh produce based in Lincolnshire. Selling the business in 2003, he returned to the North East in 2005 to the family farm business, R&M Clark Farmers, a 1,000 acre arable and beef farm, and as chairman of Nessgro Limited. He has also been an investor in several SMEs.

He was elected councillor for Inverurie & District on Aberdeen Council in a November 2016 by-election and was re-elected in May 2017. He finished second in the 2016 Scottish Parliament elections in the overlapping Aberdeenshire East constituency, and second again in Gordon at the 2015 election. His increase in the Conservative vote by 29 per cent was the largest Conservative vote increase in 2017 and the second largest in the whole of the UK by any party.

He lives with his wife and young son in Oldmeldrum in the constituency. ▪

Simon Clarke

CONSERVATIVE MP FOR MIDDLESBROUGH SOUTH
& EAST CLEVELAND

FORMER MP:	Tom Blenkinsop, Labour, stood down
MAJORITY:	1,020 (2.1%)
VOTE SHARE:	49.6%
CHANGE:	+12.6%
2ND PLACE:	Lab
EU REFERENDUM:	Leave?

www.simon-clarke.org.uk @SimonClarke84

SIMON CLARKE WAS born in in Stockton-on-Tees and educated at the independent Yarm School and Norton's Red House School. He won a scholarship to study Modern History at University College, Oxford.

At first, he followed in his solicitor father's footsteps, attending Oxford Brookes University for a Graduate Diploma in Law and Oxford BPP Law School, before joining corporate lawyers Slaughter and May in 2008. From 2010 he has worked in the House of Commons for the Conservative MP Dominic Raab and since 2013, the Beverley & Holderness MP Graham Stuart, chairman of the Education Select Committee, specialising in health and education. He fought the neighbouring Middlesbrough constituency in 2015, finishing third behind Labour and UKIP.

He is married to Hannah and they have a young son. At 6ft 7 in. he was apparently nicknamed 'Stilts' at school and is now Britain's second tallest MP, second only to Conservative colleague Daniel Kawczynski at 6ft 8.5 in. ▪

Rt Hon Sir Ed Davey

LIBERAL DEMOCRAT MP FOR KINGSTON AND SURBITON

FORMER MP:	James Berry, Conservative, defeated
MAJORITY:	4,124 (6.6%)
VOTE SHARE:	44.7%
CHANGE:	+10.3%
2ND PLACE:	Con
EU REFERENDUM:	Remain

www.voters4ed.org   @EdwardJDavey

ONE OF THE leading retreads to return in 2017, Sir Ed Davey was born in Nottinghamshire, attended the independent Nottingham High School in the year above Ed Balls, and studied at Jesus College, Oxford University, graduating in 1988 with a First in Politics, Philosophy and Economics.

His Liberal Democrat career began quickly, as he became an Economics Researcher in Parliament working for Alan Beith and Paddy Ashdown. He also studied part-time for an MSc in Economics at Birkbeck College, London University. In 1993 he joined a management consultancy called Omega Partners, specialising in postal services.

Elected to the Commons to represent Kingston and Surbiton seat in 1997, he was quickly appointed an Economic Affairs spokesman and several promotions followed. In 2010 he was appointed Junior Business Minister in the Conservative–Liberal Democrat Coalition Government, and two years later he was promoted to the Cabinet as Secretary of State for Energy and Climate Change. Defeated in 2015, he has held several roles in the intervening period: chairman of Mongoose Energy, a consultant with MHP Communications, patron of the Sustainable Futures Foundation, a non-executive director of Nord Engine Capital and in independent consultant.

He lives in Surbiton with his wife Emily Gasson, herself a former Lib Dem candidate, and their two children. ∎

Marsha de Cordova

LABOUR MP FOR BATTERSEA

FORMER MP:	Jane Ellison, Conservative, defeated
MAJORITY:	2,416 (4.4%)
VOTE SHARE:	45.9%
CHANGE:	+9.1%
2ND PLACE:	Con
EU REFERENDUM:	Remain

@Marshadecordova

MARSHA DE CORDOVA succeeded in defeating Jane Ellison, the former Financial Secretary to the Treasury, overcoming a large Conservative majority. Registered as blind after being born with the eye condition nystagmus, her mother had to fight to keep her in mainstream education after the head teacher tried to have her removed to a special school.

She is a passionate disability rights campaigner, working for Action for Blind People from 2005 until 2012, Turns2us, as chief executive of South East London Vision and, prior to her election, and as engagement and advocacy director at the Thomas Pocklington Trust.

Politically she has been a councillor for the Larkhall ward on Lambeth Council since May 2014, is a graduate of Operation Black Vote's (OBV) BME Women's Councillor Scheme and is vice-chair of Disability Labour's National Executive. She is a member of Unite and also a committed Christian. She has been strongly supportive of Jeremy Corbyn and is considered one of the new left Labour MPs. ■

Emma Dent Coad

LABOUR MP FOR KENSINGTON

FORMER MP:	Victoria Borwick, Conservative, defeated
MAJORITY:	20 (0.1%)
VOTE SHARE:	42.2%
CHANGE:	+11.1%
2ND PLACE:	Con
EU REFERENDUM:	Remain

@emmadentcoad

IT IS DOUBTFUL whether a newly elected MP has ever had to face, within a week of being elected, a tragedy in their constituency on the scale of Grenfell Tower. Just days before Emma Dent Coad had surprised most by overturning a Conservative majority of 7,020 by a winning margin of just twenty votes, after three recounts and the last constituency in election to declare, to become the 'MP for Harrods and Kensington Place, but also for the Grenfell Tower' (Patrick Kidd, *The Times*).

Born in Chelsea, the youngest of six in an Anglo-Spanish family, she attended the Sacred Heart High School in Hammersmith, the University of Liverpool in London's School of Architecture and the Royal College of Art for an MA. The mother of three is putting her PhD on hold for now. An architectural historian and writer, her politics has always been rooted in planning and housing.

She was elected to Kensington and Chelsea Council in 2006, representing Golborne ward. She served as a council-appointed board member of Kensington and Chelsea Tenant Management Organisation (TMO) from 2010 until 2012, served on the council's Housing and Property Scrutiny Committee from 2013 until 2014 and on the council's main Planning Committee since June 2014. As a councillor, she signed an open letter in 2016 supporting Jeremy Corbyn, but rebelled against the leadership in one of the first votes of her career over retaining Single Market membership. ∎

Tan Dhesi

LABOUR MP FOR SLOUGH

FORMER MP:	Fiona Mactaggart, Labour, stood down
MAJORITY:	16,998 (31.3%)
VOTE SHARE:	62.9%
CHANGE:	+14.4%
2ND PLACE:	Con
EU REFERENDUM:	Remain?

www.tsdhesi.com @TanDhesi

BORN 1978 IN Berkshire, Tan (Tanmanjeet) Dhesi was educated first at a boarding school within the Punjab, India, before returning to Gravesend, a town his parents had moved back to and where his father was president of the local Gurdwara, the largest in the UK. There he attended a grammar school in Rochester and later the Gravesend Grammar School for Boys. He studied Mathematics with Management Studies at University College London, before Applied Statistics at Keble College, Oxford University. He later gained an MPhil from Fitzwilliam College, Cambridge University.

Joining the family business, DGP Logistics Plc., he worked as a general labourer before progressing to foreman, site manager, project manager and eventually project director, including spending three years working in Edinburgh.

Elected a Gravesham Borough councillor for Northfleet North in 2007, he served as the Mayor and was the shadow cabinet member with the communities portfolio. He stood in Gravesham in 2015. His selection was controversial, apparently running contrary to the policy of replacing retiring female MPs with other women, and the retiring Fiona Mactaggart reportedly considered legal action.

He is married to Manveen, and the couple have two young boys. He is a linguist and a school governor at two local schools. He became the UK's first turban-wearing Sikh MP in 2017. ∎

Leo Docherty

CONSERVATIVE MP FOR ALDERSHOT

FORMER MP:	Sir Gerald Howarth, Conservative, stood down
MAJORITY:	11,473 (23.4%)
VOTE SHARE:	55.1%
CHANGE:	+4.5%
2ND PLACE:	Lab
EU REFERENDUM:	Leave

www.leodocherty.org.uk   @LeoDochertyUK

LEO DOCHERTY WAS born in October 1976 in Scotland and grew up in Gloucestershire. After studying Swahili and Hindi at the School of Oriental and African studies (SOAS), he attended the Royal Military Academy Sandhurst, and was commissioned into the Scots Guards, based in Aldershot, in 2001. During six years of active service in Germany, Iraq and Afghanistan, he trained as a paratrooper, completed language courses in Arabic and Pashtu, served as the aide-de-camp to the Commander of the first British forces to enter the Helmand Province in 2006 and served alongside the Afghan National Army.

Leaving the army in December 2006 he travelled extensively from Turkey to Afghanistan on horseback, bicycle and on foot for six months. He wrote a highly critical book on his experiences in Afghanistan entitled Desert of Death, saying that the Helmand operation was a 'textbook case of how to screw up a counter-insurgency'. He has been the director of the Conservative Middle East Council since 2010.

He was a South Oxfordshire District councillor between 2011 and 2015, and contested Caerphilly at the 2015 general election. He unsuccessfully stood for election to Oxfordshire County Council in May 2017, just prior to his election in Aldershot.

He is married to Lucy and they have two young children. ▪

Julia Dockerill

CONSERVATIVE MP FOR HORNCHURCH AND UPMINSTER

FORMER MP:	Dame Angela Watkinson, Conservative, stood down
MAJORITY:	17,723 (31.6%)
VOTE SHARE:	60.2%
CHANGE:	+11.2%
2ND PLACE:	Lab
EU REFERENDUM:	Leave

@JuliaDockerill

AN ESSEX GIRL by birth, Julia Dockerill was born in June 1984. She attended Herts and Essex High School before studying Social and Political Science (MA) at Queen's College, Cambridge.

She has worked closely with Mark Field, the Conservative MP for Cities of London & Westminster since 2006, as his Chief of Staff, and with him she has co-authored the book *Between the Crashes* on the aftermath of the financial crisis, and a collection of essays, *The Best of Times*. She has also worked as a freelance ghost writer since 2013 and is writing a book, *London in the Noughties*, exploring economic, social and political change in the capital from 2000 until 2010.

Having lived in Tower Hamlets, renting in Mudchute, Shadwell and Mile End, she has represented St Katharine's & Wapping on Tower Hamlets Council since 2014. She was embarrassed in November 2016 when her notes on a confidential briefing on the UK's Brexit negotiating position were photographed under her arm as she left Downing Street.

She is due to marry her partner of five years in September 2017. She is a trustee of Inspire Malawi, a non-profit organisation supporting schools and education in central Malawi, and has worked with the Westminster Foundation for Democracy to make political systems and parties more robust in developing nations. ▪

Anneliese Dodds

LABOUR MP (AND CO-OPERATIVE PARTY) FOR OXFORD EAST

FORMER MP:	Andrew Smith, Labour, stood down
MAJORITY:	23,284 (43.2%)
VOTE SHARE:	65.2%
CHANGE:	+15.1%
2ND PLACE:	Con
EU REFERENDUM:	Remain

www.anneliesedoddsmep.uk   @AnnelieseDodds

BORN IN ABERDEEN in March 1978, Anneliese Dodds moved south in 1996 to read Philosophy, Politics and Economics at St Hilda's College, Oxford, graduating with a First in 2001. She subsequently read for a Master's in Social Policy at the University of Edinburgh and a Doctorate in Government at the London School of Economics until 2006. She has lectured at the LSE and King's College, London, where she was acting director of the King's NIHR Patient Safety and Service Quality Research Centre. She was a senior lecturer in Public Policy at Aston University until her election as an MEP.

A party member since 1996, she fought the Reading East seat in 2010 and was elected as the only Labour MEP for South East England in 2014. In the European Parliament, she has sat on the Committee on Economic and Monetary Affairs, campaigning for better regulation of the financial markets and SMEs. She co-wrote a Fabian Society paper published in April 2017 on how a new deal for financial services can be reached after Brexit, 'Brexit: A New Deal for Financial Services'. She has committed to stand down as an MEP. She was appointed to the Labour frontbench as a Treasury spokesperson in July 2017.

She lives in Rose Hill, Oxford, with her partner Ed Turner, deputy leader of Labour-run Oxford City Council, and their two children, Freddie and Isabella. ■

Dr David Drew

LABOUR (AND CO-OPERATIVE PARTY) MP FOR STROUD

FORMER MP:	Neil Carmichael, Conservative, defeated
MAJORITY:	687 (1.1%)
VOTE SHARE:	47.0%
CHANGE:	+9.3%
2ND PLACE:	Con
EU REFERENDUM:	Leave?

@DavidEDrew

DAVID DREW HAS returned to Westminster, having reclaimed the seat lost to Neil Carmichael in 2010. The two have now contested five elections. Born in Gloucestershire in 1952, he attended Kingsfield School, Kingswood before studying Economics at the University of Nottingham and the University of Birmingham, where he qualified as a teacher. He went on to study for his Master's degree in Historical Studies at Bristol Polytechnic and received a Master of Education from the University of the West of England in 1994.

He began his teaching career in Warwickshire in 1976, taught in Gloucestershire, and lectured at the University of West England. He has been a member of two teaching unions, the NASUWT and NATFHE, throughout his career.

Defeated in Stroud in 1992 by the incumbent Roger Knapman, he served as a Gloucestershire County councillor, before winning the seat in 1997. He served on the Environment, Food and Rural Affairs Committee for over a decade. A member of the Socialist Campaign Group and frequent Labour backbench rebel, he is a friend of Jeremy Corbyn and supported John McDonnell's unsuccessful leadership bid in 2007. He was appointed to the Labour frontbench as a Defra spokesperson in 2017.

He is married to Anne, and they have two daughters and two sons. They've lived in the town of Stonehouse for thirty years. ∎

Rosie Duffield

LABOUR MP FOR CANTERBURY

FORMER MP:	Sir Julian Brazier, Conservative, defeated
MAJORITY:	187 (0.3%)
VOTE SHARE:	45.0%
CHANGE:	+20.5%
2ND PLACE:	Con
EU REFERENDUM:	Remain

@RosieDuffield1

ROSIE DUFFIELD'S WIN in the ancient seat of Canterbury, defeating the Conservative MP of thirty years Sir Julian Brazier, was one of the stand-out results in the 2017 general election. She is the first Labour MP ever and the first non-Conservative MP to represent the seat since it was re-constituted in 1885.

Born in July 1971, Duffield left school at the age of sixteen and worked as a teaching assistant until a year before the election, giving it up to concentrate full-time on writing political satire. She had been in the process of co-producing a pilot TV show.

The chair of the Canterbury Labour Party, she stood unsuccessfully in the Canterbury City Council elections in St Stephens ward. She is an active animal rights campaigner, has demonstrated with PETA and attended anti-fox hunt protests. She is one of the founding members of Canterbury Action Network and was part of the first Jo Cox Women in Leadership Scheme.

She is a London-born single mother of two teenage sons and has lived in Canterbury for twenty years. ∎

David Duguid

CONSERVATIVE MP FOR BANFF & BUCHAN

FORMER MP:	Dr Eilidh Whiteford, Scottish National Party (SNP), defeated
MAJORITY:	3,693 (8.9%)
VOTE SHARE:	48.0%
CHANGE:	+19.2%
2ND PLACE:	SNP
EU REFERENDUM:	Remain?

@david_duguid

DAVID DUGUID PRODUCED one of the most dramatic results in Scotland, over-turning an SNP majority of over 14,000 to take what had looked like an SNP strong-hold after thirty years. He grew up on a farm near Turriff and was educated at Banff Academy and Robert Gordon University between 1989 and 1991, studying Chemistry.

He has had a 25-year career in oil and gas, working in the UK, Europe and across the world, including Azerbaijan from 2006 until 2008, where he met his wife Rose, Angola from 2009 until 2011, Turkmenistan, UAE and Venezuela. He has worked for Servo Oil-field Chemicals in Aberdeen, SGS, BP and Hitachi Consulting, whose clients included Chevron, Centrica, DONG and Maersk.

He is relatively new to politics. In a con-stituency that is estimated to have voted 54 per cent for Brexit and which encompasses the fishing towns of Fraserburgh and Peter-head, he signed the Scottish Fishermen's Federation Brexit pledge to exit the EU and the Common Fisheries Policy during the 2017 campaign, despite reportedly having voted for Remain in the EU referendum. ∎

Vicky Ford

CONSERVATIVE MP FOR CHELMSFORD

FORMER MP:	Sir Simon Burns, Conservative, stood down
MAJORITY:	13,572 (23.9%)
VOTE SHARE:	53.7%
CHANGE:	+2.2%
2ND PLACE:	Lab
EU REFERENDUM:	Remain

www.vickyford.org   @vickyford

VICKY FORD WAS born in 1967 and raised in Omagh, County Tyrone, Northern Ireland. Her parents were both English doctors. As a child, she joined her mother campaigning with the peace movement, and her father stood in local elections for the Northern Irish Alliance Party. She attended primary school in Northern Ireland, followed by St Paul's Girls' School in England, and was awarded an academic scholarship to Marlborough College. She studied Maths and Economics at Trinity College, Cambridge, graduating in 1989.

Between 1988 and 2000, Ford worked at JP Morgan, working up from graduate trainee to be a vice-president, specialising in infrastructure and project financing. In 2000 she moved to Bear Stearns International, working as a managing director until 2002.

A party member since 1986, she stood in Birmingham Northfield in 2005, and was a South Cambridgeshire District councillor from 2006 until 2009. At the 2009 European parliamentary election, she was elected as an East of England MEP. From 2014 until 2017 she was chair of the Internal Market and Consumer Protection (IMCO) Committee, one of the most powerful economic committees of the Parliament.

She met her future husband, Hugo Ford, while they were both students in Cambridge. He is now a Consultant Oncologist at Addenbrooke's Hospital. The couple have three student-age children. ∎

James Frith

LABOUR MP FOR BURY NORTH

FORMER MP:	David Nuttall, Conservative, defeated
MAJORITY:	4,375 (9.1%)
VOTE SHARE:	53.6%
CHANGE:	+12.5%
2ND PLACE:	Con
EU REFERENDUM:	Remain

www.jamesfrith.blog   @jimmyfrith

THE SON OF a care worker mother and a clergyman father, James Frith is from Ramsbottom and was educated at Taunton School and Manchester Metropolitan University, graduating in 2000 with a 2:1 in Politics and Economics. He toured, including Glastonbury, as lead singer of rock band Finka, which he also managed. One music journalist wrote that 'Jimmy Frith sounds like the ghost of Jim Morrison having a fag with Ian McCulloch.'

Working first as a finance recruitment consultant with Badenoch & Clark from 2000, he became campaign and communications manager in 2004 for the Bolton West Labour MP, Ruth Kelly. He joined the Greater Manchester Chamber of Commerce as a policy manager in 2005, before

setting up a new business, U-Explore, for company owners following management buy-outs in 2007. In 2013 he founded and ran All Together, a social enterprise providing careers education and guidance services.

He was elected to Bury Council representing the Elton ward from 2011 until 2014. He lost Bury North to David Nuttall at the 2015 general election by only 378 votes, and secured the seat despite UKIP not standing and endorsing Nuttall. He also fought off a challenge in his selection by self-styled 'selfie queen' Karen Danczuk.

He has lived in Bury with his wife Nikki since 2009 and they have three children – Jemima, Henry and Lizzie – and a fourth is apparently on the way. ∎

Hugh Gaffney

LABOUR MP FOR COATBRIDGE, CHRYSTON & BELLSHILL

FORMER MP:	Phil Boswell, Scottish National Party (SNP), defeated
MAJORITY:	1,586 (3.5%)
VOTE SHARE:	42.6%
CHANGE:	+8.7%
2ND PLACE:	SNP
EU REFERENDUM:	Remain?

@hgaffney48

BORN IN ALPINE and raised in Birkenshaw, both in the constituency, Hugh Gaffney worked in the postal industry for twenty-five years. Arriving in Westminster on his first day, he proudly wore his old work uniform from Parcelforce Worldwide, echoing Labour's founding father Keir Hardie who was also from Lanarkshire. Gaffney revealed in his maiden speech that he is one of the founders of the Keir Hardie Society. He has served as a trade union official with the Communication Workers' Union throughout his working life, recently becoming its Scottish Political Officer. He has been secretary of the North Lanarkshire trade union council for the past fifteen years.

He was elected to the North Lanarkshire Council in 2017, representing the Thorniewood ward, and has said that he will remain a councillor for the time being, but has promised to devote his £17,000 councillor salary to buying play equipment for disabled children. He is generally considered to be on the left of the party and is likely to be a staunch Corbyn supporter.

He is married to Anne and has three sons, Paul, Matthew and Christopher. ∎

Ruth George

LABOUR MP FOR HIGH PEAK

FORMER MP:	Andrew Bingham, Conservative, defeated
MAJORITY:	2,322 (4.3%)
VOTE SHARE:	49.7%
CHANGE:	+14.4%
2ND PLACE:	Con
EU REFERENDUM:	Remain

@RuthGeorge6

RUTH GEORGE TRAINED as a tax accountant and helped to found a successful accountancy business in Chapel-en-le-Frith when in her twenties. Since 1999 she has worked as a Political Officer for the Union of Shop, Distributive and Allied Workers (Usdaw) in Manchester, setting up the Freedom from Fear campaign concerned with violence and abuse of staff in shops and campaigning against Sunday Trading and the Trade Union Act 2016.

She is married to Mark and they have four children. She has lived in the constituency for over twenty-five years, for the last ten years in Whaley Bridge. She has been a school governor in Whaley Bridge and is a committee member for the Whaley Bridge After School Club. An active local campaigner against development on greenfield sites around the local area, she was vice-chair of Chapel Vision, the first local community group to successfully produce a Neighbourhood Plan. ∎

Michelle Gildernew

SINN FÉIN MP FOR FERMANAGH & SOUTH TYRONE

FORMER MP:	Tom Elliott, Ulster Unionist Party (UUP), defeated
MAJORITY:	875 (1.6%)
VOTE SHARE:	47.2%
CHANGE:	1.8%
2ND PLACE:	UUP
EU REFERENDUM:	Remain

@gildernewm

MICHELLE GILDERNEW HAS been re-elected for a second time, but like all Sinn Féin MPs, and as before, she follows a policy of abstentionism and will not take her seat in Westminster. Born in Dungannon in March 1970, Gildernew is one of ten siblings brought up on a farm in County Tyrone. During the 1960s, the family were leading figures in the Northern Ireland Civil Rights Association. She attended St Catherine's College Armagh and later the University of Ulster, Coleraine.

She was the MP for the constituency of Fermanagh and South Tyrone from 2001 to 2015, and was a Member of the Northern Ireland Assembly (MLA) for Fermanagh and South Tyrone between June 1998 and

July 2012. She was re-elected to the Assembly in 2016 and 2017. She served as Minister for Agriculture and Rural Development in the Northern Ireland Executive. She is Sinn Féin's health spokesperson and has been a member of the party's Ard Chomhairle (National Executive).

She is married to Jimmy and is the mother of two boys, Emmet and Eunan, and one girl, Aoise. She is a speaker of the Irish language. ∎

Preet Gill

LABOUR MP (AND CO-OPERATIVE PARTY)
FOR BIRMINGHAM EDGBASTON

FORMER MP:	Gisela Stuart, Labour, stood down
MAJORITY:	6,917 (15.9%)
VOTE SHARE:	55.3%
CHANGE:	+10.5%
2ND PLACE:	Con
EU REFERENDUM:	Remain

www.preetkaurgill.com   @Preet4Edgbaston

BORN AND RAISED in Edgbaston, the daughter of a bus driver, Preet Gill attended Milford Girls followed by the University of East London, achieving a First in Sociology and Social Work, having worked India with UNICEF in India where she undertook research on street children.

She has dedicated seventeen years to social work, is team manager for the Children, Young People and Families Directorate at Birmingham City Council, has represented the St Paul's ward, Sandwell Metropolitan Borough since 2012 and has been the cabinet member for Public Health and Protection, and Mental Health Champion for the council. She'll remain a councillor but will step down from her public health portfolio.

One of her role models is the Sikh suffragette, Princess Sophia Duleep Singh, who led the movement after Emmeline Pankhurst's death – appropriate for the first elected female British Sikh MP. Birmingham Edgbaston has been represented by a female MP since Conservative Edith Pitt's by-election victory in 1953.

Gill is a director of Spring Social Housing board, a board member of the Sikh Network and a member of Sandwell Amritsar Friendship Association, as well as the Jo Cox Women in Leadership training programme.

Her husband is the team manager in Children's Services at Sandwell Metropolitan Borough Council. ∎

Paul Girvan

DEMOCRATIC UNIONIST PARTY (DUP) MP
FOR SOUTH ANTRIM

FORMER MP:	Danny Kinahan, Ulster Unionist Party (UUP), defeated
MAJORITY:	3,208 (7.4%)
VOTE SHARE:	38.2%
CHANGE:	+8.1%
2ND PLACE:	UUP
EU REFERENDUM:	Leave

@PaulGirvanMP

BORN IN JULY 1963, Paul Girvan was raised in Ballyclare in South Antrim and attended Ballyclare Secondary School and the University of Ulster. He worked as an electronics engineer and as a parliamentary assistant to William McCrea, DUP MP for South Antrim between 2005 and 2015. He owns a portfolio of residential properties throughout Northern Ireland through the Girvan Trust.

He was elected to Newtownabbey Borough Council in 1997, and served as its Mayor between 2002 and 2004. He is currently the chair of the council's Development Committee.

He was elected to the Northern Ireland Assembly, representing South Antrim from 2003 until 2007, when he had to give up his seat after failing to be selected by local party members as one of three South Antrim Assembly election candidates. He returned to the Assembly in 2010 when he was selected to replace William McCrea following his resignation, and the following year he was re-elected. He has served as the private secretary to the Office of the First Minister and Deputy First Minister. ▪

Zac Goldsmith

CONSERVATIVE MP FOR RICHMOND PARK

FORMER MP:	Sarah Olney, Liberal Democrat MP, defeated
MAJORITY:	45 (0.1%)
VOTE SHARE:	45.1%
CHANGE:	-13.1%
2ND PLACE:	Lib Dem
EU REFERENDUM:	Leave

@ZacGoldsmith

AFTER AN ABSENCE of six months, Zac Goldsmith has been returned to Parliament by a narrow margin of only forty-five votes. The son of billionaire businessman Sir James Goldsmith, his family has a long history in politics. Born in London in 1975, he was educated at Eton College and the Cambridge Centre for Sixth-form Studies. In 1998, his uncle made him editor of *The Ecologist*, a position he retained until 2007.

Selected through an open primary to contest Richmond Park against the incumbent Liberal Democrat, Susan Kramer, he was elected at the 2010 general election with a modest majority. In 2015 he increased the majority to over 23,000. As the Conservative candidate for the 2016 London mayoral election he lost convincingly to Labour's Sadiq Khan after a lacklustre and controversial campaign. He announced his resignation as an MP following the government's October 2016 decision to approve a third runway at Heathrow Airport. In the subsequent by-election, he stood as an independent candidate, and was defeated by Liberal Democrat Sarah Olney, with Brexit dominating the campaign in a strongly Remain constituency.

Goldsmith is one of the wealthiest MPs in Parliament, believed to have inherited £200–£300 million from this father's estate. He is married to banking heiress Alice Rothschild and they have daughter and a son. He has three children from his first marriage. ∎

Luke Graham

CONSERVATIVE MP FOR OCHIL & SOUTH PERTHSHIRE

FORMER MP:	Tasmina Ahmed-Sheikh, Scottish National Party (SNP), defeated
MAJORITY:	3,359 (6.2%)
VOTE SHARE:	41.5%
CHANGE:	+20.8%
2ND PLACE:	SNP
EU REFERENDUM:	Remain

@LukeGrahamMP

BORN IN JUNE 1985, Luke Graham finished his comprehensive, secondary education at Dawson School and went into sales for the Dick Lovett Group. After three years of work, he returned to education at the University of Sheffield, graduating in 2006 with a BA in Economics and Social Policy. He stayed on for a further year, working as the finance officer at Sheffield Students' Union and as director of retail trade at NUS Services Limited. Leaving Sheffield in 2007 he trained as an accountant with Tesco in London, moving to financial management roles with Tough Mudder and Marks & Spencer. He was a board member and treasurer of the British Chamber of Commerce in China between 2009 and 2011.

He was chairman of Conservative Future Sheffield. Having actively campaigned on the Better Together campaign, the following year, in 2015, he contested the seat of Ochil & South Perthshire at the general election, losing to Tasmina Ahmed-Sheikh of the SNP. In January 2016, he became director of finance at the Britain Stronger In Europe campaign during the EU referendum. Later that year he co-founded a start-up accountancy firm, Tech & the Beancounters Ltd. ∎

Bill Grant

CONSERVATIVE MP FOR AYR, CARRICK & CUMNOCK

FORMER MP:	Corri Wilson, Scottish National Party (SNP) MP, defeated
MAJORITY:	2,774 (6.0%)
VOTE SHARE:	40.1%
CHANGE:	+20.3%
2ND PLACE:	SNP
EU REFERENDUM:	Remain

@CrawleyAngela

A MINER'S SON, William 'Bill' Grant, born August 1951, was raised in Rankinston in Cumnock and educated at the local primary school and Cumnock Academy. Moving to Ayr, he spent his working life as a fire fighter, retiring after thirty-one years' service as a deputy commander in the Strathclyde Fire and Rescue Service.

He was first elected at the South Ayrshire Council elections in May 2007, serving the area of Ayr West. He stood in Ayr, Carrick & Cumnock at the 2010 general election, finishing in second place behind Labour's Sandra Osborne. He did not stand in 2015. ∎

John Grogan

LABOUR MP FOR KEIGHLEY

FORMER MP:	Kris Hopkins, Conservative, defeated
MAJORITY:	239 (0.5%)
VOTE SHARE:	46.5%
CHANGE:	+8.4%
2ND PLACE:	Con
EU REFERENDUM:	Remain

www.judithcummins.org.uk   @JudithCummins

JOHN GROGAN IS one of the retread MPs returning to Westminster in 2017 after his former seat of Selby was abolished. Born in Halifax in February 1961, the grandson of Irish migrants to Bradford, he was educated at St Michael's RC College, a Jesuit School, and St John's College, Oxford, where he read Modern History and Economics. He was president of the Oxford University Student Union.

He worked as communications coordinator for the City of Leeds Council before setting up his own conference organising business. He was research assistant to the Labour Group on Wolverhampton Borough Council between 1985 and 1987 and he also acted as the Labour Party press officer in the European Parliament in Brussels in 1995.

He unsuccessfully contested the seat of Selby in 1987 and 1992, but was elected at the third attempt in 1997. In the meantime, he stood unsuccessfully in the European parliamentary elections of 1989. He announced he would not contest the 2010 election, after the constituency of Selby was split in two, but he contested the Keighley seat in 2015.

He is vice-president of the Association of Drainage Authorities, patron of the Ukrainian British City Club, chair of the Mongolian-British Chamber of Commerce, chair of the Labour Party Yorkshire and the Humber Development board and chairman of the Hatfield Colliery Employee Benefit Trust. ∎

Kirstene Hair

CONSERVATIVE MP FOR ANGUS

FORMER MP:	Mike Weir, Scottish National Party (SNP), defeated
MAJORITY:	2,645 (6.6%)
VOTE SHARE:	45.2%
CHANGE:	+16.2%
2ND PLACE:	SNP
EU REFERENDUM:	Remain

@Kirstene4Angus

KIRSTENE HAIR WAS born in Brechin, Angus, in 1989, and grew up on the family farm at Mains of Ardovie near Brechin. She attended Brechin High School and studied Politics at the University of Aberdeen between 2007 and 2011. She has been a member of Brechin Junior Agricultural Club (JAC) for eight years and is a former club treasurer. She worked as an executive assistant to the chief executive of DC Thomson Publishing in Dundee prior to the election.

She stood as the Conservative candidate for Angus South in the 2016 Scottish Parliament election, losing to the incumbent MSP Graeme Dey, but having increased her party's share of the vote by 15 per cent. In a shock victory at the 2017 general election she defeated the SNP's chief whip Mike Weir who had served the seat for sixteen years. She will be one of the youngest MPs in the new Parliament. ∎

Emma Hardy

LABOUR MP FOR KINGSTON UPON HULL WEST & HESSLE

FORMER MP:	Alan Johnson, Labour, stood down
MAJORITY:	8,025 (23.2%)
VOTE SHARE:	53.1%
CHANGE:	3.9%
2ND PLACE:	Con
EU REFERENDUM:	Remain

@emmaannhardy

EMMA HARDY GREW up in North New-
bald, attending Wyke Sixth Form College in
Hull and the University of Liverpool, where
she studied Politics, gaining a 2:1 in 2001. Having completed her PGCE at the University of
Leeds, she taught in North East Lincolnshire
and East Riding, including at Willerby Carr
Lane primary school. Since 2015 she has been
a National Union of Teachers' organiser for
the Yorkshire Midland region.

She is a Labour town councillor in
Hessle and had already been selected as a
candidate for the 2019 East Riding Coun-
cil elections. She is the women's officer for
Hull West & Hessle Constituency Labour
Party and in 2015 was elected to the Labour
Party's National Policy Forum representing

members in Yorkshire and Humber. She sits
on the Early Years Education and Skills
Commission. She also became the deputy
general secretary of the Socialist Education
Association in 2016.

She beat David Prescott, a former Corbyn speechwriter and son of John Prescott,
and Sam Tarry, a union official and key
figure in Corbyn's leadership campaign,
to be selected to follow Alan Johnson in
this relatively safe seat. Nevertheless, she is
considered to sit on the left of the party. She
comfortably beat Michelle Dewberry, TV
personality and Lord Sugar's Apprentice in
2006, who was standing as an Independent.

She has lived in Hessle since 2004 with
her two daughters, Olivia and Isabelle. ∎

Chris Hazzard

SINN FÉIN MP FOR SOUTH DOWN

FORMER MP:	Margaret Ritchie, Social and Democratic Labour Party (SDLP), defeated
MAJORITY:	2,446 (4.8%)
VOTE SHARE:	39.9%
CHANGE:	+11.4%
2ND PLACE:	SDLP
EU REFERENDUM:	Remain

@ChrisHazzardSF

BORN IN AUGUST 1984, Chris Hazzard was raised on the outskirts of Drumaness, County Down. The eldest of four siblings, he was educated at Our Lady and St Patrick's College, Knock, before attending Queens University Belfast, where he is currently finishing his Doctorate in International Studies and Political Philosophy.

He joined his local Sinn Féin Cumann (association) as a teenager and was co-opted to the Northern Ireland Assembly when his colleague Willie Clarke retired to concentrate on his local council duties. At the time, he was the youngest MLA in the Assembly. He was re-elected in May 2016, but resigned in March 2017 along with all other nationalist MLAs. He has held positions on several committees, including the Agriculture and Rural Development Committee, Education, Justice and Enterprise, Trade and Investment committees. From May 2016 until March 2017 he was a minister in the Department for Infrastructure. Away from politics, he is a Gaelic Athletic Association member.

As with all Sinn Féin MPs, he follows a policy of abstentionism and will not take his seat in Westminster. ▪

Mike Hill

LABOUR MP FOR HARTLEPOOL

FORMER MP:	Iain Wright, Labour, stood down
MAJORITY:	7,650 (18.3%)
VOTE SHARE:	52.5%
CHANGE:	+16.9%
2ND PLACE:	Con
EU REFERENDUM:	Remain

@MikeHillMP

MIKE HILL HAS lived in Hartlepool for eighteen years and has been active in the Labour movement for decades. He studied Drama and Theatre Arts at Lancaster University, and was initially a library worker. Citing his socialist father as a key influence, he soon became a trade union activist and a Unison official.

Based in nearby Middlesbrough, he was the regional organiser for Unison until his election. He has been political lead officer for the Unison Northern Region, vice-chair of Labour North, TULO secretary, a member of the Co-operative Party and former branch secretary of Rochdale Branch Unison. He fought the seat of Richmond Yorkshire at the 2015 general election, finishing third behind the Conservatives and UKIP. With the collapse of the UKIP vote and a big uplift in the number of voters for Labour, he more than doubled the majority of retiring Labour MP, Iain Wright. He is married to Glynis. ∎

Wera Hobhouse

LIBERAL DEMOCRAT MP FOR BATH

FORMER MP:	Ben Howlett, Conservative, defeated
MAJORITY:	5,694 (11.5%)
VOTE SHARE:	47.3%
CHANGE:	+17.6%
2ND PLACE:	Con
EU REFERENDUM:	Remain

www.werahobhouse.wordpress.com   @Wera_Hobhouse

WERA HOBHOUSE WAS born in February 1960 in Hanover, Germany, and came to Britain in 1990 having met and married her English husband, William Hobhouse. They both cite the fall of the Berlin Wall, which they travelled to witness in November 1989, as a pivotal moment in their lives. She has had several diverse careers, as a radio journalist, a professional artist and, in the UK, as a teacher of modern languages, being fluent in German, English and French.

Her husband owns and runs a Rochdale-based company, Composite Textiles, and so Rochdale became her home. She has been the company secretary since 2007. She began her political career as a Conservative, elected in 2004 as a Conservative Rochdale councillor.

Her husband was also a Conservative who had stood as a Tory candidate in 1992. They both defected to the Liberal Democrats and she was re-elected in 2006 and 2010, becoming leader of the Liberal Democrat group on Rochdale Council. She stood unsuccessfully in Heywood & Middleton in 2010.

Moving to Bath to be nearer her grown-up children (they have four aged between twenty and twenty-seven), in 2015 she stood unsuccessfully in the Bath and North East Somerset Council elections and fought the North East Somerset seat. A passionate European and internationalist, she is a member of Bath for Europe. She is also member of the governing council of the Electoral Reform Society. ∎

Eddie Hughes

CONSERVATIVE MP FOR WALSALL NORTH

FORMER MP:	David Winnick, Labour, defeated
MAJORITY:	2,601 (6.8%)
VOTE SHARE:	49.6%
CHANGE:	+15.9%
2ND PLACE:	Lab
EU REFERENDUM:	Leave

www.eddiehughes.co.uk   @EddieHughes4WN

EDMUND 'EDDIE' HUGHES was born in Birmingham in October 1968, the son of an Irish immigrant bus driver. He is one of six brothers, one of whom is a Labour Birmingham City councillor. He went to Handsworth Grammar School before studying Civil Engineering at the University of Glamorgan. He was director of development and asset management for YMCA Birmingham and had been appointed assistant chief executive in January 2017.

Since 1999, he has been a Walsall councillor, representing Streetly. He has been chair of the Children's Services Scrutiny and Audit Committee and was cabinet member for Care and Safeguarding between 2015 and 2016. He has also been a local authority governor at St Anne's Catholic Primary School, served on the West Midlands Police Authority and a been a board member at whg (Walsall Housing Group) since 2012; chair since March 2016. He was selected to fight the Walsall North seat over the 2015 candidate, Douglas Hansen-Luke, who had been expected to stand again.

His wife, Clare Hughes, works for PHS Direct, suppliers of workplaces services. They live in Walsall and have two grown-up children. He is a trustee of the Walsall Wood Allotment Charity. ■

Alister Jack

CONSERVATIVE MP FOR DUMFRIES & GALLOWAY

FORMER MP:	Richard Arkless, Scottish National Party (SNP), defeated
MAJORITY:	5,643 (10.9%)
VOTE SHARE:	43.3%
CHANGE:	+13.4%
2ND PLACE:	SNP
EU REFERENDUM:	Remain

@Alister_Jack

BORN IN JULY 1963 in Dumfries, Alister Jack attended Dalbeattie Primary School, the independent Glenalmond school and Heriot-Watt University. His family have been businessmen and farmers in south-west Scotland for several generations and he farms 1,200 acres near Lockerbie.

A highly successful entrepreneur, his first venture was to co-found a tent-hire firm Field & Law in 1987. Ten years later he founded what was to become an international empire of self-storage business, largely under the brand Armadillo. He has sold several of the businesses in the UK and France since 1992, including Aardvark, Paris Lyon and Nice-based Armadillo, becoming a multi-millionaire. Closely involved in

forestry and fishing, he is chairman of Fulling Mill Limited, the River Annan Fishery Board and Trust, and Galloway Woodlands.

He stood in Tweeddale, Ettrick & Lauderdale at the 1997 general election, finishing third behind the Liberal Democrats and Labour. He is a former vice-chairman of the Scottish Conservatives.

He lives at Courance, near Lockerbie, with his wife and they have three grown-up children. ∎

Christine Jardine

LIBERAL DEMOCRAT MP FOR EDINBURGH WEST

FORMER MP:	Michelle Thomson, Scottish National Party (SNP), deselected
MAJORITY:	2,988 (5.7%)
VOTE SHARE:	34.3%
CHANGE:	+1.2%
2ND PLACE:	SNP
EU REFERENDUM:	Remain

www.christinejardine.com   @Cajardine

CHRISTINE JARDINE HAS been a journal-ist, a broadcaster, a university teacher and a media adviser. Having attended Braid-field High School in Clydebank, she studied Modern History and Politics at the University of Glasgow between 1978 and 1982. She later gained a National Council for the Training of Journalists post-graduate cer-tificate from Edinburgh Napier University in 1985.

Beginning in regional journalism, including as editor of the *Deeside Piper*, she became a senior production journalist for the BBC in Glasgow and Aberdeen between 1991 and 1997. She moved to academia at the University of Strathclyde, and spent nearly five years as a lecturer at the Scottish Centre for Journalism Studies, before returning to journalism in 2002 as the Scottish Editor for the Press Association. She served for a short period in 2011 as a media special adviser to Michael Moore MP, then Secretary of State for Scotland under the coalition govern-ment, and has been a media consultant for the Scottish Liberal Democrats ever since.

She fought the Inverness and Nairn seat in the Scottish parliamentary elections in May 2011 and stood in the Aberdeen Don-side Scottish Parliament by-election in June 2013. She also attempted to unseat Alex Salmond in Gordon at the 2015 general election, a feat achieved by the Conserv-atives in 2017.

She is married with one daughter. ∎

Darren Jones

LABOUR MP FOR BRISTOL NORTH WEST

FORMER MP:	Charlotte Leslie, Conservative, defeated
MAJORITY:	4,761 (8.8%)
VOTE SHARE:	50.7%
CHANGE:	+16.2%
2ND PLACE:	Con
EU REFERENDUM:	Remain

@darrenpjones

BORN AND RAISED in the Bristol in the constituency, 'a working-class kid from a council estate', thirty-year old Darren Jones went to school in Lawrence Weston before studying Human Bioscience at the University of Plymouth. Graduating in 2008, he studied for a Post Graduate Certificate in Leadership and Management from the Chartered Management Institute and converted to law, taking a Graduate Diploma in Law at the University of the West of England between 2009 and 2010.

As a trainee solicitor, he worked as a technology, media and communications solicitor at Bond Dickinson LLP for nearly five years, including secondments with RWE npower and BT Consumer. He remained with BT, moving to London and being appointed Legal Counsel in 2015.

He stood in Torridge & West Devon in 2010, and Bristol North West in 2015. He claims to be the first ever Darren elected to the House of Commons. He rebelled against the Labour leadership in June 2017, supporting an amendment in favour of Single Market membership.

During the EU referendum campaign, he was national chair of the Young Lawyers' Network – Stronger In. He worked on the campaign to elect Marvin Rees as Mayor of Bristol and was South West chair of Andy Burnham's Leadership campaign in 2016. He is the director of Future Labour.

He is married to Lucy, an Australian. ∎

Sarah Jones

LABOUR MP FOR CROYDON CENTRAL

FORMER MP:	Gavin Barwell, Conservative, defeated
MAJORITY:	5,652 (9.9%)
VOTE SHARE:	52.3%
CHANGE:	+9.7%
2ND PLACE:	Con
EU REFERENDUM:	Remain

www.sarah-jones.org   @LabourSJ

SARAH JONES, BORN 1972, was brought up in Croydon. She went to the independent Old Palace School in Croydon and read History at Durham University.

She has held a variety of roles in communications and campaigning, including researcher for the late Mo Mowlam MP and then Geraint Davies MP when he was MP for Croydon Central, press officer for the London Labour Party, public affairs and campaigns manager for Shelter, deputy director of communications for the NHS Confederation, director of campaigns and policy at Bond, deputy director of government Olympic communications and strategic communications adviser for Cambridge University Hospitals. Most recently,

she worked for the public affairs and communications firm Quiller Consultants.

She joined the Labour Party in 1992. She has twice stood as a candidate in Croydon Council elections. She contested Croydon Central in 2015, losing by 165 votes to Gavin Barwell, who she defeated in 2017. She is a member of Unite, the Co-operative Party and the Fawcett Society.

She lives in Shirley, Croydon, and has four children ranging in age from early twenties to toddler twins. She is a board member of a South London Housing Association and previously a school governor at Wolsey Junior School in New Addington. ▪

Gillian Keegan

CONSERVATIVE MP FOR CHICHESTER

FORMER MP:	Andrew Tyrie, Conservative, stood down
MAJORITY:	22,621 (37.8%)
VOTE SHARE:	60.1%
CHANGE:	+2.5%
2ND PLACE:	Lab
EU REFERENDUM:	Remain

www.gilliankeegan.com   @GillianKeegan

BORN IN LANCASHIRE, Gillian Keegan went to primary school in Yorkshire and attended St Augustine of Canterbury comprehensive in Huyton, Merseyside. Leaving school at sixteen, she joined Delco Electronics, a subsidiary of General Motors, in Kirby as an apprentice. GM sponsored her to study a degree in Business Studies from Liverpool John Moores University.

She had a 27-year business career as a senior executive in the manufacturing, banking, payments and travel technology sectors, working at NatWest Bank, Mondex/MasterCard International and Amadeus IT Group from 2001 until 2009 in Madrid. After spending 2010 studying for an MSc in Strategy and Leadership from the London Business School, she was Chief Marketing Officer at Travelport until 2012.

Investing in a venture capital fund targeted at technology entrepreneurs, she made the decision in 2013 to pursue a political career. She was elected a Chichester District councillor in 2014 and was cabinet member for Commercial Services. She has been the director of the Conservative's Women2Win since 2015 and fought the unwinnable seat of St Helens South & Whiston in 2015.

She is married to Michael Keegan, son of a former Conservative MP and the current chairman of Fujitsu UK, and has two stepsons in their twenties. She is godmother to two of John Bercow's children, a good friend of her husband. They live in Petworth. ■

Stephen Kerr

CONSERVATIVE MP FOR STIRLING

FORMER MP:	Steven Paterson, Scottish National Party (SNP), defeated
MAJORITY:	148 (0.3%)
VOTE SHARE:	37.1%
CHANGE:	+13.9%
2ND PLACE:	SNP
EU REFERENDUM:	Remain?

www.kerrforstirling.uk   @stephenkerrMP

STEPHEN KERR WAS born in Dundee in September 1960 and raised on a council estate in Forfar, Angus. His father was a trade butcher and worked for the local branch of the Co-op; his mother was a shop assistant. He attended Forfar West Primary School and the Forfar Academy. He left school at sixteen to work as a junior bank officer with the Royal Bank of Scotland. After returning from a two-year period of church voluntary service as a missionary in London, he studied at Stirling University, graduating with an honours degree in Business in 1986.

He has spent over thirty years working for Kimberley-Clark Professional in a variety of sales and senior executive roles in the UK, Ireland and France. More recently he has run his own sales business.

He was a Scottish Young Conservative as a teenager and was chairman of the University of Stirling Conservative Association and vice-chairman of the Scottish Federation of Conservative Students. He was chairman of the Stirling Conservative Association. He stood as the Conservative candidate in Stirling at the 2005 and 2015 general elections.

He married Yvonne in 1983 and they have four adult children. They have lived in Bridge of Allan since the early 1980s. He is a senior member of the Church of Jesus Christ of Latter-day Saints. ▪

Afzal Khan CBE

LABOUR MP FOR MANCHESTER GORTON

FORMER MP:	Gerald Kaufman, Labour, deceased
MAJORITY:	31,730 (69.0%)
VOTE SHARE:	76.3%
CHANGE:	+9.3%
2ND PLACE:	Con
EU REFERENDUM:	Remain

www.afzalkhan.org.uk   @Afzal4Gorton

BORN IN APRIL 1958 in Jhelum, Pakistan, Afzal Khan came to the UK at the age of eleven when he was adopted out of poverty as a child. After leaving school without qualifications, he worked as a labourer in a cotton mill, as a bus driver and as a Greater Manchester Police constable, before returning to education in 1989 to study law at Manchester Metropolitan University. He is now a partner in the law firm Mellor & Jackson in Oldham.

He served as a Manchester City councillor from 2000 until 2014, representing Cheetham ward and served as executive member for Children's Services. He was the first British Pakistani and Muslim Lord Mayor of Manchester in 2005. He has been an MEP representing North West England since 2014. He was selected to be Labour's candidate in the Manchester Gorton by-election, which was suspended when the 2017 snap election was called. He is Manchester's first Muslim MP.

He has served as Assistant Secretary-General of the Muslim Council of Britain and is currently its North West representative. A founding member of Hope not Hate and Unite Against Fascism, he also advised the UK Government on preventing extremism and was awarded a CBE for his work on community cohesion and race relations work.

He is married with a daughter and two sons, one of whom has also been a Manchester City councillor. ▪

Gerard Killen

LABOUR (AND CO-OPERATIVE PARTY) MP
FOR RUTHERGLEN & HAMILTON WEST

FORMER MP:	Margaret Ferrier, Scottish National Party (SNP), defeated
MAJORITY:	265 (0.5%)
VOTE SHARE:	37.5%
CHANGE:	+2.3%
2ND PLACE:	SNP
EU REFERENDUM:	Remain?

@Gedk

BORN IN MAY 1986, Gerard 'Ged' Killen attended Trinity High School and St
Columbkille's in Rutherglen. In 2008 he
started his own construction business,
Sennit Construction Limited.

He joined the Labour Party in 2007. He
stood unsuccessfully in the 2012 local elections to South Lanarkshire Council. A year
later he was elected at a by-election to represent Rutherglen South. He was re-elected in
May 2017, standing in the Rutherglen Central & North ward, but since his election to
Westminster he has confirmed that he will
stand down later in 2017. He is a prominent local leader in the LGBT community. ▪

Lesley Laird

LABOUR MP FOR KIRKCALDY & COWDENBEATH

FORMER MP:	Roger Mullin, Scottish National Party (SNP), defeated
MAJORITY:	259 (0.6%)
VOTE SHARE:	36.8%
CHANGE:	+3.5%
2ND PLACE:	SNP
EU REFERENDUM:	Remain

www.lesleylaird.com   @LesleyLaird

LESLEY LAIRD WAS appointed as shadow Secretary of State for Scotland a day before she had even been sworn in as an MP. Days before, she had only just managed to overturn an SNP majority of nearly 10,000 to recapture the former seat of Gordon Brown, to whom she dedicated the win. Born in 1958, she was educated at James Watt College, Caledonian University's Institute of Personnel Management and Napier University, graduating with a BA in Business Management and Human Resources.

She worked in the electronic, semiconductor and finance service sectors in various human resources roles. Latterly she worked for RBS Group from 2007 and as a senior talent manager between 2009 and 2012. She is a qualified executive coach from the Institute of Leadership and Management.

She was elected to Fife Council in May 2012 as councillor for Inverkeithing, Aberdour, Dalgety Bay and Hillend, appointed spokesperson for Economy and Planning in February 2013 and one year later was elected by colleagues to the deputy leader post. She is a board member of the Fife Economy Partnership, Business Gateway, Fife Coast & Countryside Trust and a trustee of the Muir Dean Trust. She is also chair of TAYplan and sits on the SESplan planning committee. She attends COSLA and is a member of the East of Scotland Advisory board and Unison. She supported Andy Burnham and Kezia Dugdale in the 2015 Labour leadership elections. ∎

Ben Lake

PLAID CYMRU MP FOR CEREDIGION

FORMER MP:	Mark Williams, Liberal Democrat, defeated
MAJORITY:	104 (0.3%)
VOTE SHARE:	29.2%
CHANGE:	+1.6%
2ND PLACE:	Lib Dem
EU REFERENDUM:	Remain

@BenMLake

BORN IN 1993, Ben Lake is the youngest MP of the 2017 intake, and the second youngest in the Commons, only older to the SNP's Mhairi Black. A Welsh-speaker brought up in Lampeter, he attended Lampeter Comprehensive School, where he was head boy, and Trinity College, Oxford University, where he studied Politics and History. He also undertook a Master of Studies postgraduate degree at Oxford into Modern British and European Studies.

Since 2016 he has worked as a Researcher for Elin Jones AM and Llyr Gruffydd AM and provided support for Plaid AMs on education, finance and transport policy. As one of four Plaid Cymru MPs, he now finds himself covering several government departments, including health, education, CLG, DCMS and DEFRA.

This was the only seat gain for Plaid Cymru in 2017; they reclaimed a constituency that they had lost to the Liberal Democrats in 2005. ▪

John Lamont

CONSERVATIVE MP FOR BERWICKSHIRE, ROXBURGH & SELKIRK

FORMER MP:	Calum Kerr, Scottish National Party (SNP), defeated
MAJORITY:	11,060 (21.1%)
VOTE SHARE:	53.9%
CHANGE:	+17.9%
2ND PLACE:	SNP
EU REFERENDUM:	Remain

www.johnlamont.org   @John2Win

AFTER THREE PREVIOUS unsuccessful attempts, in 2005, 2010 and 2015, John Lamont was confident that he would finally overturn the SNP's 328 vote majority. He announced in May 2017, shortly after the election campaign got underway, that he was standing down, after ten years, from the Scottish Parliament's corresponding seat.

Born in April 1976 in Kilwinning, Lamont is the son of Berwickshire farmer and a former local teacher. He was educated at the local Kilwinning Academy and studied at the School of Law of the University of Glasgow, leaving with a First Class degree in Commercial Law and Tax. After attending the College of Law in Chester between 1998 and 2000, he headed to London to work for the magic circle firm giant Freshfields Bruckhaus Deringer, and then Bristows. He returned to Scotland in 2005 to work at Brodies in Edinburgh.

He was first elected to Holyrood in 2007 as the Conservative MSP for Ettrick, Roxburgh & Berwickhsire. Taking over the justice brief, he rose to become the Scottish Conservative chief whip and parliamentary business manager.

Away from politics, he is a triathlete and ironman competitor, and is believed to be the first UK politician to complete an ironman triathlon. ∎

Karen Lee

LABOUR MP FOR LINCOLN

FORMER MP:	Karl McCartney, Conservative, defeated
MAJORITY:	1,538 (3.2%)
VOTE SHARE:	47.9%
CHANGE:	+8.3%
2ND PLACE:	Con
EU REFERENDUM:	Remain?

@KarenLeeMP

KAREN LEE WAS born in Lincoln and has lived in the town all of her life. She attended St Hugh's Roman Catholic school, South Park school and Lincoln College.

She has been an NHS nurse since 2003, working at Lincoln County Hospital. She has already promised to continue working as a nurse on a bank staff (zero hours) contract, donating the money she earns to food banks and other local charities.

She joined the Labour Party in 1994 and is a long-standing member of Unite and Unison, describing herself as a lifelong socialist and trade unionist. She was first elected as a Lincoln City councillor representing the Carholme ward in 2003 and served as the Mayor of Lincoln from 2012

until 2013. She is the council's representative on the Citizens Advice Bureau in Lincoln.

The former MP Karl McCartney was much criticised during the campaign when he was the only one of seven candidates who did not participate in a live election debate. A bellwether constituency, Lincoln has mirrored the national swing in UK general elections since 1974 and was the only seat in Lincolnshire to be won by Labour.

Lee is married and has four children all living in the city. ▪

Andrew Lewer MBE

CONSERVATIVE MP FOR NORTHAMPTON SOUTH

FORMER MP:	David Mackintosh, Conservative, stood down
MAJORITY:	1,159 (2.8%)
VOTE SHARE:	46.9%
CHANGE:	+5.3%
2ND PLACE:	Lab
EU REFERENDUM:	Leave

www.andrewlewer.com   @ALewerMBE

ANDREW LEWER WAS born in July 1971, and attended Queen Elizabeth's Grammar School in Ashbourne before studying History at Newcastle University and Downing College, Cambridge University.

He briefly worked in publishing locally before pursuing a political career. He was first elected to Derbyshire Dales District Council in 2003 before being elected to Derbyshire County Council in 2005, becoming first opposition leader and then leader of the council when the Conservatives gained control in 2009, the youngest county council leader in the country at the time. He was awarded an MBE for his services to local government. At the time he was chairman of the Derwent Valley Mills World Heritage Site committee, the

founding chairman of the Health and Wellbeing board and a founding director of the Local Enterprise Partnership for Derbyshire and Nottinghamshire – D2N2. He has been a vice-president of the LGA since 2014.

After Derbyshire County Council reverted to Labour control in 2003, he moved to new pastures and was elected to the European Parliament representing the East Midlands in May 2014. He was appointed to the Regional Development Committee and the Culture Committee. Although broadly Eurosceptic in outlook, he has said that he did not get elected to Brussels simply to push for Brexit, but only decided he was a 'pragmatic Leaver' after the disappointing deal negotiated by David Cameron. ∎

David Linden

SCOTTISH NATIONAL PARTY (SNP) MP FOR GLASGOW EAST

FORMER MP:	Natalie McGarry, Scottish National Party, deselected
MAJORITY:	75 (0.2%)
VOTE SHARE:	38.8%
CHANGE:	-18.1%
2ND PLACE:	Lab
EU REFERENDUM:	Remain

www.davidlinden.scot   @DavidLinden

HAVING BEEN SELECTED to replace the deselected sitting MP Natalie McGarry, David Linden was the SNP's only new MP at the 2017 general election, scraping home by a mere seventy-five votes ahead of Labour's Kate Watson. Born in May 1990 and originally from Cranhill, he moved to Garrowhill in the East End of Glasgow as a child, going to Garrowhill Primary school and then Bannerman High School in Baillieston.

He spent his early working life in the underwriting team at Access Loans & Mortgages, then undertook a qualification in Business Administration, which he completed during his years at Glasgow Credit Union.

After the SNP's 2008 Glasgow East by-election victory he worked as a caseworker in the constituency office of John Mason MP, assisting him in both Holyrood and Westminster. More recently he has worked as a parliamentary assistant to Alison Thewliss, the SNP MP for Glasgow Central since 2015.

He was National Convener of Young Scots for Independence (YSI), the youth wing of the SNP, between 2011 and 2014. He is a former branch organiser of Shettleston SNP and was the campaign manager for the successful Yes Shettleston campaign during the independence referendum.

He is married to Roslyn, a primary school teacher, and they have one young son, Isaac. ■

Emma Little-Pengelly

DEMOCRATIC UNIONIST PARTY (DUP) MP
FOR BELFAST SOUTH

FORMER MP:	Alasdair McDonnell, Social and Democratic Labour Party (SDLP), defeated
MAJORITY:	1,996 (4.6%)
VOTE SHARE:	30.4%
CHANGE:	8.2%
2ND PLACE:	SDLP
EU REFERENDUM:	Leave

www.littlepengelly.com   @little_pengelly

BORN IN DECEMBER 1979, Emma Little-Pengelly is a seasoned Democratic Unionist politician who has worked at the highest levels in the party. She studied Law at Queen's University Belfast on two scholarships and at Harvard Kennedy School. She practiced as a Barrister in Belfast between 2003 and 2007, while also working as a part-time law lecturer and tutor at the University of Ulster.

Since 2007 she has worked as a special adviser in the Office of the First Minister, first to Dr Ian Paisley and then to Peter Robinson. She was co-opted to the Northern Ireland Assembly in September 2015 to represent South Belfast. She replaced Jimmy Spratt who retired on health grounds and was appointed as a junior minister in the First Minister's Office. Following the 2016 Assembly election, she was chair of the Assembly's Finance Committee. She lost her seat in the Assembly in 2017 after a reduction in Belfast South seats, missing out by forty-nine votes. Contributing to a wipe-out of all three SDLP Westminster seats at the general election, former FM Peter Robinson was reportedly the chief strategist behind her campaign.

She is the daughter of the loyalist Noel Little, who served a prison sentence for arms trafficking. She is married to Richard Pengelly, the Permanent Secretary at the Department of Health, Social Services and Public Safety in Belfast. ▪

Stephen Lloyd

LIBERAL DEMOCRAT MP FOR EASTBOURNE

FORMER MP:	Caroline Ansell, Conservative, defeated
MAJORITY:	1,609 (2.8%)
VOTE SHARE:	46.9%
CHANGE:	+8.7%
2ND PLACE:	Con
EU REFERENDUM:	Remain

www.stephenlloyd.org.uk   @StephenLloydEBN

STEPHEN LLOYD IS one of the quartet of former Liberal Democrat MPs returning to Westminster after losing in 2015. He had originally announced this retirement from politics but supposedly reversed his decision having been canvassed by local supporters.

Born in June 1957, he was brought up in the coastal city of Mombasa, Kenya, though was educated at the independent St George's College in Weybridge from the age of eight. He is hearing-impaired, retaining only partial hearing in his right ear. Before embarking upon a political career, he worked in business for over twenty years, including as business development director between 1998 and 2005 at WPP-owned The Grass Roots Group and, until his election, at the Federation of Small Businesses.

Having contested the safe Tory seat of Beaconsfield in 2001 and Eastbourne for the first time in 2005, he was eventually elected at the 2010 general election. He served as a parliamentary private secretary to colleague Ed Davey MP, as energy secretary, but resigned after a year over the coalition government's transport strategy. Ordinarily a party loyalist, he voted against the tuition fee increases.

Having lost the seat in 2015 by 733 votes, he was appointed as the business development director for West End Studios, an international events company based in Eastbourne. ∎

Tony Lloyd

LABOUR MP FOR ROCHDALE

FORMER MP:	Simon Danczuk, Labour/Independent, defeated
MAJORITY:	14,819 (29.6%)
VOTE SHARE:	58.0%
CHANGE:	+11.9%
2ND PLACE:	Con
EU REFERENDUM:	Remain

@Tony4Rochdale

WHEN TONY LLOYD stepped down from his Stretford constituency in 2012 to successfully become the new Greater Manchester Police Commissioner, it was generally assumed that his 29-year Westminster career had ended. But having lost the Labour Party mayoral candidacy to Andy Burnham, after being interim Mayor for two years, he made a surprise return in 2017 following a last-minute selection battle.

Born in 1950, he attended Stretford Grammar School for Boys, the University of Nottingham and Manchester Business School, where he studied for an MBA degree. He lectured in Business Studies at the University of Salford, served as a Trafford councillor from 1979 until 1984, represented the Stretford constituency from 1983 until 1997 and the Manchester Central constituency from 1997 until his resignation in 2012.

He was an opposition spokesperson for ten years, a Foreign Office minister between 1997 and 1999 under Robin Cook and was chair of the Parliamentary Labour Party from 2006 until 2012. The disgraced incumbent former Labour MP Simon Danczuk could only manage fifth place in 2017, having been banned by Labour from standing. In July 2017, Lloyd was appointed as a frontbench Housing spokesperson.

He has been married to Judith since 1974 and they have three daughters and a son. ∎

Rachel Maclean

CONSERVATIVE MP FOR REDDITCH

FORMER MP:	Karen Lumley, Conservative, stood down
MAJORITY:	7,363 (16.3%)
VOTE SHARE:	52.3%
CHANGE:	+5.2%
2ND PLACE:	Lab
EU REFERENDUM:	Remain

www.rachelmaclean.org   @redditchrachel

BORN IN OCTOBER 1965 in the West Midlands, Rachel Maclean was educated at a local comprehensive. She read Experimental Psychology at St Hugh's College, Oxford University and Work and Occupational Psychology for a Master's from Aston University.

Her business career kicked off with a graduate fast track management scheme with HSBC in 1989, working in Hong Kong, Sydney and Tokyo. A couple of sales jobs followed in the technology publishing sector, including one that took her to work in Chicago, Illinois. Between 2000 and 2002 she worked part-time as a post-natal teacher at the National Childbirth Trust. She and her husband, David, set up a Birmingham-based publishing company, Packt Publishing in

2005, specialising in IT and software content. She has since helped develop several technology firms, including Air and Hollywood Monster. Since 2015 she has been a regional council member of the CBI.

With little background in politics, she was selected to fight the Birmingham Northfield seat in 2015. She co-chaired Andy Street's successful West Midlands mayoral campaign.

She has four grown children with her husband David and lives in Kings Norton. She sits on the board of trustees of local charity, Love Brum, and is the founder of Skilled and Ready, a not-for-profit education provider. She has served fifteen years as a Scout leader, been a school governor and taught Sunday School for her local church. ∎

Sandy Martin

LABOUR MP FOR IPSWICH

FORMER MP:	Ben Gummer, Conservative, defeated
MAJORITY:	836 (1.6%)
VOTE SHARE:	47.4%
CHANGE:	+10.3%
2ND PLACE:	Con
EU REFERENDUM:	Remain

@sandyofipswich

SANDY MARTIN'S VICTORY over the Conservative minister Ben Gummer was one of the high-profile results of the 2017 election. Born in May 1957, he worked at the Ipswich Community Resource Centre, a drop-in advice centre for the unemployed, and served as the coordinator for Ipswich & District Friends of the Earth, before deciding to devote himself to politics full-time.

He has been a Suffolk County councillor since 1997, representing the St John's division. He has been leader of the Labour group on the council. He served for thirteen years as an Ipswich Borough councillor and is a member of the LGBT Labour campaign. He has been a director of campaign group Labour Coast & Country, Ipswich and

Suffolk Council for Racial Equality, a director of Ipswich Disabled Advice Bureau and a school governor. In 1994 he stood for the European Parliament on Labour's regional list. He sits as one of the four East of England representatives on Labour's National Policy Forum, serving on the Transport Commission. He is a member of numerous political groups and campaigns, including Unite, the Fabian Society, SERA, Stonewall, Friends of the Earth, War on Want, CND and Amnesty International.

He has lived in Suffolk most of his life and moved to Ipswich in 1993. His partner is an actor. ▪

Paul Masterton

CONSERVATIVE MP FOR EAST RENFREWSHIRE

FORMER MP:	Kirsten Oswald, Scottish National Party (SNP), defeated
MAJORITY:	4,712 (8.8%)
VOTE SHARE:	40.0%
CHANGE:	+18.0%
2ND PLACE:	SNP
EU REFERENDUM:	Remain

www.paulmasterton.org.uk   @Masterton4EastRen

THIRTY-ONE-YEAR-OLD PAUL MAS-TERTON was educated at George Watson's College and the University of Dundee between 2003 and 2007, where he studied Scots Law. Qualifying as a solicitor in 2010, he worked for McGrigors until 2012 and Pinsent Masons in Glasgow until his election, specialising in pensions law. He is a member of the Association of Pension Lawyers.

The head of his local Conservative association branch, he stood unsuccessfully for election as an MSP at the 2016 Scottish Parliament election. He emerged victorious from a tough three-way contest with SNP incumbent Kirsten Oswald and Labour's Blair McDougall, the head of the 2014 Better Together campaign. He is the first Conservative to represent the seat since 1992 and the region's first Tory MP for two decades.

He lives in Paisley with wife Heather and baby daughter Daisy. At the start of the election campaign he adopted a more professional twitter name, having previously used @gingertwit. ∎

Elisha McCallion

SINN FÉIN MP FOR FOYLE

FORMER MP:	Mark Durkan, Social Democratic and Labour Party (SDLP), defeated
MAJORITY:	169 (0.4%)
VOTE SHARE:	39.7%
CHANGE:	+8.2%
2ND PLACE:	SDLP
EU REFERENDUM:	Remain

@GlenCentFifeSNP

BORN IN OCTOBER 1981, Elisha McCallion has been a political and community activist since her teens. She was first elected to Derry City Council in 2005 representing the Shantallow ward and became the first Mayor of the new Derry City and Strabane District Council in 2015. She successfully initiated the European Youth Capital bid, with the result that 2019 will be a year of youth in the North West region.

In March 2017, she was elected to the Northern Ireland Assembly representing Foyle, finishing top with the most first-preference votes and holding the seat previously held by the late Martin McGuinness. She won by only 169 votes, and this election was the first time that the SDLP has lost the seat since the 1983 general election. Following the well-established Sinn Féin policy of abstentionism, she will not be taking up her seat in Westminster.

She is married to Declan and the couple have three children. ∎

Barry McElduff

SINN FÉIN MP FOR WEST TYRONE

FORMER MP:	Pat Doherty, Sinn Féin MP, stood down
MAJORITY:	10,342 (23.8%)
VOTE SHARE:	50.7%
CHANGE:	+7.2%
2ND PLACE:	DUP
EU REFERENDUM:	Remain

@BarryMcElduff

BARRY MCELDUFF WAS born in August 1966 in County Tyrone. He attended the Christian Brothers Grammar School in Omagh before attending Queen's University Belfast, where he graduated in Political Science and Celtic Studies.

He is a member of Sinn Féin's Ard Comhairle and sits on the Tyrone Sinn Féin commemoration committee. At the 1992 general election, he unsuccessfully contested Mid Ulster. He was elected to the Northern Ireland Forum for the West Tyrone constituency in 1996, and has since held this seat on the Northern Ireland Assembly. In 2000 he was elected to Omagh District Council. He has chaired the Culture, Arts and Leisure Committee of the Assembly and the Committee for Education

between 2016 and 2017. As with all Sinn Féin MPs, he follows a policy of abstentionism and will not take his seat in Westminster.

He was given an eighteen-month suspended sentence in 1992 for helping in the false imprisonment of a Protestant whom the IRA suspected of being an informer. The victim was interrogated by three masked IRA men in Sinn Féin's Dungannon offices, but the court heard that McElduff had saved the victim from execution.

He is married to Paula and they have three grown up children; Niamh, Bláthnaid and Patrick. He has played Gaelic football at senior level. He has published two quirky autobiographical books: *Keep 'Er Lit* and *Sustain the Flame.* ▪

Anna McMorrin

LABOUR MP FOR CARDIFF NORTH

FORMER MP:	Craig Williams, Conservative, defeated
MAJORITY:	4,174 (8.0%)
VOTE SHARE:	50.1%
CHANGE:	+11.9%
2ND PLACE:	Con
EU REFERENDUM:	Remain

@annamcmorrin

BORN IN SEPTEMBER 1971, Anna McMorrin grew up near Brecon, and attended Brecon High School. She graduated in 1994 having studied French and Politics at the University of Southampton and in 1997, she graduated from Cardiff University, with a post-graduate diploma in Journalism.

After working as a part-time communications officer for the Labour Party in the run-up to the 1997 general election, she joined the global public affairs and communications consultancy Hill & Knowlton. In 2006, she became campaigns and communications director for Friends of the Earth Cymru.

In 2008 she joined the Welsh Government, becoming an environment and sustainability adviser to ministers, working for Rhodri Morgan, then Carwyn Jones and then Alun Davies. In 2014 she was moved to another position internally after starting a relationship with her ministerial boss, Alun Davies. After a short period working independently as a consultant, she joined Invicta Public Affairs as head of Invicta's office in Cardiff in October 2016. She is a member of the Co-operative Party. She was shortlisted for the Merthyr Tydfil & Rhymney seat to the Welsh Assembly in early 2016.

She now lives in Cardiff with Alun Davies AM, the current Minister for Lifelong Learning and the Welsh Language, and has two teenage daughters from a previous marriage. ∎

Rt Hon Esther McVey

CONSERVATIVE MP FOR TATTON

FORMER MP:	George Osborne, Conservative, stood down
MAJORITY:	14,787 (30.1%)
VOTE SHARE:	58.6%
CHANGE:	-0.1%
2ND PLACE:	Lab
EU REFERENDUM:	Leave

www.esthermcvey.com   @EstherMcVey1

ESTHER MCVEY'S DEFEAT in Wirral West was one of the headlines of the 2015 election, but now she has returned courtesy of George Osborne's old constituency of Tatton. Born in October 1967 in Liverpool, she is of Irish Catholic descent. She was educated at the independent Belvedere School, before reading Law at Queen Mary University and Radio Journalism at City University London.

Beginning as a graduate trainee with the BBC in 1991, she became a successful television presenter and producer with the BBC, ITV and Channel 4, including co-presenting GMTV. She left the media in 2001 to join her family's construction and demolition business, J G McVey & Co, as a director. She also set up her business, Making It (UK)

Ltd, providing training for SMEs. In July 2009, she graduated with an MSc (with Distinction) in Corporate Governance from Liverpool John Moores University.

Having failed at her first attempt in Wirral West in 2005, she succeeded at the next election in 2010. She served as Minister of State for Employment from 2013 to 2015, and Junior Minister for Disabled People between 2012 and 2013. Since her defeat, she has gathered a range of roles: chair of British Transport Police Authority, a special adviser to the private investment firm Floreat Group, a senior consultant with communications firm Hume Brophy, lecturer at the University of Liverpool and a Fellowship from the University of Hull. ∎

Damien Moore

CONSERVATIVE MP FOR SOUTHPORT

FORMER MP:	Dr John Pugh, Liberal Democrat, stood down
MAJORITY:	2,914 (6.1%)
VOTE SHARE:	38.7%
CHANGE:	+10.7%
2ND PLACE:	Lab
EU REFERENDUM:	Leave?

@moore4southport

BORN IN CUMBRIA, 37-year old Damien Moore moved to live in Preston in 2002 after taking up a place at the University of Central Lancashire to read History. After graduating, he took up a graduate position with Asda and has worked for sixteen years as a retail manager at various locations for national companies throughout the north-west.

He has been a councillor on Preston City Council since 2012, representing the Greyfriars ward, where he was deputy leader of the Conservative group on the council. He is a former chairman of Preston Conservative Association, currently Lancashire Area chairman. He stood unsuccessfully in Preston West at the Lancashire County elections in 2013 and 2017.

The 2017 election was his second attempt at winning the Southport seat, having stood in 2015. The seat had been represented by the Liberal Democrats since 1997. He is the only Conservative MP to be elected to the whole of Merseyside, Wirral, Halton and Warrington. ■

Layla Moran

LIBERAL DEMOCRAT MP FOR OXFORD WEST & ABINGDON

FORMER MP:	Nicola Blackwood, Conservative, defeated
MAJORITY:	816 (1.4%)
VOTE SHARE:	43.7%
CHANGE:	+14.8%
2ND PLACE:	Con
EU REFERENDUM:	Remain

www.laylamoran.com   @laylamoran

BORN TO A British diplomat father and a Christian Palestinian mother from Jerusalem in September 1982, Layla Moran is the first MP of Palestinian descent and the first female Liberal Democrat MP from a minority background. Because of her father's diplomatic career, she grew up all over the world including Belgium, Ethiopia and Greece. As a child she attended schools in Brussels, Kingston Jamaica and Brighton. She studied Physics at Imperial College, completed a PGCE at Brunel University and studied a Master's degree in Comparative Education at the Institute of Education.

She has been a maths and physics teacher at the International School of Brussels, Queensmead School in London and Southbank International School in London. Since 2009 she has worked for Oxford Study Courses, including as a part-time course tutor, a full-time academic manager and as an academic development manager.

She was selected as the Liberal Democrat candidate for Battersea at the 2010 general election, stood as a candidate for West Central at the London Assembly 2012 election and stood in the Oxford West and Abingdon seat in 2015. Elected in 2017 by only 816 votes on a strongly anti-Brexit platform, and unseating junior Health Minister Nicola Blackwood, she was named as party spokesperson for Education, Science and Young Peoples shortly after. ∎

Stephen Morgan

LABOUR MP FOR PORTSMOUTH SOUTH

FORMER MP:	Flick Drummond, Conservative, defeated
MAJORITY:	1,554 (3.5%)
VOTE SHARE:	41.0%
CHANGE:	+21.5%
2ND PLACE:	Con
EU REFERENDUM:	Remain?

www.stephenjmorgan.org   @sjmorganuk

STEPHEN MORGAN WAS born in January 1981 and grew up in Fratton. He went to Priory School and Portsmouth College before becoming the first member of his family to go to university, studying Politics and Sociology at the University of Bristol and Politics as a Master's degree at Goldsmiths in London.

He worked for various departments at Portsmouth City Council, including as the chief executive's office strategy adviser, before becoming head of community engagement for the Royal Borough of Kensington and Chelsea in 2008, commuting by train to London. In 2015 he became the chief executive of third-sector umbrella organisation, Basingstoke Voluntary Action.

A party member since the age of sixteen, once free of restrictions on standing for public office, he quickly stood for election and was elected to represent the Charles Dickens ward on Portsmouth City Council in May 2016. By the end of the year he was the leader of the Portsmouth Labour Group. He has been a local school governor and is a trustee of Age UK Portsmouth. In 2016 he was allegedly one of 600 Labour councillors who signed a petition calling for Jeremy Corbyn to stand down as party leader.

He is the first Labour MP to represent the constituency since its creation in 1918. He plans to remain a councillor at least until his current term ends in 2020. ∎

Alex Norris

LABOUR (AND CO-OPERATIVE PARTY) MP
FOR NOTTINGHAM NORTH

FORMER MP:	Graham Allen, Labour, stood down
MAJORITY:	11,160 (29.1%)
VOTE SHARE:	60.2%
CHANGE:	+5.6%
2ND PLACE:	Con
EU REFERENDUM:	Remain?

@ANorrisMP

BORN IN MANCHESTER, Alex Norris attended the independent Manchester Grammar School and the University of Nottingham, and he has remained in Nottingham ever since.

A Unison trade union organiser and member of the GMB, he has worked for the Labour Party and the former constituency MP of thirty years, Graham Allen, and Nottingham City Council.

He was elected to Nottingham City Council in 2011 representing the Basford ward. Until his election to Parliament he was a member of the executive board with responsibility for the Adults and Health portfolio and he chairs the City's Health and Wellbeing board. Until late 2015 he also had responsibility on the council for the voluntary and community sector. He is the chair of governors at Rosslyn Park Primary School. He is a member of the General Assembly of the Local Government Association and the National Society for Clean Air and Environmental Protection.

His partner is the deputy regional director of the Labour Party. ▪

Neil O'Brien OBE

CONSERVATIVE MP FOR HARBOROUGH

FORMER MP:	Sir Edward Garnier, Conservative, stood down
MAJORITY:	12,429 (21.6%)
VOTE SHARE:	52.3%
CHANGE:	-0.4%
2ND PLACE:	Lab
EU REFERENDUM:	Unknown

@NeilDotObrien

BORN IN 1978, Neil O'Brien grew up in Huddersfield, the son of two Scottish parents. After attending a local comprehensive and Greenhead College, he graduated from Christ Church College, Oxford, in 2000 with a First in PPE.

In 2000 he joined 'Business for Sterling' campaigning against UK membership of the Euro, campaigned for an EU referendum in 2003 and was the founder of the Open Europe think tank in 2005. Between 2008 and 2012 he was director of leading think tank Policy Exchange. George Osborne brought him on board in 2012 as a special adviser and he is credited with being a major influence behind the development of the Northern Powerhouse concept. He was awarded an OBE in David Cameron's resignation honours list. On entering Downing Street, Theresa May appointed him to her Policy Unit in August 2016 with responsibility for industrial strategy and the Northern Powerhouse.

He has joked that he was briefly a member of the Socialist Workers Party at seventeen, but was not any good at selling the newspaper. Undoubtedly one of the most influential political thinkers of the last ten years, he has co-authored a book *The Renewal of Government*, is a regular media commentator and has written extensively for the national press. He is the chair of governors for a primary school. ∎

Jared O'Mara

LABOUR MP FOR SHEFFIELD HALLAM

FORMER MP:	Nick Clegg, Liberal Democrat, defeated
MAJORITY:	2,125 (3.7%)
VOTE SHARE:	38.4%
CHANGE:	+2.6%
2ND PLACE:	Lib Dem
EU REFERENDUM:	Remain

@SueHayman1

JARED O'MARA'S DEFEAT of Nick Clegg, former Deputy PM and Liberal Democrat leader since 2005, was one of the key moments of the 2017 election night. Born in Sheffield in 1981, his father is a retired train driver and his mother did various jobs including working in a chip shop. He was diagnosed as having cerebral palsy when he was six months old, but has confounded early predictions that he would likely be wheelchair-bound, although he does have some mobility and dexterity restrictions. He attended Tapton School and Staffordshire University, graduating with a First in Journalism.

He worked for the British Council of Disabled People after university as a press, parliamentary and campaigns officer. He has spent the last eleven years in the music and entertainment industry, promoting bands in Sheffield and he co-founded a successful bar and music venue, West Street Live. He is a governor and trustee of Paces, a school and community resource for disabled people.

A party member since being seventeen, he stood for election to Sheffield City Council in 2016 in Ecclesfield West. He is a staunch Corbyn supporter who actively supported both his leadership campaigns. Labour have not previously held the Sheffield Hallam seat since it was formed in 1885. Labour enjoyed a modest vote share increase in this affluent constituency with a large student population, but also greatly benefited from a 10 per cent increase in the third-place Conservative vote. ∎

Fiona Onasanya

LABOUR MP FOR PETERBOROUGH

FORMER MP:	Stewart Jackson, Conservative, defeated
MAJORITY:	607 (1.3%)
VOTE SHARE:	48.1%
CHANGE:	+12.5%
2ND PLACE:	Con
EU REFERENDUM:	Remain

@FionaOnasanyaMP

BORN IN AUGUST 1983, Fiona Onasanya is of Nigerian heritage. She was educated at the Netherhall School, a comprehensive in Cambridge, as well as the University of Hertfordshire and the College of Law.

Before the election, she had been a solicitor at DC Law in St Ives, Cambridgeshire, since August 2016, undertaking general commercial and residential property work. She had previously spent three years with Eversheds in Cambridge and two years with Nockolds LLP.

She joined the Labour Party having been approached by a local party secretary who overheard her talking in a pub in the aftermath of the London riots in 2011. A Cambridgeshire County councillor for King's Hedges in Cambridge since 2013, she was deputy leader of the Labour group on the council and spokesperson for Children and Young People. She stood unsuccessfully to be the Labour mayoral candidate for the Cambridge and Peterborough mayoral contest in May 2017, won by the Conservative's James Palmer.

She lives in Paston and is a committed Christian, attending the iCAN Community Church. She has been a trustee of East Hertfordshire YMCA since 2011. ∎

Stephanie Peacock

LABOUR MP FOR BARNSLEY EAST

FORMER MP:	Michael Dugher, Labour, stood down
MAJORITY:	13,283 (32.6%)
VOTE SHARE:	59.5%
CHANGE:	+4.8%
2ND PLACE:	Con
EU REFERENDUM:	Remain

www.stephaniepeacock.co.uk @Steph_Peacock

STEPHANIE PEACOCK WAS born in December 1986 in Birmingham and was brought up in Halesowen. Her mother is an NHS worker and her father is a care worker. She attended Lordswood Girls' School Birmingham and King Edward VI College, Stourbridge. She graduated in History from Queen Mary, University of London, studying trade union and Labour history, has a PGCE from Canterbury Christ Church University and a Master's degree from the Institute of Education at the University of London.

She worked for two Labour MPs, including Sylvia Heal MP, in both their constituency offices and Westminster between 2005 and 2010. She was later to fight Sylvia Heal's old seat of Halesowen and Rowley Regis in 2015. She was as a secondary school history and politics teacher between 2010 and 2012 and worked as a trade union tutor with adults for a year. Since 2013 she worked as a GMB trade union political officer for the Birmingham and West Midlands Region.

She is a former chair of Young Labour in the West Midlands and was the Youth representative on the party's ruling National Executive Committee between 2008 and 2011. She is a West Midlands representative on Labour's National Policy Forum and a member of the Early Years, Education and Skills Policy Commission.

In 2012 the *Birmingham Mail* reported that she was the new partner of Tom Watson MP, Deputy Labour leader. ∎

Laura Pidcock

LABOUR MP FOR NORTH WEST DURHAM

FORMER MP:	Pat Glass, Labour, stood down
MAJORITY:	8,792 (18.4%)
VOTE SHARE:	52.8%
CHANGE:	+6.0%
2ND PLACE:	Con
EU REFERENDUM:	Remain?

@PidcockNWDurham

BORN IN JUNE 1988 in Cramlington, Northumberland, Laura Pidcock is a well-known figure in Labour circles in the North East. The daughter of a social worker and a Citizens Advice Bureau manager, she worked as a mental health support worker while studying politics at Manchester Metropolitan University. She spent eight years as an education worker in the North East for the campaign group, Show Racism the Red Card.

She was a Northumberland County councillor, representing Cramlington East-field, until the May 2017 elections. She is also a Cramlington Town councillor. She had been widely tipped to succeed Ronnie Campbell in Blyth Valley, which includes her home town of Cramlington, had he chosen to stand down at the election, but instead was selected from an all-women shortlist to replace Pat Glass in nearby North West Durham.

A fervent supporter of Jeremy Corbyn, she introduced him at the large Gateshead rally during the election campaign. She is a regular speaker at events organised by the Centre for Labour and Social Studies (CLASS) and sits on Unite's National and Regional Political Committee of Unite the union. She is a Northern region representative on the party's National Policy Forum, serving on the Early Years, Education and Skills Policy Commission. She is a Governor of Seaton Valley Federation. ▪

Jo Platt

LABOUR (AND CO-OPERATIVE PARTY) MP FOR LEIGH

FORMER MP:	Andy Burnham, Labour, stood down
MAJORITY:	9,554 (20.4%)
VOTE SHARE:	56.2%
CHANGE:	+2.3%
2ND PLACE:	Con
EU REFERENDUM:	Remain?

www.joplatt.me   @JoPlattMP

ANDY BURNHAM'S SUCCESSOR, Joanne 'Jo' Platt, made her name in local government and is now the town's first female MP. Elected to Wigan Council, representing Astley Mosley Common, in May 2012, she was vice-chair of the Children and Young People Scrutiny Committee between 2013 and 2014. She was appointed to the council's cabinet in June 2014 with the portfolio of Children and Young People. She was re-elected in 2016, but it is not known yet whether she will stand down ahead of the next elections in 2020.

She has been the secretary of the Leigh Constituency Labour Party and was Andy Burnham's agent at the 2015 general election. She received strong local backing from Burnham to win the selection to be Labour's Leigh candidate. She is a member of the Co-operative Party, Unite and the Association of Labour Councillors. She has volunteered with a support group for women giving up alcohol.

She is from Tyldesley and is a single mum of two, divorced from her husband Simon who ran a commercial vehicles company. ▪

Luke Pollard

LABOUR (AND CO-OPERATIVE PARTY) MP
FOR PLYMOUTH SUTTON & DEVONPORT

FORMER MP:	Oliver Colville, Conservative, defeated
MAJORITY:	6,807 (13.3%)
VOTE SHARE:	53.3%
CHANGE:	+16.6%
2ND PLACE:	Con
EU REFERENDUM:	Remain

www.lukepollard.org   @LukePollard

LUKE POLLARD WAS born in Plymouth in April 1980. His mother was a lecturer at Plymouth Marjon University and his father was a submariner in the Royal Navy. He spent his early years growing up in Devon, but moved with his family to Chester in 1992, attending Christleton High School. Returning to Devon in 1998, he graduated with a First in Politics from the University of Exeter. He spent a further year as president of Exeter's students' union.

He worked briefly in children's television for Carlton (now ITV) in Plympton, before working for David Jamieson, then Labour MP for Plymouth Devonport and George Foulkes MP. Both MPs stood down at the 2005 general election. During the 2005 election campaign,

he acted as temporary head of Labour's International Unit at Party HQ. Post-election he joined Edelman, an international communications company, as an account director working with, among others, Sainsbury's, South West Water and Cancer Research UK. In 2009 he joined ABTA, the trade association that represents travel agents and tour operators, first as head of public affairs, and from 2013, as head of European Development. From 2015 until 2017 he was a director at Field Consulting.

He fought the South West Devon seat in 2007 and Plymouth Sutton & Devonport in 2010. He is a member of the GMB, Unite, the Co-Operative Party and the Fabian Society. He has been a primary school governor for seven years. ∎

Faisal Rashid

LABOUR MP FOR WARRINGTON SOUTH

FORMER MP:	David Mowat, Conservative, defeated
MAJORITY:	2,549 (4.1%)
VOTE SHARE:	48.4%
CHANGE:	+9.3%
2ND PLACE:	Con
EU REFERENDUM:	Remain?

www.faisalrashid.com   @FaisalRashid6

FAISAL RASHID IS a former high-street banker and who has an MBA, with majors in Marketing and Management from the National College of Business Administration and Economics (NCBA&E) in Lahore, Punjab. He has more than fifteen years of commercial experience in the financial services sector, working for HBOS between 1999 and 2005, and as a relationship manager for NatWest in Warrington from 2006 until his election to Parliament.

He was elected a councillor to Warrington Borough Council in May 2011, representing Whittle Hall, renamed Chapelford & Old Hall in 2016. He was Mayor of Warrington in 2016. He has no immediate plans to stand down as a councillor. He has also been a non-executive director of Network Warrington, and was elected a Parish councillor in 2012.

He has been treasurer of Warrington South Constituency Labour Party and chair of Warrington West branch of the Labour Party for several years. He is a member of the Co-operative Party and a Unite trustee of St Rocco's Hospice.

His wife, Talat, is a personal assistant. ∎

Ellie Reeves

LABOUR MP FOR LEWISHAM WEST AND PENGE

FORMER MP:	Jim Dowd, Labour, stood down
MAJORITY:	23,162 (43.5%)
VOTE SHARE:	66.6%
CHANGE:	+16.0%
2ND PLACE:	Con
EU REFERENDUM:	Remain

www.elliereeves.org.uk   @elliereeves

ELLIE REEVES ATTENDED Adamsrill Primary School in Sydenham and Cator Park Secondary School, now Harris Academy Bromley, followed by the University of Oxford and the City Law School for a Bar vocational course. She was called to the Bar in 2004.

She started her career at OH Parsons & Partners in 2005, following her pupillage at 12 Kings Bench Walk. In 2007 she joined Thompsons Solicitors, before returning to OH Parsons in 2011 as a salaried partner/head of department. She moved to Monaco Solicitors in 2016. She specialises in employment tribunals, settlement negotiations and High Court litigation. Among her higher profile cases she represented 100 or so blacklisted construction workers. She founded WMA (Working Mum Advisory) to provide employment law advice to working mums and families.

She is vice-chair of the London Labour Party and was a member of the NEC for ten years, standing on the Progress and Labour First platform and chairing the Labour Party's Home Affairs Policy Commission, but losing to a series of pro-Corbyn candidates in 2016. She faced opposition to her selection in Lewisham West from Momentum activists.

Her sister is Rachel Reeves, Labour MP for Leeds West. She is married to John Cryer MP, chair of the Parliamentary Labour Party. They live in Lewisham and are parents to toddler Albert. ∎

Matt Rodda

LABOUR MP FOR READING EAST

FORMER MP:	Rob Wilson, Conservative, defeated
MAJORITY:	3,749 (6.8%)
VOTE SHARE:	49.0%
CHANGE:	+16.0%
2ND PLACE:	Con
EU REFERENDUM:	Remain

www.mattrodda.net @MattRodda

BORN IN DECEMBER 1966, Matt Rodda was raised in Wallingford in South Oxfordshire. After Wallingford School, the local comprehensive, he studied at Sussex University. Trained as a journalist with Thomson, he worked for the *Coventry Telegraph* and *The Independent* as an education correspondent.

He moved on to become a civil servant in the Department for Education and No. 10/ Cabinet Office, led projects in the No. 10 Strategic Communications Unit and was David Blunkett's ghost writer when he was Education Secretary. After leaving the civil service in 2007, he ran his own consultancy, assisting the 'Million+' group of UK universities. He was head of policy at the Higher Education Academy and joined Candlestar Associates in

2009, a consultancy specialising in the education and arts sector. Latterly, he worked as a voluntary sector project director for the Innovation Unit, an independent social enterprise.

He survived the Ladbroke Grove rail crash in October 1999, an event that inspired him to make a more active contribution to the community. He stood unsuccessfully for election in East Surrey in 2010, but was elected a Reading Borough councillor representing Katesgrove ward in 2011, becoming assistant lead councillor for Health. He previously stood in Reading East at the 2015 general election.

He has lived in Caversham, Reading since 2000 with his wife, a local government officer for Aylesbury Vale District Council, and their two children. ∎

Douglas Ross

CONSERVATIVE MP FOR MORAY

FORMER MP:	Angus Robertson, Scottish National Party (SNP), defeated
MAJORITY:	4,159 (8.7%)
VOTE SHARE:	47.6%
CHANGE:	+16.5%
2ND PLACE:	SNP
EU REFERENDUM:	Remain

@Douglas4Moray

IN WINNING THE seat of Moray from the SNP, Douglas Ross succeeded in ousting Angus Robertson, the deputy leader of the SNP, and probably its most effective performer in Westminster. Born in April 1983, he was educated at Forres Academy and the Scottish Agricultural College. He was a dairy farmer before entering politics.

He has served as a councillor on Moray Council, representing the Fochabers Lhanbryde ward, and became part of the Independent/Conservative administration. He has previously stood four times in Moray, in the 2010 and 2015 Westminster elections and in 2011 and 2016 Holyrood elections. He has been a regional list MSP for the Highlands and Islands region since 2016, and is a justice spokesperson.

Ross is also a football referee and has officiated as an assistant in the Scottish Premiership and at an international level. He has continued refereeing since being an MSP and has said that he will do so now as an MP. He was forced to apologise in 2016 when he missed a Justice Committee meeting in Holyrood, in which the government only won by a single vote, while he was in Portugal helping to referee a Champions League match. ▪

Danielle Rowley

LABOUR MP FOR MIDLOTHIAN

FORMER MP:	Owen Thompson, Scottish National Party (SNP), defeated
MAJORITY:	885 (2.0%)
VOTE SHARE:	36.4%
CHANGE:	+6.2%
2ND PLACE:	SNP
EU REFERENDUM:	Remain

@DaniRowley

DANIELLE ROWLEY'S HERITAGE is steeped in the history of the Labour movement. Both her grandfathers were miners and party activists. Her mother was a trade unionist and case worker for the former Midlothian Labour MP, Sir David Hamilton. Her father is Scottish Labour's deputy leader, Alex Rowley MSP. Born in 1990, she is the second youngest Labour MP. She was educated at Dalkeith High School, studied for an NHC in Radio Broadcasting at Edinburgh Telford College and a Journalism degree at Edinburgh Napier University.

After several jobs in the media and Scottish Parliament, she became campaigns coordinator in Midlothian in 2013 and the constituency media manager for Gordon Brown from June 2014 until July 2015. She worked as communications and marketing officer at ACOSVO (Association of Chief Officers of Scottish Voluntary Organisations), before becoming campaigns and public affairs officer at Shelter Scotland in 2016. She is a former press officer of the Dalkeith Festival Committee, trustee director of the Scottish Youth Parliament and a volunteer with the Midlothian Youth Platform.

She overturned a 9,859 majority to defeat the SNP's sitting MP, Owen Thompson. Although arranged before the snap election was called, she was criticised during the campaign for taking two weeks to travel to Cuba with the Cuba Solidarity Campaign as a member of a trade union delegation. ∎

Lee Rowley

CONSERVATIVE MP FOR NORTH EAST DERBYSHIRE

FORMER MP:	Natascha Engel, Labour, defeated
MAJORITY:	2,860 (5.7%)
VOTE SHARE:	49.2%
CHANGE:	+12.5%
2ND PLACE:	Lab
EU REFERENDUM:	Leave

www.lee4ned.com   @Lee4NED

LEE ROWLEY WAS born in 1980 in Chesterfield, which the North East Derbyshire constituency largely encircles. He was brought up in North Derbyshire and was educated locally at primary level and at St Mary's RC High School, where he was head boy. He was the first member of his family to attend university, studying at Lincoln College at Oxford.

He began his working life in the family business, helping his parents deliver milk in Hasland, Grassmoor and Chesterfield. He has spent the past fifteen years in various roles in the energy, education and financial sectors. He was latterly a senior manager for an insurance company, commuting daily to Manchester.

He was a Westminster councillor in London for eight years from 2006 until 2014, spending four years as a cabinet member during which time he unsuccessfully attempted to introduce controversial Sunday and weekday evening parking charges.

He fought the North East Derbyshire seat in 2015, reducing the majority to less than 2,000 and turning it into a marginal. This is the first time the seat has not been represented by a Labour MP since 1935. ∎

Chris Ruane

LABOUR MP FOR VALE OF CLWYD

FORMER MP:	James Davies, Conservative, defeated
MAJORITY:	2,379 (6.1%)
VOTE SHARE:	50.2%
CHANGE:	+11.9%
2ND PLACE:	Con
EU REFERENDUM:	Remain

@ChrisRuane2017

HAVING LOST THE Vale of Clwyd seat in 2015, Chris Ruane has returned in 2017 and has already been appointed to the Labour frontbench for the first time as spokesperson for Wales.

Born in July 1958, he attended the Blessed Edward Jones RC High School and studied economics at the University of Wales College, Aberystwyth, graduating in 1979. He went on to gain a PGCE from the University of Liverpool in 1980. He was a primary school teacher from 1982 until 1997 and a deputy head from 1991 until 1997. Active in the National Union of Teachers, he was chairman of West Clwyd NUT region.

Unsuccessfully contending Clwyd North West in 1992, he was elected to the Vale of Clwyd in 1997. He was appointed a parliamentary private secretary to Peter Hain in 2003, and resigned the position in March 2007 in protest against the decision to replace Trident, although he stressed that he was not a unilateralist. He served as an opposition whip under Ed Miliband from 2011 until 2013. After his defeat at the 2015 general election, he was a member of a task-force appointed by Harriet Harman to look at the reasons for Labour's defeat.

He has been married to Gill Roberts since 1994 and they have two daughters. ▪

Lloyd Russell-Moyle

LABOUR (AND CO-OPERATIVE PARTY) MP
FOR BRIGHTON KEMPTOWN

FORMER MP:	Simon Kirby, Conservative, defeated
MAJORITY:	9,868 (20.1%)
VOTE SHARE:	58.3%
CHANGE:	+19.2%
2ND PLACE:	Con
EU REFERENDUM:	Remain

www.russell-moyle.co.uk   @lloyd_rm

LLOYD RUSSELL-MOYLE WAS born in Brighton in September 1986. He was educated at Priory School in Lewes, Sussex Downs College, the University of Bradford, studying Peace Studies, and the University of Sussex between 2014 and 2016, earning a Master's in International Law.

He has a background in youth work, working at the National Youth Agency from 2003 until 2006, as chair and vice-chair of the Woodcraft Folk, including a year working in Brussels, and vice-president of the European Youth Forum, based in Brussels, between 2012 and 2014, while being vice-chair of the British Youth Council. He also worked for the University of Bradford as Union secretary/treasurer between 2007 and 2009. He was a children and youth participation consultant at the UN for six months in 2015.

Having been first politicised by the Woodcraft Folk, he stood in Lewes at the 2015 general election and was elected chair of Brighton & Hove Labour Party in January 2016. He has been a Brighton & Hove City councillor since 2016, representing East Brighton. He is a member of the GMB, Unite, the Co-operative Party, Brighton Momentum, CND and LGBT Labour. An enthusiastic Corbynista, he is strongly in favour of constitutional reform including electoral reform (AV+ ahead of FPTP) and abolishing the 'feudal' House of Lords. ▪

Bob Seely MBE

FORMER MP:	Andrew Turner, Conservative, stood down
MAJORITY:	21,069 (28.3%)
VOTE SHARE:	51.3%
CHANGE:	+10.6%
2ND PLACE:	Lab
EU REFERENDUM:	Leave

@IoWBobSeely

ROBERT 'BOB' SEELY comes from a long line of family members involved in politics. His great-great-uncle, General Jack Seely, is a former MP for the Isle of Wight. He has studied in the US at Harvard and is a fellow at Brown University.

He is a former foreign correspondent for *The Times* and the *Washington Post*, working in the former Soviet Union from 1990 to 1994. He served in the British Army, rising to Captain, in Iraq and completing four tours in Afghanistan. He was awarded a Joint Commanders Commendation in 2009 for his tour of Iraq and a Military MBE in 2016, having been mobilised as a reservist. Technically he remains a soldier and has been posted into various regiments and units, specialising in information warfare and non-conventional conflict, which he defines as political warfare.

He is a research associate at Oxford University's Changing Character of War programme where his area of study is Russian non-conventional warfare, and is doing a PhD at the Defence Studies Department of King's College London. He has also previously worked for seven years at MTV, launching TV stations around the world, and has been an adviser to Francis Maude and Sir Malcolm Rifkind.

Seely has been an Isle of Wight councillor since 2013, representing Central Wight, and was re-elected in May 2017. He stood in the Broxtowe seat in 2005. ▪

Eleanor Smith

LABOUR MP FOR WOLVERHAMPTON SOUTH WEST

FORMER MP:	Rob Màrris, Labour, stood down
MAJORITY:	2,185 (5.2%)
VOTE SHARE:	49.4%
CHANGE:	6.1%
2ND PLACE:	Con
EU REFERENDUM:	Remain?

www.eleanor4wolves.net   @Eleanor_SmithMP

BORN AND RAISED in Birmingham, Eleanor Smith is, surprisingly, the Midlands' first black MP. Enoch Powell was the local MP from 1950 until 1974. Her parents were encouraged to come to the UK from Barbados in the 1950s and she is the eldest of seven children. She was educated at Mount Pleasant comprehensive school in Birmingham and took a foundation nursing course at Bournville College.

A former theatre nurse at George Eliot Hospital in Nuneaton and Russell Hall Hospital in Dudley, she was a senior staff nurse at Birmingham Women's and Children's Hospital from 1985. She has spent thirty-five years working in the NHS.

She became a trade unionist in the 1990, went on to serve as chair of the Midlands Regional Trade Unions Congress and became the first ever black woman president of Unison in 2011. She is a former member of Labour's ruling National Executive Committee, where she represented the West Midlands and is chair of Unison's Labour Link. She is a member of the party's National Policy Forum and sits on the Health and Social Care Policy Commission as a Unison representative. She previously tried twice to be selected as a Labour candidate at a general election. Modestly increasing the Labour majority, she defeated the Conservative's former MP, Paul Uppal.

She has two grown up daughters. ∎

Laura Smith

LABOUR MP FOR CREWE & NANTWICH

FORMER MP:	Edward Timpson, Conservative, defeated
MAJORITY:	48 (0.1%)
VOTE SHARE:	47.1%
CHANGE:	+9.4%
2ND PLACE:	Con
EU REFERENDUM:	Unknown

www.laurasmithmp.com   @LauraSmithMP

LAURA SMITH IS a 32-year-old teacher and education campaigner. She attended Brine Leas School, South Cheshire College and Manchester Metropolitan University Cheshire Campus in Crewe. She is a former school teacher and runs the tuition business One-to-One Learning UK in Nantwich.

Although her father's best friend was apparently Labour's Gwyneth Dunwoody, who held the seat until 2008, she only recently became actively involved in politics. In only the past few months she has found herself leading a parents' campaign against local school funding cuts as part of the changes to the National Funding Formula. A Facebook post led to a public rally, a march through Nantwich and a lobby of Parliament earlier this year. She vowed to prioritise education and school funding in her parliamentary maiden speech.

Weeks later she was selected to fight the constituency, reportedly having beaten Labour's 2015 candidate in the constituency, Adrian Heald. She successfully overturned a 3,620 Conservative majority, beating incumbent Edward Timpson by forty-eight votes, incredibly still only the eighth smallest winning vote majority in 2017.

She lives in Nantwich with her partner, Steve, and they have a young son and daughter. She is a member of Unite. ∎

Alex Sobel

LABOUR (AND CO-OPERATIVE PARTY) MP
FOR LEEDS NORTH WEST

FORMER MP:	Greg Mulholland, Liberal Democrat, defeated
MAJORITY:	4,224 (9.1%)
VOTE SHARE:	44.1%
CHANGE:	+14.0%
2ND PLACE:	Lib Dem
EU REFERENDUM:	Remain

www.alexsobel.org   @alexsobel

ALEX SOBEL WAS born in the Hyde Park area of Leeds, but his family moved south in pursuit of work when he was young. Educated at the John Hampden Grammar School in Buckinghamshire, he returned to Leeds as a student, studying Information Systems at the University of Leeds. In his final year, he was elected as the full-time finance officer of Leeds University Union.

He has worked as a community development worker and now works with social enterprises, as general manager since 2009, running the regional Social Enterprise Yorkshire and the Humber.

He joined the Labour Party in 1997. He has been a Leeds City councillor representing the Meanwood and Moortown areas of the city since 2012. He stood in Beaconsfield in 2005. He was the Yorkshire and the Humber Regional Organiser for Ed Miliband's leadership campaign in 2010. He is an executive committee member of SERA, Labour's environment campaign group. Leeds North West, which includes the student heartland of Headingley, saw the biggest rise – 16 per cent – of newly registered voters.

Sobel is married to Susan, a debt manager at a local support centre, who he met while at Leeds University. They have two boys, Jakob and Zachary. He is the Governor of Chapel Allerton School. A member of the Jewish Labour Movement, his grandfather was a recruiter in the Jewish community for fighters in the Spanish Civil War. ∎

Jamie Stone

LIBERAL DEMOCRAT MP FOR CAITHNESS,
SUTHERLAND & EASTER ROSS

FORMER MP:	Paul Monaghan, Scottish National Party (SNP), defeated
MAJORITY:	2,044 (6.6%)
VOTE SHARE:	35.8%
CHANGE:	+0.7%
2ND PLACE:	SNP
EU REFERENDUM:	Remain

@Jamie4North

JAMES 'JAMIE' STONE was born in June 1954. He graduated from the University of St Andrews in 1977 having studied History and Geology. He has worked in various fields, largely in the oil industry.

He was elected as a member of Ross & Cromarty District Council in 1986, and in 1999 won the Scottish parliamentary seat of Caithness, Sutherland & Easter Ross from the opening of the Scottish Parliament, serving for twelve years, much of that time with the Liberal Democrats in coalition government with Labour. He held a wide variety of party and parliamentary roles, including spokesperson on housing and deputy spokesperson on health, and was convenor of the Subordinate Legislation Committee. He resigned from Holyrood in 2011 and revealed in 2013 that hostility from local party members had been a factor. He returned to local politics in 2012, being elected to Highland Council, and was re-elected to represent Tain & Easter Ross in May's local authority elections. He attempted a comeback in the 2016 Scottish parliamentary elections, but was beaten by the SNP's Gail Ross. Following his election to Westminster, he was announced as the Liberal Democrat spokesman for Scotland.

He is married with three children – one son and two daughters. He has been a director of Highland Fine Houses Ltd, Highland Celtic Foods and Highland Opportunity, and a trustee of Tain Guildry Trust and Tain Museum Trust. ∎

Paul Sweeney

LABOUR (AND CO-OPERATIVE PARTY) MP
FOR BARNSLEY EAST

FORMER MP:	Anne McLaughlin, Scottish National Party (SNP), defeated
MAJORITY:	242 (0.8%)
VOTE SHARE:	42.9%
CHANGE:	+9.2%
2ND PLACE:	SNP
EU REFERENDUM:	Remain

@PaulJSweeney

PAUL SWEENEY WAS educated at Turnbull High School, studied Economic History and Politics at the University of Glasgow and undertook a Certificate of Higher Education in Economics and Politics at the University of Stirling.

He has been an Army Reservist since 2006, serving in 6th Battalion, the Royal Regiment of Scotland since the age of seventeen and was a Territorial Army Sponsored Officer at both universities. He began working with BAE as an intern at Surface Ships in 2010. Having completed his degree at Glasgow University, he joined the BAE Graduate Development Framework and worked as an operations strategy coordinator until 2015. He was a senior executive account manager at Scottish Enterprise from 2015 until his election.

He joined the Labour Party at the age of sixteen and founded a project to restore Springburn's historical Winter Gardens. He was an adviser to Better Together during the independence referendum in 2014.

He is a councillor of the Institution of Engineers and Shipbuilders in Scotland, a member of the board of management of Glasgow University Union, a member of the Steering Committee of Fairfield Heritage Centre, a member of the board of directors of the Glasgow Building Preservation Trust and a STEM ambassador. ▪

Jo Swinson

LIBERAL DEMOCRAT MP FOR EAST DUNBARTONSHIRE

FORMER MP:	John Nicolson, Scottish National Party (SNP), defeated
MAJORITY:	5,339 (10.3%)
VOTE SHARE:	40.6%
CHANGE:	+4.3%
2ND PLACE:	SNP
EU REFERENDUM:	Remain

www.joswinson.org.uk   @joswinson

BORN IN GLASGOW, Jo Swinson attended the Douglas Academy in Milngavie and graduated from the London School of Economics in 2000 with a BSc in Management. Before entering Parliament, she has several roles as a marketing manager over a period of five years.

She stood against John Prescott, the then Deputy Prime Minister in 2001. She went on to win her home seat of East Dunbartonshire in 2005 and again in 2010. When she was elected at the age of twenty-five, she was the youngest MP in the 2005 UK Parliament.

After entering Parliament, she was a spokesperson on foreign affairs, equality, Scotland and the arts. She was a deputy leader of the Scottish Liberal Democrats between 2010 and 2012. In September 2012, she was appointed the Minister for Employment Relations and Consumer Affairs in the Department for Business, Innovation and Skills and Minister for Women and Equalities in the Department of Culture, Media and Sport.

Having lost her seat to the SNP's John Nicolson in 2015, she has amassed a portfolio of roles: a director of her own consultancy Equal Power Consulting Ltd, chair of the Policy Forum at CIPD, a member of the Advertising Advisory Committee at the Advertising Standards Authority, vice-chair of the Institute of Inertia at comparethemarket.com, chair at charity Maternity Action and a governor at the Ditchley Foundation. She has been a non-executive director at CLear Returns, a technology start-up. ▪

Ross Thomson

CONSERVATIVE MP FOR ABERDEEN SOUTH

FORMER MP:	Callum McCaig, Scottish National Party (SNP), defeated
MAJORITY:	4,752 (10.7%)
VOTE SHARE:	42.1%
CHANGE:	+19.3%
2ND PLACE:	SNP
EU REFERENDUM:	Leave

www.rossthomson.org.uk   @RossThomson_MP

ROSS THOMSON WAS born in Aberdeen in September 1987 and educated locally at Bridge of Don Academy. He studied Politics and International Relations at the University of Aberdeen, graduating with a First in 2009. He was the vice-chairman of the university's Conservative association. He worked as a customer adviser for the Bank of Scotland until 2011 and as a store trainer for Debenhams until 2012.

He stood in several Scottish parliamentary elections – Coatbridge and Chryston in 2007, Aberdeen Donside in 2011 and 2013 by-election – before being elected to his home seat of Aberdeen South & North Kincardine in 2016. Although the SNP retained the seat, he was elected as one of seven regional representatives. In Holyrood, he sat on the Education and Skills Committee. He has stood down from the Scottish Parliament following his election to Westminster. He was also elected to represent Hazlehead, Ashley and Queen's Cross on Aberdeen City Council in May 2012 and will continue to do so, donating his salary to two local charities. In Westminster elections, he had previously contested Gordon in 2010 and Aberdeen South in 2015. Rarely among the new Scottish Conservative MPs, he is pro-Brexit and headed up campaign organisation for Vote Leave in Scotland.

Thomson has been in a civil union with his partner, Douglas, since November 2013. He is a Governor of Robert Gordons College and a trustee of Aberdeen International Youth Festival and the Chris Anderson Trust. ▪

Liz Twist

LABOUR MP FOR BLAYDON

FORMER MP:	Labour MP, Dave Anderson, stood down
MAJORITY:	13,477 (28.0%)
VOTE SHARE:	56.1%
CHANGE:	+6.9%
2ND PLACE:	Con
EU REFERENDUM:	Remain

@LizTwistMP

BORN IN JULY 1956, Liz Twist was inspired to enter politics by her grandfather who was actively involved in the NUM in Lancashire. She herself got involved in trade union activism in 1989, becoming a Unison official. Prior to the general election she was regional head of health in the North East.

For many years, she worked in the constituency office of her predecessor, Dave Anderson, who did not stand in 2017 for personal and health reasons. She was not considered a favourite to be selected for the seat and beat, among others, Mark Ferguson, the former editor of LabourList, and Mary Foy, a member of Labour's National Policy Forum.

She was elected to Gateshead Metropolitan Borough Council in 2012, representing the Ryton, Crookhill & Stella ward. She was appointed to Gateshead's cabinet in 2015 with responsibility for housing. As a councillor she has been a director of Keelman Homes Limited and the Gateshead Housing Company, both since 2016.

She is closely involved with Stargate and Crookhill Community Centre Association, Ryton Community Library Volunteers Association and Samaritans of Tyneside. ∎

Thelma Walker

LABOUR MP FOR COLNE VALLEY

FORMER MP:	Jason McCartney, Conservative, defeated
MAJORITY:	915 (1.5%)
VOTE SHARE:	47.7%
CHANGE:	+12.7%
2ND PLACE:	Con
EU REFERENDUM:	Remain

www.thelmawalker4cv.co.uk   @Red_Thelma

THELMA WALKER WAS educated at Marple Hall Grammar School and Manchester Polytechnic, graduating in 1978 as a Bachelor of Education.

She worked in education for thirty-four years at both secondary and primary level, working in Stockton for twelve years and then moving to Kirklees in 1990. She trained as a teacher and was head of two schools, Overthorpe Church of England School and Flockton First School before setting up as an independent consultant in 2012. She has been vice-chair of Kirklees Leadership Development Group and member of Kirklees Safeguarding board and a head teacher mentor.

She is a trustee of Slaithwaite Civic Hall and is a volunteer with DASH, Destitute Asylum Seeks Huddersfield, co-ordinating the food partnership programme.

The seat of Colne Valley was Conservative between 1987 and 1997 and Labour until 2010. Walker polled the highest number of votes of any candidate in the history of the constituency.

She has lived in Colne Valley for thirty years and is married to Rob Walker, a Kirklees Labour councillor for the Colne Valley ward. They have two children. ∎

Giles Watling

CONSERVATIVE MP FOR CLACTON

FORMER UK:	Douglas Carswell, UK Independence Party (UKIP), stood down
MAJORITY:	15,828 (35.9%)
VOTE SHARE:	61.2%
CHANGE:	+24.6%
2ND PLACE:	Lab
EU REFERENDUM:	Remain

www.gileswatling.com   @GilesWatling

BORN IN FEBRUARY 1953 in Chingford, Essex, Giles Watling is an actor, director and writer. Both of his parents were actors and his two sisters are actors, too. He has worked extensively in British theatre and television since starting his career as a child actor in 1962.

He is best known as the vicar in forty-nine episodes of Carla Lane's TV sitcom, Bread, between 1988 and 1991, and has appeared in numerous TV shows and sitcoms, including 'Allo 'Allo, Upstairs Downstairs and Grange Hill. He has directed around seventy plays, appeared in numerous play productions, performed the voiceovers for numerous adverts, appeared as a celebrity contestant on game shows and chat shows and appeared in Royal Variety performances. He was the winner of the Variety Club's BBC TV Personality of the Year award in 1988.

He was adopted in the Conservative's open primary to decide the candidate to stand against Douglas Carswell in the Clacton by-election in 2014, following his defection to UKIP. Beaten again in 2015, he was comfortably elected in 2017 after the UKIP vote share collapsed from 44.4 per cent in 2015 to only 7.6 per cent. He was elected to Tendring District Council for the Frinton ward in May 2015 and has been the Council's cabinet member for regeneration.

He is married to Vanda and has two children. ■

Matt Western

LABOUR MP FOR WARWICK AND LEAMINGTON

FORMER MP:	Chris White, Conservative, defeated
MAJORITY:	1,206 (2.2%)
VOTE SHARE:	46.7%
CHANGE:	+11.8%
2ND PLACE:	Con
EU REFERENDUM:	Remain

@MattWestern_

BORN IN NOVEMBER 1962, Matt Western was educated in St Albans and graduated with a BSc degree in Geography from the University of Bristol in 1984.

Before entering politics, he worked in car manufacturer Peugeot's management team in various roles over fourteen years: fleet sales manager, advertising and media manager, manager of international communications strategy based in Paris, regional manager for Swiss and Austrian subsidiaries based in Paris and purchasing manager. He left in 2008 to become an independent consultant advising on branding, marketing communications and new business development. He also works as a volunteer careers mentor at Campion School.

He was elected to Warwickshire County Council's Leamington Willes division in 2013, and was re-elected for his second term in May 2017. He has been appointed to Warwick's Local Strategic Partnership and One World Link (Warwick).

He lives in Leamington's Old Town with Rebecca Earle, a professor of food and cultural history of Spanish America and early modern Europe at Warwick University. ∎

Martin Whitfield

LABOUR MP FOR EAST LOTHIAN

FORMER MP:	George Kerevan, Scottish National Party (SNP), defeated
MAJORITY:	3,083 (5.5%)
VOTE SHARE:	36.1%
CHANGE:	+5.1%
2ND PLACE:	SNP
EU REFERENDUM:	Remain

@MartWhitfield

MARTIN WHITFIELD WAS born in Newcastle in 1965, attending Gosforth High
School. He studied at the University of
Huddersfield, Newcastle Polytechnic and
the University of Edinburgh, becoming a
lawyer specialising in personal injury law.
After growing disillusioned with his career
in law, he became a primary school teacher,
working at Prestonpans Primary School. He
served as a council member of the General Teaching Council, and he is chairman
of Prestonpans local community council.

A father of two, he lives in Prestonpans
with his family. His wife is the marketing
manager for the local theatre. ∎

Dr Paul Williams

LABOUR MP FOR STOCKTON SOUTH

FORMER MP:	James Wharton, Conservative, defeated
MAJORITY:	888 (1.6%)
VOTE SHARE:	48.5%
CHANGE:	11.5%
2ND PLACE:	Con
EU REFERENDUM:	Remain

@PaulWilliamsMP

BORN IN EAST Anglia in August 1972, Paul Williams is the son of a teacher and a nurse. He went to Neale Wade School in Cambridgeshire and studied medicine at the University of Newcastle between 1991 and 1996. Later, he studied for a Diploma in Tropical Medicine at the University of Liverpool and an MSc in Public Health back at the University of Newcastle.

He trained at James Cook University Hospital in Middlesbrough and the University Hospital of North Tees. In 2002 he founded, along with his father, the Arrival Practice, a general practice for asylum seekers and refugees. He volunteered as a doctor for four years in western Uganda learning to speak Runyankole-Rukiga. Returning to the UK, he has been a local GP and since 2015 he was the chief executive of Hartlepool and Stockton Health GP Federation.

Although he joined the Labour Party at university, he is relatively new to frontline politics. He had been shortlisted for the nomination in the 2013 South Shields by-election. In 2017 he ousted ex-Northern Powerhouse minister James Wharton by 888 votes.

He is a trustee of ARC Theatre and Arts Centre in Stockton, and Catalyst, the voluntary development agency for Stockton's charity sector. He is patron of Justice First, which assists asylum seekers.

He is married to Vicky, a nurse, and they have two young daughters, Emmeline and Mira. He is a keen triathlete. ∎

Chris Williamson

LABOUR MP FOR DERBY NORTH

FORMER MP:	Amanda Solloway, Conservative, defeated
MAJORITY:	2,015 (4.1%)
VOTE SHARE:	48.5%
CHANGE:	12.0%
2ND PLACE:	Con
EU REFERENDUM:	Remain

www.chriswilliamson.org   @ChriswMP

CHRIS WILLIAMSON HAS returned to Parliament after a two-year absence and Jeremy Corbyn has appointed him as shadow Fire Minister under the Home Affairs team of Diane Abbott, a position he previously held under Ed Miliband's leadership until 2013. Given the Grenfell Tower tragedy and the ongoing investigations and wider implications, it is likely to be a high-profile position.

Williamson was born in Derby in September 1956 attending Castle Donnington High School and St Thomas More High School, before obtaining a CQSW in 1985 from Leicester Polytechnic. He worked as a mechanical engineering apprentice for a year before working six years as a bricklayer.

In 1983 he became a social worker before becoming a welfare rights officer from 1986.

Joining the Labour Party in 1976, he was a Derby City councillor representing the Normanton ward from 1991 until 2011 and twice was leader of the council. Elected as the MP for Derby North in 2010, he became the shadow Fire Minister, then under the CLG brief, only four months after his election, serving until 2013. He is a close ally and friend of Jeremy Corbyn and his successful election campaign was strongly supported by Momentum.

He is married to Maggie Amsbury. He is a trustee of the League Against Cruel Sports. ▪

Mohammad Yasin

LABOUR MP FOR BEDFORD

FORMER MP:	Richard Fuller, Conservative, defeated
MAJORITY:	789 (1.6%)
VOTE SHARE:	46.8%
CHANGE:	+6.6%
2ND PLACE:	Con
EU REFERENDUM:	Remain?

www.alanmak.org.uk   @AlanMak4MP @AlanMakUK

BORN IN 1971, Mohammad Yasin was a self-employed private hire driver in Milton Keynes. He has been a Bedford Borough councillor for eleven years, representing the Queen's Park ward. In 2015 he became a member of the executive of the council and portfolio holder for Adult Services. He stepped down from the portfolio within days of being elected to Westminster. He is also a former speaker of the council.

He was a director of Bedford Bereavement Care Limited from 2009 until it was dissolved in 2011. He was also a council-appointed director of Queen's Park Community Centre and Westfield School governor. He has lived in Bedford for over twenty-five years. ▪

Results by Constituency

Aberavon

LAB HOLD
Majority: 16,761, 50.4% | Turnout: 33,268, 66.7% | Electorate: 49,892 | EU Ref: 60.0% Leave

PARTY	CANDIDATE	VOTES	SHARE	CHANGE 2015
Labour	Stephen Kinnock	22,662	68.1%	19.2%
Conservative	Sadie Vidal	5,901	17.7%	5.9%
Plaid Cymru	Andrew Bennison	2,761	8.3%	-3.3%
UK Independence Party	Caroline Jones	1,345	4.0%	-11.7%
Liberal Democrat	Cen Phillips	599	1.8%	-2.6%

Aberconwy

CON HOLD
Majority: 635, 2.0% | Turnout: 32,150, 71.0% | Electorate: 45,251 | EU Ref: 53.4% Leave

PARTY	CANDIDATE	VOTES	SHARE	CHANGE 2015
Conservative	Guto Bebb	14,337	44.6%	3.1%
Labour	Emily Owen	13,702	42.6%	14.4%
Plaid Cymru	Wyn Jones	3,170	9.9%	-1.9%
Liberal Democrat	Sarah Lesiter-Burgess	941	2.9%	-1.7%

Aberdeen North

SNP HOLD

Majority: 4,139, 11.3% | Turnout: 36,757, 59.2% | Electorate: 62,130 | EU Ref: 43.1% Leave

PARTY	CANDIDATE	VOTES	SHARE	CHANGE 2015
Scottish National Party	Kirsty Blackman	15,170	41.3%	-15.2%
Labour	Orr Vinegold	11,031	30.0%	4.1%
Conservative	Grace O'Keeffe	8,341	22.7%	10.6%
Liberal Democrat	Isobel Davidson	1,693	4.6%	-0.1%
Independent	Richard Durkin	522	1.4%	1.4%

Aberdeen South

CON GAIN FROM SNP

Majority: 4,752, 10.6% | Turnout: 44,493, 68.5% | Electorate: 64,964 | EU Ref: 32.3% Leave

PARTY	CANDIDATE	VOTES	SHARE	CHANGE 2015
Conservative	Ross Thomson	18,746	42.1%	19.3%
Scottish National Party	Callum McCaig	13,994	31.5%	-10.2%
Labour	Callum O'Dwyer	9,143	20.6%	-6.2%
Liberal Democrat	Jenny Wilson	2,610	5.8%	1.2%

Airdrie & Shotts

SNP HOLD

Majority: 195, 0.5% | Turnout: 38,002, 59.2% | Electorate: 64,146 | EU Ref: 40.1% Leave

PARTY	CANDIDATE	VOTES	SHARE	CHANGE 2015
Scottish National Party	Neil Gray	14,291	37.6%	-16.3%
Labour	Helen McFarlane	14,096	37.1%	3.0%
Conservative	Jennifer Donnellan	8,813	23.2%	15.5%
Liberal Democrat	Ewan McRobert	802	2.1%	0.6%

Aldershot

CON HOLD

Majority: 11,473, 23.5% | Turnout: 48,950, 64.2% | Electorate: 76,205 | EU Ref: 58.2% Leave

PARTY	CANDIDATE	VOTES	SHARE	CHANGE 2015
Conservative	Leo Docherty	26,950	55.1%	4.5%
Labour	Gary Puffett	15,477	31.6%	13.3%
Liberal Democrat	Alan Hilliar	3,637	7.4%	-1.4%
UK Independence Party	Roy Swales	1,796	3.7%	-14.2%
Green	Donna Wallace	1,090	2.2%	-2.2%

Aldridge-Brownhills

CON HOLD

Majority: 14,307, 35.6% | Turnout: 40,235, 67.5% | Electorate: 60,363 | EU Ref: 68.0% Leave

PARTY	CANDIDATE	VOTES	SHARE	CHANGE 2015
Conservative	Wendy Morton	26,317	65.4%	13.4%
Labour	John Fisher	12,010	29.8%	7.5%
Liberal Democrat	Ian Garrett	1,343	3.3%	0.0%
Monster Raving Loony Party	Mark Beech	565	1.4%	0.9%

Altrincham & Sale West

CON HOLD

Majority: 6,426, 12.2% | Turnout: 52,790, 72.1% | Electorate: 73,226 | EU Ref: 38.5% Leave

PARTY	CANDIDATE	VOTES	SHARE	CHANGE 2015
Conservative	Graham Brady	26,933	51.0%	-2.0%
Labour	Andrew Western	20,507	38.8%	12.2%
Liberal Democrat	Jane Brophy	4,051	7.7%	-0.7%
Green	Geraldine Coggins	1,000	1.9%	-2.0%
Liberal	Neil Taylor	299	0.6%	0.6%

Alyn & Deeside

LAB HOLD

Majority: 5,235, 11.7% | Turnout: 44,760, 71.0% | Electorate: 63,013 | EU Ref: 57.7% Leave

PARTY	CANDIDATE	VOTES	SHARE	CHANGE 2015
Labour	Mark Tami	23,315	52.1%	12.1%
Conservative	Laura Knightly	18,080	40.4%	8.5%
Plaid Cymru	Jacqui Hurst	1,171	2.6%	-1.3%
UK Independence Party	David Griffiths	1,117	2.5%	-15.1%
Liberal Democrat	Pete Williams	1,077	2.4%	-1.8%

Amber Valley

CON HOLD

Majority: 8,300, 18.1% | Turnout: 45,811, 67.4% | Electorate: 68,065 | EU Ref: 65.3% Leave

PARTY	CANDIDATE	VOTES	SHARE	CHANGE 2015
Conservative	Nigel Mills	25,905	56.5%	12.6%
Labour	James Dawson	17,605	38.4%	3.6%
Liberal Democrat	Kate Smith	1,100	2.4%	-0.6%
Green	Matt McGuinness	650	1.4%	-1.0%
Independent	Daniel Bamford	551	1.2%	1.2%

Angus

CON GAIN FROM SNP

Majority: 2,645, 6.6% | Turnout: 40,192, 63.0% | Electorate: 63,840 | EU Ref: 48.1% Leave

PARTY	CANDIDATE	VOTES	SHARE	CHANGE 2015
Conservative	Kirstene Hair	18,148	45.2%	16.2%
Scottish National Party	Mike Weir	15,503	38.6%	-15.7%
Labour	William Campbell	5,233	13.0%	4.2%
Liberal Democrat	Clive Sneddon	1,308	3.3%	0.5%

Arfon

PC HOLD

Majority: 92, 0.3% | Turnout: 28,208, 68.2% | Electorate: 41,367 | EU Ref: 34.9% Leave

PARTY	CANDIDATE	VOTES	SHARE	CHANGE 2015
Plaid Cymru	Hywel Williams	11,519	40.8%	-3.1%
Labour	Mary Griffiths Clarke	11,427	40.5%	10.2%
Conservative	Phillippa Parry	4,614	16.4%	3.2%
Liberal Democrat	Calum Davies	648	2.3%	-0.4%

Argyll & Bute

SNP HOLD

Majority: 1,328, 2.8% | Turnout: 48,069, 71.5% | Electorate: 67,230 | EU Ref: 39.4% Leave

PARTY	CANDIDATE	VOTES	SHARE	CHANGE 2015
Scottish National Party	Brendan O'Hara	17,304	36.0%	-8.3%
Conservative	Gary Mulvaney	15,976	33.2%	18.3%
Liberal Democrat	Alan Reid	8,745	18.2%	-9.7%
Labour	Michael Kelly	6,044	12.6%	2.2%

Arundel & South Downs

CON HOLD

Majority: 23,883, 39.7% | Turnout: 60,256, 74.6% | Electorate: 79,478 | EU Ref: 50.7% Leave

PARTY	CANDIDATE	VOTES	SHARE	CHANGE 2015
Conservative	Nick Herbert	37,573	62.4%	1.6%
Labour	Caroline Fife	13,690	22.7%	11.5%
Liberal Democrat	Shweta Kapadia	4,783	7.9%	0.7%
Green	Jo Prior	2,542	4.2%	-2.2%
UK Independence Party	John Wallace	1,668	2.8%	-11.7%

Ashfield

LAB HOLD
Majority: 441, 0.9% | Turnout: 49,993, 64.0% | Electorate: 78,076 | EU Ref: 70.6% Leave

PARTY	CANDIDATE	VOTES	SHARE	CHANGE 2015
Labour	Gloria De Piero	21,285	42.6%	1.6%
Conservative	Tony Harper	20,844	41.7%	19.3%
Independent	Gail Turner	4,612	9.2%	9.2%
UK Independence Party	Ray Young	1,885	3.8%	-17.6%
Liberal Democrat	Bob Charlesworth	969	1.9%	-12.9%
Green	Arran Rangi	398	0.8%	0.8%

Ashford

CON HOLD
Majority: 17,478, 29.2% | Turnout: 59,879, 68.5% | Electorate: 87,387 | EU Ref: 59.7% Leave

PARTY	CANDIDATE	VOTES	SHARE	CHANGE 2015
Conservative	Rt Hon Damian Green	35,318	59.0%	6.5%
Labour	Sally Gathern	17,840	29.8%	11.4%
Liberal Democrat	Adrian Gee-Turner	3,101	5.2%	-0.8%
UK Independence Party	Gerald O'Brien	2,218	3.7%	-15.1%
Green	Mandy Rossi	1,402	2.3%	-2.0%

Ashton-Under-Lyne

LAB HOLD
Majority: 11,295, 28.4% | Turnout: 39,773, 58.8% | Electorate: 65,751 | EU Ref: 63.5% Leave

PARTY	CANDIDATE	VOTES	SHARE	CHANGE 2015
Labour	Angela Rayner	24,005	60.4%	10.6%
Conservative	Jack Rankin	12,710	32.0%	9.8%
UK Independence Party	Maurice Jackson	1,878	4.7%	-17.0%
Liberal Democrat	Carly Hicks	646	1.6%	-0.8%
Green	Andy Hunter-Rossall	534	1.3%	-2.6%

Aylesbury

CON HOLD

Majority: 14,656, 24.9% | Turnout: 58,783, 71.2% | Electorate: 82,546 | EU Ref: 52.1% Leave

PARTY	CANDIDATE	VOTES	SHARE	CHANGE 2015
Conservative	David Lidington	32,313	55.0%	4.3%
Labour	Mark Bateman	17,657	30.0%	14.9%
Liberal Democrat	Steven Lambert	5,660	9.6%	-1.0%
UK Independence Party	Vijay Srao	1,296	2.2%	-17.5%
Green	Coral Simpson	1,237	2.1%	-1.7%
Independent	Kyle Michael	620	1.1%	1.1%

Ayr, Carrick & Cumnock

CON GAIN FROM SNP

Majority: 2,774, 6.0% | Turnout: 46,222, 64.9% | Electorate: 71,241 | EU Ref: 43.0% Leave

PARTY	CANDIDATE	VOTES	SHARE	CHANGE 2015
Conservative	Bill Grant	18,550	40.1%	20.3%
Scottish National Party	Corri Wilson	15,776	34.1%	-14.7%
Labour	Carol Mochan	11,024	23.9%	-3.4%
Liberal Democrat	Callum Leslie	872	1.9%	0.2%

Banbury

CON HOLD

Majority: 12,399, 20.1% | Turnout: 61,562, 73.5% | Electorate: 83,824 | EU Ref: 50.5% Leave

PARTY	CANDIDATE	VOTES	SHARE	CHANGE 2015
Conservative	Victoria Prentis	33,388	54.2%	1.2%
Labour	Sean Woodcock	20,989	34.1%	12.8%
Liberal Democrat	John Howson	3,452	5.6%	-0.3%
UK Independence Party	Dickie Bird	1,581	2.6%	-11.3%
Green	Ian Middleton	1,225	2.0%	-2.6%
Independent	Roseanne Edwards	927	1.5%	1.5%

Banff & Buchan

CON GAIN FROM SNP

Majority: 3,693, 8.9% | Turnout: 41,643, 61.6% | Electorate: 67,601 | EU Ref: 54.0% Leave

PARTY	CANDIDATE	VOTES	SHARE	CHANGE 2015
Conservative	David Duguid	19,976	48.0%	19.2%
Scottish National Party	Eilidh Whiteford	16,283	39.1%	-21.1%
Labour	Caitlin Stott	3,936	9.5%	3.7%
Liberal Democrat	Galen Milne	1,448	3.5%	-1.7%

Barking

LAB HOLD

Majority: 21,608, 45.3% | Turnout: 47,679, 61.9% | Electorate: 77,022 | EU Ref: 60.3% Leave

PARTY	CANDIDATE	VOTES	SHARE	CHANGE 2015
Labour	Margaret Hodge	32,319	67.8%	10.1%
Conservative	Minesh Talati	10,711	22.5%	6.2%
UK Independence Party	Roger Gravett	3,031	6.4%	-15.8%
Green	Shannon Butterfield	724	1.5%	-0.6%
Liberal Democrat	Pauline Pearce	599	1.3%	0.0%
Independent	Noel Falvey	295	0.6%	0.6%

Barnsley Central

LAB HOLD

Majority: 15,546, 39.8% | Turnout: 39,087, 60.6% | Electorate: 64,204 | EU Ref: 68.4% Leave

PARTY	CANDIDATE	VOTES	SHARE	CHANGE 2015
Labour	Dan Jarvis	24,982	63.9%	8.2%
Conservative	Amanda Ford	9,436	24.1%	9.1%
UK Independence Party	Gavin Felton	3,339	8.5%	-13.2%
Green	Richard Trotman	570	1.5%	-1.1%
Liberal Democrat	David Ridgway	549	1.4%	-0.7%
English Democrats	Stephen Morris	211	0.5%	-0.8%

Barnsley East

LAB HOLD

Majority: 13,283, 32.5% | Turnout: 40,776, 58.9% | Electorate: 69,214 | EU Ref: 70.8% Leave

PARTY	CANDIDATE	VOTES	SHARE	CHANGE 2015
Labour	Stephanie Peacock	24,280	59.5%	4.8%
Conservative	Andrew Lloyd	10,997	27.0%	12.4%
UK Independence Party	James Dalton	3,247	8.0%	-15.5%
The Yorkshire Party	Tony Devoy	1,215	3.0%	1.3%
Liberal Democrat	Nicola Turner	750	1.8%	-1.3%
English Democrats	Kevin Riddiough	287	0.7%	-0.4%

Barrow & Furness

LAB HOLD

Majority: 209, 0.5% | Turnout: 47,590, 68.5% | Electorate: 69,474 | EU Ref: 56.8% Leave

PARTY	CANDIDATE	VOTES	SHARE	CHANGE 2015
Labour	John Woodcock	22,592	47.5%	5.1%
Conservative	Simon Fell	22,383	47.0%	6.5%
Liberal Democrat	Loraine Birchall	1,278	2.7%	0.0%
UK Independence Party	Alan Piper	962	2.0%	-9.7%
Green	Rob O'Hara	375	0.8%	-1.7%

Basildon & Billericay

CON HOLD

Majority: 13,400, 29.9% | Turnout: 44,918, 64.9% | Electorate: 69,149 | EU Ref: 66.9% Leave

CONSERVATIVE	JOHN BARON	27,381	61.0%	8.3%
Labour	Kayte Block	13,981	31.1%	7.5%
UK Independence Party	Tina Hughes	2,008	4.5%	-15.4%
Liberal Democrat	Antonia Harrison	1,548	3.4%	-0.4%

Basingstoke

CON HOLD

Majority: 9,466, 16.9% | Turnout: 55,960, 68.3% | Electorate: 81,875 | EU Ref: 53.6% Leave

PARTY	CANDIDATE	VOTES	SHARE	CHANGE 2015
Conservative	Maria Miller	29,510	52.7%	4.2%
Labour	Terry Bridgeman	20,044	35.8%	8.1%
Liberal Democrat	John Shaw	3,406	6.1%	-1.3%
UK Independence Party	Alan Stone	1,681	3.0%	-12.6%
Green	Richard Winter	1,106	2.0%	2.0%
Libertarian	Scott Neville	213	0.4%	0.4%

Bassetlaw

LAB HOLD

Majority: 4,852, 9.3% | Turnout: 52,250, 66.5% | Electorate: 78,540 | EU Ref: 68.3% Leave

PARTY	CANDIDATE	VOTES	SHARE	CHANGE 2015
Labour	John Mann	27,467	52.6%	3.9%
Conservative	Annette Simpson	22,615	43.3%	12.6%
Liberal Democrat	Leon Duveen	1,154	2.2%	-0.5%
Independent	Nigel Turner	1,014	1.9%	1.9%

Bath

LIB DEM GAIN FROM CON

Majority: 5,694, 11.5% | Turnout: 49,583, 74.3% | Electorate: 66,778 | EU Ref: 31.7% Leave

PARTY	CANDIDATE	VOTES	SHARE	CHANGE 2015
Liberal Democrat	Wera Hobhouse	23,436	47.3%	17.6%
Conservative	Ben Howlett	17,742	35.8%	-2.0%
Labour	Joe Rayment	7,279	14.7%	1.5%
Green	Eleanor Field	1,126	2.3%	-9.7%

Batley & Spen

LAB HOLD

Majority: 8,961, 16.7% | Turnout: 53,780, 67.1% | Electorate: 80,161 | EU Ref: 60.4% Leave

PARTY	CANDIDATE	VOTES	SHARE	CHANGE 2015
Labour	Tracy Brabin	29,844	55.5%	12.3%
Conservative	Ann Myatt	20,883	38.8%	7.6%
Liberal Democrat	John Lawson	1,224	2.3%	-2.5%
Independent	Aleks Lukic	1,076	2.0%	2.0%
Green	Alan Freeman	695	1.3%	-1.1%
Independent	Mohammed Hanif	58	0.1%	0.1%

Battersea

LAB GAIN FROM CON

Majority: 2,416, 4.4% | Turnout: 55,058, 71.0% | Electorate: 77,574 | EU Ref: 23.0% Leave

PARTY	CANDIDATE	VOTES	SHARE	CHANGE 2015
Labour	Marsha De Cordova	25,292	45.9%	9.1%
Conservative	Jane Ellison	22,876	41.5%	-10.8%
Liberal Democrat	Richard Davis	4,401	8.0%	3.6%
Independent	Chris Coghlan	1,234	2.2%	2.2%
Green	Lois Davis	866	1.6%	-1.7%
UK Independence Party	Eugene Power	357	0.6%	-2.5%
Socialist Party GB	Daniel Lambert	32	0.1%	0.1%

Beaconsfield

CON HOLD

Majority: 24,543, 43.9% | Turnout: 56,028, 72.3% | Electorate: 77,524 | EU Ref: 49.3% Leave

PARTY	CANDIDATE	VOTES	SHARE	CHANGE 2015
Conservative	Dominic Grieve	36,559	65.3%	2.0%
Labour	James English	12,016	21.4%	10.0%
Liberal Democrat	Peter Chapman	4,448	7.9%	0.6%
UK Independence Party	Jon Conway	1,609	2.9%	-10.9%
Green	Russell Secker	1,396	2.5%	-1.7%

Beckenham

CON HOLD

Majority: 15,087, 29.2% | Turnout: 51,630, 76.0% | Electorate: 67,925 | EU Ref: 47.5% Leave

PARTY	CANDIDATE	VOTES	SHARE	CHANGE 2015
Conservative	Bob Stewart	30,632	59.3%	2.0%
Labour	Marina Ahmad	15,545	30.1%	10.7%
Liberal Democrat	Julie Ireland	4,073	7.9%	1.0%
Green	Ruth Fabricant	1,380	2.7%	-1.2%

Bedford

LAB GAIN FROM CON

Majority: 789, 1.6% | Turnout: 48,480, 67.5% | Electorate: 71,829 | EU Ref: 53.7% Leave

PARTY	CANDIDATE	VOTES	SHARE	CHANGE 2015
Labour	Mohammad Yasin	22,712	46.8%	6.6%
Conservative	Richard Fuller	21,923	45.2%	2.6%
Liberal Democrat	Henry Vann	2,837	5.9%	1.6%
Green	Lucy Bywater	1,008	2.1%	-1.0%

Belfast East

DUP HOLD

Majority: 8,474, 19.8% | Turnout: 42,890, 67.5% | Electorate: 63,495 | EU Ref: Not available

PARTY	CANDIDATE	VOTES	SHARE	CHANGE 2015
Democratic Unionist Party	Gavin Robinson	23,917	55.8%	6.4%
Alliance Party	Naomi Long	15,443	36.0%	-6.8%
Ulster Unionist Party	Hazel Legge	1,408	3.3%	3.3%
Sinn Féin	Mairead O'Donnell	894	2.1%	0.0%
Green	Georgina Milne	561	1.3%	-1.4%
Conservative	Sheila Bodel	446	1.0%	-1.8%
Social Democratic & Labour Party	Seamas de Faoite	167	0.4%	0.1%
Independent	Bobby Beck	54	0.1%	0.1%

Belfast North

DUP HOLD

Majority: 2,081, 4.5% | Turnout: 45,936, 67.3% | Electorate: 68,249 | EU Ref: Not available

PARTY	CANDIDATE	VOTES	SHARE	CHANGE 2015
Democratic Unionist Party	Nigel Dodds	21,240	46.2%	-0.8%
Sinn Féin	John Finucane	19,159	41.7%	7.8%
Alliance Party	Sam Nelson	2,475	5.4%	-1.9%
Social Democratic & Labour Party	Martin McAuley	2,058	4.5%	-3.7%
Green	Malachai O'Hara	644	1.4%	1.4%
Workers Party	Gemma Weir	360	0.8%	-1.5%

Belfast South

DUP GAIN FROM SDLP

Majority: 1,996, 4.5% | Turnout: 43,705, 66.1% | Electorate: 66,105 | EU Ref: Not available

PARTY	CANDIDATE	VOTES	SHARE	CHANGE 2015
Democratic Unionist Party	Emma Little-Pengelly	13,299	30.4%	8.2%
Social Democratic & Labour Party	Alasdair McDonnell	11,303	25.9%	1.3%
Alliance Party	Paula Bradshaw	7,946	18.2%	1.0%
Sinn Féin	Mairtin O Muilleoir	7,143	16.3%	2.5%
Green	Clare Bailey	2,241	5.1%	-0.6%
Ulster Unionist Party	Michael Henderson	1,527	3.5%	-5.6%
Conservative	Clare Salier	246	0.6%	-0.9%

Belfast West

SF HOLD

Majority: 21,652, 53.3% | Turnout: 40,633, 65.1% | Electorate: 62,423 | EU Ref: Not available

PARTY	CANDIDATE	VOTES	SHARE	CHANGE 2015
Sinn Féin	Paul Maskey	27,107	66.7%	12.5%
Democratic Unionist Party	Frank McCoubrey	5,455	13.4%	5.6%
People Before Profit	Gerry Carroll	4,132	10.2%	-9.1%
Social Democratic & Labour Party	Tim Attwood	2,860	7.0%	-2.8%
Alliance Party	Sorcha Eastwood	731	1.8%	0.0%
Workers Party	Conor Campbell	348	0.9%	-0.8%

Bermondsey & Old Southwark

LAB HOLD
Majority: 12,972, 22.1% | Turnout: 58,521, 67.2% | Electorate: 87,282 | EU Ref: 27.0% Leave

PARTY	CANDIDATE	VOTES	SHARE	CHANGE 2015
Labour	Neil Coyle	31,161	53.2%	10.2%
Liberal Democrat	Simon Hughes	18,189	31.1%	-3.3%
Conservative	Siobhan Baillie	7,581	13.0%	1.2%
UK Independence Party	Elizabeth Jones	838	1.4%	-4.9%
Green	John Tyson	639	1.1%	-2.8%
Independent	James Clarke	113	0.2%	0.2%

Berwickshire, Roxburgh & Selkirk

CON GAIN FROM SNP
Majority: 11,060, 21.1% | Turnout: 52,367, 71.5% | Electorate: 73,191 | EU Ref: 43.0% Leave

PARTY	CANDIDATE	VOTES	SHARE	CHANGE 2015
Conservative	John Lamont	28,213	53.9%	17.9%
Scottish National Party	Calum Kerr	17,153	32.8%	-3.8%
Labour	Ian Davidson	4,519	8.6%	3.7%
Liberal Democrat	Caroline Burgess	2,482	4.7%	-14.0%

Berwick-Upon-Tweed

CON HOLD
Majority: 11,781, 27.9% | Turnout: 42,212, 71.8% | Electorate: 58,807 | EU Ref: 56.0% Leave

PARTY	CANDIDATE	VOTES	SHARE	CHANGE 2015
Conservative	Anne-Marie Trevelyan	22,145	52.5%	11.4%
Labour	Scott Dickinson	10,364	24.6%	9.6%
Liberal Democrat	Julie Porksen	8,916	21.1%	-7.8%
Green	Thomas Stewart	787	1.9%	-1.8%

Bethnal Green & Bow

LAB HOLD

Majority: 35,393, 59.1% | Turnout: 59,825, 69.6% | Electorate: 86,075 | EU Ref: 30.9% Leave

PARTY	CANDIDATE	VOTES	SHARE	CHANGE 2015
Labour	Rushanara Ali	42,969	71.8%	10.6%
Conservative	Charlotte Chirico	7,576	12.7%	-2.6%
Independent	Ajmal Masroor	3,888	6.5%	6.5%
Liberal Democrat	William Dyer	2,982	5.0%	0.5%
Green	Alistair Polson	1,516	2.5%	-6.7%
UK Independence Party	Ian de Wulverton	894	1.5%	-4.6%

Beverley & Holderness

CON HOLD

Majority: 14,042, 25.3% | Turnout: 55,638, 69.6% | Electorate: 80,657 | EU Ref: 58.8% Leave

PARTY	CANDIDATE	VOTES	SHARE	CHANGE 2015
Conservative	Graham Stuart	32,499	58.4%	10.2%
Labour	Johanna Boal	18,457	33.1%	8.2%
Liberal Democrat	Denis Healy	2,808	5.0%	-0.5%
The Yorkshire Party	Lee Walton	1,158	2.1%	0.8%
Green	Richard Howarth	716	1.4%	-2.1%

Bexhill & Battle

CON HOLD

Majority: 22,165, 37.3% | Turnout: 59,472, 73.1% | Electorate: 81,331 | EU Ref: 57.7% Leave

PARTY	CANDIDATE	VOTES	SHARE	CHANGE 2015
Conservative	Huw Merriman	36,854	62.0%	7.2%
Labour	Christine Bayliss	14,689	24.7%	10.6%
Liberal Democrat	Joel Kemp	4,485	7.5%	-0.1%
UK Independence Party	Geoffrey Bastin	2,006	3.4%	-15.0%
Green	Jonathan Kent	1,438	2.4%	-2.7%

Bexleyheath & Crayford

CON HOLD
Majority: 9,073, 20.1% | Turnout: 45,189, 69.2% | Electorate: 65,315 | EU Ref: 65.0% Leave

PARTY	CANDIDATE	VOTES	SHARE	CHANGE 2015
Conservative	David Evennett	25,113	55.6%	8.3%
Labour	Stef Borella	16,040	35.5%	9.3%
UK Independence Party	Mike Ferro	1,944	4.3%	-16.7%
Liberal Democrat	Simone Reynolds	1,201	2.7%	-0.3%
Green	Ivor Lobo	601	1.3%	-0.8%
British National Party	Peter Finch	290	0.6%	0.6%

Birkenhead

LAB HOLD
Majority: 25,514, 58.5% | Turnout: 43,663, 67.7% | Electorate: 64,484 | EU Ref: 51.8% Leave

PARTY	CANDIDATE	VOTES	SHARE	CHANGE 2015
Labour	Frank Field	33,558	76.9%	9.2%
Conservative	Stewart Gardiner	8,044	18.4%	3.6%
Liberal Democrat	Allan Brame	1,118	2.6%	-1.0%
Green	Jayne Clough	943	2.2%	-2.0%

Birmingham Edgbaston

LAB HOLD
Majority: 6,917, 15.8% | Turnout: 43,612, 64.1% | Electorate: 68,091 | EU Ref: 43.2% Leave

PARTY	CANDIDATE	VOTES	SHARE	CHANGE 2015
Labour	Preet Gill	24,124	55.3%	10.5%
Conservative	Caroline Squire	17,207	39.5%	1.2%
Liberal Democrat	Colin Green	1,564	3.6%	0.7%
Green	Alice Kiff	562	1.3%	-2.0%
Common Good	Dick Rodgers	155	0.4%	0.4%

Birmingham Erdington

LAB HOLD

Majority: 7,285, 19.6% | Turnout: 37,217, 57.2% | Electorate: 65,067 | EU Ref: 57.5% Leave

PARTY	CANDIDATE	VOTES	SHARE	CHANGE 2015
Labour	Jack Dromey	21,571	58.0%	12.3%
Conservative	Robert Alden	14,286	38.4%	7.6%
Liberal Democrat	Ann Holtom	750	2.0%	-0.8%
Green	James Lovatt	610	1.6%	-1.1%

Birmingham Hall Green

LAB HOLD

Majority: 33,944, 62.5% | Turnout: 54,310, 69.4% | Electorate: 78,271 | EU Ref: 43.3% Leave

PARTY	CANDIDATE	VOTES	SHARE	CHANGE 2015
Labour	Roger Godsiff	42,143	77.6%	17.8%
Conservative	Reena Ranger	8,199	15.1%	-2.6%
Liberal Democrat	Jerry Evans	3,137	5.8%	-5.8%
Green	Patrick Cox	831	1.5%	-3.1%

Birmingham Hodge Hill

LAB HOLD

Majority: 31,026, 66.9% | Turnout: 46,394, 61.3% | Electorate: 75,698 | EU Ref: 57.6% Leave

PARTY	CANDIDATE	VOTES	SHARE	CHANGE 2015
Labour	Liam Byrne	37,606	81.1%	12.7%
Conservative	Ahmereen Reza	6,580	14.2%	2.7%
UK Independence Party	Mohammed Khan	1,016	2.2%	-9.1%
Liberal Democrat	Phil Bennion	805	1.7%	-4.7%
Green	Clare Thomas	387	0.8%	-1.2%

Birmingham Ladywood

LAB HOLD

Majority: 28,714, 69.5% | Turnout: 41,307, 59.0% | Electorate: 70,023 | EU Ref: 41.1% Leave

PARTY	CANDIDATE	VOTES	SHARE	CHANGE 2015
Labour	Shabana Mahmood	34,166	82.7%	9.1%
Conservative	Andrew Browning	5,452	13.2%	0.5%
Liberal Democrat	Lee Dargue	1,156	2.8%	-1.0%
Green	Kefentse Dennis	533	1.3%	-2.9%

Birmingham Northfield

LAB HOLD

Majority: 4,667, 10.5% | Turnout: 44,348, 61.3% | Electorate: 72,322 | EU Ref: 57.5% Leave

PARTY	CANDIDATE	VOTES	SHARE	CHANGE 2015
Labour	Richard Burden	23,596	53.2%	11.6%
Conservative	Meg Powell-Chandler	18,929	42.7%	7.0%
Liberal Democrat	Roger Harmer	959	2.2%	-1.0%
Green	Eleanor Masters	864	1.9%	-0.8%

Birmingham Perry Barr

LAB HOLD

Majority: 18,383, 41.6% | Turnout: 44,197, 63.1% | Electorate: 70,106 EU Ref: 54.2% Leave

PARTY	CANDIDATE	VOTES	SHARE	CHANGE 2015
Labour	Khalid Mahmood	30,109	68.1%	10.7%
Conservative	Charlotte Hodivala	11,726	26.5%	5.0%
Liberal Democrat	Harjun Singh	1,080	2.4%	-2.4%
Socialist Labour Party	Shangara Bhatoe	592	1.3%	1.3%
Green	Vijay Rana	591	1.3%	-1.9%
Open Borders Party	Harjinder Singh	99	0.2%	0.2%

Birmingham Selly Oak

LAB HOLD

Majority: 15,207, 31.0% | Turnout: 48,985, 65.9% | Electorate: 74,370 | EU Ref: 43.6% Leave

PARTY	CANDIDATE	VOTES	SHARE	CHANGE 2015
Labour	Steve McCabe	30,836	62.9%	15.3%
Conservative	Sophie Shrubsole	15,629	31.9%	2.9%
Liberal Democrat	David Radcliffe	1,644	3.4%	-2.2%
Green	Julien Pritchard	876	1.8%	-3.3%

Birmingham Yardley

LAB HOLD

Majority: 16,574, 37.3% | Turnout: 44,502, 61.3% | Electorate: 72,581 | EU Ref: 61.3% Leave

PARTY	CANDIDATE	VOTES	SHARE	CHANGE 2015
Labour	Jess Phillips	25,398	57.1%	15.4%
Conservative	Mohammed Afzal	8,824	19.8%	5.8%
Liberal Democrat	John Hemming	7,984	17.9%	-7.7%
UK Independence Party	Paul Clayton	1,916	4.3%	-11.8%
Green	Christopher Garghan	280	0.6%	-1.1%
Independent	Abu Nowshed	100	0.2%	0.2%

Bishop Auckland

LAB HOLD

Majority: 502, 1.2% | Turnout: 43,281, 64.0% | Electorate: 67,661 | EU Ref: 60.6% Leave

PARTY	CANDIDATE	VOTES	SHARE	CHANGE 2015
Labour	Helen Goodman	20,808	48.1%	6.7%
Conservative	Christopher Adams	20,306	46.9%	14.4%
Liberal Democrat	Ciaran Morrissey	1,176	2.7%	-1.7%
British National Party	Adam Walker	991	2.3%	2.3%

Blackburn

LAB HOLD

Majority: 20,368, 42.9% | Turnout: 47,515, 67.2% | Electorate: 70,664 | EU Ref: 56.4% Leave

PARTY	CANDIDATE	VOTES	SHARE	CHANGE 2015
Labour	Kate Hollern	33,148	69.8%	13.5%
Conservative	Bob Eastwood	12,780	26.9%	-0.4%
Independent	Duncan Miller	878	1.8%	1.8%
Liberal Democrat	Irfan Ahmed	709	1.5%	-0.7%

Blackley & Broughton

LAB HOLD

Majority: 19,601, 48.8% | Turnout: 40,113, 56.0% | Electorate: 71,648 | EU Ref: 51.3% Leave

PARTY	CANDIDATE	VOTES	SHARE	CHANGE 2015
Labour	Graham Stringer	28,258	70.4%	8.5%
Conservative	David Goss	8,657	21.6%	6.5%
UK Independence Party	Martin Power	1,825	4.5%	-11.9%
Liberal Democrat	Charles Gadsden	737	1.8%	-0.5%
Green	David Jones	462	1.2%	-3.1%
Christian Peoples Alliance	Abi Ajoku	174	0.4%	0.4%

Blackpool North & Cleveleys

CON HOLD

Majority: 2,023, 4.9% | Turnout: 41,007, 64.1% | Electorate: 63,967 | EU Ref: 66.9% Leave

PARTY	CANDIDATE	VOTES	SHARE	CHANGE 2015
Conservative	Paul Maynard	20,255	49.4%	4.9%
Labour	Chris Webb	18,232	44.5%	8.5%
UK Independence Party	Paul White	1,392	3.4%	-11.4%
Liberal Democrat	Sue Close	747	1.8%	-0.6%
Green	Duncan Royle	381	0.9%	-1.3%

Blackpool South

LAB HOLD

Majority: 2,523, 7.2% | Turnout: 34,953, 59.8% | Electorate: 58,470 | EU Ref: 67.8% Leave

PARTY	CANDIDATE	VOTES	SHARE	CHANGE 2015
Labour	Gordon Marsden	17,581	50.3%	8.5%
Conservative	Peter Anthony	15,058	43.1%	9.3%
UK Independence Party	Noel Matthews	1,339	3.8%	-13.5%
Liberal Democrat	Bill Greene	634	1.8%	-0.5%
Green	John Peter Warnock	341	1.0%	-1.6%

Blaenau Gwent

LAB HOLD

Majority: 11,907, 36.8% | Turnout: 32,384, 63.2% | Electorate: 51,227 | EU Ref: 62.0% Leave

PARTY	CANDIDATE	VOTES	SHARE	CHANGE 2015
Labour	Nick Smith	18,787	58.0%	0.0%
Plaid Cymru	Nigel Copner	6,880	21.2%	12.3%
Conservative	Tracey West	4,783	14.8%	4.0%
UK Independence Party	Dennis May	973	3.0%	-14.9%
Independent	Vicki Browning	666	2.1%	2.1%
Liberal Democrat	Cameron Sullivan	295	0.9%	-1.0%

Blaydon

LAB HOLD

Majority: 13,477, 28.0% | Turnout: 48,084, 70.2% | Electorate: 68,459 | EU Ref: 56.3% Leave

PARTY	CANDIDATE	VOTES	SHARE	CHANGE 2015
Labour	Liz Twist	26,979	56.1%	6.9%
Conservative	Thomas Smith	13,502	28.1%	10.6%
Liberal Democrat	Jonathan Wallace	4,366	9.1%	-3.2%
UK Independence Party	Ray Tolley	2,459	5.1%	-12.4%
Green	Paul McNally	583	1.2%	-2.5%
Libertarian	Michael Marchetti	114	0.2%	0.2%
Space Navies Party	Lisabela Marschild	81	0.2%	0.2%

Blyth Valley

LAB HOLD

Majority: 7,915, 18.6% | Turnout: 42,490, 67.1% | Electorate: 63,415 | EU Ref: 59.9% Leave

PARTY	CANDIDATE	VOTES	SHARE	CHANGE 2015
Labour	Ronnie Campbell	23,770	55.9%	9.6%
Conservative	Ian Levy	15,855	37.3%	15.6%
Liberal Democrat	Jeff Reid	1,947	4.6%	-1.3%
Green	Dawn Furness	918	2.2%	-1.6%

Bognor Regis & Littlehampton

CON HOLD

Majority: 17,494, 34.1% | Turnout: 51,352, 67.7% | Electorate: 75,827 | EU Ref: 64.2% Leave

PARTY	CANDIDATE	VOTES	SHARE	CHANGE 2015
Conservative	Nick Gibb	30,276	59.0%	7.6%
Labour	Alan Butcher	12,782	24.9%	11.1%
Liberal Democrat	Francis Oppler	3,352	6.5%	-2.5%
Independent	Paul Sanderson	2,088	4.1%	4.1%
UK Independence Party	Patrick Lowe	1,861	3.6%	-18.1%
Green	Andrew Bishop	993	1.9%	-2.2%

Bolsover

LAB HOLD

Majority: 5,288, 11.3% | Turnout: 46,519, 63.3% | Electorate: 73,429 | EU Ref: 70.3% Leave

PARTY	CANDIDATE	VOTES	SHARE	CHANGE 2015
Labour	Dennis Skinner	24,153	51.9%	0.7%
Conservative	Helen Harrison	18,865	40.6%	16.1%
UK Independence Party	Philip Rose	2,129	4.6%	-16.4%
Liberal Democrat	Ross Shipman	1,372	2.9%	-0.4%

Bolton North East

LAB HOLD

Majority: 3,797, 8.4% | Turnout: 45,183, 67.2% | Electorate: 67,233 | EU Ref: 57.8% Leave

PARTY	CANDIDATE	VOTES	SHARE	CHANGE 2015
Labour	David Crausby	22,870	50.6%	7.7%
Conservative	James Daly	19,073	42.2%	9.4%
UK Independence Party	Harry Lamb	1,567	3.5%	-15.3%
Liberal Democrat	Warren Fox	1,316	2.9%	0.0%
Green	Liz Spencer	357	0.8%	-1.8%

Bolton South East

LAB HOLD

Majority: 13,126, 31.0% | Turnout: 42,323, 61.4% | Electorate: 68,886 | EU Ref: 63.4% Leave

PARTY	CANDIDATE	VOTES	SHARE	CHANGE 2015
Labour	Yasmin Qureshi	25,676	60.7%	10.2%
Conservative	Sarah Pochin	12,550	29.7%	9.3%
UK Independence Party	Jeff Armstrong	2,779	6.6%	-17.1%
Liberal Democrat	Frank Harasiwka	781	1.8%	-0.8%
Green	Alan Johnson	537	1.3%	-1.7%

Bolton West

CON HOLD

Majority: 936, 1.8% | Turnout: 51,054, 70.1% | Electorate: 72,797 | EU Ref: 55.5% Leave

PARTY	CANDIDATE	VOTES	SHARE	CHANGE 2015
Conservative	Christopher Green	24,459	47.9%	7.3%
Labour	Julie Hilling	23,523	46.1%	7.1%
UK Independence Party	Martin Tighe	1,587	3.1%	-12.2%
Liberal Democrat	Rebecca Forrest	1,485	2.9%	-1.1%

Bootle

LAB HOLD
Majority: 36,200, 72.0% | Turnout: 50,288, 69.2% | Electorate: 72,872 | EU Ref: 54.9% Leave

PARTY	CANDIDATE	VOTES	SHARE	CHANGE 2015
Labour	Peter Dowd	42,259	84.0%	9.6%
Conservative	Charles Fifield	6,059	12.0%	4.0%
Liberal Democrat	David Newman	837	1.7%	-0.5%
Green	Alison Gibbon	709	1.4%	-1.9%
Socialist Labour Party	Kim Bryan	424	0.8%	0.8%

Boston & Skegness

CON HOLD
Majority: 16,572, 38.6% | Turnout: 42,879, 62.7% | Electorate: 68,402 | EU Ref: 75.0% Leave

PARTY	CANDIDATE	VOTES	SHARE	CHANGE 2015
Conservative	Matt Warman	27,271	63.6%	19.8%
Labour	Paul Kenny	10,699	25.0%	8.5%
UK Independence Party	Paul Nuttall	3,308	7.7%	-26.1%
Liberal Democrat	Philip Smith	771	1.8%	-0.5%
Green	Victoria Percival	547	1.3%	-0.6%
Blue Revolution	Mike Gilbert	283	0.7%	0.7%

Bosworth

CON HOLD
Majority: 18,351, 32.6% | Turnout: 56,168, 69.6% | Electorate: 81,661 | EU Ref: 60.8% Leave

PARTY	CANDIDATE	VOTES	SHARE	CHANGE 2015
Conservative	David Tredinnick	31,864	56.7%	13.9%
Labour	Chris Kealey	13,513	24.1%	6.6%
Liberal Democrat	Michael Mullaney	9,744	17.3%	-5.0%
Green	Mick Gregg	1,047	1.9%	1.9%

Bournemouth East

CON HOLD

Majority: 7,937, 16.3% | Turnout: 48,618, 65.2% | Electorate: 74,591 | EU Ref: 53.5% Leave

PARTY	CANDIDATE	VOTES	SHARE	CHANGE 2015
Conservative	Tobias Ellwood	25,221	51.9%	2.7%
Labour	Mel Semple	17,284	35.6%	18.9%
Liberal Democrat	Jon Nicholas	3,168	6.5%	-1.9%
UK Independence Party	David Hughes	1,405	2.9%	-13.6%
Green	Alasdair Keddie	1,236	2.5%	-4.7%
Independent	Kieron Wilson	304	0.6%	0.6%

Bournemouth West

CON HOLD

Majority: 7,711, 17.3% | Turnout: 44,507, 60.8% | Electorate: 73,195 | EU Ref: 57.9% Leave

PARTY	CANDIDATE	VOTES	SHARE	CHANGE 2015
Conservative	Conor Burns	23,812	53.5%	5.3%
Labour	David Stokes	16,101	36.2%	18.5%
Liberal Democrat	Phil Dunn	2,929	6.6%	-1.3%
Green	Simon Bull	1,247	2.8%	-4.6%
Pirate Party	Jason Halsey	418	0.9%	0.9%

Bracknell

CON HOLD

Majority: 16,016, 28.6% | Turnout: 55,892, 70.6% | Electorate: 79,199 | EU Ref: 53.3% Leave

PARTY	CANDIDATE	VOTES	SHARE	CHANGE 2015
Conservative	Phillip Lee	32,882	58.8%	3.1%
Labour	Paul Bidwell	16,866	30.2%	13.3%
Liberal Democrat	Patrick Smith	4,186	7.5%	0.0%
UK Independence Party	Len Amos	1,521	2.7%	-13.0%
Independent	Olivio Barreto	437	0.8%	0.8%

Bradford East

LAB HOLD

Majority: 20,540, 45.0% | Turnout: 45,622, 64.8% | Electorate: 70,389 | EU Ref: 57.9% Leave

PARTY	CANDIDATE	VOTES	SHARE	CHANGE 2015
Labour	Imran Hussain	29,831	65.4%	18.7%
Conservative	Mark Trafford	9,291	20.4%	9.1%
Independent	David Ward	3,576	7.8%	7.8%
UK Independence Party	Jonathan Barras	1,372	3.0%	-6.9%
Liberal Democrat	Mark Jewell	843	1.8%	-27.7%
Better for Bradford	Paul Parkins	420	0.9%	0.9%
Green	Andy Stanford	289	0.6%	-1.5%

Bradford South

LAB HOLD

Majority: 6,700, 16.3% | Turnout: 41,049, 60.6% | Electorate: 67,752 | EU Ref: 62.7% Leave

PARTY	CANDIDATE	VOTES	SHARE	CHANGE 2015
Labour	Judith Cummins	22,364	54.5%	11.1%
Conservative	Tanya Graham	15,664	38.2%	11.9%
UK Independence Party	Stephen Place	1,758	4.3%	-19.8%
Liberal Democrat	Stuart Thomas	516	1.3%	-1.7%
English Democrats	Therese Hirst	377	0.9%	0.9%
Green	Darren Parkinson	370	0.9%	-2.4%

Bradford West

LAB HOLD

Majority: 21,902, 48.1% | Turnout: 45,528, 67.4% | Electorate: 67,568 | EU Ref: 49.4% Leave

PARTY	CANDIDATE	VOTES	SHARE	CHANGE 2015
Labour	Naz Shah	29,444	64.7%	15.1%
Conservative	George Grant	7,542	16.6%	1.3%
Independent	Salma Yaqoob	6,345	13.9%	13.9%
UK Independence Party	Derrick Hodgson	885	1.9%	-5.8%
Liberal Democrat	Alun Griffiths	712	1.6%	-1.3%

Green	Celia Hickson	481	1.1%	-1.6%
Independent	Hussain Khadim	65	0.1%	0.2%
Independent	Muhammad Hijazi	54	0.1%	0.1%

Braintree

CON HOLD

Majority: 18,422, 35.2% | Turnout: 52,326, 69.5% | Electorate: 75,316 | EU Ref: 61.4% Leave

PARTY	CANDIDATE	VOTES	SHARE	CHANGE 2015
Conservative	James Cleverly	32,873	62.8%	9.0%
Labour	Malcolm Fincken	14,451	27.6%	9.1%
Liberal Democrat	Peter Turner	2,251	4.3%	-0.6%
UK Independence Party	Richard Bingley	1,835	3.5%	-15.3%
Green	Thomas Pashby	916	1.8%	-1.4%

Brecon & Radnorshire

CON HOLD

Majority: 8,038, 19.5% | Turnout: 41,334, 74.6% | Electorate: 56,010 | EU Ref: 51.7% Leave

PARTY	CANDIDATE	VOTES	SHARE	CHANGE 2015
Conservative	Christopher Davies	20,081	48.6%	7.5%
Liberal Democrat	James Gibson-Watt	12,043	29.1%	0.8%
Labour	Dan Lodge	7,335	17.7%	3.0%
Plaid Cymru	Kate Heneghan	1,299	3.1%	-1.3%
UK Independence Party	Peter Gilbert	576	1.4%	-6.9%

Brent Central

LAB HOLD

Majority: 27,997, 53.6% | Turnout: 52,296, 65.0% | Electorate: 80,499 | EU Ref: 42.9% Leave

PARTY	CANDIDATE	VOTES	SHARE	CHANGE 2015
Labour	Dawn Butler	38,208	73.1%	10.9%
Conservative	Rahoul Bhansali	10,211	19.5%	-0.8%
Liberal Democrat	Anton Georgiou	2,519	4.8%	-3.6%
Green	Shaka Lish	802	1.5%	-2.5%
UK Independence Party	Janice North	556	1.1%	-2.9%

Brent North

LAB HOLD

Majority: 17,061, 30.2% | Turnout: 56,444, 68.4% | Electorate: 82,567 | EU Ref: 43.1% Leave

PARTY	CANDIDATE	VOTES	SHARE	CHANGE 2015
Labour	Barry Gardiner	35,496	62.9%	8.6%
Conservative	Ameet Jogia	18,435	32.7%	-0.9%
Liberal Democrat	Paul Lorber	1,614	2.9%	-2.1%
Green	Michaela Lichten	660	1.2%	-1.8%
Independent	Elcena Jeffers	239	0.4%	0.0%

Brentford & Isleworth

LAB HOLD

Majority: 12,182, 19.8% | Turnout: 61,629, 72.4% | Electorate: 85,164 | EU Ref: 39.5% Leave

PARTY	CANDIDATE	VOTES	SHARE	CHANGE 2015
Labour	Ruth Cadbury	35,364	57.4%	13.6%
Conservative	Mary Macleod	23,182	37.6%	-5.3%
Liberal Democrat	Joe Bourke	3,083	5.0%	1.0%

Brentwood & Ongar

CON HOLD

Majority: 24,002, 45.4% | Turnout: 52,910, 70.6% | Electorate: 75,067 | EU Ref: 60.9% Leave

PARTY	CANDIDATE	VOTES	SHARE	CHANGE 2015
Conservative	Alex Burghart	34,811	65.8%	7.0%
Labour	Gareth Barrett	10,809	20.4%	7.9%
Liberal Democrat	Karen Chilvers	4,426	8.4%	-0.5%
UK Independence Party	Michael McGough	1,845	3.5%	-13.3%
Green	Paul Jeater	915	1.7%	-1.0%
Independent	Louca Kousoulou	104	0.2%	0.2%

Bridgend

LAB HOLD

Majority: 4,700, 10.9% | Turnout: 43,255, 69.6% | Electorate: 62,185 | EU Ref: 49.7% Leave

PARTY	CANDIDATE	VOTES	SHARE	CHANGE 2015
Labour	Madeleine Moon	21,913	50.7%	13.6%
Conservative	Karen Robson	17,213	39.8%	7.6%
Plaid Cymru	Rhys Watkins	1,783	4.1%	-2.9%
Liberal Democrat	Jonathan Pratt	919	2.1%	-2.1%
UK Independence Party	Alun Williams	781	1.8%	-13.2%
Independent	Isabel Robson	646	1.5%	1.5%

Bridgwater & West Somerset

CON HOLD

Majority: 15,448, 26.5% | Turnout: 58,267, 65.3% | Electorate: 89,294 | EU Ref: 62.2% Leave

PARTY	CANDIDATE	VOTES	SHARE	CHANGE 2015
Conservative	Ian Liddell-Grainger	32,111	55.1%	9.2%
Labour	Wes Hinckes	16,663	28.6%	11.0%
Liberal Democrat	Marcus Kravis	6,332	10.9%	-1.6%
UK Independence Party	Simon Smedley	2,102	3.6%	-15.6%
Green	Kay Powell	1,059	1.8%	-3.0%

Brigg & Goole

CON HOLD

Majority: 12,363, 27.4% | Turnout: 45,057, 68.2% | Electorate: 66,069 | EU Ref: 66.2% Leave

PARTY	CANDIDATE	VOTES	SHARE	CHANGE 2015
Conservative	Andrew Percy	27,219	60.4%	7.4%
Labour	Terence Smith	14,856	33.0%	5.8%
UK Independence Party	David Jeffreys	1,596	3.5%	-11.9%
Liberal Democrat	Jerry Lonsdale	836	1.9%	0.1%
Green	Isabel Pires	550	1.2%	-0.9%

Brighton, Kemptown

LAB GAIN FROM CON

Majority: 9,868, 20.0% | Turnout: 49,207, 72.5% | Electorate: 67,893 | EU Ref: 43.4% Leave

PARTY	CANDIDATE	VOTES	SHARE	CHANGE 2015
Labour	Lloyd Russell-Moyle	28,703	58.3%	19.2%
Conservative	Simon Kirby	18,835	38.3%	-2.4%
Liberal Democrat	Emily Tester	1,457	3.0%	-0.1%
Independent	Doktor Haze	212	0.4%	0.4%

Brighton, Pavilion

GREEN HOLD

Majority: 14,699, 25.5% | Turnout: 57,687, 76.4% | Electorate: 75,486 | EU Ref: 25.7% Leave

PARTY	CANDIDATE	VOTES	SHARE	CHANGE 2015
Green	Caroline Lucas	30,149	52.3%	10.4%
Labour	Solomon Curtis	15,450	26.8%	-0.5%
Conservative	Emma Warman	11,082	19.2%	-3.6%
UK Independence Party	Ian Buchanan	630	1.1%	-3.9%
Independent	Nick Yeomans	376	0.7%	0.4%

Bristol East

LAB HOLD

Majority: 13,394, 26.3% | Turnout: 50,799, 70.2% | Electorate: 72,415 | EU Ref: 46.8% Leave

PARTY	CANDIDATE	VOTES	SHARE	CHANGE 2015
Labour	Kerry McCarthy	30,847	60.7%	21.5%
Conservative	Theo Clarke	17,453	34.4%	3.7%
Liberal Democrat	Chris Lucas	1,389	2.7%	-3.1%
Green	Lorraine Francis	1,110	2.2%	-6.1%

Bristol North West

LAB GAIN FROM CON

Majority: 4,761, 8.9% | Turnout: 54,096, 71.7% | Electorate: 75,434 | EU Ref: 41.6% Leave

PARTY	CANDIDATE	VOTES	SHARE	CHANGE 2015
Labour	Darren Jones	27,400	50.7%	16.2%
Conservative	Charlotte Leslie	22,639	41.8%	-2.1%
Liberal Democrat	Celia Downie	2,814	5.2%	-1.0%
Green	Sharmila Bousa	1,243	2.3%	-3.4%

Bristol South

LAB HOLD

Majority: 15,987, 29.4% | Turnout: 54,382, 65.5% | Electorate: 83,012 | EU Ref: 47.1% Leave

PARTY	CANDIDATE	VOTES	SHARE	CHANGE 2015
Labour	Karin Smyth	32,666	60.1%	21.7%
Conservative	Mark Weston	16,679	30.7%	6.3%
Liberal Democrat	Benjamin Nutland	1,821	3.3%	-5.3%
UK Independence Party	Ian Kealey	1,672	3.1%	-13.4%
Green	Tony Dyer	1,428	2.6%	-8.9%
Independent	John Langley	116	0.2%	0.2%

Bristol West

LAB HOLD

Majority: 37,336, 52.1% | Turnout: 71,608, 77.1% | Electorate: 93,003 | EU Ref: 20.7% Leave

PARTY	CANDIDATE	VOTES	SHARE	CHANGE 2015
Labour	Thangam Debbonaire	47,213	65.9%	30.3%
Conservative	Annabel Tall	9,877	13.8%	-1.4%
Green	Molly Scott Cato	9,216	12.9%	-14.0%
Liberal Democrat	Stephen Williams	5,201	7.3%	-11.6%
Money Free Party	Jodian Rodgers	101	0.1%	0.1%

Broadland

CON HOLD

Majority: 15,816, 28.3% | Turnout: 55,971, 72.4% | Electorate: 77,334 | EU Ref: 54.1% Leave

PARTY	CANDIDATE	VOTES	SHARE	CHANGE 2015
Conservative	Keith Simpson	32,406	57.9%	7.4%
Labour	Iain Simpson	16,590	29.6%	10.9%
Liberal Democrat	Steve Riley	4,449	7.9%	-1.8%
UK Independence Party	David Moreland	1,594	2.8%	-13.9%
Green	Andrew Boswell	932	1.7%	-2.6%

Bromley & Chislehurst

CON HOLD

Majority: 9,590, 20.6% | Turnout: 46,662, 71.6% | Electorate: 65,117 | EU Ref: 49.8% Leave

PARTY	CANDIDATE	VOTES	SHARE	CHANGE 2015
Conservative	Bob Neill	25,175	54.0%	1.0%
Labour	Sara Hyde	15,585	33.4%	11.2%
Liberal Democrat	Sam Webber	3,369	7.2%	0.8%
UK Independence Party	Emmett Jenner	1,383	3.0%	-11.3%
Green	Roisin Robertson	1,150	2.5%	-1.7%

Bromsgrove

CON HOLD
Majority: 16,573, 30.7% | Turnout: 54,040, 73.5% | Electorate: 73,571 | EU Ref: 55.4% Leave

PARTY	CANDIDATE	VOTES	SHARE	CHANGE 2015
Conservative	Sajid Javid	33,493	62.0%	8.1%
Labour	Michael Thompson	16,920	31.3%	9.1%
Liberal Democrat	Neil Lewis	2,488	4.6%	-0.4%
Green	Spoz Esposito	1,139	2.1%	-1.2%

Broxbourne

CON HOLD
Majority: 15,792, 33.3% | Turnout: 47,485, 64.6% | Electorate: 73,502 | EU Ref: 65.8% Leave

PARTY	CANDIDATE	VOTES	SHARE	CHANGE 2015
Conservative	Charles Walker	29,515	62.2%	6.1%
Labour	Selina Norgrove	13,723	28.9%	10.5%
UK Independence Party	Tony Faulkner	1,918	4.0%	-15.7%
Liberal Democrat	Andy Graham	1,481	3.1%	-0.1%
Green	Tabitha Evans	848	1.8%	-0.9%

Broxtowe

CON HOLD
Majority: 863, 1.5% | Turnout: 55,508, 75.0% | Electorate: 74,013 | EU Ref: 52.4% Leave

PARTY	CANDIDATE	VOTES	SHARE	CHANGE 2015
Conservative	Anna Soubry	25,983	46.8%	1.6%
Labour	Greg Marshall	25,120	45.3%	8.1%
Liberal Democrat	Tim Hallam	2,247	4.0%	0.1%
UK Independence Party	Fran Loi	1,477	2.7%	-8.0%
Green	Pat Morton	681	1.2%	-1.7%

Buckingham

CON HOLD (SPEAKER)

Majority: 25,725, 48.8% | Turnout: 52,679, 66.2% | Electorate: 79,615 | EU Ref: 48.7% Leave

PARTY	CANDIDATE	VOTES	SHARE	CHANGE 2015
Speaker	John Bercow	34,299	65.1%	0.6%
Green	Michael Sheppard	8,574	16.3%	2.5%
Independent	Scott Raven	5,638	10.7%	10.7%
UK Independence Party	Brian Mapletoft	4,168	7.9%	-13.8%

Burnley

LAB HOLD

Majority: 6,353, 15.7% | Turnout: 40,290, 62.2% | Electorate: 64,709 | EU Ref: 66.6% Leave

PARTY	CANDIDATE	VOTES	SHARE	CHANGE 2015
Labour	Julie Cooper	18,832	46.7%	9.1%
Conservative	Paul White	12,479	31.0%	17.5%
Liberal Democrat	Gordon Birtwistle	6,046	15.0%	-14.4%
UK Independence Party	Tom Commis	2,472	6.1%	-11.1%
Green	Laura Fisk	461	1.1%	-1.0%

Burton

CON HOLD

Majority: 10,047, 20.2% | Turnout: 49,911, 67.5% | Electorate: 73,954 | EU Ref: 64.6% Leave

PARTY	CANDIDATE	VOTES	SHARE	CHANGE 2015
Conservative	Andrew Griffiths	28,936	58.0%	8.2%
Labour	John McKiernan	18,889	37.8%	10.3%
Liberal Democrat	Dominic Hardwick	1,262	2.5%	0.0%
Green	Simon Hales	824	1.7%	-0.8%

Bury North

LAB GAIN FROM CON
Majority: 4,375, 9.1% | Turnout: 47,903, 70.9% | Electorate: 67,580 | EU Ref: 53.7% Leave

PARTY	CANDIDATE	VOTES	SHARE	CHANGE 2015
Labour	James Frith	25,683	53.6%	12.5%
Conservative	David Nuttall	21,308	44.5%	2.5%
Liberal Democrat	Richard Baum	912	1.9%	-0.2%

Bury South

LAB HOLD
Majority: 5,965, 11.7% | Turnout: 50,990, 69.2% | Electorate: 73,715 | EU Ref: 54.5% Leave

PARTY	CANDIDATE	VOTES	SHARE	CHANGE 2015
Labour	Ivan Lewis	27,165	53.3%	8.2%
Conservative	Robert Largan	21,200	41.6%	6.9%
UK Independence Party	Ian Henderson	1,316	2.6%	-10.8%
Liberal Democrat	Andrew Page	1,065	2.1%	-1.5%
Independent	Peter Wright	244	0.5%	0.5%

Bury St Edmunds

CON HOLD
Majority: 18,441, 29.7% | Turnout: 62,160, 70.8% | Electorate: 86,071 | EU Ref: 53.7% Leave

PARTY	CANDIDATE	VOTES	SHARE	CHANGE 2015
Conservative	Jo Churchill	36,794	59.2%	5.6%
Labour	Bill Edwards	18,353	29.5%	11.8%
Liberal Democrat	Helen Korfanty	3,565	5.7%	-0.3%
Green	Helen Geake	2,596	4.2%	-3.7%
Independent	Liam Byrne	852	1.4%	1.4%

Caerphilly

LAB HOLD

Majority: 12,078, 29.3% | Turnout: 41,297, 64.1% | Electorate: 64,381 | EU Ref: 55.2% Leave

PARTY	CANDIDATE	VOTES	SHARE	CHANGE 2015
Labour	Wayne David	22,491	54.5%	10.1%
Conservative	Jane Pratt	10,413	25.2%	8.6%
Plaid Cymru	Lindsay Whittle	5,962	14.4%	-0.2%
UK Independence Party	Liz Wilks	1,259	3.0%	-16.3%
Liberal Democrat	Kay David	725	1.8%	-0.6%
Green	Andrew Creak	447	1.1%	-1.2%

Caithness, Sutherland & Easter Ross

LIB DEM GAIN FROM SNP

Majority: 2,044, 6.6% | Turnout: 30,901, 65.9% | Electorate: 46,868 | EU Ref: 49.4% Leave

PARTY	CANDIDATE	VOTES	SHARE	CHANGE 2015
Liberal Democrat	Jamie Stone	11,061	35.8%	0.7%
Scottish National Party	Paul Monaghan	9,017	29.2%	-17.1%
Conservative	Struan Mackie	6,990	22.6%	15.8%
Labour	Olivia Bell	3,833	12.4%	3.5%

Calder Valley

CON HOLD

Majority: 609, 1.0% | Turnout: 58,054, 73.4% | Electorate: 79,045 | EU Ref: 51.7% Leave

PARTY	CANDIDATE	VOTES	SHARE	CHANGE 2015
Conservative	Craig Whittaker	26,790	46.1%	2.5%
Labour	Josh Fenton Glynn	26,181	45.1%	9.7%
Liberal Democrat	Janet Battye	1,952	3.4%	-1.6%
UK Independence Party	Paul Rogan	1,466	2.5%	-8.6%
Independent	Robert Holden	1,034	1.8%	1.8%
Green	Kieran Turner	631	1.1%	-2.8%

Camberwell & Peckham

LAB HOLD

Majority: 37,316, 65.0% | Turnout: 57,412, 67.1% | Electorate: 85,613 | EU Ref: 30.2% Leave

PARTY	CANDIDATE	VOTES	SHARE	CHANGE 2015
Labour	Harriet Harman	44,665	77.8%	14.5%
Conservative	Ben Spencer	7,349	12.8%	-0.4%
Liberal Democrat	Michael Bukola	3,413	5.9%	0.9%
Green	Eleanor Margolies	1,627	2.8%	-7.2%
Christian Peoples Alliance	Ray Towey	227	0.4%	0.4%
Workers Revolutionary Party	Sellu Aminata	131	0.2%	0.0%

Camborne & Redruth

CON HOLD

Majority: 1,577, 3.3% | Turnout: 48,456, 71.8% | Electorate: 68,419 | EU Ref: 57.9% Leave

PARTY	CANDIDATE	VOTES	SHARE	CHANGE 2015
Conservative	George Eustice	23,001	47.5%	7.2%
Labour	Graham Winter	21,424	44.2%	19.3%
Liberal Democrat	Geoff Williams	2,979	6.1%	-6.3%
Green	Geoff Garbett	1,052	2.2%	-3.5%

Cambridge

LAB HOLD

Majority: 12,661, 22.6% | Turnout: 55,934, 71.7% | Electorate: 78,544 | EU Ref: 26.5% Leave

PARTY	CANDIDATE	VOTES	SHARE	CHANGE 2015
Labour	Daniel Zeichner	29,032	51.9%	15.9%
Liberal Democrat	Julian Huppert	16,371	29.3%	-5.6%
Conservative	John Hayward	9,133	16.3%	0.7%
Green	Stuart Tuckwood	1,265	2.3%	-5.7%
Rebooting Democracy	Keith Garrett	133	0.2%	-0.1%

Cannock Chase

CON HOLD

Majority: 8,391, 17.6% | Turnout: 47,872, 64.2% | Electorate: 74,540 | EU Ref: 68.9% Leave

PARTY	CANDIDATE	VOTES	SHARE	CHANGE 2015
Conservative	Amanda Milling	26,318	55.0%	10.8%
Labour	Paul Dadge	17,927	37.4%	3.7%
UK Independence Party	Paul Allen	2,018	4.2%	-13.2%
Green	Paul Woodhead	815	1.7%	-0.2%
Liberal Democrat	Nat Green	794	1.7%	-1.0%

Canterbury

LAB GAIN FROM CON

Majority: 187, 0.3% | Turnout: 56,800, 72.7% | Electorate: 78,182 | EU Ref: 45.3% Leave

PARTY	CANDIDATE	VOTES	SHARE	CHANGE 2015
Labour	Rosie Duffield	25,572	45.0%	20.5%
Conservative	Julian Brazier	25,385	44.7%	1.8%
Liberal Democrat	James Flanagan	4,561	8.0%	-3.6%
Green	Henry Stanton	1,282	2.3%	-4.7%

Cardiff Central

LAB HOLD

Majority: 17,196, 42.6% | Turnout: 40,367, 68.1% | Electorate: 59,288 | EU Ref: 30.4% Leave

PARTY	CANDIDATE	VOTES	SHARE	CHANGE 2015
Labour	Jo Stevens	25,193	62.4%	22.4%
Conservative	Gregory Stafford	7,997	19.8%	5.1%
Liberal Democrat	Eluned Parrott	5,415	13.4%	-13.7%
Plaid Cymru	Mark Hooper	999	2.5%	-2.5%
Green	Benjamin Smith	420	1.0%	-5.3%
UK Independence Party	Sarul-Islam Mohammed	343	0.8%	-5.6%

Cardiff North

LAB GAIN FROM CON
Majority: 4,174, 8.0% | Turnout: 52,022, 77.4% | Electorate: 67,221 | EU Ref: 39.1% Leave

PARTY	CANDIDATE	VOTES	SHARE	CHANGE 2015
Labour	Anna McMorrin	26,081	50.1%	11.9%
Conservative	Craig Williams	21,907	42.1%	-0.3%
Plaid Cymru	Steffan Webb	1,738	3.3%	-1.2%
Liberal Democrat	Matthew Hemsley	1,714	3.3%	-0.5%
UK Independence Party	Gary Oldfield	582	1.1%	-6.6%

Cardiff South & Penarth

LAB HOLD
Majority: 14,864, 29.3% | Turnout: 50,736, 66.3% | Electorate: 76,499 | EU Ref: 44.9% Leave

PARTY	CANDIDATE	VOTES	SHARE	CHANGE 2015
Labour	Stephen Doughty	30,182	59.5%	16.7%
Conservative	Bill Rees	15,318	30.2%	3.4%
Plaid Cymru	Ian Titherington	2,162	4.3%	-3.1%
Liberal Democrat	Emma Sands	1,430	2.8%	-2.1%
UK Independence Party	Andrew Bevan	942	1.9%	-11.9%
Green	Anthony Slaughter	532	1.0%	-2.7%
Pirate Party	Jeb Hedges	170	0.3%	0.3%

Cardiff West

LAB HOLD
Majority: 12,551, 26.9% | Turnout: 46,629, 69.8% | Electorate: 66,775 | EU Ref: 44.8% Leave

PARTY	CANDIDATE	VOTES	SHARE	CHANGE 2015
Labour	Kevin Brennan	26,425	56.7%	16.0%
Conservative	Matt Smith	13,874	29.8%	4.6%
Plaid Cymru	Michael Deem	4,418	9.5%	-4.4%
Liberal Democrat	Alex Meredith	1,214	2.6%	-2.1%
UK Independence Party	Richard Lewis	698	1.5%	-9.7%

Carlisle

CON HOLD
Majority: 2,599, 6.1% | Turnout: 43,056, 69.1% | Electorate: 62,294 | EU Ref: 60.5% Leave

PARTY	CANDIDATE	VOTES	SHARE	CHANGE 2015
Conservative	John Stevenson	21,472	49.9%	5.6%
Labour	Ruth Alcroft	18,873	43.8%	6.0%
UK Independence Party	Fiona Mills	1,455	3.4%	-9.0%
Liberal Democrat	Peter Thornton	1,256	2.9%	0.4%

Carmarthen East & Dinefwr

PC HOLD
Majority: 3,908, 9.5% | Turnout: 41,029, 73.3% | Electorate: 55,976 | EU Ref: 53.8% Leave

PARTY	CANDIDATE	VOTES	SHARE	CHANGE 2015
Plaid Cymru	Jonathan Edwards	16,127	39.3%	0.9%
Labour	David Darkin	12,219	29.8%	5.6%
Conservative	Havard Hughes	10,778	26.3%	5.1%
UK Independence Party	Neil Hamilton	985	2.4%	-8.7%
Liberal Democrat	Lesley Prosser	920	2.2%	-0.1%

Carmarthen West & South Pembrokeshire

CON HOLD
Majority: 3,110, 7.3% | Turnout: 42,226, 72.1% | Electorate: 58,565 | EU Ref: 55.4% Leave

PARTY	CANDIDATE	VOTES	SHARE	CHANGE 2015
Conservative	Simon Hart	19,771	46.8%	3.1%
Labour	Marc Tierney	16,661	39.5%	10.8%
Plaid Cymru	Abi Thomas	3,933	9.3%	-1.1%
Liberal Democrat	Alistair Cameron	956	2.3%	-0.1%
UK Independence Party	Phil Edwards	905	2.1%	-9.5%

Carshalton & Wallington

LIB DEM HOLD
Majority: 1,369, 2.7% | Turnout: 50,753, 71.6% | Electorate: 70,849 | EU Ref: 56.3% Leave

PARTY	CANDIDATE	VOTES	SHARE	CHANGE 2015
Liberal Democrat	Tom Brake	20,819	41.0%	6.1%
Conservative	Matthew Maxwell Scott	19,450	38.3%	6.6%
Labour	Emina Ibrahim	9,360	18.4%	3.4%
Green	Shasha Khan	501	1.0%	-2.1%
Independent	Nick Mattey	434	0.9%	0.9%
Christian Peoples Alliance	Ashley Dickenson	189	0.4%	0.0%

Castle Point

CON HOLD
Majority: 18,872, 42.2% | Turnout: 44,710, 64.4% | Electorate: 69,470 | EU Ref: 72.7% Leave

PARTY	CANDIDATE	VOTES	SHARE	CHANGE 2015
Conservative	Rebecca Harris	30,076	67.3%	16.4%
Labour	Joe Cooke	11,204	25.1%	11.2%
UK Independence Party	David Kurten	2,381	5.3%	-25.9%
Liberal Democrat	Tom Holder	1,049	2.3%	0.6%

Central Ayrshire

SNP HOLD
Majority: 1,267, 2.8% | Turnout: 45,087, 65.3% | Electorate: 68,999 | EU Ref: 42.7% Leave

PARTY	CANDIDATE	VOTES	SHARE	CHANGE 2015
Scottish National Party	Philippa Whitford	16,771	37.2%	-16.0%
Conservative	Caroline Hollins Martin	15,504	34.4%	17.0%
Labour	Nairn McDonald	11,762	26.1%	-0.3%
Liberal Democrat	Tom Inglis	1,050	2.3%	0.5%

Central Devon

CON HOLD

Majority: 15,680, 27.1% | Turnout: 57,844, 77.8% | Electorate: 74,370 | EU Ref: 51.2% Leave

PARTY	CANDIDATE	VOTES	SHARE	CHANGE 2015
Conservative	Mel Stride	31,278	54.1%	1.8%
Labour	Lisa Robillard Webb	15,598	27.0%	14.1%
Liberal Democrat	Alex White	6,770	11.7%	-0.5%
Green	Andy Williamson	1,531	2.6%	-6.3%
UK Independence Party	Tim Matthews	1,326	2.3%	-10.9%
National Health Action	John Dean	871	1.5%	1.5%
Liberal	Lloyd Knight	470	0.8%	0.8%

Central Suffolk & North Ipswich

CON HOLD

Majority: 17,185, 30.4% | Turnout: 56,524, 72.4% | Electorate: 78,116 | EU Ref: 54.5% Leave

PARTY	CANDIDATE	VOTES	SHARE	CHANGE 2015
Conservative	Daniel Poulter	33,992	60.1%	4.1%
Labour	Elizabeth Hughes	16,807	29.7%	10.9%
Liberal Democrat	Aidan Van de Weyer	2,431	4.3%	-1.8%
Green	Regan Scott	1,659	2.9%	-2.0%
UK Independence Party	Stephen Searle	1,635	2.9%	-10.9%

Ceredigion

PC GAIN FROM LIB DEM

Majority: 104, 0.3% | Turnout: 39,767, 73.3% | Electorate: 54,262 | EU Ref: 45.4% Leave

PARTY	CANDIDATE	VOTES	SHARE	CHANGE 2015
Plaid Cymru	Ben Lake	11,623	29.2%	1.6%
Liberal Democrat	Mark Williams	11,519	29.0%	-6.9%
Labour	Dinah Mulholland	8,017	20.2%	10.5%
Conservative	Ruth Davis	7,307	18.4%	7.4%
UK Independence Party	Tom Harrison	602	1.5%	-8.7%

| Green | Grenville Ham | 542 | 1.4% | -4.2% |
| Monster Raving Loony Party | The Crazed Sir Dudley | 157 | 0.4% | 0.4% |

Charnwood

CON HOLD

Majority: 16,341, 29.6% | Turnout: 55,176, 70.7% | Electorate: 78,071 | EU Ref: 58.3% Leave

PARTY	CANDIDATE	VOTES	SHARE	CHANGE 2015
Conservative	Edward Argar	33,318	60.4%	6.1%
Labour	Sean Kelly-Walsh	16,977	30.8%	8.9%
Liberal Democrat	Simon Sansome	2,052	3.7%	-3.2%
UK Independence Party	Victoria Connor	1,471	2.7%	-13.3%
Green	Nick Cox	1,036	1.9%	1.9%
British National Party	Stephen Denham	322	0.6%	0.4%

Chatham & Aylesford

CON HOLD

Majority: 10,458, 23.3% | Turnout: 44,890, 63.7% | Electorate: 70,419 | EU Ref: 64.7% Leave

PARTY	CANDIDATE	VOTES	SHARE	CHANGE 2015
Conservative	Tracey Crouch	25,587	57.0%	6.8%
Labour	Vince Maple	15,129	33.7%	10.1%
UK Independence Party	Nicole Bushill	2,225	5.0%	-15.0%
Liberal Democrat	Thomas Quinton	1,116	2.5%	-0.7%
Green	Bernard Hyde	573	1.3%	-1.3%
Christian Peoples Alliance	John Gibson	260	0.6%	0.3%

Cheadle

CON HOLD

Majority: 4,507, 8.3% | Turnout: 54,572, 74.3% | Electorate: 73,406 | EU Ref: 41.9% Leave

PARTY	CANDIDATE	VOTES	SHARE	CHANGE 2015
Conservative	Mary Robinson	24,331	44.6%	1.5%
Liberal Democrat	Mark Hunter	19,824	36.3%	5.4%
Labour	Martin Miller	10,417	19.1%	2.8%

Chelmsford

CON HOLD

Majority: 13,572, 23.9% | Turnout: 56,860, 70.2% | Electorate: 81,032 | EU Ref: 50.5% Leave

PARTY	CANDIDATE	VOTES	SHARE	CHANGE 2015
Conservative	Vicky Ford	30,525	53.7%	2.2%
Labour	Chris Vince	16,953	29.8%	12.2%
Liberal Democrat	Stephen Robinson	6,916	12.2%	0.3%
UK Independence Party	Nigel Carter	1,645	2.9%	-11.3%
Green	Reza Hossain	821	1.4%	-2.1%

Chelsea & Fulham

CON HOLD

Majority: 8,188, 19.4% | Turnout: 42,128, 66.1% | Electorate: 63,728 | EU Ref: 29.2% Leave

PARTY	CANDIDATE	VOTES	SHARE	CHANGE 2015
Conservative	Greg Hands	22,179	52.6%	-10.3%
Labour	Alan De'Ath	13,991	33.2%	10.1%
Liberal Democrat	Louise Rowntree	4,627	11.0%	5.8%
Green	Bill Cashmore	807	1.9%	-1.7%
UK Independence Party	Alasdair Seton-Marsden	524	1.2%	-3.8%

Cheltenham

CON HOLD

Majority: 2,569, 4.5% | Turnout: 57,012, 72.2% | Electorate: 78,878 | EU Ref: 42.8% Leave

PARTY	CANDIDATE	VOTES	SHARE	CHANGE 2015
Conservative	Alex Chalk	26,615	46.7%	0.5%
Liberal Democrat	Martin Horwood	24,046	42.2%	8.2%
Labour	Keith White	5,408	9.5%	2.2%
Green	Adam Van Coevorden	943	1.7%	-3.4%

Chesham & Amersham

CON HOLD
Majority: 22,140, 40.1% | Turnout: 55,252, 77.1% | Electorate: 71,654 | EU Ref: 45.0% Leave

PARTY	CANDIDATE	VOTES	SHARE	CHANGE 2015
Conservative	Cheryl Gillan	33,514	60.7%	1.7%
Labour	Nina Dluzewska	11,374	20.6%	7.9%
Liberal Democrat	Peter Jones	7,179	13.0%	4.0%
Green	Alan Booth	1,660	3.0%	-2.5%
UK Independence Party	David Meacock	1,525	2.8%	-10.9%

Chesterfield

LAB HOLD
Majority: 9,605, 20.0% | Turnout: 47,927, 66.5% | Electorate: 72,069 | EU Ref: 59.3% Leave

PARTY	CANDIDATE	VOTES	SHARE	CHANGE 2015
Labour	Toby Perkins	26,266	54.8%	6.9%
Conservative	Spencer Pitfield	16,661	34.8%	16.7%
Liberal Democrat	Tom Snowdon	2,612	5.4%	-8.4%
UK Independence Party	Stuart Bent	1,611	3.4%	-13.1%
Green	David Wadsworth	777	1.6%	-1.3%

Chichester

CON HOLD
Majority: 22,621, 37.7% | Turnout: 59,918, 70.4% | Electorate: 84,991 | EU Ref: 50.6% Leave

PARTY	CANDIDATE	VOTES	SHARE	CHANGE 2015
Conservative	Gillian Keegan	36,032	60.1%	2.5%
Labour	Mark Farwell	13,411	22.4%	10.2%
Liberal Democrat	Jonathan Brown	6,749	11.3%	2.7%
Green	Heather Barrie	1,992	3.3%	-3.2%
UK Independence Party	Andrew Moncreiff	1,650	2.8%	-12.2%
Patria	Andrew Emerson	84	0.1%	0.0%

Chingford & Woodford Green

CON HOLD
Majority: 2,438, 5.2% | Turnout: 46,961, 71.1% | Electorate: 65,958 | EU Ref: 49.2% Leave

PARTY	CANDIDATE	VOTES	SHARE	CHANGE 2015
Conservative	Iain Duncan Smith	23,076	49.1%	1.2%
Labour	Bilal Mahmood	20,638	43.9%	15.2%
Liberal Democrat	Deborah Unger	2,043	3.4%	-1.1%
Green	Sinead King	1,204	2.6%	-1.7%

Chippenham

CON HOLD
Majority: 16,630, 29.1% | Turnout: 57,140, 74.8% | Electorate: 76,432 | EU Ref: 52.3% Leave

PARTY	CANDIDATE	VOTES	SHARE	CHANGE 2015
Conservative	Michelle Donelan	31,267	54.7%	7.2%
Liberal Democrat	Helen Belcher	14,637	25.6%	-3.8%
Labour	Andrew Newman	11,236	19.7%	11.4%

Chipping Barnet

CON HOLD
Majority: 353, 0.6% | Turnout: 55,423, 71.8% | Electorate: 77,218 | EU Ref: 40.9% Leave

PARTY	CANDIDATE	VOTES	SHARE	CHANGE 2015
Conservative	Theresa Villiers	25,679	46.3%	-2.3%
Labour	Emma Whysall	25,326	45.7%	11.5%
Liberal Democrat	Marisha Ray	3,012	5.4%	0.9%
Green	Phil Fletcher	1,406	2.5%	-2.2%

Chorley

LAB HOLD

Majority: 7,512, 13.5% | Turnout: 55,634, 72.7% | Electorate: 76,404 | EU Ref: 56.6% Leave

PARTY	CANDIDATE	VOTES	SHARE	CHANGE 2015
Labour	Lindsay Hoyle	30,745	55.3%	10.2%
Conservative	Caroline Moon	23,233	41.8%	5.4%
Liberal Democrat	Stephen Fenn	1,126	2.0%	-0.6%
Green	Peter Lageard	530	1.0%	-1.2%

Christchurch

CON HOLD

Majority: 25,171, 49.7% | Turnout: 50,634, 72.0% | Electorate: 70,309 | EU Ref: 59.9% Leave

PARTY	CANDIDATE	VOTES	SHARE	CHANGE 2015
Conservative	Christopher Chope	35,230	69.6%	11.5%
Labour	Patrick Canavan	10,059	19.9%	10.3%
Liberal Democrat	Michael Cox	4,020	7.9%	1.4%
Green	Chris Rugby	1,325	2.6%	-1.7%

Cities of London & Westminster

CON HOLD

Majority: 3,148, 8.2% | Turnout: 38,654, 62.8% | Electorate: 61,533 | EU Ref: 28.6% Leave

PARTY	CANDIDATE	VOTES	SHARE	CHANGE 2015
Conservative	Mark Field	18,005	46.6%	-7.5%
Labour	Ibrahim Dogus	14,857	38.4%	11.1%
Liberal Democrat	Bridget Fox	4,270	11.0%	4.1%
Green	Lawrence McNally	821	2.1%	-3.3%
UK Independence Party	Anil Bhatti	426	1.1%	-4.1%
Independent	Tim Lord	173	0.4%	0.4%
Independent	Ankit Love The Maharaja of Kashmir	59	0.2%	0.2%
Young People's Party	Benjamin Weenen	43	0.1%	0.1%

City of Chester

LAB HOLD
Majority: 9,176, 16.3% | Turnout: 56,421, 77.4% | Electorate: 72,859 | EU Ref: 42.7% Leave

PARTY	CANDIDATE	VOTES	SHARE	CHANGE 2015
Labour	Chris Matheson	32,023	56.8%	13.5%
Conservative	Will Gallagher	22,847	40.5%	-2.6%
Liberal Democrat	Lizzie Jewkes	1,551	2.7%	-2.9%

City of Durham

LAB HOLD
Majority: 12,364, 25.6% | Turnout: 48,324, 67.9% | Electorate: 71,132 | EU Ref: 44.4% Leave

PARTY	CANDIDATE	VOTES	SHARE	CHANGE 2015
Labour	Roberta Blackman-Woods	26,772	55.4%	8.1%
Conservative	Richard Lawrie	14,408	29.8%	7.6%
Liberal Democrat	Amanda Hopgood	4,787	9.9%	-1.4%
UK Independence Party	Malcolm Bint	1,116	2.3%	-9.1%
Green	Jonathan Elmer	797	1.6%	-4.2%
Independent	Jim Clark	399	0.8%	0.8%
Young People's Party	Jon Collings	45	0.1%	0.1%

Clacton

CON GAIN FROM UKIP
Majority: 15,828, 35.8% | Turnout: 44,145, 63.7% | Electorate: 68,566 | EU Ref: 71.1% Leave

PARTY	CANDIDATE	VOTES	SHARE	CHANGE 2015
Conservative	Giles Watling	27,031	61.2%	24.6%
Labour	Tasha Osben	11,203	25.4%	11.0%
UK Independence Party	Paul Oakley	3,357	7.6%	-36.8%
Liberal Democrat	David Grace	887	2.0%	0.2%
Green	Chris Southall	719	1.6%	-1.0%
Independent	Caroline Shearer	449	1.0%	1.0%
English Democrats	Robin Tilbrook	289	0.7%	0.7%
Independent	Nick Martin	210	0.5%	0.5%

Cleethorpes

CON HOLD

Majority: 10,400, 21.7% | Turnout: 47,844, 65.5% | Electorate: 72,711 | EU Ref: 68.4% Leave

PARTY	CANDIDATE	VOTES	SHARE	CHANGE 2015
Conservative	Martin Vickers	27,321	57.1%	10.5%
Labour	Peter Keith	16,921	35.4%	6.2%
UK Independence Party	Tony Blake	2,022	4.2%	-14.3%
Liberal Democrat	Roy Horobin	1,110	2.3%	-0.7%
Green	Loyd Emmerson	470	1.0%	-1.3%

Clwyd South

LAB HOLD

Majority: 4,356, 11.6% | Turnout: 37,474, 68.9% | Electorate: 53,729 | EU Ref: 60.3% Leave

PARTY	CANDIDATE	VOTES	SHARE	CHANGE 2015
Labour	Susan Elan Jones	19,002	50.7%	13.5%
Conservative	Simon Baynes	14,646	39.1%	8.7%
Plaid Cymru	Christopher Allen	2,293	6.1%	-4.2%
UK Independence Party	Jeanette Bassford-Barton	802	2.1%	-13.5%
Liberal Democrat	Bruce Roberts	731	2.0%	-1.9%

Clwyd West

CON HOLD

Majority: 3,437, 8.5% | Turnout: 40,654, 69.8% | Electorate: 58,263 | EU Ref: 52.5% Leave

PARTY	CANDIDATE	VOTES	SHARE	CHANGE 2015
Conservative	David Jones	19,541	48.1%	4.8%
Labour	Gareth Thomas	16,104	39.6%	14.0%
Plaid Cymru	Dilwyn Roberts	3,918	9.6%	-2.6%
Liberal Democrat	Victor Babu	1,091	2.7%	-1.0%

Coatbridge, Chryston & Bellshill

LAB GAIN FROM SNP
Majority: 1,586, 3.5% | Turnout: 45,040, 63.3% | Electorate: 71,198 | EU Ref: 38.7% Leave

PARTY	CANDIDATE	VOTES	SHARE	CHANGE 2015
Labour	Hugh Gaffney	19,193	42.6%	8.7%
Scottish National Party	Phil Boswell	17,607	39.1%	-17.5%
Conservative	Robyn Halbert	7,318	16.2%	9.9%
Liberal Democrat	David Bennie	922	2.0%	1.0%

Colchester

CON HOLD
Majority: 5,677, 10.6% | Turnout: 53,545, 66.9% | Electorate: 79,996 | EU Ref: 51.1% Leave

PARTY	CANDIDATE	VOTES	SHARE	CHANGE 2015
Conservative	Will Quince	24,565	45.9%	6.9%
Labour	Tim Young	18,888	35.3%	19.1%
Liberal Democrat	Bob Russell	9,087	17.0%	-10.5%
Green	Mark Goacher	828	1.5%	-3.6%
Christian Peoples Alliance	Robin Rennie	177	0.3%	0.1%

Colne Valley

LAB GAIN FROM CON
Majority: 915, 1.5% | Turnout: 60,420, 71.6% | Electorate: 84,387 | EU Ref: 49.8% Leave

PARTY	CANDIDATE	VOTES	SHARE	CHANGE 2015
Labour	Thelma Walker	28,818	47.7%	12.7%
Conservative	Jason McCartney	27,903	46.2%	1.7%
Liberal Democrat	Cahal Burke	2,494	4.1%	-1.9%
Green	Sonia King	892	1.5%	-1.9%
Independent	Patricia Sadio	313	0.5%	0.5%

Congleton

CON HOLD
Majority: 12,619, 22.4% | Turnout: 56,231, 73.3% | Electorate: 76,694 | EU Ref: 52.7% Leave

PARTY	CANDIDATE	VOTES	SHARE	CHANGE 2015
Conservative	Fiona Bruce	31,830	56.6%	3.3%
Labour	Sam Corcoran	19,211	34.2%	13.8%
Liberal Democrat	Peter Hirst	2,902	5.2%	-3.9%
UK Independence Party	Mark Davies	1,289	2.3%	-11.3%
Green	Alexander Heath	999	1.8%	-1.9%

Copeland

CON HOLD
Majority: 1,695, 4.0% | Turnout: 42,927, 70.2% | Electorate: 61,751 | EU Ref: 59.8% Leave

PARTY	CANDIDATE	VOTES	SHARE	CHANGE 2015
Conservative	Trudy Harrison	21,062	49.1%	13.3%
Labour	Gillian Troughton	19,367	45.1%	2.9%
Liberal Democrat	Rebecca Hanson	1,404	3.3%	-0.2%
UK Independence Party	Herbert Crossman	1,094	2.5%	-13.0%

Corby

CON HOLD
Majority: 2,690, 4.5% | Turnout: 59,997, 72.8% | Electorate: 83,020 | EU Ref: 60.1% Leave

PARTY	CANDIDATE	VOTES	SHARE	CHANGE 2015
Conservative	Tom Pursglove	29,534	49.2%	6.5%
Labour	Beth Miller	26,844	44.7%	6.3%
Liberal Democrat	Chris Stanbra	1,545	2.6%	0.0%
UK Independence Party	Sam Watts	1,495	2.5%	-11.2%
Green	Steven Scrutton	579	1.0%	-1.5%

Coventry North East

LAB HOLD

Majority: 15,580, 33.5% | Turnout: 46,508, 61.4% | Electorate: 75,759 | EU Ref: 59.2% Leave

PARTY	CANDIDATE	VOTES	SHARE	CHANGE 2015
Labour	Colleen Fletcher	29,499	63.4%	11.3%
Conservative	Timothy Mayer	13,919	29.9%	6.8%
UK Independence Party	Avtar Taggar	1,350	2.9%	-12.0%
Liberal Democrat	Russell Field	1,157	2.5%	-2.3%
Green	Matthew Handley	502	1.1%	-1.9%
Independent	Afzal Mahmood	81	0.2%	0.2%

Coventry North West

LAB HOLD

Majority: 8,580, 17.3% | Turnout: 49,849, 66.3% | Electorate: 75,196 | EU Ref: 58.7% Leave

PARTY	CANDIDATE	VOTES	SHARE	CHANGE 2015
Labour	Geoffrey Robinson	26,894	54.0%	12.9%
Conservative	Resham Kotecha	18,314	36.7%	5.7%
UK Independence Party	Michael Gee	1,525	3.1%	-12.6%
Liberal Democrat	Andrew Hilton	1,286	2.6%	-1.4%
Independent	Ciaran Norris	1,164	2.3%	2.3%
Green	Stephen Gray	666	1.3%	-3.0%

Coventry South

LAB HOLD

Majority: 7,947, 16.9% | Turnout: 47,009, 66.4% | Electorate: 70,736 | EU Ref: 48.9% Leave

PARTY	CANDIDATE	VOTES	SHARE	CHANGE 2015
Labour	Jim Cunningham	25,874	55.0%	12.8%
Conservative	Michelle Lowe	17,927	38.1%	3.2%
Liberal Democrat	Greg Judge	1,343	2.9%	-1.2%
UK Independence Party	Ian Rogers	1,037	2.2%	-10.9%
Green	Aimee Challenor	604	1.3%	-2.6%
Independent	Sandra Findlay	224	0.5%	0.5%

Crawley

CON HOLD

Majority: 2,457, 4.9% | Turnout: 50,273, 68.5% | Electorate: 73,425 | EU Ref: 58.4% Leave

PARTY	CANDIDATE	VOTES	SHARE	CHANGE 2015
Conservative	Henry Smith	25,426	50.6%	3.6%
Labour	Tim Lunnon	22,969	45.7%	12.1%
Liberal Democrat	Marko Scepanovic	1,878	3.7%	1.0%

Crewe & Nantwich

LAB GAIN FROM CON

Majority: 48, 0.1% | Turnout: 55,027, 69.7% | Electorate: 78,895 | EU Ref: 59.0% Leave

PARTY	CANDIDATE	VOTES	SHARE	CHANGE 2015
Labour	Laura Smith	25,928	47.1%	9.4%
Conservative	Edward Timpson	25,880	47.0%	2.0%
UK Independence Party	Michael Stanley	1,885	3.4%	-11.1%
Liberal Democrat	David Crowther	1,334	2.4%	-0.3%

Croydon Central

LAB GAIN FROM CON

Majority: 5,652, 9.9% | Turnout: 57,091, 71.3% | Electorate: 80,045 | EU Ref: 50.3% Leave

PARTY	CANDIDATE	VOTES	SHARE	CHANGE 2015
Labour	Sarah Jones	29,873	52.3%	9.7%
Conservative	Gavin Barwell	24,221	42.4%	-0.6%
Liberal Democrat	Gill Hickson	1,083	1.9%	-0.3%
UK Independence Party	Peter Staveley	1,040	1.8%	-7.3%
Green	Tracey Hague	626	1.1%	-1.6%
Christian Peoples Alliance	John Boadu	177	0.3%	0.3%
Independent	Don Locke	71	0.1%	0.1%

Croydon North

LAB HOLD
Majority: 32,365, 54.3% | Turnout: 59,623, 68.2% | Electorate: 87,461 | EU Ref: 42.6% Leave

PARTY	CANDIDATE	VOTES	SHARE	CHANGE 2015
Labour	Steve Reed	44,213	74.2%	11.5%
Conservative	Samuel Kasumu	11,848	19.9%	-2.8%
Liberal Democrat	Maltby Pindar	1,656	2.8%	-0.8%
Green	Peter Underwood	983	1.6%	-3.1%
UK Independence Party	Michael Swadling	753	1.3%	-4.2%
Independent	Lee Berks	170	0.3%	0.0%

Croydon South

CON HOLD
Majority: 11,406, 18.6% | Turnout: 61,257, 73.3% | Electorate: 83,518 | EU Ref: 45.9% Leave

PARTY	CANDIDATE	VOTES	SHARE	CHANGE 2015
Conservative	Chris Philp	33,334	54.4%	-0.1%
Labour	Jennifer Brathwaite	21,928	35.8%	11.0%
Liberal Democrat	Anna Jones	3,541	5.8%	-0.2%
Green	Catherine Shelley	1,125	1.8%	-1.9%
UK Independence Party	Kathleen Garner	1,116	1.8%	-8.7%
Christian Peoples Alliance	David Omamogho	213	0.3%	0.3%

Cumbernauld, Kilsyth & Kirkintilloch East

SNP HOLD
Majority: 4,264, 9.7% | Turnout: 43,833, 65.9% | Electorate: 66,554 | EU Ref: 37.9% Leave

PARTY	CANDIDATE	VOTES	SHARE	CHANGE 2015
Scottish National Party	Stuart C McDonald	19,122	43.6%	-16.3%
Labour	Elisha Fisher	14,858	33.9%	3.9%
Conservative	Stephen Johnston	8,010	18.3%	10.4%
Liberal Democrat	Rod Ackland	1,238	2.8%	0.6%
UK Independence Party	Carl Pearson	605	1.4%	1.4%

Cynon Valley

LAB HOLD
Majority: 13,238, 41.6% | Turnout: 31,802, 62.0% | Electorate: 51,334 | EU Ref: 57.0% Leave

PARTY	CANDIDATE	VOTES	SHARE	CHANGE 2015
Labour	Ann Clwyd	19,404	61.0%	13.3%
Conservative	Keith Dewhurst	6,166	19.4%	7.3%
Plaid Cymru	Liz Walters	4,376	13.8%	-3.1%
UK Independence Party	Ian McLean	1,271	4.0%	-12.3%
Liberal Democrat	Nicola Knight	585	1.8%	-0.9%

Dagenham & Rainham

LAB HOLD
Majority: 4,652, 10.2% | Turnout: 45,843, 64.9% | Electorate: 70,616 | EU Ref: 69.9% Leave

PARTY	CANDIDATE	VOTES	SHARE	CHANGE 2015
Labour	Jon Cruddas	22,958	50.1%	8.7%
Conservative	Julie Marson	18,306	39.9%	15.6%
UK Independence Party	Peter Harris	3,246	7.1%	-22.8%
Green	Denis Breading	544	1.2%	-0.7%
Liberal Democrat	Jonathan Fryer	465	1.0%	-0.7%
British National Party	Paul Sturdy	239	0.5%	0.2%
Concordia	Terence London	85	0.2%	0.2%

Darlington

LAB HOLD
Majority: 3,280, 7.3% | Turnout: 44,817, 67.6% | Electorate: 66,341 | EU Ref: 58.1% Leave

PARTY	CANDIDATE	VOTES	SHARE	CHANGE 2015
Labour	Jenny Chapman	22,681	50.6%	7.7%
Conservative	Peter Cuthbertson	19,401	43.3%	8.1%
UK Independence Party	Kevin Brack	1,180	2.6%	-10.5%
Liberal Democrat	Anne-Marie Curry	1,031	2.3%	-2.5%
Green	Matthew Snedker	524	1.2%	-2.3%

Dartford

CON HOLD
Majority: 13,186, 24.4% | Turnout: 54,224, 69.8% | Electorate: 78,506 | EU Ref: 64.0% Leave

PARTY	CANDIDATE	VOTES	SHARE	CHANGE 2015
Conservative	Gareth Johnson	31,210	57.6%	8.6%
Labour	Bachchu Kaini	18,024	33.2%	7.8%
UK Independence Party	Ben Fryer	2,544	4.7%	-15.2%
Liberal Democrat	Simon Beard	1,428	2.6%	-0.1%
Green	Andrew Blatchford	807	1.5%	-1.0%
Independent	Ola Adewunmi	211	0.4%	0.4%

Daventry

CON HOLD
Majority: 21,734, 39.0% | Turnout: 55,663, 74.0% | Electorate: 75,268 | EU Ref: 58.8% Leave

PARTY	CANDIDATE	VOTES	SHARE	CHANGE 2015
Conservative	Chris Heaton-Harris	35,464	63.7%	5.5%
Labour	Aiden Ramsey	13,730	24.7%	6.6%
Liberal Democrat	Andrew Simpson	4,015	7.2%	2.7%
UK Independence Party	Ian Gibbins	1,497	2.7%	-13.1%
Green	Jamie Wildman	957	1.7%	-1.8%

Delyn

LAB HOLD
Majority: 4,240, 10.8% | Turnout: 39,418, 72.8% | Electorate: 54,090 | EU Ref: 54.8% Leave

PARTY	CANDIDATE	VOTES	SHARE	CHANGE 2015
Labour	David Hanson	20,573	52.2%	11.6%
Conservative	Matt Wright	16,333	41.4%	8.7%
Plaid Cymru	Paul Rowlinson	1,481	3.8%	-1.1%
Liberal Democrat	Tom Rippeth	1,031	2.6%	-1.1%

Denton & Reddish

LAB HOLD

Majority: 14,077, 35.5% | Turnout: 39,599, 61.1% | Electorate: 67,674 | EU Ref: 61.9% Leave

PARTY	CANDIDATE	VOTES	SHARE	CHANGE 2015
Labour	Andrew Gwynne	25,161	63.5%	12.7%
Conservative	Rozila Kana	11,084	28.0%	4.3%
UK Independence Party	Josh Seddon	1,798	4.5%	-14.1%
Liberal Democrat	Catherine Ankers	853	2.2%	-0.3%
Green	Gareth Hayes	486	1.2%	-2.6%
Monster Raving Loony Party	Farmin Lord Dave	217	0.5%	0.5%

Derby North

LAB GAIN FROM CON

Majority: 2,015, 4.1% | Turnout: 48,672, 69.1% | Electorate: 69,919 | EU Ref: 53.7% Leave

PARTY	CANDIDATE	VOTES	SHARE	CHANGE 2015
Labour	Chris Williamson	23,622	48.5%	12.0%
Conservative	Amanda Solloway	21,607	44.4%	7.7%
Liberal Democrat	Lucy Care	2,262	4.6%	-3.9%
UK Independence Party	Bill Piper	1,181	2.4%	-12.2%

Derby South

LAB HOLD

Majority: 11,248, 24.8% | Turnout: 45,306, 64.4% | Electorate: 69,918 | EU Ref: 61.6% Leave

PARTY	CANDIDATE	VOTES	SHARE	CHANGE 2015
Labour	Margaret Beckett	26,430	58.3%	9.3%
Conservative	Evonne Williams	15,182	33.5%	6.1%
UK Independence Party	Alan Graves	2,011	4.4%	-11.1%
Liberal Democrat	Joe Naitta	1,229	2.7%	-1.5%
Green	Ian Sleeman	454	1.0%	-2.0%

Derbyshire Dales

CON HOLD
Majority: 14,327, 28.9% | Turnout: 49,571, 77.0% | Electorate: 64,430 | EU Ref: 51.3% Leave

PARTY	CANDIDATE	VOTES	SHARE	CHANGE 2015
Conservative	Patrick McLoughlin	29,744	60.0%	7.6%
Labour	Andy Botham	15,417	31.1%	8.4%
Liberal Democrat	Andrew Hollyer	3,126	6.3%	-2.1%
Green	Matthew Buckler	1,002	2.0%	-2.6%
Humanity	Robin Greenwood	282	0.6%	0.3%

Devizes

CON HOLD
Majority: 21,136, 41.7% | Turnout: 50,593, 71.1% | Electorate: 72,184 | EU Ref: 51.5% Leave

PARTY	CANDIDATE	VOTES	SHARE	CHANGE 2015
Conservative	Claire Perry	31,744	62.7%	5.0%
Labour	Imtiyaz Shaikh	10,608	21.0%	8.0%
Liberal Democrat	Christopher Coleman	4,706	9.3%	1.2%
UK Independence Party	Timothy Page	1,706	3.4%	-12.0%
Green	Emma Dawnay	1,606	3.2%	-2.6%
Wessex Regionalists	Jim Gunter	223	0.4%	0.4%

Dewsbury

LAB HOLD
Majority: 3,321, 5.9% | Turnout: 56,545, 69.5% | Electorate: 81,343 | EU Ref: 57.3% Leave

PARTY	CANDIDATE	VOTES	SHARE	CHANGE 2015
Labour	Paula Sherriff	28,814	51.0%	9.2%
Conservative	Beth Prescott	25,493	45.1%	6.0%
Liberal Democrat	Ednan Hussain	1,214	2.1%	-1.4%
Green	Simon Cope	1,024	1.8%	-0.7%

Don Valley

LAB HOLD

Majority: 5,169, 11.3% | Turnout: 45,988, 62.2% | Electorate: 73,990 | EU Ref: 68.6% Leave

PARTY	CANDIDATE	VOTES	SHARE	CHANGE 2015
Labour	Caroline Flint	24,351	53.0%	6.8%
Conservative	Aaron Bell	19,182	41.7%	16.4%
The Yorkshire Party	Stevie Manion	1,599	3.5%	3.5%
Liberal Democrat	Anthony Smith	856	1.9%	-1.6%

Doncaster Central

LAB HOLD

Majority: 10,131, 23.5% | Turnout: 43,024, 60.0% | Electorate: 71,718 | EU Ref: 66.3% Leave

PARTY	CANDIDATE	VOTES	SHARE	CHANGE 2015
Labour	Rosie Winterton	24,915	57.9%	8.8%
Conservative	Tom Hunt	14,784	34.4%	13.6%
The Yorkshire Party	Chris Whitwood	1,346	3.1%	3.1%
Independent	Eddie Todd	1,006	2.3%	2.3%
Liberal Democrat	Alison Breslford	973	2.3%	-2.0%

Doncaster North

LAB HOLD

Majority: 14,024, 33.2% | Turnout: 42,312, 58.5% | Electorate: 72,377 | EU Ref: 72.1% Leave

PARTY	CANDIDATE	VOTES	SHARE	CHANGE 2015
Labour	Ed Miliband	25,711	60.8%	8.3%
Conservative	Shade Adoh	11,687	27.6%	9.3%
UK Independence Party	Kim Parkinson	2,738	6.5%	-16.1%
The Yorkshire Party	Charlie Bridges	741	1.8%	1.8%
Liberal Democrat	Robert Adamson	706	1.7%	-0.9%
Independent	Frank Calladine	366	0.9%	0.9%
English Democrats	David Allen	363	0.9%	0.3%

Dover

CON HOLD
Majority: 6,437, 12.4% | Turnout: 51,966, 69.7% | Electorate: 74,564 | EU Ref: 63.1% Leave

PARTY	CANDIDATE	VOTES	SHARE	CHANGE 2015
Conservative	Charlie Elphicke	27,211	52.4%	9.1%
Labour	Stacey Blair	20,774	40.0%	9.2%
UK Independence Party	Piers Wauchope	1,722	3.3%	-16.9%
Liberal Democrat	Simon Dodd	1,336	2.6%	-0.6%
Green	Beccy Sawbridge	923	1.8%	-0.8%

Dudley North

LAB HOLD
Majority: 22, 0.1% | Turnout: 38,910, 62.7% | Electorate: 62,043 | EU Ref: 69.2% Leave

PARTY	CANDIDATE	VOTES	SHARE	CHANGE 2015
Labour	Ian Austin	18,090	46.5%	4.7%
Conservative	Les Jones	18,068	46.4%	15.6%
UK Independence Party	Bill Etheridge	2,144	5.5%	-18.5%
Liberal Democrat	Ben France	368	0.9%	-0.3%
Green	Andrew Nixon	240	0.6%	-0.7%

Dudley South

CON HOLD
Majority: 7,730, 20.2% | Turnout: 38,244, 62.4% | Electorate: 61,323 | EU Ref: 70.2% Leave

PARTY	CANDIDATE	VOTES	SHARE	CHANGE 2015
Conservative	Mike Wood	21,588	56.4%	12.7%
Labour	Natasha Millward	13,858	36.2%	3.6%
UK Independence Party	Mitch Bolton	1,791	4.7%	-14.3%
Liberal Democrat	Jon Bramall	625	1.6%	-0.5%
Green	Jenny Maxwell	382	1.0%	-1.5%

Dulwich & West Norwood

LAB HOLD

Majority: 28,129, 50.1% | Turnout: 56,116, 71.9% | Electorate: 78,037 | EU Ref: 22.1% Leave

PARTY	CANDIDATE	VOTES	SHARE	CHANGE 2015
Labour	Helen Hayes	39,069	69.6%	15.6%
Conservative	Rachel Wolf	10,940	19.5%	-3.2%
Liberal Democrat	Gail Kent	4,475	8.0%	-1.9%
Green	Rashid Nix	1,408	2.5%	-6.9%
Independent	Robin Lambert	121	0.2%	0.0%
Independent	Yen Lin Chong	103	0.2%	0.2%

Dumfries & Galloway

CON GAIN FROM SNP

Majority: 5,643, 11.0% | Turnout: 51,599, 69.5% | Electorate: 74,206 | EU Ref: 45.4% Leave

PARTY	CANDIDATE	VOTES	SHARE	CHANGE 2015
Conservative	Alister Jack	22,344	43.4%	13.4%
Scottish National Party	Richard Arkless	16,701	32.4%	-9.0%
Labour	Daniel Goodare	10,775	20.9%	-3.8%
Liberal Democrat	Joan Mitchell	1,241	2.4%	0.7%
Independent	Yen Hongmei Jin	538	1.0%	1.0%

Dumfriesshire, Clydesdale & Tweeddale

CON HOLD

Majority: 9,441, 19.3% | Turnout: 48,964, 72.4% | Electorate: 67,672 | EU Ref: 43.9% Leave

PARTY	CANDIDATE	VOTES	SHARE	CHANGE 2015
Conservative	David Mundell	24,177	49.4%	9.6%
Scottish National Party	Mairi McAllan	14,736	30.1%	-8.2%
Labour	Douglas Beattie	8,102	16.5%	1.8%
Liberal Democrat	John Ferry	1,949	4.0%	1.3%

Dundee East

SNP HOLD

Majority: 6,645, 15.4% | Turnout: 42,928, 65.2% | Electorate: 65,854 | EU Ref: 38.3% Leave

PARTY	CANDIDATE	VOTES	SHARE	CHANGE 2015
Scottish National Party	Stewart Hosie	18,391	42.8%	-16.9%
Conservative	Eleanor Price	11,746	27.4%	12.4%
Labour	Lesley Brennan	11,176	26.0%	6.1%
Liberal Democrat	Christopher McIntyre	1,615	3.8%	0.9%

Dundee West

SNP HOLD

Majority: 5,262, 13.6% | Turnout: 38,677, 61.7% | Electorate: 62,644 | EU Ref: 41.2% Leave

PARTY	CANDIDATE	VOTES	SHARE	CHANGE 2015
Scottish National Party	Chris Law	18,045	46.7%	-15.3%
Labour	Alan Cowan	12,783	33.1%	9.4%
Conservative	Darren Cormack	6,257	16.2%	7.6%
Liberal Democrat	Jenny Blain	1,189	3.1%	0.7%
Independent	Sean Dobson	403	1.0%	1.0%

Dunfermline & West Fife

SNP HOLD

Majority: 844, 1.6% | Turnout: 51,010, 67.4% | Electorate: 75,672 | EU Ref: 40.0% Leave

PARTY	CANDIDATE	VOTES	SHARE	CHANGE 2015
Scottish National Party	Doug Chapman	18,121	35.5%	-14.7%
Labour	Cara Hilton	17,277	33.9%	2.1%
Conservative	Belinda Hacking	12,593	24.7%	12.8%
Liberal Democrat	James Calder	3,019	5.9%	1.9%

Dwyfor Meirionnydd

PC HOLD

Majority: 4,850, 16.0% | Turnout: 30,348, 67.9% | Electorate: 44,699 | EU Ref: 48.4% Leave

PARTY	CANDIDATE	VOTES	SHARE	CHANGE 2015
Plaid Cymru	Liz Saville Roberts	13,687	45.1%	4.3%
Conservative	Neil Fairlamb	8,837	29.1%	6.5%
Labour	Matthew Norman	6,273	20.7%	7.2%
Liberal Democrat	Stephen Churchman	937	3.1%	-0.9%
UK Independence Party	Frank Wykes	614	2.0%	-8.8%

Ealing Central & Acton

LAB HOLD

Majority: 13,807, 25.0% | Turnout: 55,342, 74.6% | Electorate: 74,200 | EU Ref: 28.2% Leave

PARTY	CANDIDATE	VOTES	SHARE	CHANGE 2015
Labour	Rupa Huq	33,037	59.7%	16.5%
Conservative	Joy Morrissey	19,230	34.7%	-7.9%
Liberal Democrat	Jon Ball	3,075	5.6%	-0.5%

Ealing North

LAB HOLD

Majority: 19,693, 37.5% | Turnout: 52,516, 70.2% | Electorate: 74,764 | EU Ref: 48.8% Leave

PARTY	CANDIDATE	VOTES	SHARE	CHANGE 2015
Labour	Stephen Pound	34,635	66.0%	10.8%
Conservative	Isobel Grant	14,942	28.5%	-1.3%
Liberal Democrat	Humaira Sanders	1,275	2.4%	-0.8%
UK Independence Party	Peter Mcilvenna	921	1.8%	-6.3%
Green	Meena Hans	743	1.4%	-2.0%

Ealing Southall

LAB HOLD
Majority: 22,090, 49.0% | Turnout: 45,145, 69.3% | Electorate: 65,188 | EU Ref: 44.3% Leave

PARTY	CANDIDATE	VOTES	SHARE	CHANGE 2015
Labour	Virendra Sharma	31,720	70.3%	5.3%
Conservative	Fabio Conti	9,630	21.3%	-0.3%
Liberal Democrat	Nigel Bakhai	1,892	4.2%	0.6%
Green	Peter Ward	1,037	2.3%	-2.3%
UK Independence Party	John Poynton	504	1.1%	-3.0%
Workers Revolutionary Party	Arjinder Thiara	362	0.8%	0.8%

Easington

LAB HOLD
Majority: 14,892, 41.0% | Turnout: 36,364, 58.3% | Electorate: 62,385 | EU Ref: 66.6% Leave

PARTY	CANDIDATE	VOTES	SHARE	CHANGE 2015
Labour	Grahame Morris	23,152	63.7%	2.6%
Conservative	Barney Campbell	8,260	22.7%	9.8%
North East Party	Susan McDonnell	2,355	6.5%	4.1%
UK Independence Party	Allyn Roberts	1,727	4.7%	-14.0%
Liberal Democrat	Tom Hancock	460	1.3%	-1.1%
Green	Martie Warin	410	1.1%	-1.0%

East Antrim

DUP HOLD
Majority: 15,923, 41.7% | Turnout: 38,143, 60.6% | Electorate: 62,908 | EU Ref: Not available

PARTY	CANDIDATE	VOTES	SHARE	CHANGE 2015
Democratic Unionist Party	Sammy Wilson	21,873	57.3%	21.2%
Alliance Party	Stewart Dickson	5,950	15.6%	0.6%
Ulster Unionist Party	John Stewart	4,524	11.9%	-7.0%
Sinn Féin	Oliver McMullan	3,555	9.3%	2.4%
Social Democratic & Labour Party	Margaret McKillop	1,278	3.4%	-1.5%
Conservative	Mark Logan	963	2.5%	0.9%

East Devon

CON HOLD

Majority: 8,036, 13.3% | Turnout: 60,382, 73.3% | Electorate: 82,369 | EU Ref: 50.5% Leave

PARTY	CANDIDATE	VOTES	SHARE	CHANGE 2015
Conservative	Hugo Swire	29,306	48.5%	2.1%
Independent	Claire Wright	21,270	35.2%	11.2%
Labour	Jan Ross	6,857	11.4%	1.1%
Liberal Democrat	Alison Eden	1,468	2.4%	-4.4%
UK Independence Party	Brigitte Graham	1,203	2.0%	-10.6%
Independent	Peter Faithfull	150	0.2%	0.2%
Independent	Michael Val Davies	128	0.2%	0.2%

East Dunbartonshire

LIB DEM GAIN FROM SNP

Majority: 5,339, 10.3% | Turnout: 51,801, 78.8% | Electorate: 66,300 | EU Ref: 26.7% Leave

PARTY	CANDIDATE	VOTES	SHARE	CHANGE 2015
Liberal Democrat	Jo Swinson	21,023	40.6%	4.3%
Scottish National Party	John Nicolson	15,684	30.3%	-10.0%
Conservative	Sheila Mechan	7,563	14.6%	6.0%
Labour	Callum McNally	7,531	14.5%	2.2%

East Ham

LAB HOLD

Majority: 39,883, 70.4% | Turnout: 56,633, 67.5% | Electorate: 83,928 | EU Ref: 46.9% Leave

PARTY	CANDIDATE	VOTES	SHARE	CHANGE 2015
Labour	Stephen Timms	47,124	83.2%	5.6%
Conservative	Kirsty Finlayson	7,241	12.8%	0.7%
UK Independence Party	Daniel Oxley	697	1.2%	-3.8%
Liberal Democrat	Glanville Williams	656	1.2%	-0.5%
Green	Chidi Oti-Obihara	474	0.8%	-1.6%
Friends Party	Choudhry Afzal	311	0.5%	0.5%
Independent	Mirza Rahman	130	0.2%	0.2%

East Hampshire

CON HOLD

Majority: 25,852, 46.6% | Turnout: 55,408, 75.6% | Electorate: 74,151 | EU Ref: 48.7% Leave

PARTY	CANDIDATE	VOTES	SHARE	CHANGE 2015
Conservative	Damian Hinds	35,263	63.6%	3.0%
Labour	Rohit Dasgupta	9,411	17.0%	6.9%
Liberal Democrat	Richard Robinson	8,403	15.2%	4.1%
Green	Richard Knight	1,760	3.2%	-3.0%
Justice & Anti-Corruption Party	Susan Jerrard	571	1.0%	1.0%

East Kilbride, Strathaven & Lesmahagow

SNP HOLD

Majority: 3,866, 7.2% | Turnout: 54,102, 67.3% | Electorate: 80,442 | EU Ref: 38.0% Leave

PARTY	CANDIDATE	VOTES	SHARE	CHANGE 2015
Scottish National Party	Lisa Cameron	21,023	38.9%	-16.8%
Labour	Monique McAdams	17,157	31.7%	3.4%
Conservative	Mark McGeever	13,704	25.3%	13.6%
Liberal Democrat	Paul McGarry	1,590	2.9%	1.2%
UK Independence Party	Janice MacKay	628	1.2%	-0.9%

East Londonderry

DUP HOLD

Majority: 8,842, 21.6% | Turnout: 41,030, 61.2% | Electorate: 67,038 | EU Ref: Not available

PARTY	CANDIDATE	VOTES	SHARE	CHANGE 2015
Democratic Unionist Party	Gregory Campbell	19,723	48.1%	5.8%
Sinn Fein	Dermot Nicholl	10,881	26.5%	6.8%
Social Democratic & Labour Party	Stephanie Quigley	4,423	10.8%	-1.5%
Ulster Unionist Party	Richard Holmes	3,135	7.6%	-7.7%
Alliance Party	Chris McCaw	2,538	6.2%	-1.4%
Conservative	Liz St Clair-Legge	330	0.8%	-0.4%

East Lothian

LAB GAIN FROM SNP
Majority: 3,083, 5.5% | Turnout: 55,878, 70.6% | Electorate: 79,093 | EU Ref: 35.4% Leave

PARTY	CANDIDATE	VOTES	SHARE	CHANGE 2015
Labour	Martin Whitfield	20,158	36.1%	5.1%
Scottish National Party	George Kerevan	17,075	30.6%	-12.0%
Conservative	Sheila Low	16,540	29.6%	10.1%
Liberal Democrat	Elizabeth Wilson	1,738	3.1%	0.5%
Independent	Mike Allan	367	0.7%	0.7%

East Renfrewshire

CON GAIN FROM SNP
Majority: 4,712, 8.8% | Turnout: 53,738, 76.7% | Electorate: 70,067 | EU Ref: 25.7% Leave

PARTY	CANDIDATE	VOTES	SHARE	CHANGE 2015
Conservative	Paul Masterton	21,496	40.0%	18.0%
Scottish National Party	Kirsten Oswald	16,784	31.2%	-9.3%
Labour	Blair McDougall	14,346	26.7%	-7.3%
Liberal Democrat	Aileen Morton	1,112	2.1%	0.2%

East Surrey

CON HOLD
Majority: 23,914, 40.4% | Turnout: 59,203, 74.9% | Electorate: 82,004 | EU Ref: 54.2% Leave

PARTY	CANDIDATE	VOTES	SHARE	CHANGE 2015
Conservative	Sam Gyimah	35,310	59.6%	2.2%
Labour	Hitesh Taylor	11,396	19.2%	7.4%
Liberal Democrat	David Lee	6,197	10.5%	1.2%
Independent	Andy Parr	2,973	5.0%	5.0%
UK Independence Party	Helena Windsor	2,227	3.8%	-13.3%
Green	Benedict Southworth	1,100	1.9%	-2.0%

East Worthing & Shoreham

CON HOLD
Majority: 5,106, 9.6% | Turnout: 53,117, 70.7% | Electorate: 75,525 | EU Ref: 53.7% Leave

PARTY	CANDIDATE	VOTES	SHARE	CHANGE 2015
Conservative	Tim Loughton	25,988	48.9%	-0.5%
Labour	Sophie Cook	20,882	39.3%	19.8%
Liberal Democrat	Oli Henman	2,523	4.7%	-2.0%
UK Independence Party	Mike Glennon	1,444	2.7%	-13.8%
Green	Leslie Groves Williams	1,273	2.4%	-2.8%
National Health Action	Carl Walker	575	1.1%	-1.4%
Independent	Andy Lutwyche	432	0.8%	0.8%

East Yorkshire

CON HOLD
Majority: 15,006, 27.8% | Turnout: 53,956, 67.0% | Electorate: 81,065 | EU Ref: 63.3% Leave

PARTY	CANDIDATE	VOTES	SHARE	CHANGE 2015
Conservative	Greg Knight	31,442	58.3%	7.7%
Labour	Alan Clark	16,436	30.5%	9.8%
Liberal Democrat	Carl Minns	2,134	4.0%	-2.0%
UK Independence Party	Andrew Dennis	1,986	3.7%	-14.2%
The Yorkshire Party	Timothy Norman	1,015	1.9%	0.4%
Green	Michael Jackson	943	1.7%	-1.7%

Eastbourne

LIB DEM GAIN FROM CON
Majority: 1,609, 2.8% | Turnout: 57,420, 72.9% | Electorate: 78,754 | EU Ref: 57.6% Leave

PARTY	CANDIDATE	VOTES	SHARE	CHANGE 2015
Liberal Democrat	Stephen Lloyd	26,924	46.9%	8.7%
Conservative	Caroline Ansell	25,315	44.1%	4.5%
Labour	Jake Lambert	4,671	8.1%	0.3%
Green	Alex Hough	510	0.9%	-1.7%

Eastleigh

CON HOLD
Majority: 14,179, 24.7% | Turnout: 57,280, 70.5% | Electorate: 81,212 | EU Ref: 54.0% Leave

PARTY	CANDIDATE	VOTES	SHARE	CHANGE 2015
Conservative	Mims Davies	28,889	50.4%	8.2%
Liberal Democrat	Mike Thornton	14,710	25.7%	-0.1%
Labour	Jill Payne	11,454	20.0%	7.1%
UK Independence Party	Malcolm Jones	1,477	2.6%	-13.2%
Green	Ron Meldrum	750	1.3%	-1.4%

Eddisbury

CON HOLD
Majority: 11,942, 23.3% | Turnout: 51,319, 73.0% | Electorate: 70,272 | EU Ref: 52.2% Leave

PARTY	CANDIDATE	VOTES	SHARE	CHANGE 2015
Conservative	Antoinette Sandbach	29,192	56.9%	5.8%
Labour	Cathy Reynolds	17,250	33.6%	10.0%
Liberal Democrat	Ian Priestner	2,804	5.5%	-3.6%
UK Independence Party	John Bickley	1,109	2.2%	-10.0%
Green	Mark Green	785	1.5%	-1.9%
Pirate Party	Morgan Hill	179	0.3%	0.3%

Edinburgh East

SNP HOLD
Majority: 3,425, 7.8% | Turnout: 43,523, 66.0% | Electorate: 65,896 | EU Ref: 27.6% Leave

PARTY	CANDIDATE	VOTES	SHARE	CHANGE 2015
Scottish National Party	Tommy Sheppard	18,509	42.5%	-6.7%
Labour	Patsy King	15,084	34.7%	4.8%
Conservative	Katie Mackie	8,081	18.6%	8.6%
Liberal Democrat	Tristan Gray	1,849	4.2%	1.4%

Edinburgh North & Leith

SNP HOLD
Majority: 1,625, 2.8% | Turnout: 56,552, 71.2% | Electorate: 79,473 | EU Ref: 21.8% Leave

PARTY	CANDIDATE	VOTES	SHARE	CHANGE 2015
Scottish National Party	Deidre Brock	19,243	34.0%	-6.9%
Labour	Gordon Munro	17,618	31.2%	-0.1%
Conservative	Iain McGill	15,385	27.2%	11.0%
Liberal Democrat	Martin Veart	2,579	4.6%	0.0%
Green	Lorna Slater	1,727	3.1%	-2.4%

Edinburgh South

LAB HOLD
Majority: 15,514, 32.4% | Turnout: 47,840, 74.1% | Electorate: 64,553 | EU Ref: 22.2% Leave

PARTY	CANDIDATE	VOTES	SHARE	CHANGE 2015
Labour	Ian Murray	26,269	54.9%	15.8%
Scottish National Party	Jim Eadie	10,755	22.5%	-11.3%
Conservative	Stephanie Smith	9,428	19.7%	2.2%
Liberal Democrat	Alan Beal	1,388	2.9%	-0.8%

Edinburgh South West

SNP HOLD
Majority: 1,097, 2.2% | Turnout: 49,390, 69.4% | Electorate: 71,178 | EU Ref: 27.9% Leave

PARTY	CANDIDATE	VOTES	SHARE	CHANGE 2015
Scottish National Party	Joanna Cherry	17,575	35.6%	-7.4%
Conservative	Miles Briggs	16,478	33.4%	13.1%
Labour	Foysol Choudbury	13,213	26.8%	-0.4%
Liberal Democrat	Aisha Mir	2,124	4.3%	0.6%

Edinburgh West

LIB DEM GAIN FROM SNP

Majority: 2,988, 5.7% | Turnout: 52,795, 73.8% | Electorate: 71,500 | EU Ref: 28.8% Leave

PARTY	CANDIDATE	VOTES	SHARE	CHANGE 2015
Liberal Democrat	Christine Jardine	18,108	34.3%	1.2%
Scottish National Party	Toni Giugliano	15,120	28.6%	-10.3%
Conservative	Sandy Batho	11,559	21.9%	9.6%
Labour	Mandy Telford	7,876	14.9%	3.2%
Scotland's Independence Referendum Party	Mark Whittet	132	0.3%	0.3%

Edmonton

LAB HOLD

Majority: 21,115, 48.4% | Turnout: 43,678, 66.6% | Electorate: 65,777 | EU Ref: 48.2% Leave

PARTY	CANDIDATE	VOTES	SHARE	CHANGE 2015
Labour	Kate Osamor	31,221	71.5%	10.1%
Conservative	Gonul Daniels	10,106	23.1%	-1.0%
UK Independence Party	Nigel Sussman	860	2.0%	-6.2%
Liberal Democrat	David Schmitz	858	2.0%	-0.2%
Green	Benjamin Gill	633	1.4%	-1.8%

Ellesmere Port & Neston

LAB HOLD

Majority: 11,390, 22.4% | Turnout: 50,939, 74.2% | Electorate: 68,666 | EU Ref: 57.8% Leave

PARTY	CANDIDATE	VOTES	SHARE	CHANGE 2015
Labour	Justin Madders	30,137	59.2%	11.4%
Conservative	Nigel Jones	18,747	36.8%	2.5%
Liberal Democrat	Ed Gough	892	1.8%	-1.6%
UK Independence Party	Fred Fricker	821	1.6%	-10.4%
Green	Steven Baker	342	0.7%	-1.4%

Elmet & Rothwell

CON HOLD

Majority: 9,805, 16.4% | Turnout: 59,542, 74.2% | Electorate: 80,291 | EU Ref: 56.4% Leave

PARTY	CANDIDATE	VOTES	SHARE	CHANGE 2015
Conservative	Alec Shelbrooke	32,352	54.3%	5.9%
Labour	David Patrick Nagle	22,547	37.9%	4.1%
Liberal Democrat	Stewart Golton	2,606	4.4%	-0.2%
The Yorkshire Party	Matthew Clover	1,042	1.8%	1.8%
Green	Dylan Brown	995	1.7%	-0.5%

Eltham

LAB HOLD

Majority: 6,296, 13.6% | Turnout: 46,155, 71.6% | Electorate: 64,474 | EU Ref: 52.8% Leave

PARTY	CANDIDATE	VOTES	SHARE	CHANGE 2015
Labour	Clive Efford	25,128	54.4%	11.8%
Conservative	Matt Hartley	18,832	40.8%	4.4%
Liberal Democrat	David Hall-Matthews	1,457	3.2%	0.1%
British National Party	John Clarke	738	1.6%	1.6%

Enfield North

LAB HOLD

Majority: 10,247, 21.1% | Turnout: 48,565, 71.5% | Electorate: 68,076 | EU Ref: 47.9% Leave

PARTY	CANDIDATE	VOTES	SHARE	CHANGE 2015
Labour	Joan Ryan	28,177	58.0%	14.3%
Conservative	Nick De Bois	17,930	36.9%	-4.4%
Liberal Democrat	Nicholas Da Costa	1,036	2.1%	-0.2%
UK Independence Party	Deborah Cairns	848	1.7%	-7.2%
Green	Bill Linton	574	1.2%	-1.6%

Enfield Southgate

LAB GAIN FROM CON

Majority: 4,355, 9.0% | Turnout: 48,328, 74.3% | Electorate: 65,210 | EU Ref: 37.4% Leave

PARTY	CANDIDATE	VOTES	SHARE	CHANGE 2015
Labour	Bambos Charalambous	24,989	51.7%	12.7%
Conservative	David Burrowes	20,634	42.7%	-6.7%
Liberal Democrat	Pippa Morgan	1,925	4.0%	0.7%
Green	David Flint	780	1.6%	-2.1%

Epping Forest

CON HOLD

Majority: 18,243, 36.0% | Turnout: 50,779, 67.9% | Electorate: 74,737 | EU Ref: 61.1% Leave

PARTY	CANDIDATE	VOTES	SHARE	CHANGE 2015
Conservative	Eleanor Laing	31,462	62.0%	7.2%
Labour	Liam Preston	13,219	26.0%	9.9%
Liberal Democrat	Jon Whitehouse	2,884	5.7%	-1.3%
UK Independence Party	Patrick O'Flynn	1,871	3.7%	-14.7%
Green	Simon Heap	1,233	2.4%	-1.2%
Young People's Party	Thomas Hall	110	0.2%	0.1%

Epsom & Ewell

CON HOLD

Majority: 20,475, 34.6% | Turnout: 59,266, 74.1% | Electorate: 80,029 | EU Ref: 48.0% Leave

PARTY	CANDIDATE	VOTES	SHARE	CHANGE 2015
Conservative	Chris Grayling	35,313	59.6%	1.3%
Labour	Ed Mayne	14,838	25.0%	9.5%
Liberal Democrat	Steve Gee	7,401	12.5%	3.7%
Green	Janice Baker	1,714	2.9%	-0.8%

Erewash

CON HOLD

Majority: 4,534, 9.1% | Turnout: 49,781, 68.2% | Electorate: 72,995 | EU Ref: 63.3% Leave

PARTY	CANDIDATE	VOTES	SHARE	CHANGE 2015
Conservative	Maggie Throup	25,939	52.1%	9.4%
Labour	Catherine Atkinson	21,405	43.0%	7.7%
Liberal Democrat	Martin Garnett	1,243	2.5%	-0.9%
Green	Ralph Hierons	675	1.4%	-1.1%
Independent	Roy Dunn	519	1.0%	1.0%

Erith & Thamesmead

LAB HOLD

Majority: 10,014, 22.5% | Turnout: 44,464, 63.8% | Electorate: 69,724 | EU Ref: 54.3% Leave

PARTY	CANDIDATE	VOTES	SHARE	CHANGE 2015
Labour	Teresa Pearce	25,585	57.5%	7.8%
Conservative	Edward Baxter	15,571	35.0%	7.6%
UK Independence Party	Ronie Johnson	1,728	3.9%	-13.4%
Liberal Democrat	Simon Waddington	750	1.7%	-0.6%
Green	Claudine Letsae	507	1.1%	-1.1%
Christian Peoples Alliance	Temi Olodu	243	0.5%	-0.1%
Independent	Doro Oddiri	80	0.2%	0.2%

Esher & Walton

CON HOLD
Majority: 23,298, 38.9% | Turnout: 59,842, 75.4% | Electorate: 80,938 | EU Ref: 41.6% Leave

PARTY	CANDIDATE	VOTES	SHARE	CHANGE 2015
Conservative	Dominic Raab	35,071	58.6%	-4.3%
Labour	Lana Hylands	11,773	19.7%	7.0%
Liberal Democrat	Andrew Davis	10,374	17.3%	7.9%
Green	Olivia Palmer	1,074	1.8%	-2.3%
UK Independence Party	David Ions	1,034	1.7%	-8.0%
Monster Raving Loony Party	Baron Badger	318	0.5%	0.5%
Independent	Della Reynolds	198	0.3%	-0.1%

Exeter

LAB HOLD
Majority: 16,117, 29.1% | Turnout: 55,423, 71.7% | Electorate: 77,330 | EU Ref: 44.7% Leave

PARTY	CANDIDATE	VOTES	SHARE	CHANGE 2015
Labour	Ben Bradshaw	34,336	62.0%	15.6%
Conservative	James Taghdissian	18,219	32.9%	-0.2%
Liberal Democrat	Vanessa Newcombe	1,562	2.8%	-1.5%
Green	Joe Levy	1,027	1.9%	-4.6%
Independent	Jonathan West	212	0.4%	0.4%
Independent	Jonathan Bishop	67	0.1%	0.1%

Falkirk

SNP HOLD
Majority: 4,923, 9.1% | Turnout: 53,809, 65.4% | Electorate: 82,240 | EU Ref: 42.0% Leave

PARTY	CANDIDATE	VOTES	SHARE	CHANGE 2015
Scottish National Party	John McNally	20,952	38.9%	-18.8%
Labour	Craig Martin	16,029	29.8%	4.7%
Conservative	Callum Laidlaw	14,088	26.2%	14.0%
Liberal Democrat	Austin Reid	1,120	2.1%	0.1%
Green	Debra Pickering	908	1.7%	1.7%
UK Independence Party	Stuart Martin	712	1.3%	-1.7%

Fareham

CON HOLD

Majority: 21,555, 39.8% | Turnout: 57,014, 72.3% | Electorate: 78,837 | EU Ref: 55.4% Leave

PARTY	CANDIDATE	VOTES	SHARE	CHANGE 2015
Conservative	Suella Fernandes	35,915	65.0%	6.9%
Labour	Matthew Randall	14,360	25.2%	10.9%
Liberal Democrat	Matthew Winnington	3,896	6.8%	-2.0%
UK Independence Party	Tony Blewett	1,541	2.7%	-12.7%
Green	Miles Grindey	1,302	2.3%	-1.6%

Faversham & Mid Kent

CON HOLD

Majority: 17,413, 35.0% | Turnout: 49,749, 65.5% | Electorate: 66,425 | EU Ref: 58.2% Leave

PARTY	CANDIDATE	VOTES	SHARE	CHANGE 2015
Conservative	Helen Whately	30,390	61.1%	6.7%
Labour	Michael Desmond	12,977	26.1%	9.9%
Liberal Democrat	David Naghi	3,249	6.5%	-0.1%
UK Independence Party	Mark McGiffin	1,702	3.4%	-14.6%
Green	Alastair Gould	1,431	2.9%	-1.0%

Feltham & Heston

LAB HOLD

Majority: 15,603, 29.4% | Turnout: 53,027, 64.9% | Electorate: 81,714 | EU Ref: 59.4% Leave

PARTY	CANDIDATE	VOTES	SHARE	CHANGE 2015
Labour	Seema Malhotra	32,462	61.2%	8.9%
Conservative	Samir Jassal	16,859	31.8%	2.7%
UK Independence Party	Stuart Agnew	1,510	2.8%	-9.7%
Liberal Democrat	Hina Malik	1,387	2.6%	-0.6%
Green	Tony Firkins	809	1.5%	-1.3%

Fermanagh & South Tyrone

SF GAIN FROM UUP

Majority: 875, 1.7% | Turnout: 53,481, 75.8% | Electorate: 70,601 | EU Ref: Not available

PARTY	CANDIDATE	VOTES	SHARE	CHANGE 2015
Sinn Féin	Michelle Gildernew	25,230	47.2%	1.8%
Ulster Unionist Party	Tom Elliott	24,355	45.5%	-0.9%
Social Democratic & Labour Party	Mary Garrity	2,587	4.8%	-0.5%
Alliance Party	Noreen Campbell	886	1.7%	0.4%
Green	Tanya Jones	423	0.8%	-0.8%

Filton & Bradley Stoke

CON HOLD

Majority: 4,190, 8.3% | Turnout: 50,702, 70.0% | Electorate: 72,483 | EU Ref: 48.0% Leave

PARTY	CANDIDATE	VOTES	SHARE	CHANGE 2015
Conservative	Jack Lopresti	25,339	50.0%	3.3%
Labour	Naomi Rylatt	21,149	41.7%	15.1%
Liberal Democrat	Eva Fielding	3,052	6.0%	-1.3%
Green	Diana Warner	1,162	2.3%	-2.3%

Finchley & Golders Green

CON HOLD

Majority: 1,657, 3.2% | Turnout: 52,385, 71.7% | Electorate: 73,329 | EU Ref: 30.9% Leave

PARTY	CANDIDATE	VOTES	SHARE	CHANGE 2015
Conservative	Mike Freer	24,599	47.0%	-3.9%
Labour	Jeremy Newmark	22,942	43.8%	4.1%
Liberal Democrat	Jonathan Davies	3,463	6.6%	3.3%
Green	Adele Ward	919	1.8%	-0.9%
UK Independence Party	Andrew Price	462	0.9%	-2.5%

Folkestone & Hythe

CON HOLD

Majority: 15,411, 26.2% | Turnout: 58,875, 68.3% | Electorate: 86,272 | EU Ref: 61.8% Leave

PARTY	CANDIDATE	VOTES	SHARE	CHANGE 2015
Conservative	Damian Collins	32,197	54.7%	6.8%
Labour	Laura Davison	16,786	28.5%	14.1%
Liberal Democrat	Lynne Beaumont	4,222	7.2%	-1.7%
UK Independence Party	Stephen Priestley	2,565	4.4%	-18.4%
Green	Martin Whybrow	2,498	4.2%	-1.1%
Independent	David Plumstead	493	0.8%	0.8%
Independent	Naomi Slade	114	0.2%	0.2%

Forest of Dean

CON HOLD

Majority: 9,502, 18.4% | Turnout: 51,767, 73.0% | Electorate: 70,898 | EU Ref: 58.1% Leave

PARTY	CANDIDATE	VOTES	SHARE	CHANGE 2015
Conservative	Mark Harper	28,096	54.3%	7.4%
Labour	Shaun Stammers	18,594	35.9%	11.3%
Liberal Democrat	Janet Ellard	2,029	3.9%	-1.4%
Green	James Greenwood	1,241	2.4%	-3.1%
UK Independence Party	Ernie Warrender	1,237	2.4%	-15.4%
Independent	Julian Burrett	570	1.1%	1.1%

Foyle

SF GAIN FROM SDLP

Majority: 169, 0.4% | Turnout: 45,965, 65.4% | Electorate: 70,324 | EU Ref: Not available

PARTY	CANDIDATE	VOTES	SHARE	CHANGE 2015
Sinn Féin	Elisha McCallion	18,256	39.7%	8.2%
Social Democratic & Labour Party	Mark Durkan	18,087	39.3%	-8.6%
Democratic Unionist Party	Gary Middleton	7,398	16.1%	3.7%
People Before Profit	Shaun Harkin	1,377	3.0%	3.0%
Alliance Party	John Doherty	847	1.8%	-0.4%

Fylde

CON HOLD
Majority: 11,805, 25.4% | Turnout: 46,467, 70.5% | Electorate: 65,937 | EU Ref: 56.6% Leave

PARTY	CANDIDATE	VOTES	SHARE	CHANGE 2015
Conservative	Mark Menzies	27,334	58.8%	9.7%
Labour	Jed Sullivan	15,529	33.4%	14.6%
Liberal Democrat	Freddie Van Mierlo	2,341	5.0%	1.3%
Green	Tina Rothery	1,263	2.7%	-0.5%

Gainsborough

CON HOLD
Majority: 17,023, 33.1% | Turnout: 51,425, 67.6% | Electorate: 75,893 | EU Ref: 62.0% Leave

PARTY	CANDIDATE	VOTES	SHARE	CHANGE 2015
Conservative	Edward Leigh	31,790	61.8%	9.1%
Labour	Catherine Tite	14,767	28.7%	7.4%
Liberal Democrat	Lesley Rollings	3,630	7.1%	0.4%
Green	Vicky Pearson	1,238	2.4%	-0.2%

Garston & Halewood

LAB HOLD
Majority: 32,149, 60.0% | Turnout: 53,522, 71.1% | Electorate: 75,248 | EU Ref: 47.9% Leave

PARTY	CANDIDATE	VOTES	SHARE	CHANGE 2015
Labour	Maria Eagle	41,599	77.7%	8.6%
Conservative	Adam Marsden	9,450	17.7%	4.0%
Liberal Democrat	Anna Martin	1,723	3.2%	-1.4%
Green	Lawrence Brown	750	1.4%	-2.0%

Gateshead

LAB HOLD

Majority: 17,350, 41.2% | Turnout: 42,103, 64.6% | Electorate: 65,186 | EU Ref: 56.0% Leave

PARTY	CANDIDATE	VOTES	SHARE	CHANGE 2015
Labour	Ian Mearns	27,426	65.1%	8.4%
Conservative	Lauren Hankinson	10,076	23.9%	9.4%
UK Independence Party	Mark Bell	2,281	5.4%	-12.4%
Liberal Democrat	Frank Hindle	1,709	4.1%	-2.8%
Green	Andy Redfern	611	1.5%	-2.6%

Gedling

LAB HOLD

Majority: 4,694, 9.1% | Turnout: 51,682, 72.5% | Electorate: 71,223 | EU Ref: 56.2% Leave

PARTY	CANDIDATE	VOTES	SHARE	CHANGE 2015
Labour	Vernon Coaker	26,833	51.9%	9.6%
Conservative	Carolyn Abbott	22,139	42.8%	6.8%
UK Independence Party	Lee Waters	1,143	2.2%	-12.2%
Liberal Democrat	Robert Swift	1,052	2.0%	-1.9%
Green	Rebecca Connick	515	1.0%	-2.2%

Gillingham & Rainham

CON HOLD

Majority: 9,430, 19.3% | Turnout: 48,868, 66.9% | Electorate: 72,903 | EU Ref: 64.0% Leave

PARTY	CANDIDATE	VOTES	SHARE	CHANGE 2015
Conservative	Rehman Chishti	27,091	55.4%	7.5%
Labour	Andrew Stamp	17,661	36.1%	10.5%
UK Independence Party	Martin Cook	2,097	4.3%	-15.2%
Liberal Democrat	Paul Chaplin	1,372	2.8%	-0.8%
Green	Clive Gregory	520	1.1%	-1.3%
Christian Peoples Alliance	Roger Peacock	127	0.3%	0.3%

Glasgow Central

SNP HOLD

SNP HOLD

Majority: 2,267, 6.3% | Turnout: 35,984, 55.9% | Electorate: 64,346 | EU Ref: 28.8% Leave

PARTY	CANDIDATE	VOTES	SHARE	CHANGE 2015
Scottish National Party	Alison Thewliss	16,096	44.7%	-7.8%
Labour	Faten Hameed	13,829	38.4%	5.4%
Conservative	Charlotte Fairbanks	5,014	13.9%	7.9%
Liberal Democrat	Isabel Nelson	1,045	2.9%	1.3%

Glasgow East

SNP HOLD

Majority: 75, 0.2% | Turnout: 36,166, 54.6% | Electorate: 66,242 | EU Ref: 43.8% Leave

PARTY	CANDIDATE	VOTES	SHARE	CHANGE 2015
Scottish National Party	David Linden	14,024	38.8%	-18.1%
Labour	Kate Watson	13,949	38.6%	6.2%
Conservative	Thomas Kerr	6,816	18.8%	12.8%
Liberal Democrat	Matthew Clark	567	1.6%	0.8%
UK Independence Party	John Ferguson	504	1.4%	-1.2%
Independent	Karin Finegan	158	0.4%	0.4%
Social Democratic Party	Steven Marshall	148	0.4%	0.4%

Glasgow North

SNP HOLD

Majority: 1,060, 3.1% | Turnout: 33,473, 62.1% | Electorate: 53,862 | EU Ref: 21.6% Leave

PARTY	CANDIDATE	VOTES	SHARE	CHANGE 2015
Scottish National Party	Patrick Grady	12,597	37.6%	-15.5%
Labour	Pam Duncan-Glancy	11,537	34.5%	6.5%
Conservative	Stuart Cullen	4,935	14.7%	6.9%
Green	Patrick Harvie	3,251	9.7%	3.5%
Liberal Democrat	Calum Shepherd	1,153	3.4%	0.7%

Glasgow North East

LAB GAIN FROM SNP

Majority: 242, 0.7% | Turnout: 31,775, 53.0% | Electorate: 59,931 | EU Ref: 40.7% Leave

PARTY	CANDIDATE	VOTES	SHARE	CHANGE 2015
Labour	Paul Sweeney	13,637	42.9%	9.2%
Scottish National Party	Anne McLaughlin	13,395	42.2%	-15.9%
Conservative	Jack Wylie	4,106	12.9%	8.2%
Liberal Democrat	Daniel Donaldson	637	2.0%	1.2%

Glasgow North West

SNP HOLD

Majority: 2,561, 6.6% | Turnout: 38,844, 60.9% | Electorate: 63,773 | EU Ref: 31.5% Leave

PARTY	CANDIDATE	VOTES	SHARE	CHANGE 2015
Scottish National Party	Carol Monaghan	16,508	42.5%	-12.0%
Labour	Michael Shanks	13,947	35.9%	5.0%
Conservative	Christopher Land	7,002	18.0%	9.6%
Liberal Democrat	James Speirs	1,387	3.6%	0.8%

Glasgow South

SNP HOLD

Majority: 2,027, 4.5% | Turnout: 44,550, 64.4% | Electorate: 69,126 | EU Ref: 28.2% Leave

PARTY	CANDIDATE	VOTES	SHARE	CHANGE 2015
Scottish National Party	Stewart M McDonald	18,312	41.1%	-13.8%
Labour	Eileen Dinning	16,285	36.6%	6.8%
Conservative	Taylor Muir	8,506	19.1%	9.4%
Liberal Democrat	Ewan Hoyle	1,447	3.2%	1.2%

Glasgow South West

SNP HOLD
Majority: 60, 0.2% | Turnout: 35,378, 56.2% | Electorate: 62,991 | EU Ref: 40.9% Leave

PARTY	CANDIDATE	VOTES	SHARE	CHANGE 2015
Scottish National Party	Chris Stephens	14,386	40.7%	-16.5%
Labour	Matt Kerr	14,326	40.5%	7.7%
Conservative	Thomas Haddow	5,524	15.6%	10.6%
Liberal Democrat	Ben Denton-Cardew	661	1.9%	0.9%
UK Independence Party	Sarah Hemy	481	1.4%	-1.0%

Glenrothes

SNP HOLD
Majority: 3,267, 8.1% | Turnout: 40,399, 60.9% | Electorate: 66,378 | EU Ref: 46.5% Leave

PARTY	CANDIDATE	VOTES	SHARE	CHANGE 2015
Scottish National Party	Peter Grant	17,291	42.8%	-17.0%
Labour	Altany Craik	14,024	34.7%	4.1%
Conservative	Andrew Brown	7,876	19.5%	11.8%
Liberal Democrat	Rebecca Hall	1,208	3.0%	1.1%

Gloucester

CON HOLD
Majority: 5,520, 10.2% | Turnout: 54,071, 65.0% | Electorate: 82,965 | EU Ref: 58.6% Leave

PARTY	CANDIDATE	VOTES	SHARE	CHANGE 2015
Conservative	Richard Graham	27,208	50.3%	5.0%
Labour	Barry Kirby	21,688	40.1%	8.6%
Liberal Democrat	Jeremy Hilton	2,716	5.0%	-0.4%
UK Independence Party	Daniel Wolf	1,495	2.8%	-11.5%
Green	Gerald Hartley	754	1.4%	-1.4%
Monster Raving Loony Party	George Ridgeon	210	0.4%	0.0%

Gordon

CON GAIN FROM SNP

Majority: 2,607, 4.8% | Turnout: 53,685, 68.4% | Electorate: 78,531 | EU Ref: 44.6% Leave

PARTY	CANDIDATE	VOTES	SHARE	CHANGE 2015
Conservative	Colin Clark	21,861	40.7%	29.0%
Scottish National Party	Alex Salmond	19,254	35.9%	-11.8%
Labour	Kirsten Muat	6,340	11.8%	5.9%
Liberal Democrat	David Evans	6,230	11.6%	-21.1%

Gosport

CON HOLD

Majority: 17,211, 34.7% | Turnout: 49,481, 67.0% | Electorate: 74,152 | EU Ref: 62.0% Leave

PARTY	CANDIDATE	VOTES	SHARE	CHANGE 2015
Conservative	Caroline Dinenage	30,647	61.9%	6.6%
Labour	Alan Durrant	13,436	27.2%	12.6%
Liberal Democrat	Bruce Tennent	2,328	4.7%	-2.2%
UK Independence Party	Chloe Palmer	1,790	3.6%	-15.8%
Green	Monica Cassidy	1,024	2.1%	-1.5%
Independent	Jeffrey Roberts	256	0.5%	0.3%

Gower

LAB GAIN FROM CON

Majority: 3,269, 7.2% | Turnout: 45,576, 73.3% | Electorate: 62,163 | EU Ref: 50.2% Leave

PARTY	CANDIDATE	VOTES	SHARE	CHANGE 2015
Labour	Antonia (Tonia) Antoniazzi	22,727	49.9%	12.8%
Conservative	Bryon Davies	19,458	42.7%	5.6%
Plaid Cymru	Harri Roberts	1,669	3.7%	-3.5%
Liberal Democrat	Howard Evans	931	2.0%	-1.6%
UK Independence Party	Ross Ford	642	1.4%	-9.8%
Pirate Party	Jason Winstanley	149	0.3%	0.3%

Grantham & Stamford

CON HOLD

Majority: 20,094, 35.5% | Turnout: 56,593, 69.2% | Electorate: 81,740 | EU Ref: 61.0% Leave

PARTY	CANDIDATE	VOTES	SHARE	CHANGE 2015
Conservative	Nick Boles	35,090	62.0%	9.2%
Labour	Barrie Fairbairn	14,996	26.5%	9.6%
Liberal Democrat	Anita Day	3,120	5.5%	-0.6%
UK Independence Party	Marietta King	1,745	3.1%	-14.4%
Independent	Tariq Mahmood	860	1.5%	1.5%
Green	Becca Thackray	782	1.4%	-2.1%

Gravesham

CON HOLD

Majority: 9,347, 19.1% | Turnout: 48,997, 67.2% | Electorate: 72,954 | EU Ref: 65.4% Leave

PARTY	CANDIDATE	VOTES	SHARE	CHANGE 2015
Conservative	Adam Holloway	27,237	55.6%	8.8%
Labour	Mandy Garford	17,890	36.5%	6.4%
UK Independence Party	Emmanuel Feyisetan	1,742	3.6%	-15.0%
Liberal Democrat	James Willis	1,210	2.5%	0.3%
Green	Marna Gilligan	723	1.5%	-0.8%
Independent	Michael Rogan	195	0.4%	0.4%

Great Grimsby

LAB HOLD

Majority: 2,565, 7.2% | Turnout: 35,521, 57.5% | Electorate: 61,743 | EU Ref: 70.2% Leave

PARTY	CANDIDATE	VOTES	SHARE	CHANGE 2015
Labour	Melanie Onn	17,545	49.4%	9.6%
Conservative	Jo Gideon	14,980	42.2%	15.9%
UK Independence Party	Mike Hookem	1,648	4.6%	-20.3%
Liberal Democrat	Steve Beasant	954	2.7%	-2.3%
Independent	Christina McGilligan-Fell	394	1.1%	1.1%

Great Yarmouth

CON HOLD
Majority: 7,973, 18.0% | Turnout: 44,146, 61.8% | Electorate: 71,408 | EU Ref: 71.5% Leave

PARTY	CANDIDATE	VOTES	SHARE	CHANGE 2015
Conservative	Brandon Lewis	23,901	54.1%	11.2%
Labour	Mike Smith-Clare	15,928	36.1%	7.0%
UK Independence Party	Catherine Blaiklock	2,767	6.3%	-16.8%
Liberal Democrat	James Joyce	987	2.2%	-0.1%
Green	Harry Webb	563	1.3%	-0.9%

Greenwich & Woolwich

LAB HOLD
Majority: 20,714, 39.0% | Turnout: 53,106, 68.8% | Electorate: 77,190 | EU Ref: 35.7% Leave

PARTY	CANDIDATE	VOTES	SHARE	CHANGE 2015
Labour	Matthew Pennycook	34,215	64.4%	12.2%
Conservative	Caroline Attfield	13,501	25.4%	-1.2%
Liberal Democrat	Chris Adams	3,785	7.1%	1.5%
Green	Daniel Garrun	1,605	3.0%	-3.4%

Guildford

CON HOLD
Majority: 17,040, 30.7% | Turnout: 55,509, 73.7% | Electorate: 75,291 | EU Ref: 41.2% Leave

PARTY	CANDIDATE	VOTES	SHARE	CHANGE 2015
Conservative	Anne Milton	30,295	54.6%	-2.5%
Liberal Democrat	Zoe Franklin	13,255	23.9%	8.4%
Labour	Howard Smith	10,545	19.0%	6.9%
Green	Mark Bray-Parry	1,152	2.1%	-2.7%
Peace Party	John Morris	205	0.4%	-0.1%
Independent	Semi Essessi	57	0.1%	0.1%

Hackney North & Stoke Newington

LAB HOLD

Majority: 35,139, 62.4% | Turnout: 56,298, 67.1% | Electorate: 85,058 | EU Ref: 20.9% Leave

PARTY	CANDIDATE	VOTES	SHARE	CHANGE 2015
Labour	Diane Abbott	42,265	75.1%	12.2%
Conservative	Amy Gray	7,126	12.7%	-2.1%
Liberal Democrat	Joe Richards	3,817	6.8%	1.8%
Green	Alastair Binnie-Lubbock	2,606	4.6%	-10.0%
Animal Welfare Party	Jonathan Homan	222	0.4%	0.0%
Independent	Abraham Spielmann	203	0.4%	0.4%
Friends Party	Coraline Corlis-Khan	59	0.1%	0.1%

Hackney South & Shoreditch

LAB HOLD

Majority: 37,931, 68.5% | Turnout: 55,354, 67.6% | Electorate: 83,099 | EU Ref: 22.2% Leave

PARTY	CANDIDATE	VOTES	SHARE	CHANGE 2015
Labour	Meg Hillier	43,974	79.4%	15.1%
Conservative	Luke Parker	6,043	10.9%	-2.6%
Liberal Democrat	Dave Raval	3,168	5.7%	1.1%
Green	Rebecca Johnson	1,522	2.7%	-8.8%
Animal Welfare Party	Vanessa Hudson	226	0.4%	0.4%
Independent	Russell Higgs	143	0.3%	0.1%
Christian Peoples Alliance	Angel Watt	113	0.2%	-0.3%
Workers Revolutionary Party	Jonty Leff	86	0.2%	0.0%
Independent	Hugo Sugg	50	0.1%	0.1%
Independent	Dale Kalamazad	29	0.1%	0.1%

Halesowen & Rowley Regis

CON HOLD
Majority: 5,253, 11.9% | Turnout: 44,379, 64.5% | Electorate: 68,856 | EU Ref: 66.3% Leave

PARTY	CANDIDATE	VOTES	SHARE	CHANGE 2015
Conservative	James Morris	23,012	51.9%	8.6%
Labour	Ian Cooper	17,759	40.0%	3.8%
UK Independence Party	Stuart Henley	2,126	4.8%	-11.8%
Liberal Democrat	Jamie Scott	859	1.9%	-0.1%
Green	James Robertson	440	1.0%	-0.9%
Independent	Tim Weller	183	0.4%	0.4%

Halifax

LAB HOLD
Majority: 5,376, 11.1% | Turnout: 48,276, 67.8% | Electorate: 71,224 | EU Ref: 60.4% Leave

PARTY	CANDIDATE	VOTES	SHARE	CHANGE 2015
Labour	Holly Lynch	25,507	52.8%	12.8%
Conservative	Chris Pearson	20,131	41.7%	2.7%
UK Independence Party	Mark Weedon	1,568	3.2%	-9.6%
Liberal Democrat	James Baker	1,070	2.2%	-1.5%

Haltemprice & Howden

CON HOLD
Majority: 15,405, 30.0% | Turnout: 51,440, 72.4% | Electorate: 71,519 | EU Ref: 55.5% Leave

PARTY	CANDIDATE	VOTES	SHARE	CHANGE 2015
Conservative	David Davis	31,355	61.0%	6.8%
Labour	Hollie Devanney	15,950	31.0%	10.0%
Liberal Democrat	David Nolan	2,482	4.8%	-1.4%
The Yorkshire Party	Diana Wallis	942	1.8%	0.8%
Green	Carole Needham	711	1.4%	-2.3%

Halton

LAB HOLD

Majority: 25,405, 51.3% | Turnout: 49,518, 67.4% | Electorate: 73,457 | EU Ref: 57.8% Leave

PARTY	CANDIDATE	VOTES	SHARE	CHANGE 2015
Labour	Derek Twigg	36,115	72.9%	10.1%
Conservative	Matthew Lloyd	10,710	21.6%	3.8%
UK Independence Party	Glyn Redican	1,488	3.0%	-11.1%
Liberal Democrat	Ryan Bate	896	1.8%	-0.6%
Independent	Vic Turton	309	0.6%	0.0%

Hammersmith

LAB HOLD

Majority: 18,651, 35.7% | Turnout: 52,252, 71.8% | Electorate: 72,803 | EU Ref: 31.0% Leave

PARTY	CANDIDATE	VOTES	SHARE	CHANGE 2015
Labour	Andy Slaughter	33,375	63.9%	13.9%
Conservative	Charlie Dewhirst	14,724	28.2%	-8.2%
Liberal Democrat	Joyce Onstad	2,802	5.4%	0.7%
Green	Alex Horn	800	1.5%	-2.9%
UK Independence Party	Jack Bovill	507	1.0%	-3.4%
Independent	Jagdeosingh Hauzaree	44	0.1%	0.1%

Hampstead & Kilburn

LAB HOLD

Majority: 15,560, 26.6% | Turnout: 58,407, 70.4% | Electorate: 82,957 | EU Ref: 23.5% Leave

PARTY	CANDIDATE	VOTES	SHARE	CHANGE 2015
Labour	Tulip Siddiq	34,464	59.0%	14.6%
Conservative	Claire-Louise Leyland	18,904	32.4%	-10.0%
Liberal Democrat	Kirsty Allan	4,100	7.0%	1.4%
Green	John Mansook	742	1.3%	-3.2%
Independent	Hugh Easterbrook	136	0.2%	0.2%
Independent	Rainbow George Weiss	61	0.1%	0.1%

Harborough

CON HOLD

Majority: 12,429, 21.6% | Turnout: 57,598, 73.1% | Electorate: 78,810 | EU Ref: 52.2% Leave

PARTY	CANDIDATE	VOTES	SHARE	CHANGE 2015
Conservative	Neil O'Brien	30,135	52.3%	-0.4%
Labour	Andy Thomas	17,706	30.7%	15.4%
Liberal Democrat	Zuffar Haq	7,286	12.6%	-0.8%
UK Independence Party	Teck Khong	1,361	2.4%	-12.0%
Green	Darren Woodiwiss	1,110	1.9%	-2.2%

Harlow

CON HOLD

Majority: 7,031, 15.6% | Turnout: 44,846, 66.2% | Electorate: 67,699 | EU Ref: 68.0% Leave

PARTY	CANDIDATE	VOTES	SHARE	CHANGE 2015
Conservative	Robert Halfon	24,230	54.0%	5.2%
Labour	Phil Waite	17,199	38.4%	8.4%
UK Independence Party	Mark Gough	1,787	4.0%	-12.3%
Liberal Democrat	Geoffrey Seef	970	2.2%	0.1%
Green	Hannah Clare	660	1.5%	-0.7%

Harrogate & Knaresborough

CON HOLD

Majority: 18,168, 32.0% | Turnout: 56,740, 73.4% | Electorate: 77,280 | EU Ref: 47.2% Leave

PARTY	CANDIDATE	VOTES	SHARE	CHANGE 2015
Conservative	Andrew Jones	31,477	55.5%	2.7%
Liberal Democrat	Helen Flynn	13,309	23.5%	1.4%
Labour	Mark Sewards	11,395	20.1%	9.9%
Independent	Donald Fraser	559	1.0%	1.0%

Harrow East

CON HOLD
Majority: 1,757, 3.4% | Turnout: 50,845, 70.9% | Electorate: 71,755 | EU Ref: 47.5% Leave

PARTY	CANDIDATE	VOTES	SHARE	CHANGE 2015
Conservative	Bob Blackman	25,129	49.4%	-0.9%
Labour	Navin Shah	23,372	46.0%	5.3%
Liberal Democrat	Adam Bernard	1,573	3.1%	1.0%
Green	Emma Wallace	771	1.5%	-0.2%

Harrow West

LAB HOLD
Majority: 13,314, 26.4% | Turnout: 50,355, 72.1% | Electorate: 69,797 | EU Ref: 41.4% Leave

PARTY	CANDIDATE	VOTES	SHARE	CHANGE 2015
Labour	Gareth Thomas	30,640	60.8%	13.9%
Conservative	Hannah David	17,326	34.4%	-7.8%
Liberal Democrat	Christopher Noyce	1,267	2.5%	-0.8%
Green	Rowan Langley	652	1.3%	-1.5%
UK Independence Party	Rathy Alagaratnam	470	0.9%	-3.5%

Hartlepool

LAB HOLD
Majority: 7,650, 18.3% | Turnout: 41,835, 59.2% | Electorate: 70,718 | EU Ref: 69.6% Leave

PARTY	CANDIDATE	VOTES	SHARE	CHANGE 2015
Labour	Mike Hill	21,969	52.5%	16.9%
Conservative	Carl Jackson	14,319	34.2%	13.3%
UK Independence Party	Phillip Broughton	4,801	11.5%	-16.5%
Liberal Democrat	Andy Hagon	746	1.8%	0.1%

Harwich & North Essex

CON HOLD

Majority: 14,356, 28.1% | Turnout: 51,141, 71.7% | Electorate: 71,294 | EU Ref: 61.1% Leave

PARTY	CANDIDATE	VOTES	SHARE	CHANGE 2015
Conservative	Bernard Jenkin	29,921	58.5%	7.5%
Labour	Rosalind Scott	15,565	30.4%	10.7%
Liberal Democrat	Dominic Graham	2,787	5.4%	-1.9%
UK Independence Party	Aaran Hammond	1,685	3.3%	-14.2%
Green	Blake Roberts	1,042	2.0%	-2.3%
Christian Peoples Alliance	Stephen Todd	141	0.3%	0.3%

Hastings & Rye

CON HOLD

Majority: 346, 0.7% | Turnout: 54,766, 69.9% | Electorate: 78,319 | EU Ref: 56.2% Leave

PARTY	CANDIDATE	VOTES	SHARE	CHANGE 2015
Conservative	Amber Rudd	25,668	46.9%	2.3%
Labour	Peter Chowney	25,322	46.2%	11.1%
Liberal Democrat	Nicholas Perry	1,885	3.4%	0.3%
UK Independence Party	Michael Phillips	1,479	2.7%	-10.6%
Independent	Nicholas Wilson	412	0.8%	0.8%

Havant

CON HOLD

Majority: 15,956, 34.5% | Turnout: 46,314, 63.9% | Electorate: 72,470 | EU Ref: 62.5% Leave

PARTY	CANDIDATE	VOTES	SHARE	CHANGE 2015
Conservative	Alan Mak	27,676	59.8%	8.1%
Labour	Graham Giles	11,720	25.3%	9.4%
Liberal Democrat	Paul Gray	2,801	6.0%	-0.5%
UK Independence Party	John Perry	2,011	4.3%	-16.3%
Green	Tim Dawes	1,122	2.4%	-2.8%
Independent	Ann Buckley	984	2.1%	2.1%

Hayes & Harlington

LAB HOLD

Majority: 18,115, 37.9% | Turnout: 47,802, 65.2% | Electorate: 73,268 | EU Ref: 59.4% Leave

PARTY	CANDIDATE	VOTES	SHARE	CHANGE 2015
Labour	John McDonnell	31,796	66.5%	6.9%
Conservative	Greg Smith	13,681	28.6%	3.9%
UK Independence Party	Cliff Dixon	1,153	2.4%	-9.5%
Liberal Democrat	Bill Newton Dunn	601	1.3%	-0.7%
Green	John Bowman	571	1.2%	-0.6%

Hazel Grove

CON HOLD

Majority: 5,514, 12.5% | Turnout: 44,132, 69.9% | Electorate: 63,166 | EU Ref: 51.4% Leave

PARTY	CANDIDATE	VOTES	SHARE	CHANGE 2015
Conservative	William Wragg	20,047	45.4%	4.0%
Liberal Democrat	Lisa Smart	14,533	32.9%	6.7%
Labour	Nav Mishra	9,036	20.5%	2.9%
Green	Robbie Lee	516	1.2%	-1.5%

Hemel Hempstead

CON HOLD

Majority: 9,445, 18.1% | Turnout: 52,282, 69.7% | Electorate: 74,415 | EU Ref: 55.2% Leave

PARTY	CANDIDATE	VOTES	SHARE	CHANGE 2015
Conservative	Mike Penning	28,735	55.0%	2.1%
Labour	Mandi Tattershall	19,290	36.9%	13.1%
Liberal Democrat	Sally Symington	3,233	6.2%	1.3%
Green	Sherief Hassan	1,024	2.0%	-1.4%

Hemsworth

LAB HOLD

Majority: 10,174, 22.1% | Turnout: 45,944, 63.9% | Electorate: 71,870 | EU Ref: 67.5% Leave

PARTY	CANDIDATE	VOTES	SHARE	CHANGE 2015
Labour	Jon Trickett	25,740	56.0%	4.7%
Conservative	Mike Jordan	15,566	33.9%	11.0%
UK Independence Party	David Dews	2,591	5.6%	-14.6%
The Yorkshire Party	Martin Roberts	1,135	2.5%	0.1%
Liberal Democrat	Joan MacQueen	912	2.0%	-1.2%

Hendon

CON HOLD

Majority: 1,072, 2.0% | Turnout: 52,215, 68.5% | Electorate: 76,522 | EU Ref: 41.9% Leave

PARTY	CANDIDATE	VOTES	SHARE	CHANGE 2015
Conservative	Matthew Offord	25,078	48.0%	-1.0%
Labour	Mike Katz	24,006	46.0%	4.5%
Liberal Democrat	Alasdair Hill	1,985	3.8%	1.6%
Green	Carmen Legarda	578	1.1%	-0.9%
UK Independence Party	Sabriye Warsame	568	1.1%	-4.1%

Henley

CON HOLD

Majority: 22,294, 39.0% | Turnout: 57,099, 76.1% | Electorate: 74,997 | EU Ref: 43.1% Leave

PARTY	CANDIDATE	VOTES	SHARE	CHANGE 2015
Conservative	John Howell	33,749	59.1%	0.6%
Labour	Oliver Kavanagh	11,455	20.1%	7.5%
Liberal Democrat	Laura Coyle	8,485	14.9%	3.6%
Green	Robin Bennett	1,864	3.3%	-3.6%
UK Independence Party	Tim Scott	1,154	2.0%	-8.9%
The Radical Party	Patrick Gray	392	0.7%	0.7%

Hereford & South Herefordshire

CON HOLD

Majority: 15,013, 29.7% | Turnout: 50,484, 71.0% | Electorate: 71,088 | EU Ref: 60.2% Leave

PARTY	CANDIDATE	VOTES	SHARE	CHANGE 2015
Conservative	Jesse Norman	27,004	53.5%	0.9%
Labour	Anna Coda	11,991	23.8%	11.0%
Independent	Jim Kenyon	5,560	11.0%	11.0%
Liberal Democrat	Lucy Hurds	3,556	7.0%	-3.5%
Green	Diana Toynbee	1,220	2.4%	-4.8%
UK Independence Party	Gwyn Price	1,153	2.3%	-14.5%

Hertford & Stortford

CON HOLD

Majority: 19,035, 31.7% | Turnout: 59,992, 72.8% | Electorate: 82,339 | EU Ref: 49.2% Leave

PARTY	CANDIDATE	VOTES	SHARE	CHANGE 2015
Conservative	Mark Prisk	36,184	60.3%	4.2%
Labour	Katherine Chibah	17,149	28.6%	10.7%
Liberal Democrat	Mark Argent	4,845	8.1%	0.3%
Green	David Woollcombe	1,814	3.0%	-1.7%

Hertsmere

CON HOLD

Majority: 16,951, 32.4% | Turnout: 52,253, 71.0% | Electorate: 73,561 | EU Ref: 50.8% Leave

PARTY	CANDIDATE	VOTES	SHARE	CHANGE 2015
Conservative	Oliver Dowden	31,928	61.1%	1.8%
Labour	Fiona Smith	14,977	28.7%	6.2%
Liberal Democrat	Joe Jordan	2,794	5.3%	-0.2%
UK Independence Party	David Hoy	1,564	3.0%	-9.7%
Green	Sophie Summerhayes	990	1.9%	1.9%

Hexham

CON HOLD

Majority: 9,236, 20.0% | Turnout: 46,224, 75.8% | Electorate: 61,053 | EU Ref: 45.4% Leave

PARTY	CANDIDATE	VOTES	SHARE	CHANGE 2015
Conservative	Guy Opperman	24,996	54.1%	1.4%
Labour	Stephen Powers	15,760	34.1%	9.2%
Liberal Democrat	Fiona Hall	3,285	7.1%	0.3%
Green	Wesley Foot	1,253	2.7%	-2.9%
UK Independence Party	Francis Miles	930	2.0%	-7.9%

Heywood & Middleton

LAB HOLD

Majority: 7,617, 15.3% | Turnout: 49,865, 62.4% | Electorate: 79,901 | EU Ref: 62.2% Leave

PARTY	CANDIDATE	VOTES	SHARE	CHANGE 2015
Labour	Liz McInnes	26,578	53.3%	10.2%
Conservative	Chris Clarkson	18,961	38.0%	18.9%
UK Independence Party	Lee Seville	3,239	6.5%	-25.7%
Liberal Democrat	Bill Winlow	1,087	2.2%	-1.1%

High Peak

LAB GAIN FROM CON

Majority: 2,322, 4.3% | Turnout: 53,853, 73.5% | Electorate: 73,248 | EU Ref: 50.5% Leave

PARTY	CANDIDATE	VOTES	SHARE	CHANGE 2015
Labour	Ruth George	26,753	49.7%	14.4%
Conservative	Andrew Bingham	24,431	45.4%	0.4%
Liberal Democrat	Charles Lawley	2,669	5.0%	0.3%

Hitchin & Harpenden

CON HOLD

Majority: 12,031, 20.5% | Turnout: 58,783, 77.4% | Electorate: 75,916 | EU Ref: 39.2% Leave

PARTY	CANDIDATE	VOTES	SHARE	CHANGE 2015
Conservative	Bim Afolami	31,189	53.1%	-3.8%
Labour	John Hayes	19,158	32.6%	11.9%
Liberal Democrat	Hugh Annand	6,236	10.6%	2.5%
Green	Richard Cano	1,329	2.3%	-3.3%
Independent	Ray Blake	629	1.1%	1.1%
Christian Peoples Alliance	Sid Cordle	242	0.4%	0.4%

Holborn & St Pancras

LAB HOLD

Majority: 30,509, 51.7% | Turnout: 58,997, 67.0% | Electorate: 88,088 | EU Ref: 27.4% Leave

PARTY	CANDIDATE	VOTES	SHARE	CHANGE 2015
Labour	Keir Starmer	41,343	70.1%	17.2%
Conservative	Tim Barnes	10,834	18.4%	-3.5%
Liberal Democrat	Stephen Crosher	4,020	6.8%	0.3%
Green	Sian Berry	1,980	3.4%	-9.4%
UK Independence Party	Giles Game	727	1.2%	-3.8%
English Democrats	Janus Polenceus	93	0.2%	0.2%

Hornchurch & Upminster

CON HOLD

Majority: 17,723, 31.6% | Turnout: 56,045, 69.4% | Electorate: 80,802 | EU Ref: 69.5% Leave

PARTY	CANDIDATE	VOTES	SHARE	CHANGE 2015
Conservative	Julia Dockerill	33,750	60.2%	11.2%
Labour	Rocky Gill	16,027	28.6%	8.5%
UK Independence Party	Lawrence Webb	3,502	6.2%	-19.1%
Liberal Democrat	Jonathan Mitchell	1,371	2.4%	-0.3%
Green	Peter Caton	1,077	1.9%	-0.6%
British National Party	David Furness	318	0.7%	0.3%

Hornsey & Wood Green

LAB HOLD

Majority: 30,738, 49.3% | Turnout: 62,293, 77.9% | Electorate: 79,946 | EU Ref: 18.5% Leave

PARTY	CANDIDATE	VOTES	SHARE	CHANGE 2015
Labour	Catherine West	40,738	65.4%	14.5%
Liberal Democrat	Dawn Barnes	10,000	16.1%	-15.7%
Conservative	Emma Lane	9,246	14.8%	5.6%
Green	Sam Hall	1,181	1.9%	-3.5%
Women's Equality Party	Nimco Ali	551	0.9%	0.9%
UK Independence Party	Ruth Price	429	0.7%	-1.5%
Christian Peoples Alliance	Helen Spiby-Vann	93	0.1%	-0.1%
Workers Revolutionary Party	Anna Athow	55	0.1%	-0.1%

Horsham

CON HOLD

Majority: 23,484, 37.8% | Turnout: 61,987, 74.9% | Electorate: 82,772 | EU Ref: 48.7% Leave

PARTY	CANDIDATE	VOTES	SHARE	CHANGE 2015
Conservative	Jeremy Quin	36,906	59.5%	2.2%
Labour	Susannah Brady	13,422	21.7%	10.2%
Liberal Democrat	Morwen Millson	7,644	12.3%	0.7%
Green	Catherine Ross	1,844	3.0%	-0.9%
UK Independence Party	Roger Arthur	1,533	2.5%	-11.5%
Something New	James Smith	375	0.6%	-0.1%
Peace Party	Jim Duggan	263	0.4%	-0.1%

Houghton & Sunderland South

LAB HOLD

Majority: 12,341, 29.8% | Turnout: 41,480, 60.9% | Electorate: 68,123 | EU Ref: 64.7% Leave

PARTY	CANDIDATE	VOTES	SHARE	CHANGE 2015
Labour	Bridget Phillipson	24,665	59.5%	4.3%
Conservative	Paul Howell	12,324	29.7%	11.3%
UK Independence Party	Michael Joyce	2,379	5.7%	-15.8%
Liberal Democrat	Paul Edgeworth	908	2.2%	0.1%
Green	Richard Bradley	725	1.7%	-1.1%
Independent	Mick Watson	479	1.2%	1.2%

Hove

LAB HOLD

Majority: 18,757, 32.5% | Turnout: 57,596, 77.6% | Electorate: 74,236 | EU Ref: 33.9% Leave

PARTY	CANDIDATE	VOTES	SHARE	CHANGE 2015
Labour	Peter Kyle	36,942	64.1%	21.8%
Conservative	Kristy Adams	18,185	31.6%	-8.4%
Liberal Democrat	Caroline Hynds	1,311	2.3%	-1.3%
Green	Phelim Mac Cafferty	971	1.7%	-5.1%
Independent	Charley Sabel	187	0.3%	0.3%

Huddersfield

LAB HOLD

Majority: 12,005, 27.4% | Turnout: 43,834, 65.4% | Electorate: 67,037 | EU Ref: 51.1% Leave

PARTY	CANDIDATE	VOTES	SHARE	CHANGE 2015
Labour	Barry Sheerman	26,470	60.4%	15.5%
Conservative	Scott Benton	14,465	33.0%	6.2%
Green	Andrew Cooper	1,395	3.2%	-3.7%
Liberal Democrat	Zulfiqar Ali	1,155	2.6%	-3.2%
The Yorkshire Party	Bikatshi Katenga	274	0.6%	0.6%
Independent	Marteen Thokkudubiyyapu	75	0.2%	0.2%

Huntingdon

CON HOLD
Majority: 14,475, 24.2% | Turnout: 59,720, 70.8% | Electorate: 84,273 | EU Ref: 53.3% Leave

PARTY	CANDIDATE	VOTES	SHARE	CHANGE 2015
Conservative	Jonathan Djanogly	32,915	55.1%	2.1%
Labour	Nik Johnson	18,440	30.9%	12.6%
Liberal Democrat	Rod Cantrill	5,090	8.5%	0.7%
UK Independence Party	Paul Bullen	2,180	3.7%	-13.3%
Green	Tom Maclennan	1,095	1.8%	-2.1%

Hyndburn

LAB HOLD
Majority: 5,815, 12.9% | Turnout: 45,202, 61.8% | Electorate: 73,111 | EU Ref: 65.8% Leave

PARTY	CANDIDATE	VOTES	SHARE	CHANGE 2015
Labour	Graham Jones	24,120	53.4%	11.2%
Conservative	Kevin Horkin	18,305	40.5%	8.6%
UK Independence Party	Janet Brown	1,953	4.3%	-17.0%
Liberal Democrat	Les Jones	824	1.8%	-0.2%

Ilford North

LAB HOLD
Majority: 9,639, 18.2% | Turnout: 52,941, 72.5% | Electorate: 70,791 | EU Ref: 52.6% Leave

PARTY	CANDIDATE	VOTES	SHARE	CHANGE 2015
Labour	Wes Streeting	30,589	57.8%	13.9%
Conservative	Lee Scott	20,950	39.6%	-3.1%
Liberal Democrat	Richard Clare	1,034	2.0%	-0.4%
Independent	Doris Osen	368	0.7%	0.5%

Ilford South

LAB HOLD

Majority: 31,647, 54.9% | Turnout: 57,657, 67.5% | Electorate: 82,487 | EU Ref: 43.9% Leave

PARTY	CANDIDATE	VOTES	SHARE	CHANGE 2015
Labour	Mike Gapes	43,724	75.8%	11.8%
Conservative	Chris Chapman	12,077	20.9%	-5.0%
Liberal Democrat	Farid Ahmed	772	1.3%	-0.6%
Green	Rosemary Warrington	542	0.9%	-2.0%
UK Independence Party	Tariq Saeed	477	0.8%	-4.4%
Friends Party	Kane Khan	65	0.1%	0.1%

Inverclyde

SNP HOLD

Majority: 384, 1.0% | Turnout: 39,093, 66.4% | Electorate: 58,853 | EU Ref: 36.2% Leave

PARTY	CANDIDATE	VOTES	SHARE	CHANGE 2015
Scottish National Party	Ronnie Cowan	15,050	38.5%	-16.6%
Labour	Martin McCluskey	14,666	37.5%	7.2%
Conservative	David Wilson	8,399	21.5%	11.5%
Liberal Democrat	David Stevens	978	2.5%	0.0%

Inverness, Nairn, Badenoch & Strathspey

SNP HOLD

Majority: 4,924, 9.4% | Turnout: 52,801, 68.7% | Electorate: 76,844 | EU Ref: 41.4% Leave

PARTY	CANDIDATE	VOTES	SHARE	CHANGE 2015
Scottish National Party	Drew Hendry	21,042	39.9%	-10.2%
Conservative	Nicholas Tulloch	16,118	30.5%	24.6%
Labour	Mike Robb	8,552	16.2%	8.7%
Liberal Democrat	Ritchie Cunningham	6,477	12.3%	-19.0%
Christian Party	Donald Boyd	612	1.2%	0.4%

Ipswich

LAB GAIN FROM CON

Majority: 836, 1.7% | Turnout: 51,154, 67.6% | Electorate: 75,668 | EU Ref: 56.6% Leave

PARTY	CANDIDATE	VOTES	SHARE	CHANGE 2015
Labour	Sandy Martin	24,235	47.4%	10.3%
Conservative	Ben Gummer	23,399	45.7%	1.0%
UK Independence Party	Tony Gould	1,372	2.7%	-9.0%
Liberal Democrat	Adrian Hyyrylainen-Trett	1,187	2.3%	-0.6%
Green	Charlotte Armstrong	840	1.6%	-1.9%
Independent	David Tabane	121	0.2%	0.2%

Isle of Wight

CON HOLD

Majority: 21,069, 28.3% | Turnout: 74,479, 67.2% | Electorate: 110,683 | EU Ref: 61.9% Leave

PARTY	CANDIDATE	VOTES	SHARE	CHANGE 2015
Conservative	Bob Seely	38,190	51.3%	10.6%
Labour	Julian Critchley	17,121	23.0%	10.2%
Green	Vix Lowthion	12,915	17.3%	4.0%
Liberal Democrat	Nick Belfitt	2,740	3.7%	-3.8%
UK Independence Party	Daryll Pitcher	1,921	2.6%	-18.6%
Independent	Julie Jones-Evans	1,592	2.1%	2.1%

Islington North

LAB HOLD

Majority: 33,215, 60.5% | Turnout: 54,928, 73.3% | Electorate: 74,831 | EU Ref: 23.5% Leave

PARTY	CANDIDATE	VOTES	SHARE	CHANGE 2015
Labour	Jeremy Corbyn	40,086	73.0%	12.7%
Conservative	James Clark	6,871	12.5%	-4.7%
Liberal Democrat	Keith Angus	4,946	9.0%	0.9%
Green	Caroline Russell	2,229	4.1%	-6.2%
UK Independence Party	Keith Fraser	413	0.8%	-3.3%
Independent	Michael Foster	208	0.4%	0.4%

Monster Raving Loony Party	Knigel Knapp	106	0.2%	0.2%
Independent	Susanne Cameron-Blackie	41	0.1%	0.1%
Socialist Party GB	Bill Martin	21	0.0%	-0.2%
Communist League	Andres Mendoza	7	0.0%	0.0%

Islington South & Finsbury

LAB HOLD

Majority: 20,263, 42.1% | Turnout: 48,049, 69.0% | Electorate: 69,536 | EU Ref: 26.1% Leave

PARTY	CANDIDATE	VOTES	SHARE	CHANGE 2015
Labour	Emily Thornberry	30,188	62.8%	11.9%
Conservative	Jason Charalambous	9,925	20.7%	-1.6%
Liberal Democrat	Alain Desmier	5,809	12.1%	1.2%
Green	Benali Hamdache	1,198	2.5%	-5.1%
UK Independence Party	Pete Muswell	929	1.9%	-5.7%

Islwyn

LAB HOLD

Majority: 11,412, 31.6% | Turnout: 36,093, 64.2% | Electorate: 56,256 | EU Ref: 58.9% Leave

PARTY	CANDIDATE	VOTES	SHARE	CHANGE 2015
Labour	Chris Evans	21,238	58.8%	9.9%
Conservative	Dan Thomas	9,826	27.2%	12.1%
Plaid Cymru	Darren Jones	2,739	7.6%	-3.1%
UK Independence Party	Joe Smyth	1,605	4.4%	-15.1%
Liberal Democrat	Matthew Kidner	685	1.9%	-0.8%

Jarrow

LAB HOLD

Majority: 17,263, 40.1% | Turnout: 43,023, 66.4% | Electorate: 64,778 | EU Ref: 61.6% Leave

PARTY	CANDIDATE	VOTES	SHARE	CHANGE 2015
Labour	Stephen Hepburn	28,020	65.1%	9.5%
Conservative	Robin Gwynn	10,757	25.0%	7.9%
UK Independence Party	James Askwith	2,338	5.4%	-14.2%
Liberal Democrat	Peter Maughan	1,163	2.7%	-0.5%
Green	David Herbert	745	1.7%	-1.7%

Keighley

LAB GAIN FROM CON

Majority: 239, 0.5% | Turnout: 51,714, 72.4% | Electorate: 71,429 | EU Ref: 53.5% Leave

PARTY	CANDIDATE	VOTES	SHARE	CHANGE 2015
Labour	John Grogan	24,056	46.5%	8.4%
Conservative	Kris Hopkins	23,817	46.0%	1.7%
UK Independence Party	Paul Latham	1,291	2.5%	-9.0%
Liberal Democrat	Matt Walker	1,226	2.4%	-0.3%
Green	Ros Brown	790	1.5%	-1.9%
Independent	David Crabtree	534	1.0%	1.0%

Kenilworth & Southam

CON HOLD

Majority: 18,076, 35.2% | Turnout: 51,321, 77.4% | Electorate: 66,319 | EU Ref: 46.6% Leave

PARTY	CANDIDATE	VOTES	SHARE	CHANGE 2015
Conservative	Jeremy Wright	31,207	60.8%	2.4%
Labour	Bally Singh	13,131	25.6%	10.3%
Liberal Democrat	Richard Dickson	4,921	9.6%	-0.5%
Green	Rob Ballantyne	1,133	2.2%	-1.8%
UK Independence Party	Harry Cottam	929	1.8%	-9.4%

Kensington

LAB GAIN FROM CON

Majority: 20, 0.0% | Turnout: 38,677, 63.8% | Electorate: 60,588 | EU Ref: 31.4% Leave

PARTY	CANDIDATE	VOTES	SHARE	CHANGE 2015
Labour	Emma Dent Coad	16,333	42.2%	11.1%
Conservative	Victoria Borwick	16,313	42.2%	-10.1%
Liberal Democrat	Annable Mullin	4,724	12.2%	6.6%
Green	Jennifer Nadel	767	2.0%	-3.1%
Independent	James Torrance	393	1.0%	1.0%
Independent	Peter Marshall	98	0.3%	0.3%
Alliance for Green Socialism	John Lloyd	49	0.1%	-0.2%

Kettering

CON HOLD

Majority: 10,562, 21.4% | Turnout: 49,404, 69.1% | Electorate: 71,440 | EU Ref: 61.0% Leave

PARTY	CANDIDATE	VOTES	SHARE	CHANGE 2015
Conservative	Philip Hollobone	28,616	57.9%	6.1%
Labour	Mick Scrimshaw	18,054	36.5%	11.4%
Liberal Democrat	Suzanna Austin	1,618	3.3%	0.1%
Green	Rob Reeves	1,116	2.3%	-1.2%

Kilmarnock & Loudoun

SNP HOLD

Majority: 6,269, 13.4% | Turnout: 46,509, 63.4% | Electorate: 73,327 | EU Ref: 39.6% Leave

PARTY	CANDIDATE	VOTES	SHARE	CHANGE 2015
Scottish National Party	Alan Brown	19,690	42.3%	-13.3%
Labour	Laura Dover	13,421	28.9%	-1.5%
Conservative	Alison Harper	12,404	26.7%	14.1%
Liberal Democrat	Irene Lang	994	2.1%	0.7%

Kingston & Surbiton

LIB DEM GAIN FROM CON
Majority: 4,124, 6.6% | Turnout: 62,178, 76.2% | Electorate: 81,588 | EU Ref: 41.6% Leave

PARTY	CANDIDATE	VOTES	SHARE	CHANGE 2015
Liberal Democrat	Ed Davey	27,810	44.7%	10.3%
Conservative	James Berry	23,686	38.1%	-1.1%
Labour	Laurie South	9,203	14.8%	0.3%
UK Independence Party	Graham Matthews	675	1.1%	-6.2%
Green	Chris Walker	536	0.9%	-3.1%
Monster Raving Loony Party	Chinners	168	0.3%	0.3%
Independent	Michael Basman	100	0.2%	0.2%

Kingston upon Hull East

LAB HOLD
Majority: 10,396, 28.4% | Turnout: 36,638, 55.5% | Electorate: 65,959 | EU Ref: 73.0% Leave

PARTY	CANDIDATE	VOTES	SHARE	CHANGE 2015
Labour	Karl Turner	21,355	58.3%	6.6%
Conservative	Simon Burton	10,959	29.9%	14.0%
UK Independence Party	Mark Fox	2,573	7.0%	-15.3%
Liberal Democrat	Andrew Marchington	1,258	3.4%	-3.1%
Green	Julia Brown	493	1.3%	-0.9%

Kingston upon Hull North

LAB HOLD
Majority: 14,322, 38.6% | Turnout: 37,122, 57.4% | Electorate: 64,665 | EU Ref: 60.0% Leave

PARTY	CANDIDATE	VOTES	SHARE	CHANGE 2015
Labour	Diana Johnson	23,685	63.8%	11.0%
Conservative	Lia Nici-Townend	9,363	25.2%	10.2%
Liberal Democrat	Mike Ross	1,869	5.0%	-4.0%
UK Independence Party	John Kitchener	1,601	4.3%	-12.0%
Green	Martin Deane	604	1.6%	-4.2%

Kingston upon Hull West & Hessle

LAB HOLD

Majority: 8,025, 23.3% | Turnout: 34,565, 57.4% | Electorate: 60,181 | EU Ref: 68.0% Leave

PARTY	CANDIDATE	VOTES	SHARE	CHANGE 2015
Labour	Emma Hardy	18,342	53.1%	3.9%
Conservative	Christine Mackay	10,317	29.8%	12.4%
Liberal Democrat	Claire Thomas	2,210	6.4%	-3.6%
Independent	Michelle Dewberry	1,898	5.5%	5.5%
UK Independence Party	Gary Shores	1,399	4.0%	-15.8%
Green	Mike Lammiman	332	1.0%	-2.0%
Libertarian	Will Taylor	67	0.2%	0.2%

Kingswood

CON HOLD

Majority: 7,500, 15.4% | Turnout: 48,741, 70.2% | Electorate: 69,368 | EU Ref: 56.8% Leave

PARTY	CANDIDATE	VOTES	SHARE	CHANGE 2015
Conservative	Chris Skidmore	26,754	54.9%	6.6%
Labour	Mhairi Threlfall	19,254	39.5%	9.9%
Liberal Democrat	Karen Wilkinson	1,749	3.6%	-0.2%
Green	Matt Furey-King	984	2.0%	-0.8%

Kirkcaldy & Cowdenbeath

LAB GAIN FROM SNP

Majority: 259, 0.5% | Turnout: 46,193, 63.5% | Electorate: 72,721 | EU Ref: 41.7% Leave

PARTY	CANDIDATE	VOTES	SHARE	CHANGE 2015
Labour	Lesley Laird	17,016	36.8%	3.5%
Scottish National Party	Roger Mullin	16,757	36.3%	-16.0%
Conservative	Dave Dempsey	10,762	23.3%	13.4%
Liberal Democrat	Malcolm Wood	1,118	2.4%	0.2%
UK Independence Party	David Coburn	540	1.2%	-1.2%

Knowsley

LAB HOLD
Majority: 42,214, 76.0% | Turnout: 55,483, 67.8% | Electorate: 81,760 | EU Ref: 52.4% Leave

PARTY	CANDIDATE	VOTES	SHARE	CHANGE 2015
Labour	George Howarth	47,351	85.3%	7.2%
Conservative	James Spencer	5,137	9.3%	2.6%
UK Independence Party	Neil Miney	1,285	2.3%	-7.5%
Liberal Democrat	Carl Cashman	1,189	2.1%	-0.8%
Green	Steve Baines	521	0.9%	-1.6%

Lagan Valley

DUP HOLD
Majority: 19,229, 42.8% | Turnout: 44,926, 62.1% | Electorate: 72,380 | EU Ref: Not available

PARTY	CANDIDATE	VOTES	SHARE	CHANGE 2015
Democratic Unionist Party	Jeffrey Donaldson	26,762	59.6%	11.7%
Ulster Unionist Party	Robbie Butler	7,533	16.8%	1.6%
Alliance Party	Aaron McIntyre	4,996	11.1%	-2.8%
Social Democratic & Labour Party	Pat Catney	3,384	7.5%	1.3%
Sinn Fein	Jacqui Russell	1,567	3.5%	0.6%
Conservative	Ian Nickels	462	1.0%	-0.6%
Independent	Jonny Orr	222	0.5%	-1.4%

Lanark & Hamilton East

SNP HOLD
Majority: 266, 0.5% | Turnout: 50,470, 65.3% | Electorate: 77,313 | EU Ref: 35.5% Leave

PARTY	CANDIDATE	VOTES	SHARE	CHANGE 2015
Scottish National Party	Angela Crawley	16,444	32.6%	-16.2%
Conservative	Poppy Corbett	16,178	32.1%	16.2%
Labour	Andrew Hilland	16,084	31.9%	1.3%
Liberal Democrat	Colin Robb	1,214	2.4%	0.2%
UK Independence Party	Donald Mackay	550	1.1%	-1.5%

Lancaster & Fleetwood

LAB HOLD

Majority: 6,661, 14.5% | Turnout: 45,989, 68.7% | Electorate: 67,154 | EU Ref: 50.9% Leave

PARTY	CANDIDATE	VOTES	SHARE	CHANGE 2015
Labour	Cat Smith	25,342	55.1%	12.8%
Conservative	Eric Ollerenshaw	18,681	40.6%	1.4%
Liberal Democrat	Robin Long	1,170	2.5%	-0.8%
Green	Rebecca Novell	796	1.7%	-3.3%

Leeds Central

LAB HOLD

Majority: 23,698, 49.7% | Turnout: 47,673, 53.2% | Electorate: 89,537 | EU Ref: 47.4% Leave

PARTY	CANDIDATE	VOTES	SHARE	CHANGE 2015
Labour	Hilary Benn	33,453	70.2%	15.2%
Conservative	Gareth Davies	9,755	20.5%	3.2%
UK Independence Party	Bill Palfreman	2,056	4.3%	-11.4%
Green	Ed Carlisle	1,189	2.5%	-5.4%
Liberal Democrat	Andy Nash	1,063	2.2%	-1.2%
Christian Peoples Alliance	Alex Coetzee	157	0.3%	0.3%

Leeds East

LAB HOLD

Majority: 12,752, 30.8% | Turnout: 41,441, 62.8% | Electorate: 65,950 | EU Ref: 60.9% Leave

PARTY	CANDIDATE	VOTES	SHARE	CHANGE 2015
Labour	Richard Burgon	25,428	61.4%	7.6%
Conservative	Matthew Robinson	12,676	30.6%	9.7%
UK Independence Party	Paul Spivey	1,742	4.2%	-14.8%
Liberal Democrat	Ed Sanderson	739	1.8%	-1.6%
Green	Jaimes Moran	434	1.0%	-1.9%
The Yorkshire Party	John Otley	422	1.0%	1.0%

Leeds North East

LAB HOLD

Majority: 16,991, 32.1% | Turnout: 52,999, 75.6% | Electorate: 70,112 | EU Ref: 37.3% Leave

PARTY	CANDIDATE	VOTES	SHARE	CHANGE 2015
Labour	Fabian Hamilton	33,436	63.1%	15.2%
Conservative	Ryan Stephenson	16,445	31.0%	-1.9%
Liberal Democrat	Jon Hannah	1,952	3.7%	-1.6%
Green	Ann Forsaith	680	1.3%	-4.0%
The Yorkshire Party	Tess Seddon	303	0.6%	0.6%
Alliance for Green Socialism	Celia Foote	116	0.2%	-0.7%
hristian Peoples Alliance	Tim Mutamiri	67	0.1%	0.1%

Leeds North West

LAB GAIN FROM LIB DEM

Majority: 4,224, 9.1% | Turnout: 46,287, 67.9% | Electorate: 68,152 | EU Ref: 35.4% Leave

PARTY	CANDIDATE	VOTES	SHARE	CHANGE 2015
Labour	Alex Sobel	20,416	44.1%	14.0%
Liberal Democrat	Greg Mulholland	16,192	35.0%	-1.8%
Conservative	Alan Lamb	9,097	19.7%	1.0%
Green	Martin Hemingway	582	1.3%	-5.8%

Leeds West

LAB HOLD

Majority: 15,965, 37.8% | Turnout: 42,229, 62.1% | Electorate: 67,955 | EU Ref: 55.0% Leave

PARTY	CANDIDATE	VOTES	SHARE	CHANGE 2015
Labour	Rachel Reeves	27,013	64.0%	15.9%
Conservative	Zoe Metcalfe	11,048	26.2%	6.0%
UK Independence Party	Mark Thackray	1,815	4.3%	-14.2%
Green	Andrew Pointon	1,023	2.4%	-6.0%
Liberal Democrat	Alisdair McGregor	905	2.1%	-1.7%
The Yorkshire Party	Ed Jones	378	0.9%	0.9%
Alliance for Green Socialism	Mike Davies	47	0.1%	0.1%

Leicester East

LAB HOLD

Majority: 22,428, 42.8% | Turnout: 52,424, 67.4% | Electorate: 77,788 | EU Ref: 53.2% Leave

PARTY	CANDIDATE	VOTES	SHARE	CHANGE 2015
Labour	Keith Vaz	35,116	67.0%	5.9%
Conservative	Edward He	12,688	24.2%	1.2%
Independent	Sujata Barot	1,753	3.3%	3.3%
Liberal Democrat	Nitesh Dave	1,343	2.6%	0.0%
Green	Melanie Wakley	1,070	2.0%	-1.0%

Leicester South

LAB HOLD

Majority: 26,261, 52.0% | Turnout: 50,517, 66.9% | Electorate: 75,534 | EU Ref: 42.6% Leave

PARTY	CANDIDATE	VOTES	SHARE	CHANGE 2015
Labour	Jonathan Ashworth	37,157	73.6%	13.8%
Conservative	Meera Sonecha	10,896	21.6%	0.6%
Liberal Democrat	Harrish Bisnauthsing	1,287	2.5%	-2.1%
Green	Mags Lewis	1,177	2.3%	-3.2%

Leicester West

LAB HOLD

Majority: 11,060, 29.4% | Turnout: 37,512, 57.9% | Electorate: 64,843 | EU Ref: 51.7% Leave

PARTY	CANDIDATE	VOTES	SHARE	CHANGE 2015
Labour	Liz Kendall	22,823	60.8%	14.3%
Conservative	Jack Hickey	11,763	31.4%	5.7%
UK Independence Party	Stuart Young	1,406	3.7%	-13.5%
Liberal Democrat	Ian Bradwell	792	2.1%	-2.3%
Green	Mel Gould	607	1.6%	-3.8%
Independent	David Bowley	121	0.3%	0.3%

Leigh

LAB HOLD

Majority: 9,554, 20.4% | Turnout: 46,874, 61.5% | Electorate: 76,202 | EU Ref: 63.5% Leave

PARTY	CANDIDATE	VOTES	SHARE	CHANGE 2015
Labour	Joanne Platt	26,347	56.2%	2.3%
Conservative	James Grundy	16,793	35.8%	13.2%
UK Independence Party	Mark Bradley	2,783	5.9%	-13.8%
Liberal Democrat	Richard Kilpatrick	951	2.0%	-0.5%

Lewes

CON HOLD

Majority: 5,508, 10.2% | Turnout: 54,192, 76.4% | Electorate: 70,941 | EU Ref: 47.0% Leave

PARTY	CANDIDATE	VOTES	SHARE	CHANGE 2015
Conservative	Maria Caulfield	26,820	49.5%	11.5%
Liberal Democrat	Kelly-Marie Blundell	21,312	39.3%	3.5%
Labour	Daniel Chapman	6,060	11.2%	1.3%

Lewisham Deptford

LAB HOLD

Majority: 34,899, 63.3% | Turnout: 55,112, 70.2% | Electorate: 78,468 | EU Ref: 25.0% Leave

PARTY	CANDIDATE	VOTES	SHARE	CHANGE 2015
Labour	Vicky Foxcroft	42,461	77.0%	16.8%
Conservative	Melanie McLean	7,562	13.7%	-1.2%
Liberal Democrat	Bobby Dean	2,911	5.3%	0.0%
Green	John Coughlin	1,640	3.0%	-9.5%
Christian Peoples Alliance	Malcolm Martin	252	0.5%	-0.2%
Animal Welfare Party	Laura McAnea	225	0.4%	0.4%
The Realists' Party	Jane Lawrence	61	0.1%	0.1%

Lewisham East

LAB HOLD

Majority: 21,213, 44.9% | Turnout: 47,201, 69.3% | Electorate: 68,124 | EU Ref: 35.0% Leave

PARTY	CANDIDATE	VOTES	SHARE	CHANGE 2015
Labour	Heidi Alexander	32,072	67.9%	12.3%
Conservative	Peter Fortune	10,859	23.0%	0.7%
Liberal Democrat	Emily Frith	2,086	4.4%	-1.3%
Green	Storm Poorun	803	1.7%	-4.0%
UK Independence Party	Keith Forster	798	1.7%	-7.4%
Independent	Willow Winston	355	0.8%	0.8%
Christian Peoples Alliance	Maureen Martin	228	0.5%	-0.2%

Lewisham West & Penge

LAB HOLD

Majority: 23,162, 43.6% | Turnout: 53,196, 73.0% | Electorate: 72,899 | EU Ref: 34.0% Leave

PARTY	CANDIDATE	VOTES	SHARE	CHANGE 2015
Labour	Ellie Reeves	35,411	66.6%	16.0%
Conservative	Shaun Bailey	12,249	23.0%	-1.1%
Liberal Democrat	John Russell	3,317	6.2%	-1.5%
Green	Karen Wheller	1,144	2.2%	-6.3%
UK Independence Party	Hoong-Wai Cheah	700	1.3%	-6.5%
Christian Peoples Alliance	Katherine Hortense	325	0.6%	0.6%
Populist Party	Russell White	50	0.1%	0.1%

Leyton & Wanstead

LAB HOLD

Majority: 22,607, 49.0% | Turnout: 46,173, 70.7% | Electorate: 65,149 | EU Ref: 35.0% Leave

PARTY	CANDIDATE	VOTES	SHARE	CHANGE 2015
Labour	John Cryer	32,234	69.8%	11.2%
Conservative	Laura Farris	9,627	20.8%	-1.1%
Liberal Democrat	Ben Sims	2,961	6.4%	0.8%
Green	Ashley Gunstock	1,351	2.9%	-4.4%

Lichfield

CON HOLD
Majority: 18,581, 34.8% | Turnout: 53,524, 71.9% | Electorate: 74,430 | EU Ref: 57.6% Leave

PARTY	CANDIDATE	VOTES	SHARE	CHANGE 2015
Conservative	Michael Fabricant	34,018	63.6%	8.4%
Labour	Chris Worsey	15,437	28.8%	9.0%
Liberal Democrat	Paul Ray	2,653	5.0%	-0.3%
Green	Robert Pass	1,416	2.6%	-1.2%

Lincoln

LAB GAIN FROM CON
Majority: 1,538, 3.2% | Turnout: 48,718, 66.6% | Electorate: 73,111 | EU Ref: 57.3% Leave

PARTY	CANDIDATE	VOTES	SHARE	CHANGE 2015
Labour	Karen Lee	23,333	47.9%	8.3%
Conservative	Karl McCartney	21,795	44.7%	2.1%
UK Independence Party	Nick Smith	1,287	2.6%	-9.6%
Liberal Democrat	Caroline Kenyon	1,284	2.6%	-1.6%
Green	Benjamin Loryman	583	1.2%	1.2%
Independent	Phil Gray	312	0.6%	0.6%
Independent	Iain Scott-Burdon	124	0.3%	0.3%

Linlithgow & East Falkirk

SNP HOLD
Majority: 2,919, 5.2% | Turnout: 56,094, 64.7% | Electorate: 86,186 | EU Ref: 41.6% Leave

PARTY	CANDIDATE	VOTES	SHARE	CHANGE 2015
Scottish National Party	Martyn Day	20,388	36.3%	-15.7%
Labour	Joan Coombes	17,469	31.1%	0.1%
Conservative	Charles Kennedy	16,311	29.1%	17.1%
Liberal Democrat	Sally Pattle	1,926	3.4%	1.4%

Liverpool Riverside

LAB HOLD

Majority: 35,947, 74.8% | Turnout: 48,020, 62.9% | Electorate: 76,332 | EU Ref: 26.9% Leave

PARTY	CANDIDATE	VOTES	SHARE	CHANGE 2015
Labour	Louise Ellman	40,599	84.5%	17.1%
Conservative	Pamela Hall	4,652	9.7%	0.1%
Green	Stephanie Pitchers	1,582	3.3%	-8.8%
Liberal Democrat	Tom Sebire	1,187	2.5%	-1.4%

Liverpool Walton

LAB HOLD

Majority: 32,551, 77.1% | Turnout: 42,197, 67.3% | Electorate: 62,738 | EU Ref: 53.8% Leave

PARTY	CANDIDATE	VOTES	SHARE	CHANGE 2015
Labour	Dan Carden	36,175	85.7%	4.4%
Conservative	Laura Evans	3,624	8.6%	3.9%
Independent	Terry May	1,237	2.9%	2.9%
Liberal Democrat	Kris Brown	638	1.5%	-0.8%
Green	Colm Feeley	523	1.2%	-1.2%

Liverpool Wavertree

LAB HOLD

Majority: 29,466, 67.6% | Turnout: 43,640, 69.9% | Electorate: 62,411 | EU Ref: 35.8% Leave

PARTY	CANDIDATE	VOTES	SHARE	CHANGE 2015
Labour	Luciana Berger	34,717	79.6%	10.2%
Conservative	Denise Haddad	5,251	12.0%	2.0%
Liberal Democrat	Richard Kemp	2,858	6.5%	0.6%
Green	Ted Grant	598	1.4%	-3.9%
Independent	Adam Heatherington	216	0.5%	0.5%

Liverpool West Derby

LAB HOLD

Majority: 32,908, 72.8% | Turnout: 45,163, 69.3% | Electorate: 65,164 | EU Ref: 50.3% Leave

PARTY	CANDIDATE	VOTES	SHARE	CHANGE 2015
Labour	Stephen Twigg	37,371	82.7%	7.6%
Conservative	Paul Richardson	4,463	9.9%	3.3%
Liberal	Steve Radford	2,150	4.8%	-0.2%
Liberal Democrat	Paul Parr	545	1.2%	-1.1%
Green	Will Ward	329	0.7%	-1.7%
Independent	Graham Hughes	305	0.7%	0.7%

Livingston

SNP HOLD

Majority: 3,878, 7.4% | Turnout: 52,505, 64.7% | Electorate: 81,208 | EU Ref: 43.8% Leave

PARTY	CANDIDATE	VOTES	SHARE	CHANGE 2015
Scottish National Party	Hannah Bardell	21,036	40.1%	-16.8%
Labour	Rhea Wolfson	17,158	32.7%	5.1%
Conservative	Damian Timson	12,799	24.4%	14.1%
Liberal Democrat	Charles Dundas	1,512	2.9%	0.7%

Llanelli

LAB HOLD

Majority: 12,024, 29.8% | Turnout: 40,342, 67.9% | Electorate: 59,434 | EU Ref: 55.5% Leave

PARTY	CANDIDATE	VOTES	SHARE	CHANGE 2015
Labour	Nia Griffith	21,568	53.5%	12.1%
Conservative	Stephen Davies	9,544	23.7%	9.3%
Plaid Cymru	Mari Arthur	7,351	18.2%	-4.7%
UK Independence Party	Ken Rees	1,331	3.3%	-13.0%
Liberal Democrat	Rory Daniels	548	1.4%	-0.6%

Loughborough

CON HOLD

Majority: 4,269, 7.9% | Turnout: 54,148, 68.0% | Electorate: 79,607 | EU Ref: 49.7% Leave

PARTY	CANDIDATE	VOTES	SHARE	CHANGE 2015
Conservative	Nicky Morgan	27,022	49.9%	0.4%
Labour	Jewel Miah	22,753	42.0%	10.1%
Liberal Democrat	David Walker	1,937	3.6%	-0.5%
UK Independence Party	Andy McWilliam	1,465	2.7%	-8.3%
Green	Philip Leicester	971	1.8%	-1.8%

Louth & Horncastle

CON HOLD

Majority: 19,641, 37.2% | Turnout: 52,771, 66.8% | Electorate: 79,007 | EU Ref: 69.4% Leave

PARTY	CANDIDATE	VOTES	SHARE	CHANGE 2015
Conservative	Victoria Atkins	33,733	63.9%	12.8%
Labour	Julie Speed	14,092	26.7%	8.7%
UK Independence Party	Jonathan Noble	2,460	4.7%	-16.8%
Liberal Democrat	Lisa Gabriel	1,990	3.8%	-0.7%
Monster Raving Loony party	The Iconic Arty-Pole	496	0.9%	0.4%

Ludlow

CON HOLD

Majority: 19,286, 38.6% | Turnout: 49,970, 73.4% | Electorate: 68,034 | EU Ref: 58.6% Leave

PARTY	CANDIDATE	VOTES	SHARE	CHANGE 2015
Conservative	Philip Dunne	31,433	62.9%	8.6%
Labour	Julia Buckley	12,147	24.3%	12.0%
Liberal Democrat	Heather Kidd	5,336	10.7%	-2.8%
Green	Hilary Wendt	1,054	2.1%	-3.0%

Luton North

LAB HOLD

Majority: 14,364, 30.8% | Turnout: 46,622, 71.0% | Electorate: 66,811 | EU Ref: 58.2% Leave

PARTY	CANDIDATE	VOTES	SHARE	CHANGE 2015
Labour	Kelvin Hopkins	29,765	63.8%	11.6%
Conservative	Caroline Kerswell	15,401	33.0%	3.1%
Liberal Democrat	Rabi Martins	808	1.7%	-1.3%
Green	Simon Hall	648	1.4%	-0.9%

Luton South

LAB HOLD

Majority: 13,925, 30.1% | Turnout: 46,133, 70.3% | Electorate: 67,188 | EU Ref: 55.4% Leave

PARTY	CANDIDATE	VOTES	SHARE	CHANGE 2015
Labour	Gavin Shuker	28,804	62.4%	18.2%
Conservative	Dean Russell	14,879	32.3%	1.6%
Liberal Democrat	Andrew Strange	1,056	2.3%	-5.3%
UK Independence Party	Ujjawal Ub	795	1.7%	-10.4%
Green	Marc Sheimann	439	1.0%	-2.0%
Independent	Abid Ali	160	0.3%	0.3%

Macclesfield

CON HOLD

Majority: 8,608, 15.9% | Turnout: 54,307, 72.2% | Electorate: 75,228 | EU Ref: 48.2% Leave

PARTY	CANDIDATE	VOTES	SHARE	CHANGE 2015
Conservative	David Rutley	28,595	52.7%	0.1%
Labour	Neil Puttick	19,987	36.8%	14.1%
Liberal Democrat	Richard Flowers	3,350	6.2%	-1.6%
Green	James Booth	1,213	2.2%	-2.6%
Independent	Mark Johnson	1,162	2.1%	2.1%

Maidenhead

CON HOLD
Majority: 26,457, 45.5% | Turnout: 58,239, 76.4% | Electorate: 76,076 | EU Ref: 45.4% Leave

PARTY	CANDIDATE	VOTES	SHARE	CHANGE 2015
Conservative	Theresa May	37,718	64.8%	-1.1%
Labour	Pat McDonald	11,261	19.3%	7.5%
Liberal Democrat	Tony Hill	6,540	11.2%	1.3%
Green	Derek Wall	907	1.6%	-2.0%
UK Independence Party	Gerard Batten	871	1.5%	-6.9%
Animal Welfare Party	Andrew Knight	282	0.5%	0.5%
Independent	Lord Buckethead	249	0.4%	0.4%
Independent	Grant Smith	152	0.3%	0.3%
Monster Raving Loony Party	Howling 'Laud' Hope	119	0.2%	0.2%
Christian Peoples Alliance	Edmonds Victor	69	0.1%	0.1%
The Just Political Party	Julian Reid	52	0.1%	0.1%
Independent	Yemi Hailemariam	16	0.0%	0.0%
Independent	Bobby Smith	3	0.0%	0.0%

Maidstone & the Weald

CON HOLD
Majority: 17,723, 34.3% | Turnout: 51,717, 68.7% | Electorate: 75,334 | EU Ref: 55.9% Leave

PARTY	CANDIDATE	VOTES	SHARE	CHANGE 2015
Conservative	Helen Grant	29,156	56.4%	10.9%
Labour	Allen Simpson	11,433	22.1%	11.6%
Liberal Democrat	Emily Fermor	8,455	16.3%	-7.7%
UK Independence Party	Pamela Watts	1,613	3.1%	-12.7%
Green	Stuart Jeffery	888	1.7%	-1.1%
Independent	Yolande Kenward	172	0.3%	0.3%

Makerfield

LAB HOLD
Majority: 13,542, 28.9% | Turnout: 46,933, 63.2% | Electorate: 74,259 | EU Ref: 65.0% Leave

PARTY	CANDIDATE	VOTES	SHARE	CHANGE 2015
Labour	Yvonne Fovargue	28,245	60.2%	8.4%
Conservative	Adam Carney	14,703	31.3%	11.8%
Independent	Bob Brierley	2,663	5.7%	5.7%
Liberal Democrat	John Skipworth	1,322	2.8%	-0.8%

Maldon

CON HOLD
Majority: 23,430, 46.6% | Turnout: 50,202, 75.0% | Electorate: 71,470 | EU Ref: 61.3% Leave

PARTY	CANDIDATE	VOTES	SHARE	CHANGE 2015
Conservative	John Whittingdale	34,111	67.9%	7.4%
Labour	Peter Edwards	10,681	21.3%	9.4%
Liberal Democrat	Zoe O'Connell	2,181	4.3%	-0.1%
UK Independence Party	Jesse Pryke	1,899	3.8%	-10.9%
Green	Steven Betteridge	1,073	2.1%	-1.0%
British National Party	Richard Perry	257	0.5%	0.5%

Manchester Central

LAB HOLD
Majority: 31,445, 63.2% | Turnout: 49,720, 55.1% | Electorate: 90,261 | EU Ref: 36.7% Leave

PARTY	CANDIDATE	VOTES	SHARE	CHANGE 2015
Labour	Lucy Powell	38,490	77.4%	16.1%
Conservative	Xingang Wang	7,045	14.2%	0.6%
Liberal Democrat	John Bridges	1,678	3.4%	-0.7%
UK Independence Party	Kalvin Chapman	1,469	3.0%	-8.1%
Green	Rachael Shah	846	1.7%	-6.8%
Pirate Party	Neil Blackburn	192	0.4%	-0.4%

Manchester Gorton

LAB HOLD

Majority: 31,730, 69.0% | Turnout: 45,953, 61.0% | Electorate: 75,362 | EU Ref: 37.9% Leave

PARTY	CANDIDATE	VOTES	SHARE	CHANGE 2015
Labour	Afzal Khan	35,085	76.3%	9.3%
Conservative	Shaden Jaradat	3,355	7.3%	-2.4%
Independent	George Galloway	2,615	5.7%	5.7%
Liberal Democrat	Jackie Pearcey	2,597	5.7%	1.4%
Green	Jess Mayo	1,038	2.3%	-7.5%
UK Independence Party	Phil Eckersley	952	2.1%	-6.1%
Christian Peoples Alliance	Kemi Abidogun	233	0.5%	0.5%
Independent	David Hopkins	51	0.1%	0.1%
Communist League	Peter Clifford	27	0.1%	0.1%

Manchester Withington

LAB HOLD

Majority: 29,875, 55.8% | Turnout: 53,602, 71.9% | Electorate: 74,654 | EU Ref: 26.3% Leave

PARTY	CANDIDATE	VOTES	SHARE	CHANGE 2015
Labour	Jeff Smith	38,424	71.7%	18.0%
Liberal Democrat	John Leech	8,549	15.9%	-8.0%
Conservative	Sarah Heald	5,530	10.3%	0.6%
Green	Laura Bannister	865	1.6%	-6.5%
Women's Equality Party	Sally Carr	234	0.4%	0.4%

Mansfield

CON GAIN FROM LAB
Majority: 1,057, 2.1% | Turnout: 50,157, 64.5% | Electorate: 77,811 | EU Ref: 70.9% Leave

PARTY	CANDIDATE	VOTES	SHARE	CHANGE 2015
Conservative	Ben Bradley	23,392	46.6%	18.5%
Labour	Alan Meale	22,335	44.5%	5.1%
UK Independence Party	Sid Pepper	2,654	5.3%	-19.8%
Independent	Philip Shields	1,079	2.2%	2.2%
Liberal Democrat	Anita Prabhakar	697	1.4%	-2.1%

Meon Valley

CON HOLD
Majority: 25,692, 47.4% | Turnout: 54,192, 73.0% | Electorate: 74,246 | EU Ref: 52.9% Leave

PARTY	CANDIDATE	VOTES	SHARE	CHANGE 2015
Conservative	George Hollingbery	35,624	65.7%	4.7%
Labour	Sheena King	9,932	18.3%	7.4%
Liberal Democrat	Martin Tod	5,900	10.9%	1.2%
UK Independence Party	Paul Bailey	1,435	2.6%	-12.2%
Green	Andrew Hayward	1,301	2.4%	-1.1%

Meriden

CON HOLD
Majority: 19,198, 35.1% | Turnout: 54,643, 67.6% | Electorate: 81,443 | EU Ref: 58.1% Leave

PARTY	CANDIDATE	VOTES	SHARE	CHANGE 2015
Conservative	Caroline Spelman	33,873	62.0%	7.3%
Labour	Tom McNeil	14,675	26.9%	7.9%
Liberal Democrat	Antony Rogers	2,663	4.9%	-0.1%
UK Independence Party	Leslie Kaye	2,016	3.7%	-13.2%
Green	Alison Gavin	1,416	2.6%	-1.5%

Merthyr Tydfil & Rhymney

LAB HOLD
Majority: 16,334, 48.7% | Turnout: 33,545, 60.5% | Electorate: 55,463 | EU Ref: 58.4% Leave

PARTY	CANDIDATE	VOTES	SHARE	CHANGE 2015
Labour	Gerald Jones	22,407	66.8%	12.9%
Conservative	Pauline Jorgensen	6,073	18.1%	8.0%
Plaid Cymru	Amy Kitcher	2,740	8.2%	-1.3%
UK Independence Party	David Rowlands	1,484	4.4%	-14.2%
Liberal Democrat	Bob Griffin	841	2.5%	-1.6%

Mid Bedfordshire

CON HOLD
Majority: 20,983, 33.3% | Turnout: 63,138, 75.0% | Electorate: 84,161 | EU Ref: 52.3% Leave

PARTY	CANDIDATE	VOTES	SHARE	CHANGE 2015
Conservative	Nadine Dorries	38,936	61.7%	5.6%
Labour	Rhiannon Meades	17,953	28.4%	12.6%
Liberal Democrat	Lisa French	3,788	6.0%	-1.2%
Green	Gareth Ellis	1,794	2.8%	-1.4%
Monster Raving Loony party	Ann Kelly	667	1.1%	0.5%

Mid Derbyshire

CON HOLD
Majority: 11,616, 22.1% | Turnout: 50,371, 74.6% | Electorate: 67,466 | EU Ref: 52.5% Leave

PARTY	CANDIDATE	VOTES	SHARE	CHANGE 2015
Conservative	Pauline Latham	29,513	58.6%	6.4%
Labour	Alison Martin	17,897	36.5%	10.1%
Liberal Democrat	Adam Wain	1,793	3.6%	-1.2%
Green	Sue Macfarlane	1,168	2.3%	-1.7%

Mid Dorset & North Poole

CON HOLD

Majority: 15,339, 31.7% | Turnout: 48,254, 74.2% | Electorate: 65,050 | EU Ref: 57.9% Leave

PARTY	CANDIDATE	VOTES	SHARE	CHANGE 2015
Conservative	Michael Tomlinson	28,585	59.2%	8.4%
Liberal Democrat	Vikki Slade	13,246	27.5%	-0.7%
Labour	Steve Brew	6,423	13.3%	7.4%

Mid Norfolk

CON HOLD

Majority: 16,086, 28.9% | Turnout: 55,668, 69.6% | Electorate: 80,027 | EU Ref: 60.6% Leave

PARTY	CANDIDATE	VOTES	SHARE	CHANGE 2015
Conservative	George Freeman	32,828	59.0%	6.9%
Labour	Sarah Simpson	16,742	30.1%	11.7%
Liberal Democrat	Fionna Tod	2,848	5.1%	-1.2%
UK Independence Party	Tracy Knowles	2,092	3.8%	-15.3%
Green	Hannah Lester	1,158	2.1%	-2.1%

Mid Sussex

CON HOLD

Majority: 19,673, 31.9% | Turnout: 61,632, 72.8% | Electorate: 84,170 | EU Ref: 46.7% Leave

PARTY	CANDIDATE	VOTES	SHARE	CHANGE 2015
Conservative	Nicholas Soames	35,082	56.9%	0.8%
Labour	Greg Mountain	15,409	25.0%	11.1%
Liberal Democrat	Sarah Osborne	7,855	12.7%	1.3%
Green	Chris Jerrey	1,571	2.5%	-1.7%
UK Independence Party	Toby Brothers	1,251	2.0%	-10.0%
Monster Raving Loony Party	Baron Von Thunderclap	464	0.8%	0.2%

Mid Ulster

SF HOLD

Majority: 12,890, 27.6% | Turnout: 46,694, 68.2% | Electorate: 68,485 | EU Ref: Not available

PARTY	CANDIDATE	VOTES	SHARE	CHANGE 2015
Sinn Féin	Francie Molloy	25,455	54.5%	5.8%
Democratic Unionist Party	Keith Buchanan	12,565	26.9%	13.6%
Social Democratic & Labour Party	Malachy Quinn	4,563	9.8%	-2.6%
Ulster Unionist Party	Mark Glasgow	3,017	6.5%	-9.0%
Alliance Party	Fay Watson	1,094	2.3%	0.4%

Mid Worcestershire

CON HOLD

Majority: 23,326, 42.4% | Turnout: 55,089, 72.4% | Electorate: 76,057 | EU Ref: 58.9% Leave

PARTY	CANDIDATE	VOTES	SHARE	CHANGE 2015
Conservative	Nigel Huddleston	35,967	65.3%	8.3%
Labour	Fred Grindrod	12,641	22.9%	8.5%
Liberal Democrat	Margaret Rowley	3,450	6.3%	-0.9%
UK Independence Party	David Greenwood	1,660	3.0%	-14.7%
Green	Fay Whitfield	1,371	2.5%	-1.2%

Middlesbrough

LAB HOLD

Majority: 13,873, 39.0% | Turnout: 35,637, 58.3% | Electorate: 61,059 | EU Ref: 64.9% Leave

PARTY	CANDIDATE	VOTES	SHARE	CHANGE 2015
Labour	Andy McDonald	23,404	65.7%	8.9%
Conservative	Jacob Young	9,531	26.7%	10.3%
UK Independence Party	David Hodgson	1,452	4.1%	-14.6%
Independent	Terry Lawton	632	1.8%	1.8%
Liberal Democrat	Dawud Islam	368	1.0%	-2.7%
Green	Carl Martinez	250	0.7%	-3.6%

Middlesbrough South & East Cleveland

CON GAIN FROM LAB
Majority: 1,020, 2.1% | Turnout: 47,620, 65.8% | Electorate: 72,336 | EU Ref: 65.0% Leave

PARTY	CANDIDATE	VOTES	SHARE	CHANGE 2015
Conservative	Simon Clarke	23,643	49.6%	12.6%
Labour	Tracy Harvey	22,623	47.5%	5.5%
Liberal Democrat	Chris Foote-Wood	1,354	2.8%	-0.6%

Midlothian

LAB GAIN FROM SNP
Majority: 885, 2.0% | Turnout: 45,273, 66.3% | Electorate: 68,328 | EU Ref: 37.9% Leave

PARTY	CANDIDATE	VOTES	SHARE	CHANGE 2015
Labour	Danielle Rowley	16,458	36.4%	6.2%
Scottish National Party	Owen Thompson	15,573	34.4%	-16.2%
Conservative	Chris Donnelly	11,521	25.4%	13.5%
Liberal Democrat	Ross Laird	1,721	3.8%	1.5%

Milton Keynes North

CON HOLD
Majority: 1,915, 3.0% | Turnout: 63,864, 71.6% | Electorate: 89,207 | EU Ref: 49.8% Leave

PARTY	CANDIDATE	VOTES	SHARE	CHANGE 2015
Conservative	Mark Lancaster	30,307	47.5%	0.2%
Labour	Charlynne Pullen	28,392	44.5%	14.1%
Liberal Democrat	Imogen Shepherd-Dubey	2,499	3.9%	-2.3%
UK Independence Party	Jeff Wyatt	1,390	2.2%	-9.7%
Green	Alan Francis	1,107	1.7%	-2.2%
Christian Peoples Alliance	Venetia Sams	169	0.3%	0.3%

Milton Keynes South

CON HOLD

Majority: 1,725, 2.6% | Turnout: 64,486, 69.8% | Electorate: 92,417 | EU Ref: 53.0% Leave

PARTY	CANDIDATE	VOTES	SHARE	CHANGE 2015
Conservative	Iain Stewart	30,652	47.5%	0.7%
Labour	Hannah O'Neill	28,927	44.9%	12.7%
Liberal Democrat	Tahir Maher	1,895	2.9%	-1.0%
UK Independence Party	Vince Peddle	1,833	2.8%	-10.4%
Green	Graham Findlay	1,179	1.8%	-1.5%

Mitcham & Morden

LAB HOLD

Majority: 21,375, 44.5% | Turnout: 48,118, 70.0% | Electorate: 68,705 | EU Ref: 49.1% Leave

PARTY	CANDIDATE	VOTES	SHARE	CHANGE 2015
Labour	Siobhain McDonagh	33,039	68.7%	8.0%
Conservative	Alicia Kearns	11,664	24.2%	1.1%
Liberal Democrat	Claire Mathys	1,494	3.1%	0.1%
UK Independence Party	Richard Hilton	1,054	2.2%	-7.3%
Green	Laura Collins	644	1.3%	-1.8%
Christian Peoples Alliance	Des Coke	223	0.5%	0.0%

Mole Valley

CON HOLD

Majority: 24,137, 42.6% | Turnout: 56,726, 76.1% | Electorate: 74,545 | EU Ref: 47.6% Leave

PARTY	CANDIDATE	VOTES	SHARE	CHANGE 2015
Conservative	Paul Beresford	35,092	61.9%	1.2%
Liberal Democrat	Paul Kennedy	10,955	19.3%	4.8%
Labour	Marc Green	7,864	13.9%	5.6%
Green	Jacquetta Fewster	1,463	2.6%	-2.8%
UK Independence Party	Judy Moore	1,352	2.4%	-8.8%

Monmouth

CON HOLD
Majority: 8,206, 16.5% | Turnout: 49,734, 76.6% | Electorate: 64,909 | EU Ref: 47.8% Leave

PARTY	CANDIDATE	VOTES	SHARE	CHANGE 2015
Conservative	David TC Davies	26,411	53.1%	3.2%
Labour	Ruth Jones	18,205	36.6%	9.8%
Liberal Democrat	Veronica German	2,064	4.2%	-1.1%
Plaid Cymru	Carole Damon	1,338	2.7%	-1.3%
Green	Ian Chandler	954	1.9%	-1.5%
UK Independence Party	Roy Neale	762	1.5%	-8.9%

Montgomeryshire

CON HOLD
Majority: 9,285, 26.6% | Turnout: 34,891, 70.1% | Electorate: 50,755 | EU Ref: 56.0% Leave

PARTY	CANDIDATE	VOTES	SHARE	CHANGE 2015
Conservative	Glyn Davies	18,075	51.8%	6.8%
Liberal Democrat	Jane Dodds	8,790	25.2%	-4.1%
Labour	Iwan Jones	5,542	15.9%	10.3%
Plaid Cymru	Aled Hughes	1,960	5.6%	0.4%
Green	Richard Chaloner	524	1.5%	-2.2%

Moray

CON GAIN FROM SNP
Majority: 4,159, 8.8% | Turnout: 47,605, 67.4% | Electorate: 70,649 | EU Ref: 49.9% Leave

PARTY	CANDIDATE	VOTES	SHARE	CHANGE 2015
Conservative	Douglas Ross	22,637	47.6%	16.5%
Scottish National Party	Angus Robertson	18,478	38.8%	-10.7%
Labour	Jo Kirby	5,208	10.9%	1.0%
Liberal Democrat	Alex Linklater	1,078	2.3%	-0.6%
Independent	Anne Glen	204	0.4%	0.4%

Morecambe & Lunesdale

CON HOLD

Majority: 1,399, 3.1% | Turnout: 45,657, 68.3% | Electorate: 66,818 | EU Ref: 58.9% Leave

PARTY	CANDIDATE	VOTES	SHARE	CHANGE 2015
Conservative	David Morris	21,773	47.7%	2.2%
Labour	Vikki Singleton	20,374	44.6%	9.7%
Liberal Democrat	Matthew Severn	1,699	3.7%	0.0%
UK Independence Party	Robert Gillespie	1,333	2.9%	-9.5%
Green	Cait Sinclair	478	1.0%	-2.2%

Morley & Outwood

CON HOLD

Majority: 2,104, 4.0% | Turnout: 52,357, 68.4% | Electorate: 76,495 | EU Ref: 59.8% Leave

PARTY	CANDIDATE	VOTES	SHARE	CHANGE 2015
Conservative	Andrea Jenkyns	26,550	50.7%	11.8%
Labour	Neil Dawson	24,446	46.7%	8.7%
Liberal Democrat	Craig Dobson	1,361	2.6%	0.4%

Motherwell & Wishaw

SNP HOLD

Majority: 318, 0.7% | Turnout: 41,926, 61.5% | Electorate: 68,215 | EU Ref: 37.0% Leave

PARTY	CANDIDATE	VOTES	SHARE	CHANGE 2015
Scottish National Party	Marion Fellows	16,150	38.5%	-18.0%
Labour	Angela Feeney	15,832	37.8%	5.9%
Conservative	Meghan Gallacher	8,490	20.2%	12.6%
Liberal Democrat	Yvonne Finlayson	920	2.2%	0.9%
UK Independence Party	Neil Wilson	534	1.3%	-1.4%

Na h-Eileanan an Iar

SNP HOLD

Majority: 1,007, 6.8% | Turnout: 14,818, 69.6% | Electorate: 21,301 | EU Ref: 44.8% Leave

PARTY	CANDIDATE	VOTES	SHARE	CHANGE 2015
Scottish National Party	Angus MacNeil	6,013	40.6%	-13.8%
Labour	Ealasaid MacDonald	5,006	33.8%	5.2%
Conservative	Dan McCroskrie	2,441	16.5%	8.8%
Christian Party	John Cormack	1,108	7.5%	0.9%
Liberal Democrat	James Paterson	250	1.7%	-1.2%

Neath

LAB HOLD

Majority: 12,631, 33.0% | Turnout: 38,285, 68.5% | Electorate: 55,862 | EU Ref: 54.2% Leave

PARTY	CANDIDATE	VOTES	SHARE	CHANGE 2015
Labour	Christina Rees	21,713	56.7%	12.9%
Conservative	Orla Lowe	9,082	23.7%	8.4%
Plaid Cymru	Daniel Williams	5,339	13.9%	-4.2%
UK Independence Party	Richard Pritchard	1,419	3.7%	-12.7%
Liberal Democrat	Frank Little	732	1.9%	-1.2%

New Forest East

CON HOLD

Majority: 21,995, 42.8% | Turnout: 51,366, 71.4% | Electorate: 72,602 | EU Ref: 59.5% Leave

PARTY	CANDIDATE	VOTES	SHARE	CHANGE 2015
Conservative	Julian Lewis	32,162	62.6%	6.4%
Labour	Julie Renyard	10,167	19.8%	7.6%
Liberal Democrat	David Harrison	7,786	15.2%	5.8%
Green	Henry Mellor	1,251	2.4%	-2.3%

New Forest West

CON HOLD
Majority: 23,431, 47.2% | Turnout: 49,627, 72.8% | Electorate: 68,786 | EU Ref: 55.9% Leave

PARTY	CANDIDATE	VOTES	SHARE	CHANGE 2015
Conservative	Desmond Swayne	33,170	66.8%	6.9%
Labour	Jo Graham	9,739	19.6%	8.8%
Liberal Democrat	Terry Scriven	4,781	9.6%	2.7%
Green	Janet Richards	1,454	2.9%	-2.9%
Pirate Party	Des Hjerling	483	1.0%	1.0%

Newark

CON HOLD
Majority: 18,149, 33.0% | Turnout: 55,042, 72.9% | Electorate: 75,510 | EU Ref: 55.8% Leave

PARTY	CANDIDATE	VOTES	SHARE	CHANGE 2015
Conservative	Robert Jenrick	34,493	62.7%	5.6%
Labour	Chantal Lee	16,344	29.7%	8.0%
Liberal Democrat	David Watts	2,786	5.1%	0.5%
UK Independence Party	Xandra Arundel	1,419	2.6%	-9.5%

Newbury

CON HOLD
Majority: 24,380, 40.1% | Turnout: 60,849, 73.4% | Electorate: 82,924 | EU Ref: 47.5% Leave

PARTY	CANDIDATE	VOTES	SHARE	CHANGE 2015
Conservative	Richard Benyon	37,399	61.5%	0.4%
Liberal Democrat	Judith Bunting	13,019	21.4%	6.4%
Labour	Alex Skirvin	8,596	14.1%	5.7%
Green	Paul Field	1,531	2.5%	-1.5%
Apoltical Democrats	Dave Yates	304	0.5%	0.1%

Newcastle upon Tyne Central

LAB HOLD

Majority: 14,937, 40.3% | Turnout: 37,094, 66.8% | Electorate: 55,368 | EU Ref: 48.4% Leave

PARTY	CANDIDATE	VOTES	SHARE	CHANGE 2015
Labour	Chi Onwurah	24,071	64.9%	9.9%
Conservative	Steve Kyte	9,134	24.6%	5.7%
Liberal Democrat	Nick Cott	1,812	4.9%	-1.4%
UK Independence Party	David Muat	1,482	4.0%	-10.9%
Green	Peter Thomson	595	1.6%	-3.3%

Newcastle upon Tyne East

LAB HOLD

Majority: 19,261, 46.3% | Turnout: 41,637, 66.8% | Electorate: 61,989 | EU Ref: 41.1% Leave

PARTY	CANDIDATE	VOTES	SHARE	CHANGE 2015
Labour	Nick Brown	28,127	67.6%	18.1%
Conservative	Simon Kitchen	8,866	21.3%	3.7%
Liberal Democrat	Wendy Taylor	2,574	6.2%	-4.9%
UK Independence Party	Tony Sanderson	1,315	3.2%	-9.4%
Green	Alistair Ford	755	1.8%	-6.9%

Newcastle upon Tyne North

LAB HOLD

Majority: 10,349, 21.5% | Turnout: 48,288, 72.8% | Electorate: 66,073 | EU Ref: 57.1% Leave

PARTY	CANDIDATE	VOTES	SHARE	CHANGE 2015
Labour	Catherine McKinnell	26,729	55.4%	9.3%
Conservative	Duncan Crute	16,380	33.9%	10.5%
Liberal Democrat	Anita Lower	2,533	5.2%	-4.5%
UK Independence Party	Timothy Marron	1,780	3.7%	-12.9%
Green	Alison Whalley	513	1.1%	-2.3%
North of England Community Alliance	Brian Moore	353	0.7%	0.7%

Newcastle-under-Lyme

LAB HOLD

Majority: 30, 0.1% | Turnout: 43,842, 66.9% | Electorate: 65,596 | EU Ref: 61.7% Leave

PARTY	CANDIDATE	VOTES	SHARE	CHANGE 2015
Labour	Paul Farrelly	21,124	48.2%	9.8%
Conservative	Owen Meredith	21,094	48.1%	11.2%
Liberal Democrat	Nigel Jones	1,624	3.7%	-0.5%

Newport East

LAB HOLD

Majority: 8,003, 21.7% | Turnout: 36,820, 64.3% | Electorate: 57,233 | EU Ref: 60.3% Leave

PARTY	CANDIDATE	VOTES	SHARE	CHANGE 2015
Labour	Jessica Morden	20,804	56.5%	15.8%
Conservative	Natasha Asghar	12,801	34.8%	7.5%
UK Independence Party	Ian Gorman	1,180	3.2%	-15.2%
Liberal Democrat	Pete Brown	966	2.6%	-3.8%
Plaid Cymru	Cameron Wixcey	881	2.4%	-1.1%
Independent	Nadeem Ahmed	188	0.5%	0.5%

Newport West

LAB HOLD

Majority: 5,658, 13.0% | Turnout: 43,438, 67.5% | Electorate: 64,399 | EU Ref: 53.0% Leave

PARTY	CANDIDATE	VOTES	SHARE	CHANGE 2015
Labour	Paul Flynn	22,723	52.3%	11.1%
Conservative	Angela Jones-Evans	17,065	39.3%	6.8%
UK Independence Party	Stan Edwards	1,100	2.5%	-12.7%
Plaid Cymru	Morgan Bowler-Brown	1,077	2.5%	-1.5%
Liberal Democrat	Sarah Lockyer	976	2.2%	-1.7%
Green	Pippa Bartolotti	497	1.1%	-2.0%

Newry & Armagh

SF HOLD

Majority: 12,489, 23.3% | Turnout: 53,579, 68.5% | Electorate: 78,266 | EU Ref: Not available

PARTY	CANDIDATE	VOTES	SHARE	CHANGE 2015
Sinn Féin	Mickey Brady	25,666	47.9%	6.8%
Democratic Unionist Party	William Irwin	13,177	24.6%	24.6%
Social Democratic & Labour Party	Justin McNulty	9,055	16.9%	-7.2%
Ulster Unionist Party	Sam Nicholson	4,425	8.3%	-24.4%
Alliance Party	Jackie Coade	1,256	2.3%	0.7%

Newton Abbot

CON HOLD

Majority: 17,160, 33.3% | Turnout: 51,637, 72.0% | Electorate: 71,714 | EU Ref: 56.1% Leave

PARTY	CANDIDATE	VOTES	SHARE	CHANGE 2015
Conservative	Anne-Marie Morris	28,635	55.5%	8.2%
Labour	James Osben	11,475	22.2%	12.4%
Liberal Democrat	Marie Chadwick	10,601	20.5%	-3.4%
Green	Kathryn Driscoll	926	1.8%	-2.8%

Normanton, Pontefract & Castleford

LAB HOLD

Majority: 14,499, 29.5% | Turnout: 49,191, 60.3% | Electorate: 81,641 | EU Ref: 70.8% Leave

PARTY	CANDIDATE	VOTES	SHARE	CHANGE 2015
Labour	Yvette Cooper	29,268	59.5%	4.6%
Conservative	Andrew Lee	14,769	30.0%	9.2%
UK Independence Party	Lewis Thompson	3,030	6.2%	-15.2%
The Yorkshire Party	Daniel Gascoigne	1,431	2.9%	2.9%
Liberal Democrat	Clarke Roberts	693	1.4%	-1.5%

North Antrim

DUP HOLD

Majority: 20,643, 42.6% | Turnout: 48,460, 64.1% | Electorate: 75,657 | EU Ref: Not available

PARTY	CANDIDATE	VOTES	SHARE	CHANGE 2015
Democratic Unionist Party	Ian Paisley	28,521	58.9%	15.6%
Sinn Féin	Cara McShane	7,878	16.3%	4.0%
Ulster Unionist Party	Jackson Minford	3,482	7.2%	-4.9%
Traditionalist Unionist Voice	Timothy Gaston	3,282	6.8%	-8.9%
Alliance Party	Patricia O'Lynn	2,723	5.6%	0.0%
Social Democratic & Labour Party	Declan O'Loan	2,574	5.3%	-1.7%

North Ayrshire & Arran

SNP HOLD

Majority: 3,633, 7.7% | Turnout: 47,433, 64.8% | Electorate: 73,176 | EU Ref: 42.3% Leave

PARTY	CANDIDATE	VOTES	SHARE	CHANGE 2015
Scottish National Party	Patricia Gibson	18,451	38.9%	-14.3%
Conservative	David Rocks	14,818	31.2%	16.4%
Labour	Chris Rimicans	13,040	27.5%	-0.5%
Liberal Democrat	Mark Dickson	1,124	2.4%	0.7%

North Cornwall

CON HOLD

Majority: 7,200, 14.1% | Turnout: 50,944, 74.0% | Electorate: 68,844 | EU Ref: 60.3% Leave

PARTY	CANDIDATE	VOTES	SHARE	CHANGE 2015
Conservative	Scott Mann	25,835	50.7%	5.8%
Liberal Democrat	Daniel Rogerson	18,635	36.6%	5.3%
Labour	Joy Bassett	6,151	12.1%	6.6%
Christian Peoples Alliance	John Allman	185	0.4%	0.4%
Socialist Labour Party	Robert Hawkins	138	0.3%	0.3%

North Devon

CON HOLD
Majority: 4,332, 7.8% | Turnout: 55,705, 73.2% | Electorate: 75,801 | EU Ref: 57.0% Leave

PARTY	CANDIDATE	VOTES	SHARE	CHANGE 2015
Conservative	Peter Heaton-Jones	25,517	45.8%	3.1%
Liberal Democrat	Nick Harvey	21,185	38.0%	8.6%
Labour	Mark Cann	7,063	12.7%	5.6%
UK Independence Party	Stephen Crowther	1,187	2.1%	-12.6%
Green	Ricky Knight	753	1.4%	-4.4%

North Dorset

CON HOLD
Majority: 25,777, 46.3% | Turnout: 55,724, 74.0% | Electorate: 76,324 | EU Ref: 56.4% Leave

PARTY	CANDIDATE	VOTES	SHARE	CHANGE 2015
Conservative	Simon Hoare	36,169	64.9%	8.3%
Labour	Pat Osborne	10,392	18.6%	9.7%
Liberal Democrat	Thomas Panton	7,556	13.6%	1.9%
Green	John Tutton	1,607	2.9%	-2.8%

North Down

INDEPENDENT HOLD
Majority: 1,208, 3.1% | Turnout: 39,185, 60.9% | Electorate: 64,334 | EU Ref: Not available

PARTY	CANDIDATE	VOTES	SHARE	CHANGE 2015
Independent	Sylvia Hermon	16,148	41.2%	-8.0%
Democratic Unionist Party	Alex Easton	14,940	38.1%	14.5%
Alliance Party	Andrew Muir	3,639	9.3%	0.7%
Green	Steven Agnew	2,549	6.5%	1.1%
Conservative	Frank Shivers	941	2.4%	-2.0%
Sinn Fein	Frank Shivers	531	1.4%	0.6%
Social Democratic & Labour Party	Therese McCartney	400	1.0%	0.0%
Independent	Caoimhe McNeill	37	0.1%	0.1%

North Durham

LAB HOLD
Majority: 12,939, 29.9% | Turnout: 43,284, 64.6% | Electorate: 66,970 | EU Ref: 60.1% Leave

PARTY	CANDIDATE	VOTES	SHARE	CHANGE 2015
Labour	Kevan Jones	25,917	59.9%	5.0%
Conservative	Laetitia Glossop	12,978	30.0%	9.1%
UK Independence Party	Kenneth Rollings	2,408	5.6%	-10.4%
Liberal Democrat	Craig Martin	1,981	4.6%	-0.5%

North East Bedfordshire

CON HOLD
Majority: 20,862, 32.4% | Turnout: 64,220, 73.8% | Electorate: 87,505 | EU Ref: 53.3% Leave

PARTY	CANDIDATE	VOTES	SHARE	CHANGE 2015
Conservative	Alistair Burt	39,139	60.9%	1.5%
Labour	Julian Vaughan	18,277	28.5%	12.7%
Liberal Democrat	Stephen Rutherford	3,693	5.8%	-0.1%
UK Independence Party	Duncan Strachan	1,896	3.0%	-11.7%
Green	Philippa Fleming	1,215	1.9%	-2.4%

North East Cambridgeshire

CON HOLD
Majority: 21,270, 39.9% | Turnout: 53,284, 63.1% | Electorate: 84,414 | EU Ref: 69.4% Leave

PARTY	CANDIDATE	VOTES	SHARE	CHANGE 2015
Conservative	Steve Barclay	34,340	64.4%	9.4%
Labour	Ken Rustidge	13,070	24.5%	10.1%
Liberal Democrat	Darren Fower	2,383	4.5%	0.0%
UK Independence Party	Robin Talbot	2,174	4.1%	-18.4%
Green	Ruth Johnson	1,024	1.9%	-1.6%
English Democrats	Stephen Goldspink	293	0.5%	0.5%

North East Derbyshire

CON GAIN FROM LAB

Majority: 2,860, 5.7% | Turnout: 50,380, 69.9% | Electorate: 72,097 | EU Ref: 62.2% Leave

PARTY	CANDIDATE	VOTES	SHARE	CHANGE 2015
Conservative	Lee Rowley	24,783	49.2%	12.5%
Labour	Natascha Engel	21,923	43.5%	2.9%
UK Independence Party	James Bush	1,565	3.1%	-12.8%
Liberal Democrat	David Lomax	1,390	2.8%	-1.4%
Green	David Kesteven	719	1.4%	-0.8%

North East Fife

SNP HOLD

Majority: 2, 0.0% | Turnout: 41,822, 71.3% | Electorate: 58,685 | EU Ref: 38.1% Leave

PARTY	CANDIDATE	VOTES	SHARE	CHANGE 2015
Scottish National Party	Stephen Gethins	13,743	32.9%	-8.1%
Liberal Democrat	Elizabeth Riches	13,741	32.9%	1.5%
Conservative	Tony Niklinski	10,088	24.1%	7.8%
Labour	Rosalind Garton	4,026	9.6%	1.9%
Independent Sovereign Democratic Britain	Mike Scott-Hayward	224	0.5%	0.5%

North East Hampshire

CON HOLD

Majority: 27,772, 48.2% | Turnout: 57,627, 76.3% | Electorate: 74,576 | EU Ref: 45.9% Leave

PARTY	CANDIDATE	VOTES	SHARE	CHANGE 2015
Conservative	Ranil Jayawardena	37,754	65.5%	-0.4%
Labour	Barry Jones	9,982	17.3%	7.5%
Liberal Democrat	Graham Cockarill	6,987	12.1%	1.6%
Green	Chas Spradbery	1,476	2.6%	-1.8%
UK Independence Party	Mike Gascoigne	1,061	1.8%	-6.9%
Independent	Robert Blay	367	0.6%	0.6%

North East Hertfordshire

CON HOLD

Majority: 16,835, 30.3% | Turnout: 55,580, 73.2% | Electorate: 75,965 | EU Ref: 51.4% Leave

PARTY	CANDIDATE	VOTES	SHARE	CHANGE 2015
Conservative	Oliver Heald	32,587	58.6%	3.3%
Labour	Doug Swanney	15,752	28.3%	9.5%
Liberal Democrat	Nicky Shepard	4,276	7.7%	0.1%
Green	Tim Lee	2,965	5.3%	0.0%

North East Somerset

CON HOLD

Majority: 10,235, 18.9% | Turnout: 54,043, 75.7% | Electorate: 71,355 | EU Ref: 52.1% Leave

PARTY	CANDIDATE	VOTES	SHARE	CHANGE 2015
Conservative	Jacob Rees-Mogg	28,992	53.6%	3.9%
Labour	Robin Moss	18,757	34.7%	9.9%
Liberal Democrat	Manda Rigby	4,461	8.3%	0.4%
Green	Sally Calverley	1,245	2.3%	-3.2%
Independent	Shaun Hughes	588	1.1%	1.1%

North Herefordshire

CON HOLD

Majority: 21,602, 43.1% | Turnout: 50,177, 74.1% | Electorate: 67,751 | EU Ref: 58.3% Leave

PARTY	CANDIDATE	VOTES	SHARE	CHANGE 2015
Conservative	Bill Wiggin	31,097	62.0%	6.3%
Labour	Roger Page	9,495	18.9%	7.5%
Liberal Democrat	Jeanie Falconer	5,874	11.7%	-0.3%
Green	Ellie Chowns	2,771	5.5%	-1.4%
Independent	Sasha Norris	577	1.1%	1.1%
Independent	Arthur Devine	363	0.7%	0.7%

North Norfolk

LIB DEM HOLD

Majority: 3,512, 6.7% | Turnout: 52,188, 75.3% | Electorate: 69,271 | EU Ref: 58.3% Leave

PARTY	CANDIDATE	VOTES	SHARE	CHANGE 2015
Liberal Democrat	Norman Lamb	25,260	48.4%	9.3%
Conservative	James Wild	21,748	41.7%	10.8%
Labour	Stephen Burke	5,180	9.9%	-0.3%

North Shropshire

CON HOLD

Majority: 16,355, 29.4% | Turnout: 55,599, 69.0% | Electorate: 80,535 | EU Ref: 59.5% Leave

PARTY	CANDIDATE	VOTES	SHARE	CHANGE 2015
Conservative	Owen Paterson	33,642	60.5%	9.1%
Labour	Graeme Currie	17,287	31.1%	11.0%
Liberal Democrat	Tom Thornhill	2,948	5.3%	-0.7%
Green	Duncan Kerr	1,722	3.1%	-1.8%

North Somerset

CON HOLD

Majority: 17,103, 27.6% | Turnout: 61,994, 76.9% | Electorate: 80,529 | EU Ref: 48.0% Leave

PARTY	CANDIDATE	VOTES	SHARE	CHANGE 2015
Conservative	Liam Fox	33,605	54.2%	0.7%
Labour	Greg Chambers	16,502	26.6%	12.3%
Liberal Democrat	Richard Foord	5,982	9.6%	-3.1%
Independent	Donald Davies	3,929	6.3%	6.3%
Green	Charley Pattison	1,976	3.2%	-3.3%

North Swindon

CON HOLD
Majority: 8,335, 15.2% | Turnout: 54,911, 68.5% | Electorate: 80,168 | EU Ref: 57.4% Leave

PARTY	CANDIDATE	VOTES	SHARE	CHANGE 2015
Conservative	Justin Tomlinson	29,431	53.6%	3.3%
Labour	Mark Dempsey	21,096	38.4%	10.6%
Liberal Democrat	Liz Webster	1,962	3.6%	0.3%
UK Independence Party	Steve Halden	1,564	2.8%	-12.5%
Green	Andy Bentley	858	1.6%	-1.7%

North Thanet

CON HOLD
Majority: 10,738, 22.2% | Turnout: 48,325, 66.5% | Electorate: 72,651 | EU Ref: 65.0% Leave

PARTY	CANDIDATE	VOTES	SHARE	CHANGE 2015
Conservative	Sir Roger Gale	27,163	56.2%	7.2%
Labour	Frances Rehal	16,425	34.0%	16.1%
UK Independence Party	Clive Egan	2,198	4.5%	-21.2%
Liberal Democrat	Martyn Pennington	1,586	3.3%	-0.2%
Green	Ed Targett	825	1.7%	-1.9%
Christian Peoples Alliance	Iris White	128	0.3%	0.3%

North Tyneside

LAB HOLD
Majority: 19,284, 37.2% | Turnout: 51,892, 65.7% | Electorate: 78,914 | EU Ref: 59.4% Leave

PARTY	CANDIDATE	VOTES	SHARE	CHANGE 2015
Labour	Mary Glindon	33,456	64.5%	8.5%
Conservative	Henry Newman	14,172	27.3%	8.1%
UK Independence Party	Gary Legg	2,101	4.0%	-12.2%
Liberal Democrat	Greg Stone	1,494	2.9%	-1.6%
Green	Martin Collins	669	1.3%	-1.8%

North Warwickshire

CON HOLD
Majority: 8,510, 18.0% | Turnout: 47,178, 65.3% | Electorate: 72,277 | EU Ref: 67.8% Leave

PARTY	CANDIDATE	VOTES	SHARE	CHANGE 2015
Conservative	Craig Tracey	26,860	56.9%	14.6%
Labour	Julie Jackson	18,350	38.9%	2.9%
Liberal Democrat	James Cox	1,028	2.2%	0.1%
Green	Keith Kondakor	940	2.0%	0.1%

North West Cambridgeshire

CON HOLD
Majority: 18,008, 28.1% | Turnout: 63,991, 68.8% | Electorate: 93,221 | EU Ref: 57.0% Leave

PARTY	CANDIDATE	VOTES	SHARE	CHANGE 2015
Conservative	Shailesh Vara	37,529	58.6%	6.2%
Labour	Ian Ramsbottom	19,521	30.5%	12.6%
Liberal Democrat	Bridget Smith	3,168	5.0%	-0.7%
UK Independence Party	John Whitby	2,518	3.9%	-16.2%
Green	Greg Guthrie	1,255	2.0%	-1.6%

North West Durham

LAB HOLD
Majority: 8,792, 18.3% | Turnout: 47,902, 66.5% | Electorate: 71,918 | EU Ref: 55.0% Leave

PARTY	CANDIDATE	VOTES	SHARE	CHANGE 2015
Labour	Laura Pidcock	25,308	52.8%	6.0%
Conservative	Sally-Ann Hart	16,516	34.5%	11.1%
Liberal Democrat	Owen Temple	3,398	7.1%	-2.0%
UK Independence Party	Alan Breeze	2,150	4.5%	-12.5%
Green	Dominic Horsman	530	1.1%	-2.6%

North West Hampshire

CON HOLD

Majority: 22,679, 38.6% | Turnout: 58,772, 72.1% | Electorate: 81,430 | EU Ref: 54.5% Leave

PARTY	CANDIDATE	VOTES	SHARE	CHANGE 2015
Conservative	Kit Malthouse	36,471	62.1%	4.0%
Labour	Andy Fitchet	13,792	23.5%	10.2%
Liberal Democrat	Alex Payton	5,708	9.7%	0.4%
UK Independence Party	Roger Clark	1,467	2.5%	-12.2%
Green	Dan Hill	1,334	2.3%	-2.3%

North West Leicestershire

CON HOLD

Majority: 13,286, 24.8% | Turnout: 53,541, 71.0% | Electorate: 75,362 | EU Ref: 60.7% Leave

PARTY	CANDIDATE	VOTES	SHARE	CHANGE 2015
Conservative	Andrew Bridgen	31,153	58.2%	8.7%
Labour	Sean Sheahan	17,867	33.4%	6.0%
Liberal Democrat	Michael Wyatt	3,420	6.4%	2.4%
Green	Mia Woolley	1,101	2.1%	0.2%

North West Norfolk

CON HOLD

Majority: 13,788, 28.2% | Turnout: 48,811, 67.7% | Electorate: 72,062 | EU Ref: 66.1% Leave

PARTY	CANDIDATE	VOTES	SHARE	CHANGE 2015
Conservative	Henry Bellingham	29,408	60.2%	8.1%
Labour	Jo Rust	15,620	32.0%	9.2%
UK Independence Party	Michael Stone	1,539	3.2%	-14.6%
Liberal Democrat	Rupert Moss-Eccardt	1,393	2.9%	-0.7%
Green	Andrew De Whalley	851	1.7%	-2.0%

North Wiltshire

CON HOLD
Majority: 22,877, 42.6% | Turnout: 53,706, 76.1% | Electorate: 71,408 | EU Ref: 50.4% Leave

PARTY	CANDIDATE	VOTES	SHARE	CHANGE 2015
Conservative	James Gray	32,398	60.3%	3.1%
Liberal Democrat	Brian Mathew	9,521	17.7%	2.1%
Labour	Peter Baldrey	9,399	17.5%	7.7%
Green	Phil Chamberlain	1,141	2.1%	-2.5%
UK Independence Party	Paddy Singh	871	1.6%	-9.9%
Independent	Lisa Tweedie	376	0.7%	0.7%

Northampton North

CON HOLD
Majority: 807, 2.0% | Turnout: 40,378, 68.6% | Electorate: 58,861 | EU Ref: 60.7% Leave

PARTY	CANDIDATE	VOTES	SHARE	CHANGE 2015
Conservative	Michael Ellis	19,065	47.2%	4.8%
Labour	Sally Keeble	18,258	45.2%	11.1%
UK Independence Party	Jonathan Bullock	1,404	3.5%	-12.6%
Liberal Democrat	George Smid	1,015	2.5%	-1.0%
Green	Steve Miller	636	1.6%	-2.2%

Northampton South

CON HOLD
Majority: 1,159, 2.9% | Turnout: 41,034, 66.5% | Electorate: 61,766 | EU Ref: 59.6% Leave

PARTY	CANDIDATE	VOTES	SHARE	CHANGE 2015
Conservative	Andrew Lewer	19,231	46.9%	5.3%
Labour	Kevin McKeever	18,072	44.0%	12.2%
UK Independence Party	Rose Gibbins	1,630	4.0%	-14.3%
Liberal Democrat	Jill Hope	1,405	3.4%	-0.9%
Green	Scott Mabbutt	696	1.7%	-1.9%

Norwich North

CON HOLD

Majority: 507, 1.1% | Turnout: 45,895, 68.6% | Electorate: 66,924 | EU Ref: 57.3% Leave

PARTY	CANDIDATE	VOTES	SHARE	CHANGE 2015
Conservative	Chloe Smith	21,900	47.7%	4.0%
Labour	Chris Jones	21,393	46.6%	13.1%
Liberal Democrat	Hugh Lanham	1,480	3.2%	-1.1%
Green	Adrian Holmes	782	1.7%	-2.7%
Pirate Party	Liam Matthews	340	0.7%	0.7%

Norwich South

LAB HOLD

Majority: 15,596, 30.4% | Turnout: 51,359, 69.2% | Electorate: 74,182 | EU Ref: 40.4% Leave

PARTY	CANDIDATE	VOTES	SHARE	CHANGE 2015
Labour	Clive Lewis	31,311	61.0%	21.7%
Conservative	Lana Hempsall	15,715	30.6%	7.1%
Liberal Democrat	James Wright	2,841	5.5%	-8.1%
Green	Richard Bearman	1,492	2.9%	-11.0%

Nottingham East

LAB HOLD

Majority: 19,590, 49.9% | Turnout: 39,327, 63.7% | Electorate: 61,760 | EU Ref: 42.8% Leave

PARTY	CANDIDATE	VOTES	SHARE	CHANGE 2015
Labour	Christopher Leslie	28,102	71.5%	16.9%
Conservative	Simon Murray	8,512	21.6%	0.9%
Liberal Democrat	Barry Holliday	1,003	2.6%	-1.6%
UK Independence Party	Robert Hall-Palmer	817	2.1%	-7.9%
Green	Kat Boettge	698	1.8%	-8.1%
Church of the Militant Elvis Party	David Bishop	195	0.5%	0.5%

Nottingham North

LAB HOLD

Majority: 11,160, 29.1% | Turnout: 38,319, 57.3% | Electorate: 66,886 | EU Ref: 63.8% Leave

PARTY	CANDIDATE	VOTES	SHARE	CHANGE 2015
Labour	Alex Norris	23,067	60.2%	5.6%
Conservative	Jack Tinley	11,907	31.1%	10.1%
UK Independence Party	Stephen Crosby	2,133	5.6%	-12.9%
Liberal Democrat	Tad Jones	674	1.8%	-0.6%
Green	Kirsty Jones	538	1.4%	-1.7%

Nottingham South

LAB HOLD

Majority: 15,162, 31.5% | Turnout: 48,129, 67.6% | Electorate: 71,182 | EU Ref: 46.5% Leave

PARTY	CANDIDATE	VOTES	SHARE	CHANGE 2015
Labour	Lillian Greenwood	30,013	62.4%	14.7%
Conservative	Jane Hunt	14,851	30.9%	-0.8%
Liberal Democrat	Tony Sutton	1,564	3.2%	-0.3%
UK Independence Party	David Hollas	1,103	2.3%	-9.0%
Green	Adam McGregor	598	1.2%	-4.2%

Nuneaton

CON HOLD

Majority: 4,739, 10.3% | Turnout: 46,067, 66.6% | Electorate: 69,201 | EU Ref: 64.8% Leave

PARTY	CANDIDATE	VOTES	SHARE	CHANGE 2015
Conservative	Marcus Jones	23,755	51.6%	6.0%
Labour	Philip Johnson	19,016	41.3%	6.4%
UK Independence Party	Craig Carpenter	1,619	3.5%	-10.9%
Liberal Democrat	Richard Brighton-Knight	914	2.0%	0.2%
Green	Chris Brookes	763	1.7%	-1.1%

Ochil & South Perthshire

CON GAIN FROM SNP
Majority: 3,359, 6.2% | Turnout: 54,168, 70.6% | Electorate: 76,767 | EU Ref: 39.3% Leave

PARTY	CANDIDATE	VOTES	SHARE	CHANGE 2015
Conservative	Luke Graham	22,469	41.5%	20.8%
Scottish National Party	Tasmina Ahmed-Sheikh	19,110	35.3%	-10.7%
Labour	Joanne Ross	10,847	20.0%	-8.4%
Liberal Democrat	Iliyan Stefanov	1,742	3.2%	0.7%

Ogmore

LAB HOLD
Majority: 13,871, 37.3% | Turnout: 37,204, 65.1% | Electorate: 57,125 | EU Ref: 59.8% Leave

PARTY	CANDIDATE	VOTES	SHARE	CHANGE 2015
Labour	Chris Elmore	23,225	62.4%	9.5%
Conservative	Jamie Wallis	9,354	25.1%	9.2%
Plaid Cymru	Huw Marshall	2,796	7.5%	-2.6%
UK Independence Party	Glenda Davies	1,235	3.3%	-12.1%
Liberal Democrat	Gerald Francis	594	1.6%	-1.4%

Old Bexley & Sidcup

CON HOLD
Majority: 15,466, 32.2% | Turnout: 48,042, 72.8% | Electorate: 66,005 | EU Ref: 63.2% Leave

PARTY	CANDIDATE	VOTES	SHARE	CHANGE 2015
Conservative	James Brokenshire	29,545	61.5%	8.7%
Labour	Danny Hackett	14,079	29.3%	10.3%
UK Independence Party	Freddy Vachha	1,619	3.4%	-14.9%
Liberal Democrat	Drew Hefferman	1,572	3.3%	-0.2%
Green	Derek Moran	820	1.7%	-1.2%
British National Party	Michael Jones	324	0.7%	0.2%
Christian Peoples Alliance	Chinwe Nwadikeduruibe	83	0.2%	0.2%

Oldham East & Saddleworth

LAB HOLD
Majority: 8,182, 17.4% | Turnout: 47,037, 65.1% | Electorate: 72,184 | EU Ref: 57.3% Leave

PARTY	CANDIDATE	VOTES	SHARE	CHANGE 2015
Labour	Debbie Abrahams	25,629	54.5%	15.1%
Conservative	Kashif Ali	17,447	37.1%	11.2%
UK Independence Party	Ian Bond	2,278	4.8%	-14.4%
Liberal Democrat	Jonathan Smith	1,683	3.6%	-9.3%

Oldham West & Royton

LAB HOLD
Majority: 17,198, 37.6% | Turnout: 45,788, 63.2% | Electorate: 72,401 | EU Ref: 62.7% Leave

PARTY	CANDIDATE	VOTES	SHARE	CHANGE 2015
Labour	Jim McMahon	29,846	65.2%	10.4%
Conservative	Christopher Glenny	12,648	27.6%	8.6%
UK Independence Party	Ruth Keating	1,899	4.1%	-16.5%
Liberal Democrat	Garth Harkness	956	2.1%	-1.6%
Green	Adam King	439	1.0%	-1.0%

Orkney & Shetland

LIB DEM HOLD
Majority: 4,563, 19.6% | Turnout: 23,277, 68.1% | Electorate: 34,164 | EU Ref: 40.3% Leave

PARTY	CANDIDATE	VOTES	SHARE	CHANGE 2015
Liberal Democrat	Alistair Carmichael	11,312	48.6%	7.2%
Scottish National Party	Miriam Brett	6,749	29.0%	-8.8%
Labour	Robina Barton	2,664	11.4%	4.3%
Conservative	Jamie Halcro Johnston	2,024	8.7%	-0.2%
UK Independence Party	Robert Smith	283	1.2%	-3.5%
Independent	Stuart Hill	245	1.1%	1.1%

Orpington

CON HOLD
Majority: 19,461, 38.5% | Turnout: 50,461, 74.3% | Electorate: 67,902 | EU Ref: 56.0% Leave

PARTY	CANDIDATE	VOTES	SHARE	CHANGE 2015
Conservative	Jo Johnson	31,762	62.9%	5.5%
Labour	Nigel De Gruchy	12,301	24.4%	8.8%
Liberal Democrat	Alex Feakes	3,315	6.6%	-0.2%
UK Independence Party	Brian Philp	2,023	4.0%	-12.7%
Green	Tamara Galloway	1,060	2.1%	-1.4%

Oxford East

LAB HOLD
Majority: 23,284, 43.2% | Turnout: 53,896, 68.8% | Electorate: 78,350 | EU Ref: 32.3% Leave

PARTY	CANDIDATE	VOTES	SHARE	CHANGE 2015
Labour	Anneliese Dodds	35,118	65.2%	15.1%
Conservative	Suzanne Bartington	11,834	22.0%	2.1%
Liberal Democrat	Kirsten Johnson	4,904	9.1%	-1.7%
Green	Larry Sanders	1,785	3.3%	-8.3%
Independent	Chaka Artwell	255	0.5%	0.2%

Oxford West & Abingdon

LIB DEM GAIN FROM CON
Majority: 816, 1.3% | Turnout: 60,020, 75.7% | Electorate: 75,574 | EU Ref: 38.2% Leave

PARTY	CANDIDATE	VOTES	SHARE	CHANGE 2015
Liberal Democrat	Layla Moran	26,256	43.7%	14.8%
Conservative	Nicola Blackwood	25,440	42.4%	-3.3%
Labour	Marie Tidball	7,573	12.6%	-0.1%
UK Independence Party	Alan Harris	751	1.3%	-5.7%

Paisley & Renfrewshire North

SNP HOLD
Majority: 2,613, 5.6% | Turnout: 46,615, 69.1% | Electorate: 67,436 | EU Ref: 36.1% Leave

PARTY	CANDIDATE	VOTES	SHARE	CHANGE 2015
Scottish National Party	Gavin Newlands	17,455	37.4%	-13.3%
Labour	Alison Taylor	14,842	31.8%	-0.9%
Conservative	David Gardiner	12,842	27.5%	15.3%
Liberal Democrat	John Boyd	1,476	3.2%	1.1%

Paisley & Renfrewshire South

SNP HOLD
Majority: 2,541, 6.1% | Turnout: 41,712, 68.0% | Electorate: 61,344 | EU Ref: 34.2% Leave

PARTY	CANDIDATE	VOTES	SHARE	CHANGE 2015
Scottish National Party	Mhairi Black	16,964	40.7%	-10.3%
Labour	Alison Dowling	14,423	34.6%	-4.1%
Conservative	Amy Thomson	8,122	19.5%	11.8%
Liberal Democrat	Eileen McCartin	1,327	3.2%	1.0%
Independent	Paul Mack	876	2.1%	2.1%

Pendle

CON HOLD
Majority: 1,279, 2.8% | Turnout: 44,854, 69.0% | Electorate: 64,962 | EU Ref: 63.2% Leave

PARTY	CANDIDATE	VOTES	SHARE	CHANGE 2015
Conservative	Andrew Stephenson	21,986	49.0%	1.8%
Labour	Wayne Blackburn	20,707	46.2%	11.2%
Liberal Democrat	Gordon Lishman	941	2.1%	-1.2%
British National Party	Brian Parker	718	1.6%	1.6%
Green	Ian Barnett	502	1.1%	-1.2%

Penistone & Stocksbridge

LAB HOLD

Majority: 1,322, 2.6% | Turnout: 49,787, 69.8% | Electorate: 71,293 | EU Ref: 61.3% Leave

PARTY	CANDIDATE	VOTES	SHARE	CHANGE 2015
Labour	Angela C Smith	22,807	45.8%	3.8%
Conservative	Nicola Wilson	21,485	43.2%	15.5%
UK Independence Party	John Booker	3,453	6.9%	-16.0%
Liberal Democrat	Penny Baker	2,042	4.1%	-2.2%

Penrith & The Border

CON HOLD

Majority: 15,910, 34.2% | Turnout: 46,470, 71.3% | Electorate: 65,139 | EU Ref: 55.4% Leave

PARTY	CANDIDATE	VOTES	SHARE	CHANGE 2015
Conservative	Rory Stewart	28,078	60.4%	0.8%
Labour	Lola McEvoy	12,168	26.2%	11.8%
Liberal Democrat	Neil Hughes	3,641	7.8%	-0.7%
UK Independence Party	Kerryanne Wilde	1,142	2.5%	-9.7%
Green	Douglas Lawson	1,029	2.2%	-3.1%
Independent	Jonathan Davies	412	0.9%	0.9%

Perth & North Perthshire

SNP HOLD

Majority: 21, 0.0% | Turnout: 51,525, 71.8% | Electorate: 71,762 | EU Ref: 40.2% Leave

PARTY	CANDIDATE	VOTES	SHARE	CHANGE 2015
Scottish National Party	Pete Wishart	21,804	42.3%	-8.2%
Conservative	Ian Duncan	21,783	42.3%	9.5%
Labour	David Roemmele	5,349	10.4%	2.2%
Liberal Democrat	Peter Barrett	2,589	5.0%	1.2%

Peterborough

LAB GAIN FROM CON
Majority: 607, 1.3% | Turnout: 47,738, 67.5% | Electorate: 71,522 | EU Ref: 62.9% Leave

PARTY	CANDIDATE	VOTES	SHARE	CHANGE 2015
Labour	Fiona Onasanya	22,950	48.1%	12.5%
Conservative	Stewart Jackson	22,343	46.8%	7.1%
Liberal Democrat	Beki Sellick	1,597	3.3%	-0.4%
Green	Fiona Radic	848	1.8%	-0.8%

Plymouth Moor View

CON HOLD
Majority: 5,019, 11.1% | Turnout: 45,417, 65.5% | Electorate: 69,342 | EU Ref: 66.4% Leave

PARTY	CANDIDATE	VOTES	SHARE	CHANGE 2015
Conservative	Johnny Mercer	23,567	51.9%	14.3%
Labour	Sue Dann	18,548	40.8%	5.6%
UK Independence Party	Wendy Noble	1,849	4.1%	-17.4%
Liberal Democrat	Graham Reed	917	2.0%	-0.9%
Green	Joshua Pope	536	1.2%	-1.2%

Plymouth Sutton & Devonport

LAB GAIN FROM CON
Majority: 6,807, 13.3% | Turnout: 51,208, 66.9% | Electorate: 76,584 | EU Ref: 54.4% Leave

PARTY	CANDIDATE	VOTES	SHARE	CHANGE 2015
Labour	Luke Pollard	27,283	53.3%	16.6%
Conservative	Oliver Colvile	20,476	40.0%	2.2%
UK Independence Party	Richard Ellison	1,364	2.7%	-11.4%
Liberal Democrat	Henrietta Bewley	1,244	2.4%	-1.8%
Green	Daniel Sheaff	604	1.2%	-5.9%
Independent	Danny Bamping	237	0.5%	0.5%

Pontypridd

LAB HOLD

Majority: 11,448, 28.7% | Turnout: 39,894, 65.9% | Electorate: 60,564 | EU Ref: 45.8% Leave

PARTY	CANDIDATE	VOTES	SHARE	CHANGE 2015
Labour	Owen Smith	22,103	55.4%	14.3%
Conservative	Juliette Ash	10,655	26.7%	9.4%
Plaid Cymru	Ffur Elin	4,102	10.3%	-1.2%
Liberal Democrat	Michael Powell	1,963	4.9%	-8.0%
UK Independence Party	Robin Hunter-Clarke	1,071	2.7%	-10.7%

Poole

CON HOLD

Majority: 14,209, 28.5% | Turnout: 49,850, 67.5% | Electorate: 73,796 | EU Ref: 56.9% Leave

PARTY	CANDIDATE	VOTES	SHARE	CHANGE 2015
Conservative	Robert Syms	28,888	57.9%	7.8%
Labour	Katie Taylor	14,679	29.4%	16.6%
Liberal Democrat	Mike Plummer	4,433	8.9%	-2.9%
Green	Adrian Oliver	1,299	2.6%	-2.0%
Demos Direct Initiative	Marty Caine	551	1.1%	1.1%

Poplar & Limehouse

LAB HOLD

Majority: 27,712, 47.2% | Turnout: 58,814, 67.5% | Electorate: 87,331 | EU Ref: 34.2% Leave

PARTY	CANDIDATE	VOTES	SHARE	CHANGE 2015
Labour	Jim Fitzpatrick	39,558	67.3%	8.7%
Conservative	Christopher Wilford	11,846	20.1%	-5.3%
Liberal Democrat	Elaine Bagshaw	3,959	6.7%	2.5%
Independent	Oliur Rahman	1,477	2.5%	2.5%
Green	Bethan Lant	989	1.7%	-3.1%
UK Independence Party	Nicholas McQueen	849	1.4%	-4.7%
Independent	David Barker	136	0.2%	0.2%

Portsmouth North

CON HOLD

Majority: 9,965, 21.1% | Turnout: 47,210, 66.1% | Electorate: 71,374 | EU Ref: 66.2% Leave

PARTY	CANDIDATE	VOTES	SHARE	CHANGE 2015
Conservative	Penny Mordaunt	25,860	54.8%	7.8%
Labour	Rumal Khan	15,895	33.7%	9.9%
Liberal Democrat	Darren Sanders	2,608	5.5%	-0.7%
UK Independence Party	Mike Fitzgerald	1,926	4.1%	-15.0%
Green	Ken Hawkins	791	1.7%	-1.5%
Libertarian	Joe Jenkins	130	0.3%	0.3%

Portsmouth South

LAB GAIN FROM CON

Majority: 1,554, 3.4% | Turnout: 44,566, 63.9% | Electorate: 69,785 | EU Ref: 51.8% Leave

PARTY	CANDIDATE	VOTES	SHARE	CHANGE 2015
Labour	Stephen Morgan	18,290	41.0%	21.5%
Conservative	Flick Drummond	16,736	37.6%	2.7%
Liberal Democrat	Gerald Vernon-Jackson	7,699	17.3%	-5.0%
UK Independence Party	Kevan Chippindall-Higgin	1,129	2.5%	-10.8%
Green	Ian McCulloch	712	1.6%	-5.9%

Preseli Pembrokeshire

CON HOLD

Majority: 314, 0.8% | Turnout: 42,197, 72.1% | Electorate: 58,554 | EU Ref: 55.8% Leave

PARTY	CANDIDATE	VOTES	SHARE	CHANGE 2015
Conservative	Stephen Crabb	18,302	43.4%	3.0%
Labour	Philippa Thompson	17,988	42.6%	14.5%
Plaid Cymru	Owain Williams	2,711	6.4%	0.2%
Independent	Chris Overton	1,209	2.9%	-6.3%
Liberal Democrat	Bob Kilmister	1,106	2.6%	0.7%
UK Independence Party	Susan Bale	850	2.0%	-8.5%
New Society of Worth	Rodney Maile	31	0.1%	0.0%

Preston

LAB HOLD

Majority: 15,723, 44.2% | Turnout: 35,597, 61.6% | Electorate: 57,791 | EU Ref: 56.9% Leave

PARTY	CANDIDATE	VOTES	SHARE	CHANGE 2015
Labour	Mark Hendrick	24,210	68.0%	12.0%
Conservative	Kevin Beaty	8,487	23.8%	3.9%
UK Independence Party	Simon Platt	1,348	3.8%	-11.6%
Liberal Democrat	Neil Darby	1,204	3.4%	-0.3%
Green	Anne Power	348	1.0%	-3.9%

Pudsey

CON HOLD

Majority: 331, 0.7% | Turnout: 53,959, 74.3% | Electorate: 72,622 | EU Ref: 48.4% Leave

PARTY	CANDIDATE	VOTES	SHARE	CHANGE 2015
Conservative	Stuart Andrew	25,550	47.4%	0.9%
Labour	Ian McCargo	25,219	46.7%	9.2%
Liberal Democrat	Allen Nixon	1,761	3.3%	-0.5%
The Yorkshire Party	Bob Buxton	1,138	2.1%	2.1%
Independent	Michael Wharton	291	0.5%	0.5%

Putney

CON HOLD

Majority: 1,554, 3.3% | Turnout: 46,894, 72.2% | Electorate: 65,031 | EU Ref: 26.9% Leave

PARTY	CANDIDATE	VOTES	SHARE	CHANGE 2015
Conservative	Justine Greening	20,679	44.1%	-9.7%
Labour	Neeraj Patil	19,125	40.8%	10.8%
Liberal Democrat	Ryan Mercer	5,448	11.6%	5.3%
Green	Ben Fletcher	1,107	2.4%	-2.5%
UK Independence Party	Patricia Ward	477	1.0%	-3.6%
Independent	Lotta Quizeen	58	0.1%	0.1%

Rayleigh & Wickford

CON HOLD

Majority: 23,450, 42.4% | Turnout: 55,323, 70.4% | Electorate: 78,556 | EU Ref: 67.9% Leave

PARTY	CANDIDATE	VOTES	SHARE	CHANGE 2015
Conservative	Mark Francois	36,914	66.7%	12.1%
Labour	Mark Daniels	13,464	24.3%	11.7%
UK Independence Party	Peter Smith	2,326	4.2%	-18.1%
Liberal Democrat	Ron Tindall	1,557	2.8%	-0.2%
Green	Paul Hill	1,062	1.9%	-1.0%

Reading East

LAB GAIN FROM CON

Majority: 3,749, 6.7% | Turnout: 55,238, 73.1% | Electorate: 75,537 | EU Ref: 38.2% Leave

PARTY	CANDIDATE	VOTES	SHARE	CHANGE 2015
Labour	Matt Rodda	27,093	49.0%	16.0%
Conservative	Rob Wilson	23,344	42.3%	-3.7%
Liberal Democrat	Jenny Woods	3,378	6.1%	-1.2%
Green	Kizzi Johannessen	1,093	2.0%	-4.4%
Independent	Michael Turberville	188	0.3%	0.3%
Movement for Active Democracy	Andy Kirkwood	142	0.3%	0.3%

Reading West

CON HOLD

Majority: 2,876, 5.6% | Turnout: 51,766, 69.5% | Electorate: 74,523 | EU Ref: 52.7% Leave

PARTY	CANDIDATE	VOTES	SHARE	CHANGE 2015
Conservative	Alok Sharma	25,311	48.9%	1.2%
Labour	Olivia Bailey	22,435	43.3%	9.4%
Liberal Democrat	Meri O'Connell	3,041	5.9%	1.0%
Green	Jamie Whitham	979	1.9%	-1.0%

Redcar

LAB HOLD

Majority: 9,485, 22.3% | Turnout: 42,560, 63.7% | Electorate: 66,836 | EU Ref: 67.6% Leave

PARTY	CANDIDATE	VOTES	SHARE	CHANGE 2015
Labour	Anna Turley	23,623	55.5%	11.6%
Conservative	Peter Gibson	14,138	33.2%	17.0%
Liberal Democrat	Josh Mason	2,849	6.7%	-11.8%
UK Independence Party	Chris Gallacher	1,950	4.6%	-13.8%

Redditch

CON HOLD

Majority: 7,363, 16.3% | Turnout: 45,203, 70.3% | Electorate: 64,413 | EU Ref: 61.4% Leave

PARTY	CANDIDATE	VOTES	SHARE	CHANGE 2015
Conservative	Rachel Maclean	23,652	52.3%	5.2%
Labour	Rebecca Blake	16,289	36.0%	4.9%
National Health Action	Neil Stote	2,239	5.0%	5.0%
UK Independence Party	Paul Swansborough	1,371	3.0%	-13.1%
Liberal Democrat	Susan Juned	1,173	2.6%	-0.5%
Green	Kevin White	380	0.8%	-1.3%
Independent	Sally Woodhall	99	0.2%	0.2%

Reigate

CON HOLD

Majority: 17,614, 32.7% | Turnout: 53,823, 72.1% | Electorate: 74,628 | EU Ref: 47.8% Leave

PARTY	CANDIDATE	VOTES	SHARE	CHANGE 2015
Conservative	Crispin Blunt	30,896	57.4%	0.6%
Labour	Toby Brampton	13,282	24.7%	11.9%
Liberal Democrat	Anna Tarrant	5,889	10.9%	0.5%
Green	Jonathan Essex	2,214	4.1%	-2.6%
UK Independence Party	Joseph Fox	1,542	2.9%	-10.4%

Rhondda

LAB HOLD

Majority: 13,746, 41.8% | Turnout: 32,936, 65.2% | Electorate: 50,514 | EU Ref: 61.2% Leave

PARTY	CANDIDATE	VOTES	SHARE	CHANGE 2015
Labour	Chris Bryant	21,096	64.1%	13.4%
Plaid Cymru	Branwen Cennard	7,350	22.3%	-4.7%
Conservative	Virginia Crosbie	3,333	10.1%	3.4%
UK Independence Party	Janet Kenrick	880	2.7%	-10.0%
Liberal Democrat	Karen Roberts	277	0.8%	-0.7%

Ribble Valley

CON HOLD

Majority: 13,199, 23.9% | Turnout: 55,200, 70.8% | Electorate: 77,968 | EU Ref: 58.7% Leave

PARTY	CANDIDATE	VOTES	SHARE	CHANGE 2015
Conservative	Nigel Evans	31,919	57.8%	9.2%
Labour	David Hinder	18,720	33.9%	11.3%
Liberal Democrat	Allan Knox	3,247	5.9%	0.6%
Green	Graham Sowter	1,314	2.4%	-1.8%

Richmond Park

CON GAIN FROM LIB DEM

Majority: 45, 0.0% | Turnout: 63,330, 79.1% | Electorate: 80,025 | EU Ref: 28.0% Leave

PARTY	CANDIDATE	VOTES	SHARE	CHANGE 2015
Conservative	Zac Goldsmith	28,588	45.1%	-13.1%
Liberal Democrat	Sarah Olney	28,543	45.1%	25.8%
Labour	Cate Tuitt	5,773	9.1%	-3.2%
UK Independence Party	Peter Jewell	426	0.7%	-3.5%

Richmond Yorkshire

CON HOLD

Majority: 23,108, 40.5% | Turnout: 57,013, 70.5% | Electorate: 80,905 | EU Ref: 55.0% Leave

PARTY	CANDIDATE	VOTES	SHARE	CHANGE 2015
Conservative	Rishi Sunak	36,458	63.9%	12.6%
Labour	Dan Perry	13,350	23.4%	10.2%
Liberal Democrat	Tobie Abel	3,360	5.9%	-0.5%
The Yorkshire Party	Chris Pearson	2,106	3.7%	3.7%
Green	Fiona Yorke	1,739	3.1%	-1.2%

Rochdale

LAB HOLD

Majority: 14,819, 29.6% | Turnout: 50,044, 64.1% | Electorate: 78,064 | EU Ref: 57.7% Leave

PARTY	CANDIDATE	VOTES	SHARE	CHANGE 2015
Labour	Tony Lloyd	29,035	58.0%	11.9%
Conservative	Jane Howard	14,216	28.4%	11.4%
Liberal Democrat	Andy Kelly	4,027	8.0%	-2.2%
UK Independence Party	Christopher Baksa	1,641	3.3%	-15.5%
Independent	Simon Danczuk	883	1.8%	1.8%
Greater Manchester Homeless Voice	Andy Littlewood	242	0.5%	0.5%

Rochester & Strood

CON HOLD

Majority: 9,850, 18.4% | Turnout: 53,769, 64.9% | Electorate: 82,702 | EU Ref: 63.1% Leave

PARTY	CANDIDATE	VOTES	SHARE	CHANGE 2015
Conservative	Kelly Tolhurst	29,232	54.4%	10.3%
Labour	Teresa Murray	19,382	36.0%	16.3%
UK Independence Party	David Allen	2,893	5.4%	-25.1%
Liberal Democrat	Bart Ricketts	1,189	2.2%	-0.2%
Green	Sonia Hyner	781	1.5%	-1.4%
Christian Peoples Alliance	Steve Benson	163	0.3%	0.3%
Independent	Primerose Chiguri	129	0.2%	0.2%

Rochford & Southend East

CON HOLD
Majority: 5,548, 11.7% | Turnout: 47,248, 64.3% | Electorate: 73,501 | EU Ref: 60.5% Leave

PARTY	CANDIDATE	VOTES	SHARE	CHANGE 2015
Conservative	James Duddridge	23,013	48.7%	2.3%
Labour	Ashley Dalton	17,465	37.0%	12.3%
Independent	Ron Woodley	2,924	6.2%	6.2%
UK Independence Party	Neil Hookway	1,777	3.8%	-16.8%
Liberal Democrat	Peter Gwizdala	1,265	2.7%	-0.7%
Green	Simon Cross	804	1.7%	-3.3%

Romford

CON HOLD
Majority: 13,778, 27.6% | Turnout: 49,944, 67.9% | Electorate: 73,493 | EU Ref: 67.8% Leave

PARTY	CANDIDATE	VOTES	SHARE	CHANGE 2015
Conservative	Andrew Rosindell	29,671	59.4%	8.4%
Labour	Angelina Leatherbarrow	15,893	31.8%	10.9%
UK Independence Party	Andrew Beadle	2,350	4.7%	-18.1%
Liberal Democrat	Ian Sanderson	1,215	2.4%	-0.4%
Green	David Hughes	815	1.6%	-0.9%

Romsey & Southampton North

CON HOLD
Majority: 18,046, 36.0% | Turnout: 50,128, 74.6% | Electorate: 67,186 | EU Ref: 45.8% Leave

PARTY	CANDIDATE	VOTES	SHARE	CHANGE 2015
Conservative	Caroline Nokes	28,668	57.2%	2.9%
Liberal Democrat	Catherine Royce	10,622	21.2%	3.5%
Labour	Darren Paffey	9,614	19.2%	7.3%
Green	Ian Callaghan	953	1.9%	-2.8%
Justice & Anti-Corruption Party	Don Jerrard	271	0.5%	0.5%

Ross, Skye & Lochaber

SNP HOLD

Majority: 5,919, 15.4% | Turnout: 38,454, 71.7% | Electorate: 53,638 | EU Ref: 43.4% Leave

PARTY	CANDIDATE	VOTES	SHARE	CHANGE 2015
Scottish National Party	Ian Blackford	15,480	40.3%	-7.9%
Conservative	Robert Mackenzie	9,561	24.9%	18.6%
Liberal Democrat	Jean Davis	8,042	20.9%	-15.0%
Labour	Peter O'Donnghaile	4,695	12.2%	7.3%
Independent	Ronnie the Crofter Campbell	499	1.3%	0.8%
Something New	Stick Sturrock	177	0.5%	0.5%

Rossendale & Darwen

CON HOLD

Majority: 3,216, 6.4% | Turnout: 50,156, 69.2% | Electorate: 72,486 | EU Ref: 58.6% Leave

PARTY	CANDIDATE	VOTES	SHARE	CHANGE 2015
Conservative	Jake Berry	25,499	50.8%	4.2%
Labour	Alyson Barnes	22,283	44.4%	9.4%
Liberal Democrat	Sean Bonner	1,550	3.1%	1.4%
Green	John Payne	824	1.6%	-0.5%

Rother Valley

LAB HOLD

Majority: 3,882, 7.8% | Turnout: 49,488, 65.8% | Electorate: 75,230 | EU Ref: 66.9% Leave

PARTY	CANDIDATE	VOTES	SHARE	CHANGE 2015
Labour	Kevin Barron	23,821	48.1%	4.5%
Conservative	Bethan Eddy	19,939	40.3%	17.0%
UK Independence Party	Lee Hunter	3,704	7.5%	-20.6%
Liberal Democrat	Katie Pruszynski	1,155	2.3%	-1.9%
Green	Paul Martin	869	1.8%	1.8%

Rotherham

LAB HOLD
Majority: 11,387, 30.0% | Turnout: 37,923, 60.0% | Electorate: 63,237 | EU Ref: 68.2% Leave

PARTY	CANDIDATE	VOTES	SHARE	CHANGE 2015
Labour	Sarah Champion	21,404	56.4%	3.9%
Conservative	James Bellis	10,017	26.4%	14.1%
UK Independence Party	Allen Cowles	3,316	8.7%	-21.4%
Liberal Democrat	Adam Carter	1,754	4.6%	1.7%
The Yorkshire Party	Mick Bower	1,432	3.8%	3.8%

Rugby

CON HOLD
Majority: 8,212, 16.0% | Turnout: 51,336, 71.1% | Electorate:72,175 | EU Ref: 58.4% Leave

PARTY	CANDIDATE	VOTES	SHARE	CHANGE 2015
Conservative	Mark Pawsey	27,872	54.3%	5.2%
Labour	Claire Edwards	19,660	38.3%	10.4%
Liberal Democrat	Jerry Roodhouse	2,851	5.6%	-0.1%
Green	Graham Bliss	953	1.9%	-1.0%

Ruislip, Northwood & Pinner

CON HOLD
Majority: 13,980, 26.2% | Turnout: 53,382, 72.9% | Electorate: 73,427 | EU Ref: 49.0% Leave

PARTY	CANDIDATE	VOTES	SHARE	CHANGE 2015
Conservative	Nick Hurd	30,555	57.2%	-2.3%
Labour	Rebecca Lury	16,575	31.0%	10.9%
Liberal Democrat	Alex Cunliffe	3,813	7.1%	2.2%
Green	Sarah Green	1,268	2.4%	-1.1%
UK Independence Party	Richard Braine	1,171	2.2%	-8.7%

Runnymede & Weybridge

CON HOLD
Majority: 18,050, 35.0% | Turnout: 51,609, 68.1% | Electorate: 74,888 | EU Ref: 49.8% Leave

PARTY	CANDIDATE	VOTES	SHARE	CHANGE 2015
Conservative	Philip Hammond	31,436	60.9%	1.2%
Labour	Fiona Dent	13,386	25.9%	10.4%
Liberal Democrat	John Vincent	3,765	7.3%	0.6%
UK Independence Party	Nicholas Wood	1,675	3.2%	-10.6%
Green	Lee-Anne Lawrence	1,347	2.6%	-1.5%

Rushcliffe

CON HOLD
Majority: 8,010, 13.7% | Turnout: 58,311, 78.0% | Electorate: 74,738 | EU Ref: 41.3% Leave

PARTY	CANDIDATE	VOTES	SHARE	CHANGE 2015
Conservative	Kenneth Clarke	30,223	51.8%	0.4%
Labour	David Mellen	22,213	38.1%	11.8%
Liberal Democrat	Jayne Phoenix	2,759	4.7%	-0.3%
Green	George Mallender	1,626	2.8%	-3.7%
UK Independence Party	Matthew Faithfull	1,490	2.6%	-8.2%

Rutherglen & Hamilton West

LAB GAIN FROM SNP
Majority: 265, 0.5% | Turnout: 50,872, 63.5% | Electorate: 80,098 | EU Ref: 37.3% Leave

PARTY	CANDIDATE	VOTES	SHARE	CHANGE 2015
Labour	Ged Killen	19,101	37.5%	2.3%
Scottish National Party	Margaret Ferrier	18,836	37.0%	-15.5%
Conservative	Ann Le Blond	9,941	19.5%	12.0%
Liberal Democrat	Robert Brown	2,158	4.2%	2.4%
UK Independence Party	Caroline Santos	465	0.9%	-1.3%
Independent	Andy Dixon	371	0.7%	0.7%

Rutland & Melton

CON HOLD

Majority: 23,104, 40.1% | Turnout: 57,569, 73.4% | Electorate: 78,463 | EU Ref: 54.0% Leave

PARTY	CANDIDATE	VOTES	SHARE	CHANGE 2015
Conservative	Alan Duncan	36,169	62.8%	7.2%
Labour	Heather Peto	13,065	22.7%	7.3%
Liberal Democrat	Ed Reynolds	4,711	8.2%	0.1%
UK Independence Party	John Scutter	1,869	3.2%	-12.6%
Green	Alastair McQuillan	1,755	3.0%	-1.2%

Saffron Walden

CON HOLD

Majority: 24,966, 41.0% | Turnout: 60,911, 73.1% | Electorate: 83,072 | EU Ref: 50.9% Leave

PARTY	CANDIDATE	VOTES	SHARE	CHANGE 2015
Conservative	Kemi Badenoch	37,629	61.8%	4.6%
Labour	Jane Berney	12,663	20.8%	9.0%
Liberal Democrat	Mike Hibbs	8,528	14.0%	3.4%
UK Independence Party	Lorna Howe	2,091	3.4%	-10.4%

Salford & Eccles

LAB HOLD

Majority: 19,132, 40.2% | Turnout: 47,619, 60.8% | Electorate: 78,080 | EU Ref: 53.0% Leave

PARTY	CANDIDATE	VOTES	SHARE	CHANGE 2015
Labour	Rebecca Long Bailey	31,168	65.5%	16.1%
Conservative	Jason Sugarman	12,036	25.3%	4.9%
UK Independence Party	Christopher Barnes	2,320	4.9%	-13.2%
Liberal Democrat	John Reid	1,286	2.7%	-1.0%
Green	Wendy Olsen	809	1.7%	-3.5%

Salisbury

CON HOLD
Majority: 17,333, 32.6% | Turnout: 53,311, 74.1% | Electorate: 72,892 | EU Ref: 50.3% Leave

PARTY	CANDIDATE	VOTES	SHARE	CHANGE 2015
Conservative	John Glen	30,952	58.1%	2.5%
Labour	Tom Corbin	13,619	25.5%	10.2%
Liberal Democrat	Paul Sample	5,982	11.2%	1.2%
UK Independence Party	Dean Palethorpe	1,191	2.2%	-9.9%
Green	Brig Oubridge	1,152	2.2%	-3.3%
Independent	King Arthur Pendragon	415	0.8%	-0.7%

Scarborough & Whitby

CON HOLD
Majority: 3,435, 6.8% | Turnout: 50,449, 68.6% | Electorate: 73,599 | EU Ref: 61.4% Leave

PARTY	CANDIDATE	VOTES	SHARE	CHANGE 2015
Conservative	Robert Goodwill	24,401	48.4%	5.2%
Labour	Eric Broadbent	20,966	41.6%	11.4%
UK Independence Party	Sam Cross	1,682	3.3%	-13.8%
Liberal Democrat	Robert Lockwood	1,354	2.7%	-1.8%
Green	David Malone	915	1.8%	-2.8%
Independent	John Freeman	680	1.3%	1.3%
The Yorkshire Party	Bill Black	369	0.7%	0.7%
Independent	Gordon Johnson	82	0.2%	0.2%

Scunthorpe

LAB HOLD
Majority: 3,431, 8.5% | Turnout: 40,202, 65.3% | Electorate: 61,578 | EU Ref: 69.1% Leave

PARTY	CANDIDATE	VOTES	SHARE	CHANGE 2015
Labour	Nic Dakin	20,916	52.0%	10.4%
Conservative	Holly Mumby-Croft	17,485	43.5%	10.3%
UK Independence Party	Andy Talliss	1,247	3.1%	-14.0%
Liberal Democrat	Ryk Downes	554	1.4%	0.7%

Sedgefield

LAB HOLD

Majority: 6,059, 14.6% | Turnout: 41,591, 65.1% | Electorate: 63,889 | EU Ref: 58.9% Leave

PARTY	CANDIDATE	VOTES	SHARE	CHANGE 2015
Labour	Phil Wilson	22,202	53.4%	6.2%
Conservative	Dehenna Davison	16,143	38.8%	9.3%
UK Independence Party	John Grant	1,763	4.2%	-12.4%
Liberal Democrat	Stephen Psallidas	797	1.9%	-1.6%
Green	Melissa Wilson	686	1.6%	-1.5%

Sefton Central

LAB HOLD

Majority: 15,618, 30.0% | Turnout: 52,079, 75.5% | Electorate: 69,019 | EU Ref: 45.1% Leave

PARTY	CANDIDATE	VOTES	SHARE	CHANGE 2015
Labour	Bill Esterson	32,830	63.0%	9.3%
Conservative	Jade Marsden	17,212	33.0%	3.4%
Liberal Democrat	Daniel Lewis	1,381	2.7%	-1.6%
Green	Mike Carter	656	1.3%	-1.2%

Selby & Ainsty

CON HOLD

Majority: 13,772, 24.6% | Turnout: 56,076, 74.0% | Electorate: 75,918 | EU Ref: 57.8% Leave

PARTY	CANDIDATE	VOTES	SHARE	CHANGE 2015
Conservative	Nigel Adams	32,921	58.7%	6.2%
Labour	David Bowgett	19,149	34.1%	7.3%
Liberal Democrat	Callum Delhoy	2,293	4.1%	0.5%
UK Independence Party	Tony Pycroft	1,713	3.1%	-10.9%

Sevenoaks

CON HOLD
Majority: 21,917, 42.8% | Turnout: 51,218, 72.1% | Electorate: 71,565 | EU Ref: 53.9% Leave

PARTY	CANDIDATE	VOTES	SHARE	CHANGE 2015
Conservative	Michael Fallon	32,644	63.7%	6.8%
Labour	Chris Clark	10,727	20.9%	8.1%
Liberal Democrat	Alan Bullion	4,280	8.4%	0.5%
UK Independence Party	Graham Cushway	1,894	3.7%	-14.2%
Green	Philip Dodd	1,673	3.3%	-1.2%

Sheffield Brightside & Hillsborough

LAB HOLD
Majority: 19,143, 45.7% | Turnout: 41,870, 59.6% | Electorate: 70,344 | EU Ref: 61.0% Leave

PARTY	CANDIDATE	VOTES	SHARE	CHANGE 2015
Labour	Gill Furniss	28,193	67.3%	10.8%
Conservative	Michael Naughton	9,050	21.6%	10.6%
UK Independence Party	Shane Harper	2,645	6.3%	-15.8%
Liberal Democrat	Simon Clement-Jones	1,061	2.5%	-2.0%
Green	Christine Gilligan Kubo	737	1.8%	-2.5%
Workers Revolutionary Party	Mike Driver	137	0.3%	0.3%
Social Democratic Party	Muzafar Rahman	47	0.1%	0.1%

Sheffield Central

LAB HOLD

Majority: 27,748, 57.9% | Turnout: 47,877, 62.0% | Electorate: 77,560 | EU Ref: 30.4% Leave

PARTY	CANDIDATE	VOTES	SHARE	CHANGE 2015
Labour	Paul Blomfield	33,963	70.9%	15.9%
Conservative	Stephanie Roe	6,215	13.0%	1.8%
Green	Natalie Bennett	3,848	8.0%	-7.8%
Liberal Democrat	Shaffaq Mohammed	2,465	5.1%	-4.5%
UK Independence Party	Dominic Cook	1,060	2.2%	-5.2%
The Yorkshire Party	Jack Carrington	197	0.4%	0.4%
Pirate Party	Robert Moran	91	0.2%	-0.1%
Social Democratic Party	Joe Westridge	38	0.1%	0.1%

Sheffield Hallam

LAB GAIN FROM LIB DEM

Majority: 2,125, 3.8% | Turnout: 57,020, 77.8% | Electorate: 73,455 | EU Ref: 36.0% Leave

PARTY	CANDIDATE	VOTES	SHARE	CHANGE 2015
Labour	Jared O'Mara	21,881	38.4%	2.6%
Liberal Democrat	Nick Clegg	19,756	34.6%	-5.4%
Conservative	Ian Walker	13,561	23.8%	10.2%
UK Independence Party	John Thurley	929	1.6%	-4.8%
Green	Logan Robin	823	1.4%	-1.8%
Social Democratic Party	Steven Winstone	70	0.1%	0.1%

Sheffield Heeley

LAB HOLD
Majority: 13,828, 31.3% | Turnout: 44,226, 65.1% | Electorate: 68,040 | EU Ref: 58.0% Leave

PARTY	CANDIDATE	VOTES	SHARE	CHANGE 2015
Labour	Louise Haigh	26,524	60.0%	11.8%
Conservative	Gordon Gregory	12,696	28.7%	12.6%
Liberal Democrat	Joe Otten	2,022	4.6%	-6.7%
UK Independence Party	Howard Denby	1,977	4.5%	-12.9%
Green	Declan Walsh	943	2.1%	-4.0%
Social Democratic Party	Jaspreet Oberoi	64	0.1%	0.1%

Sheffield South East

LAB HOLD
Majority: 11,798, 27.0% | Turnout: 43,596, 63.3% | Electorate: 68,945 | EU Ref: 66.5% Leave

PARTY	CANDIDATE	VOTES	SHARE	CHANGE 2015
Labour	Clive Betts	25,520	58.5%	7.1%
Conservative	Lindsey Cawrey	13,722	31.5%	14.1%
UK Independence Party	Dennise Dawson	2,820	6.5%	-15.4%
Liberal Democrat	Colin Ross	1,432	3.3%	-2.1%
Social Democratic Party	Ishleen Oberoi	102	0.2%	0.2%

Sherwood

CON HOLD
Majority: 5,198, 9.7% | Turnout: 53,364, 70.0% | Electorate: 76,196 | EU Ref: 63.8% Leave

PARTY	CANDIDATE	VOTES	SHARE	CHANGE 2015
Conservative	Mark Spencer	27,492	51.5%	6.5%
Labour	Mike Pringle	22,294	41.8%	5.9%
UK Independence Party	Stuart Bestwick	1,801	3.4%	-11.2%
Liberal Democrat	Becky Thomas	1,113	2.1%	-0.1%
Green	Morris Findley	664	1.2%	-0.9%

Shipley

CON HOLD
Majority: 4,681, 8.7% | Turnout: 53,395, 73.0% | Electorate: 73,133 | EU Ref: 52.2% Leave

PARTY	CANDIDATE	VOTES	SHARE	CHANGE 2015
Conservative	Philip Davies	27,417	51.3%	1.4%
Labour	Steve Clapcote	22,736	42.6%	11.6%
Liberal Democrat	Caroline Jones	2,202	4.1%	0.3%
Women's Equality Party	Sophie Walker	1,040	1.9%	1.9%

Shrewsbury & Atcham

CON HOLD
Majority: 6,627, 11.4% | Turnout: 58,203, 73.6% | Electorate: 79,043 | EU Ref: 53.0% Leave

PARTY	CANDIDATE	VOTES	SHARE	CHANGE 2015
Conservative	Daniel Kawczynski	29,073	50.0%	4.4%
Labour	Laura Davies	22,446	38.6%	10.7%
Liberal Democrat	Hannah Fraser	4,254	7.3%	-0.6%
UK Independence Party	Edward Higginbottom	1,363	2.3%	-12.1%
Green	Emma Bullard	1,067	1.8%	-2.3%

Sittingbourne & Sheppey

CON HOLD
Majority: 15,211, 29.6% | Turnout: 51,389, 62.7% | Electorate: 81,717 | EU Ref: 65.8% Leave

PARTY	CANDIDATE	VOTES	SHARE	CHANGE 2015
Conservative	Gordon Henderson	30,911	60.2%	10.7%
Labour	Mike Rolfe	15,700	30.6%	11.0%
Independent	Mike Baldock	2,133	4.2%	4.2%
Liberal Democrat	Keith Nevols	1,392	2.7%	-0.5%
Green	Mark Richard Lindop	558	1.1%	-1.3%
Monster Raving Loony Party	Mad Mike Young	403	0.8%	0.2%
Independent	Lee McCall	292	0.6%	0.6%

Skipton & Ripon

CON HOLD

Majority: 19,985, 34.4% | Turnout: 58,138, 74.4% | Electorate: 78,104 | EU Ref: 53.0% Leave

PARTY	CANDIDATE	VOTES	SHARE	CHANGE 2015
Conservative	Julian Smith	36,425	62.7%	7.2%
Labour	Alan Woodhead	16,440	28.3%	10.9%
Green	Andy Brown	3,734	6.4%	0.7%
The Yorkshire Party	Jack Render	1,539	2.6%	2.6%

Sleaford & North Hykeham

CON HOLD

Majority: 25,237, 38.4% | Turnout: 65,797, 72.4% | Electorate: 90,929 | EU Ref: 61.5% Leave

PARTY	CANDIDATE	VOTES	SHARE	CHANGE 2015
Conservative	Caroline Johnson	42,245	64.2%	8.0%
Labour	Jim Clarke	17,008	25.8%	8.6%
Liberal Democrat	Ross Pepper	2,722	4.1%	-1.5%
UK Independence Party	Sally Chadd	1,954	3.0%	-12.7%
Green	Fiona McKenna	968	1.5%	1.5%
Independent	Paul Coyne	900	1.4%	1.4%

Slough

LAB HOLD

Majority: 16,998, 31.3% | Turnout: 54,295, 65.2% | Electorate: 83,272 | EU Ref: 54.1% Leave

PARTY	CANDIDATE	VOTES	SHARE	CHANGE 2015
Labour	Tan Dhesi	34,170	62.9%	14.4%
Conservative	Mark Vivis	17,172	31.6%	-1.7%
Liberal Democrat	Tom McCann	1,308	2.4%	-0.2%
UK Independence Party	Karen Perez	1,228	2.3%	-10.7%
Independent	Paul Janik	417	0.8%	0.8%

Solihull

CON HOLD

Majority: 20,571, 36.2% | Turnout: 56,748, 73.4% | Electorate: 77,789 | EU Ref: 54.3% Leave

PARTY	CANDIDATE	VOTES	SHARE	CHANGE 2015
Conservative	Julian Knight	32,985	58.1%	8.9%
Labour	Nigel Knowles	12,414	21.9%	11.5%
Liberal Democrat	Ade Adeyemo	8,901	15.7%	-10.0%
UK Independence Party	Andrew Garcarz	1,291	2.3%	-9.3%
Green	Max McLoughlin	1,157	2.0%	-0.9%

Somerton & Frome

CON HOLD

Majority: 22,906, 35.8% | Turnout: 63,892, 75.7% | Electorate: 84,437 | EU Ref: 51.0% Leave

PARTY	CANDIDATE	VOTES	SHARE	CHANGE 2015
Conservative	David Warburton	36,231	56.7%	3.7%
Liberal Democrat	Mark Blackburn	13,325	20.9%	1.5%
Labour	Sean Dromgoole	10,998	17.2%	9.9%
Green	Theo Simon	2,347	3.7%	-5.3%
Independent	Richard Hadwin	991	1.6%	1.6%

South Antrim

DUP GAIN FROM UUP

Majority: 3,208, 7.4% | Turnout: 43,170, 63.3% | Electorate: 68,244 | EU Ref: Not available

PARTY	CANDIDATE	VOTES	SHARE	CHANGE 2015
Democratic Unionist Party	Paul Girvan	16,508	38.2%	8.1%
Ulster Unionist Party	Danny Kinahan	13,300	30.8%	-1.9%
Sinn Féin	Declan Kearney	7,797	18.1%	5.2%
Alliance Party	Neil Kelly	3,203	7.4%	-2.4%
Social Democratic & Labour Party	Roisin Lynch	2,362	5.5%	-2.7%

South Basildon & East Thurrock

CON HOLD
Majority: 11,490, 24.4% | Turnout: 47,120, 64.4% | Electorate: 73,537 | EU Ref: 73.1% Leave

PARTY	CANDIDATE	VOTES	SHARE	CHANGE 2015
Conservative	Stephen Metcalfe	26,811	56.9%	13.5%
Labour	Byron Taylor	15,321	32.5%	7.3%
UK Independence Party	Peter Whittle	3,193	6.8%	-19.8%
Liberal Democrat	Reetendra Banerji	732	1.6%	-1.4%
Green	Sim Harman	680	1.4%	1.4%
British National Party	Paul Borg	383	0.8%	0.8%

South Cambridgeshire

CON HOLD
Majority: 15,952, 24.6% | Turnout: 64,924, 76.2% | Electorate: 85,257 | EU Ref: 38.4% Leave

PARTY	CANDIDATE	VOTES	SHARE	CHANGE 2015
Conservative	Heidi Allen	33,631	51.8%	0.7%
Labour	Dan Greef	17,679	27.2%	9.6%
Liberal Democrat	Susan van de Ven	12,102	18.6%	3.4%
Green	Simon Saggers	1,512	2.3%	-3.9%

South Derbyshire

CON HOLD
Majority: 11,970, 22.7% | Turnout: 52,631, 68.9% | Electorate: 76,380 | EU Ref: 60.4% Leave

PARTY	CANDIDATE	VOTES	SHARE	CHANGE 2015
Conservative	Heather Wheeler	30,907	58.7%	9.3%
Labour	Robert Pearson	18,937	36.0%	9.2%
Liberal Democrat	Lorraine Johnson	1,870	3.6%	-0.2%
Green	Marten Kats	917	1.7%	-0.7%

South Dorset

CON HOLD

Majority: 11,695, 22.5% | Turnout: 51,906, 68.7% | Electorate: 72,323 | EU Ref: 59.5% Leave

PARTY	CANDIDATE	VOTES	SHARE	CHANGE 2015
Conservative	Richard Drax	29,135	56.1%	7.2%
Labour	Tashi Warr	17,440	33.6%	9.4%
Liberal Democrat	Howard Legg	3,053	5.9%	-0.1%
Green	Jon Orrell	2,278	4.4%	-0.3%

South Down

SF GAIN FROM SDLP

Majority: 2,446, 4.8% | Turnout: 50,893, 67.2% | Electorate: 75,685 | EU Ref: Not available

PARTY	CANDIDATE	VOTES	SHARE	CHANGE 2015
Sinn Féin	Chris Hazzard	20,328	39.9%	11.4%
Social Democratic & Labour Party	Margaret Ritchie	17,882	35.1%	-7.2%
Democratic Unionist Party	Diane Forsythe	8,867	17.4%	9.3%
Ulster Unionist Party	Harold McKee	2,002	3.9%	-5.4%
Alliance Party	Andrew McMurray	1,814	3.6%	-0.2%

South East Cambridgeshire

CON HOLD

Majority: 16,158, 25.6% | Turnout: 63,002, 73.2% | Electorate: 86,121 | EU Ref: 45.0% Leave

PARTY	CANDIDATE	VOTES	SHARE	CHANGE 2015
Conservative	Lucy Frazer	33,601	53.3%	4.9%
Labour	Huw Jones	17,443	27.7%	12.5%
Liberal Democrat	Lucy Nethsingha	11,958	19.0%	-1.2%

South East Cornwall

CON HOLD
Majority: 17,443, 32.8% | Turnout: 53,224, 74.0% | Electorate: 71,880 | EU Ref: 54.9% Leave

PARTY	CANDIDATE	VOTES	SHARE	CHANGE 2015
Conservative	Sheryll Murray	29,493	55.4%	4.9%
Labour	Gareth Derrick	12,050	22.6%	13.3%
Liberal Democrat	Phil Hutty	10,346	19.4%	2.6%
Green	Martin Corney	1,335	2.5%	-2.9%

South Holland & The Deepings

CON HOLD
Majority: 24,897, 49.5% | Turnout: 50,315, 65.8% | Electorate: 76,374 | EU Ref: 71.2% Leave

PARTY	CANDIDATE	VOTES	SHARE	CHANGE 2015
Conservative	John Hayes	35,179	69.9%	10.4%
Labour	Voyteck Kowalewski	10,282	20.4%	8.0%
UK Independence Party	Nicola Smith	2,185	4.3%	-17.5%
Liberal Democrat	Julia Cambridge	1,433	2.8%	-0.1%
Green	Daniel Wilshire	894	1.8%	-1.4%
Independent	Rick Stringer	342	0.7%	0.7%

South Leicestershire

CON HOLD
Majority: 18,631, 32.9% | Turnout: 56,689, 71.8% | Electorate: 78,985 | EU Ref: 58.2% Leave

PARTY	CANDIDATE	VOTES	SHARE	CHANGE 2015
Conservative	Alberto Costa	34,795	61.4%	8.2%
Labour	Shabbir Aslam	16,164	28.5%	6.5%
Liberal Democrat	Gregory Webb	2,403	4.2%	-3.2%
UK Independence Party	Roger Helmer	2,235	3.9%	-13.4%
Green	Mary Morgan	1,092	1.9%	1.9%

South Norfolk

Majority: 16,678, 27.3% | Turnout: 61,111, 73.6% | Electorate: 83,055 | EU Ref: 51.1% Leave

PARTY	CANDIDATE	VOTES	SHARE	CHANGE 2015
Conservative	Richard Bacon	35,580	58.2%	4.0%
Labour	Danielle Glavin	18,902	30.9%	12.5%
Liberal Democrat	Christopher Brown	5,074	8.3%	0.1%
Green	Catherine Rowett	1,555	2.5%	-2.9%

South Northamptonshire

Majority: 22,840, 35.2% | Turnout: 64,998, 75.9% | Electorate: 85,759 | EU Ref: 52.7% Leave

PARTY	CANDIDATE	VOTES	SHARE	CHANGE 2015
Conservative	Andrea Leadsom	40,599	62.5%	2.3%
Labour	Sophie Johnson	17,759	27.3%	10.6%
Liberal Democrat	Chris Lofts	3,623	5.6%	-0.4%
UK Independence Party	Nigel Wickens	1,363	2.1%	-11.4%
Green	Denise Donaldson	1,357	2.1%	-1.6%
Independent	Josh Phillips	297	0.5%	0.5%

South Ribble

Majority: 7,421, 13.6% | Turnout: 54,833, 72.4% | Electorate: 75,752 | EU Ref: 56.9% Leave

PARTY	CANDIDATE	VOTES	SHARE	CHANGE 2015
Conservative	Seema Kennedy	28,980	52.9%	6.4%
Labour	Julie Gibson	21,559	39.3%	4.2%
Liberal Democrat	John Wright	2,073	3.8%	-0.6%
UK Independence Party	Mark Smith	1,387	2.5%	-11.6%
Green	Andrew Wight	493	0.9%	0.9%
National Health Action	Mark Jarnell	341	0.6%	0.6%

South Shields

LAB HOLD

Majority: 14,508, 35.6% | Turnout: 40,772, 64.3% | Electorate: 63,433 | EU Ref: 62.8% Leave

PARTY	CANDIDATE	VOTES	SHARE	CHANGE 2015
Labour	Emma Lewell-Buck	25,078	61.5%	10.2%
Conservative	Felicity Buchan	10,570	25.9%	9.3%
UK Independence Party	Richard Elvin	3,006	7.4%	-14.6%
Green	Shirley Ford	1,437	3.5%	-0.9%
Liberal Democrat	Gita Gordon	681	1.7%	-0.1%

South Staffordshire

CON HOLD

Majority: 22,733, 44.5% | Turnout: 51,109, 69.6% | Electorate: 73,441 | EU Ref: 65.3% Leave

PARTY	CANDIDATE	VOTES	SHARE	CHANGE 2015
Conservative	Gavin Williamson	35,656	69.8%	10.3%
Labour	Adam Freeman	12,923	25.3%	6.9%
Liberal Democrat	Hilary Myers	1,348	2.6%	-0.3%
Green	Claire McIlvenna	1,182	2.3%	-0.3%

South Suffolk

CON HOLD

Majority: 17,749, 32.7% | Turnout: 54,235, 71.8% | Electorate: 75,485 | EU Ref: 54.2% Leave

PARTY	CANDIDATE	VOTES	SHARE	CHANGE 2015
Conservative	James Cartlidge	32,829	60.5%	7.5%
Labour	Emma Bishton	15,080	27.8%	8.5%
Liberal Democrat	Andrew Aalders-Dunthorne	3,154	5.8%	-2.0%
Green	Robert Lindsay	1,723	3.2%	-1.2%
UK Independence Party	Aidan Powlesland	1,449	2.7%	-12.5%

South Swindon

CON HOLD
Majority: 2,464, 4.8% | Turnout: 51,271, 70.8% | Electorate: 72,372 | EU Ref: 51.6% Leave

PARTY	CANDIDATE	VOTES	SHARE	CHANGE 2015
Conservative	Robert Buckland	24,809	48.4%	2.2%
Labour	Sarah Church	22,345	43.6%	9.1%
Liberal Democrat	Stan Pajak	2,079	4.1%	0.4%
UK Independence Party	Martin Costello	1,291	2.5%	-9.5%
Green	Talis Kimberley-Fairbourn	747	1.5%	-2.1%

South Thanet

CON HOLD
Majority: 6,387, 12.9% | Turnout: 49,753, 68.8% | Electorate: 72,334 | EU Ref: 61.6% Leave

PARTY	CANDIDATE	VOTES	SHARE	CHANGE 2015
Conservative	Craig Mackinlay	25,262	50.8%	12.6%
Labour	Raushan Ara	18,875	37.9%	14.2%
UK Independence Party	Stuart Piper	2,997	6.0%	-26.4%
Liberal Democrat	Jordan Williams	1,514	3.0%	1.2%
Green	Trevor Roper	809	1.6%	-0.6%
Independent	Tim Garbutt	181	0.4%	0.4%
Christian Peoples Alliance	Faith Fisher	115	0.2%	0.2%

South West Bedfordshire

CON HOLD
Majority: 14,168, 25.4% | Turnout: 55,635, 69.8% | Electorate: 79,658 | EU Ref: 58.6% Leave

PARTY	CANDIDATE	VOTES	SHARE	CHANGE 2015
Conservative	Andrew Selous	32,961	59.2%	4.3%
Labour	Daniel Scott	18,793	33.8%	13.5%
Liberal Democrat	Daniel Norton	2,630	4.7%	-0.4%
Green	Morvern Rennie	950	1.7%	-2.4%
Christian Peoples Alliance	Morenike Mafoh	301	0.5%	0.5%

South West Devon

CON HOLD

Majority: 15,816, 29.9% | Turnout: 52,857, 74.2% | Electorate: 71,260 | EU Ref: 55.2% Leave

PARTY	CANDIDATE	VOTES	SHARE	CHANGE 2015
Conservative	Gary Streeter	31,634	59.8%	3.3%
Labour	Philippa Davey	15,818	29.9%	13.3%
Liberal Democrat	Caroline Voaden	2,732	5.2%	-2.3%
UK Independence Party	Ian Ross	1,540	2.9%	-11.6%
Green	Win Scutt	1,133	2.1%	-2.6%

South West Hertfordshire

CON HOLD

Majority: 19,550, 32.2% | Turnout: 60,653, 75.5% | Electorate: 81,087 | EU Ref: 46.4% Leave

PARTY	CANDIDATE	VOTES	SHARE	CHANGE 2015
Conservative	David Gauke	35,128	57.9%	1.0%
Labour	Robert Wakely	15,578	25.7%	9.4%
Liberal Democrat	Christopher Townsend	7,078	11.7%	1.4%
Green	Paul De Hoest	1,576	2.6%	-1.9%
UK Independence Party	Mark Anderson	1,293	2.1%	-9.4%

South West Norfolk

CON HOLD

Majority: 18,312, 35.0% | Turnout: 52,416, 67.3% | Electorate: 77,874 | EU Ref: 66.3% Leave

PARTY	CANDIDATE	VOTES	SHARE	CHANGE 2015
Conservative	Elizabeth Truss	32,894	62.8%	11.8%
Labour	Peter Smith	14,582	27.8%	10.6%
UK Independence Party	David Williams	2,575	4.9%	-18.3%
Liberal Democrat	Stephen Gordon	2,365	4.5%	0.1%

South West Surrey

CON HOLD

Majority: 21,590, 35.7% | Turnout: 60,432, 77.4% | Electorate: 78,042 | EU Ref: 40.6% Leave

PARTY	CANDIDATE	VOTES	SHARE	CHANGE 2015
Conservative	Jeremy Hunt	33,683	55.7%	-4.1%
National Health Action	Louise Irvine	12,093	20.0%	11.5%
Labour	David Black	7,606	12.6%	3.1%
Liberal Democrat	Ollie Purkiss	5,967	9.9%	3.6%
UK Independence Party	Mark Webber	1,083	1.8%	-8.1%

South West Wiltshire

CON HOLD

Majority: 18,326, 33.5% | Turnout: 54,751, 72.0% | Electorate: 76,898 | EU Ref: 57.7% Leave

PARTY	CANDIDATE	VOTES	SHARE	CHANGE 2015
Conservative	Andrew Murrison	32,841	60.0%	7.3%
Labour	Laura Pictor	14,515	26.5%	13.1%
Liberal Democrat	Trevor Carbin	5,360	9.8%	-0.8%
Green	Christopher Walford	1,445	2.6%	-3.1%
Independent	Liam Silcocks	590	1.1%	1.1%

Southampton Itchen

CON HOLD

Majority: 31, 0.0% | Turnout: 46,783, 65.2% | Electorate: 71,722 | EU Ref: 60.0% Leave

PARTY	CANDIDATE	VOTES	SHARE	CHANGE 2015
Conservative	Royston Smith	21,773	46.5%	4.8%
Labour	Simon Letts	21,742	46.5%	9.9%
Liberal Democrat	Eleanor Bell	1,421	3.0%	-0.5%
UK Independence Party	Kim Rose	1,122	2.4%	-11.0%
Green	Rosie Pearce	725	1.5%	-2.6%

Southampton Test

LAB HOLD

Majority: 11,503, 24.6% | Turnout: 46,903, 66.8% | Electorate: 70,199 | EU Ref: 50.7% Leave

PARTY	CANDIDATE	VOTES	SHARE	CHANGE 2015
Labour	Alan Whitehead	27,509	58.7%	17.4%
Conservative	Paul Holmes	16,006	34.1%	1.6%
Liberal Democrat	Thomas Gravatt	1,892	4.0%	-0.8%
Southampton Independents	Andrew Pope	816	1.7%	1.7%
Independent	Keith Morrell	680	1.4%	1.4%

Southend West

CON HOLD

Majority: 10,000, 21.2% | Turnout: 47,191, 69.7% | Electorate: 67,677 | EU Ref: 57.2% Leave

PARTY	CANDIDATE	VOTES	SHARE	CHANGE 2015
Conservative	David Amess	26,046	55.2%	5.4%
Labour	Julian Ware-Lane	16,046	34.0%	15.7%
Liberal Democrat	Lucy Salek	2,110	4.5%	-4.8%
UK Independence Party	John Stansfield	1,666	3.5%	-14.0%
Green	Dominic Ellis	831	1.8%	-2.9%
Southend Independent Association	Tino Callaghan	305	0.6%	0.6%
Independent	Jason Pilley	187	0.4%	0.4%

Southport

CON GAIN FROM LIB DEM

Majority: 2,914, 6.1% | Turnout: 47,956, 69.1% | Electorate: 69,400 | EU Ref: 45.5% Leave

PARTY	CANDIDATE	VOTES	SHARE	CHANGE 2015
Conservative	Damien Moore	18,541	38.7%	10.7%
Labour	Liz Savage	15,627	32.6%	13.4%
Liberal Democrat	Sue McGuire	12,661	26.4%	-4.6%
UK Independence Party	Terry Durrance	1,127	2.4%	-14.5%

Spelthorne

CON HOLD

Majority: 13,425, 26.8% | Turnout: 50,115, 69.0% | Electorate: 72,641 | EU Ref: 60.3% Leave

PARTY	CANDIDATE	VOTES	SHARE	CHANGE 2015
Conservative	Kwasi Kwarteng	28,692	57.3%	7.6%
Labour	Rebecca Geach	15,267	30.5%	11.9%
Liberal Democrat	Rosamund Shimell	2,755	5.5%	-0.9%
UK Independence Party	Redvers Cunningham	2,296	4.6%	-16.3%
Green	Paul Jacobs	1,105	2.2%	-1.3%

St Albans

CON HOLD

Majority: 6,109, 10.7% | Turnout: 56,998, 78.3% | Electorate: 72,811 | EU Ref: 38.0% Leave

PARTY	CANDIDATE	VOTES	SHARE	CHANGE 2015
Conservative	Anne Main	24,571	43.1%	-3.5%
Liberal Democrat	Daisy Cooper	18,462	32.4%	13.9%
Labour	Kerry Pollard	13,137	23.0%	-0.2%
Green	Jack Easton	828	1.5%	-2.3%

St Austell & Newquay

CON HOLD

Majority: 11,142, 20.5% | Turnout: 54,212, 69.0% | Electorate: 78,609 | EU Ref: 63.5% Leave

PARTY	CANDIDATE	VOTES	SHARE	CHANGE 2015
Conservative	Steve Double	26,856	49.5%	9.3%
Labour	Kevin Neil	15,714	29.0%	18.8%
Liberal Democrat	Stephen Gilbert	11,642	21.5%	-2.5%

St Helens North

LAB HOLD

Majority: 18,406, 36.6% | Turnout: 50,222, 66.0% | Electorate: 76,088 | EU Ref: 58.3% Leave

PARTY	CANDIDATE	VOTES	SHARE	CHANGE 2015
Labour	Conor McGinn	32,012	63.7%	6.7%
Conservative	Jackson Ng	13,606	27.1%	7.4%
UK Independence Party	Peter Peers	2,097	4.2%	-10.9%
Liberal Democrat	Tom Morrison	1,287	2.6%	-1.9%
Green	Rachel Parkinson	1,220	2.4%	-1.4%

St Helens South & Whiston

LAB HOLD

Majority: 24,343, 46.0% | Turnout: 52,886, 66.9% | Electorate: 79,036 | EU Ref: 56.1% Leave

PARTY	CANDIDATE	VOTES	SHARE	CHANGE 2015
Labour	Marie Rimmer	35,879	67.8%	8.0%
Conservative	Ed McRandal	11,536	21.8%	5.9%
Liberal Democrat	Brian Spencer	2,101	4.0%	-1.7%
UK Independence Party	Mark Hitchen	1,953	3.7%	-10.3%
Green	Jess Northey	1,417	2.7%	-1.9%

St Ives

CON HOLD

Majority: 312, 0.6% | Turnout: 51,226, 75.9% | Electorate: 67,145 | EU Ref: 55.1% Leave

PARTY	CANDIDATE	VOTES	SHARE	CHANGE 2015
Conservative	Derek Thomas	22,120	43.2%	4.9%
Liberal Democrat	Andrew George	21,808	42.6%	9.4%
Labour	Christopher Drew	7,298	14.2%	4.9%

Stafford

CON HOLD

Majority: 7,729, 14.8% | Turnout: 51,924, 75.9% | Electorate: 68,445 | EU Ref: 57.2% Leave

PARTY	CANDIDATE	VOTES	SHARE	CHANGE 2015
Conservative	Jeremy Lefroy	28,424	54.7%	6.3%
Labour	David Williams	20,695	39.9%	10.3%
Liberal Democrat	Christine Tinker	1,540	3.0%	0.2%
Green	Tony Pearce	1,265	2.4%	-0.4%

Staffordshire Moorlands

CON HOLD

Majority: 10,830, 24.2% | Turnout: 44,655, 67.6% | Electorate: 63,260 | EU Ref: 64.6% Leave

PARTY	CANDIDATE	VOTES	SHARE	CHANGE 2015
Conservative	Karen Bradley	25,963	58.1%	7.0%
Labour	Dave Jones	15,133	33.9%	6.7%
Independent	Nicholas Sheldon	1,524	3.4%	3.4%
Liberal Democrat	Henry Jebb	1,494	3.3%	-0.8%
Green	Mike Shone	541	1.2%	-1.7%

Stalybridge & Hyde

LAB HOLD

Majority: 8,084, 19.1% | Turnout: 42,457, 59.4% | Electorate: 71,409 | EU Ref: 58.5% Leave

PARTY	CANDIDATE	VOTES	SHARE	CHANGE 2015
Labour	Jonathan Reynolds	24,277	57.2%	12.2%
Conservative	Tom Dowse	16,193	38.1%	9.5%
Liberal Democrat	Paul Ankers	996	2.3%	-0.7%
Green	Julie Wood	991	2.3%	-2.2%

Stevenage

CON HOLD

Majority: 3,386, 6.9% | Turnout: 49,327, 69.7% | Electorate: 70,765 | EU Ref: 57.1% Leave

PARTY	CANDIDATE	VOTES	SHARE	CHANGE 2015
Conservative	Stephen McPartland	24,798	50.3%	5.7%
Labour	Sharon Taylor	21,412	43.4%	9.2%
Liberal Democrat	Barbara Gibson	2,032	4.1%	0.8%
Green	Victoria Snelling	1,085	2.2%	-0.7%

Stirling

CON GAIN FROM SNP

Majority: 148, 0.3% | Turnout: 49,356, 74.3% | Electorate: 66,415 | EU Ref: 32.3% Leave

PARTY	CANDIDATE	VOTES	SHARE	CHANGE 2015
Conservative	Stephen Kerr	18,291	37.1%	13.9%
Scottish National Party	Steven Paterson	18,143	36.8%	-8.9%
Labour	Chris Kane	10,902	22.1%	-3.4%
Liberal Democrat	Wendy Chamberlain	1,683	3.4%	0.7%
Women's Equality Party	Kirstein Rummery	337	0.7%	0.7%

Stockport

LAB HOLD

Majority: 14,477, 34.9% | Turnout: 41,544, 64.7% | Electorate: 64,236 | EU Ref: 48.2% Leave

PARTY	CANDIDATE	VOTES	SHARE	CHANGE 2015
Labour	Ann Coffey	26,282	63.3%	13.4%
Conservative	Daniel Hamilton	11,805	28.4%	3.9%
Liberal Democrat	Daniel Hawthorne	1,778	4.3%	-3.4%
UK Independence Party	John Kelly	1,088	2.6%	-10.5%
Green	Gary Lawson	591	1.4%	-3.0%

Stockton North

LAB HOLD

Majority: 8,715, 20.4% | Turnout: 42,731, 64.5% | Electorate: 66,285 | EU Ref: 66.5% Leave

PARTY	CANDIDATE	VOTES	SHARE	CHANGE 2015
Labour	Alex Cunningham	24,304	56.9%	7.8%
Conservative	Mark Fletcher	15,589	36.5%	8.5%
UK Independence Party	Ted Strike	1,834	4.3%	-14.9%
Liberal Democrat	Sarah Brown	646	1.5%	-0.7%
Green	Emma Robson	358	0.8%	0.8%

Stockton South

LAB GAIN FROM CON

Majority: 888, 1.7% | Turnout: 53,824, 71.2% | Electorate: 75,625 | EU Ref: 57.8% Leave

PARTY	CANDIDATE	VOTES	SHARE	CHANGE 2015
Labour	Paul Williams	26,102	48.5%	11.5%
Conservative	James Wharton	25,214	46.8%	0.1%
UK Independence Party	David Outterside	1,186	2.2%	-8.4%
Liberal Democrat	Drew Durning	951	1.8%	-0.9%
Green	Jo Fitzgerald	371	0.7%	-1.1%

Stoke-on-Trent Central

LAB HOLD

Majority: 3,897, 11.7% | Turnout: 33,145, 58.2% | Electorate: 56,915 | EU Ref: 65.0% Leave

PARTY	CANDIDATE	VOTES	SHARE	CHANGE 2015
Labour	Gareth Snell	17,083	51.5%	12.2%
Conservative	Daniel Jellyman	13,186	39.8%	17.2%
UK Independence Party	Mick Harold	1,608	4.9%	-17.8%
Liberal Democrat	Peter Andras	680	2.1%	-2.1%
Green	Adam Colclough	378	1.1%	-2.5%
Independent	Barbara Fielding	210	0.6%	0.6%

Stoke-on-Trent North

LAB HOLD

Majority: 2,359, 5.6% | Turnout: 41,786, 57.7% | Electorate: 71,558 | EU Ref: 72.1% Leave

PARTY	CANDIDATE	VOTES	SHARE	CHANGE 2015
Labour	Ruth Smeeth	21,272	50.9%	11.0%
Conservative	Ben Adams	18,913	45.3%	17.9%
Liberal Democrat	Richard Whelan	916	2.2%	-0.7%
Green	Douglas Rouxel	685	1.6%	-1.2%

Stoke-on-Trent South

CON GAIN FROM LAB

Majority: 663, 1.6% | Turnout: 41,690, 63.1% | Electorate: 66,057 | EU Ref: 70.8% Leave

PARTY	CANDIDATE	VOTES	SHARE	CHANGE 2015
Conservative	Jack Brereton	20,451	49.1%	16.4%
Labour	Rob Flello	19,788	47.5%	8.3%
Liberal Democrat	Ian Wilkes	808	1.9%	-1.4%
Green	Jan Zablocki	643	1.5%	-1.1%

Stone

CON HOLD

Majority: 17,495, 35.0% | Turnout: 50,032, 73.8% | Electorate: 67,824 | EU Ref: 58.0% Leave

PARTY	CANDIDATE	VOTES	SHARE	CHANGE 2015
Conservative	William Cash	31,614	63.2%	8.5%
Labour	Sam Hale	14,119	28.2%	8.1%
Liberal Democrat	Martin Lewis	2,222	4.4%	-0.8%
UK Independence Party	Edward Whitfield	1,370	2.7%	-13.5%
Green	Samantha Pancheri	707	1.4%	-1.1%

Stourbridge

CON HOLD
Majority: 7,654, 16.2% | Turnout: 47,135, 67.2% | Electorate: 70,215 | EU Ref: 65.1% Leave

PARTY	CANDIDATE	VOTES	SHARE	CHANGE 2015
Conservative	Margot James	25,706	54.5%	8.5%
Labour	Pete Lowe	18,052	38.3%	6.8%
UK Independence Party	Glen Wilson	1,801	3.8%	-13.1%
Liberal Democrat	Christopher Bramall	1,083	2.3%	-1.0%
Green	Andi Mohr	493	1.0%	-1.2%

Strangford

DUP HOLD
Majority: 18,343, 47.3% | Turnout: 38,749, 60.2% | Electorate: 64,327 | EU Ref: Not available

PARTY	CANDIDATE	VOTES	SHARE	CHANGE 2015
Democratic Unionist Party	Jim Shannon	24,036	62.0%	17.7%
Alliance Party	Kellie Armstrong	5,693	14.7%	0.9%
Ulster Unionist Party	Mike Nesbitt	4,419	11.4%	-2.9%
Social Democratic & Labour Party	Joe Boyle	2,404	6.2%	-0.7%
Sinn Fein	Carole Murphy	1,083	2.8%	0.2%
Green	Ricky Bamford	607	1.6%	1.6%
Conservative	Claire Hiscott	507	1.3%	-5.1%

Stratford-on-Avon

CON HOLD
Majority: 21,958, 41.0% | Turnout: 53,532, 73.9% | Electorate: 72,572 | EU Ref: 51.2% Leave

PARTY	CANDIDATE	VOTES	SHARE	CHANGE 2015
Conservative	Nadhim Zahawi	33,657	62.9%	5.2%
Labour	Jeff Kenner	11,699	21.9%	8.9%
Liberal Democrat	Elizabeth Adams	6,357	11.9%	0.1%
Green	Dominic Giles	1,345	2.5%	-1.6%
Independent	Jandy Spurway	255	0.5%	0.5%
Independent	Tom Darwood	219	0.4%	0.4%

Streatham

LAB HOLD

Majority: 26,285, 47.1% | Turnout: 55,795, 70.9% | Electorate: 78,649 | EU Ref: 20.5% Leave

PARTY	CANDIDATE	VOTES	SHARE	CHANGE 2015
Labour	Chuka Umunna	38,212	68.5%	15.5%
Conservative	Kim Caddy	11,927	21.4%	-3.7%
Liberal Democrat	Alex Davies	3,611	6.5%	-2.5%
Green	Nicole Griffiths	1,696	3.0%	-5.8%
UK Independence Party	Robert Stephenson	349	0.6%	-2.6%

Stretford & Urmston

LAB HOLD

Majority: 19,705, 39.3% | Turnout: 50,191, 69.9% | Electorate: 71,833 | EU Ref: 48.5% Leave

PARTY	CANDIDATE	VOTES	SHARE	CHANGE 2015
Labour	Kate Green	33,519	66.8%	13.7%
Conservative	Lisa Cooke	13,814	27.5%	-0.3%
UK Independence Party	Andrew Beaumont	1,094	2.2%	-8.7%
Liberal Democrat	Anna Fryer	1,001	2.0%	-0.9%
Green	Michael Ingleson	641	1.3%	-3.4%
Christian Peoples Alliance	Rose Doman	122	0.2%	0.2%

Stroud

LAB GAIN FROM CON
Majority: 687, 1.1% | Turnout: 63,816, 77.0% | Electorate: 82,839 | EU Ref: 46.0% Leave

PARTY	CANDIDATE	VOTES	SHARE	CHANGE 2015
Labour	David Drew	29,994	47.0%	9.3%
Conservative	Neil Carmichael	29,307	45.9%	0.2%
Liberal Democrat	Max Wilkinson	2,053	3.2%	-0.2%
Green	Sarah Lunnon	1,423	2.2%	-2.3%
UK Independence Party	Glenville Gogerly	1,039	1.6%	-6.3%

Suffolk Coastal

CON HOLD
Majority: 16,012, 27.6% | Turnout: 58,074, 73.2% | Electorate: 79,366 | EU Ref: 55.8% Leave

PARTY	CANDIDATE	VOTES	SHARE	CHANGE 2015
Conservative	Therese Coffey	33,713	58.1%	6.1%
Labour	Cameron Matthews	17,701	30.5%	12.5%
Liberal Democrat	James Sandbach	4,048	7.0%	-1.6%
Green	Eamonn O'Nolan	1,802	3.1%	-2.8%
Independent	Philip Young	810	1.4%	1.4%

Sunderland Central

LAB HOLD
Majority: 9,997, 22.1% | Turnout: 45,111, 62.0% | Electorate: 72,728 | EU Ref: 54.7% Leave

PARTY	CANDIDATE	VOTES	SHARE	CHANGE 2015
Labour	Julie Elliott	25,056	55.5%	5.4%
Conservative	Robert Oliver	15,059	33.4%	10.0%
UK Independence Party	Gary Leighton	2,209	4.9%	-14.3%
Liberal Democrat	Niall Hodson	1,777	3.9%	1.3%
Green	Rachel Featherstone	705	1.6%	-2.5%
Independent	Sean Cockburn	305	0.7%	0.7%

Surrey Heath

CON HOLD
Majority: 24,943, 43.1% | Turnout: 57,822, 71.6% | Electorate: 80,764 | EU Ref: 52.0% Leave

PARTY	CANDIDATE	VOTES	SHARE	CHANGE 2015
Conservative	Michael Gove	37,118	64.2%	4.3%
Labour	Laween Altroshi	12,175	21.1%	9.8%
Liberal Democrat	Anne-Marie Barker	6,271	10.8%	1.8%
Green	Sharon Galliford	2,258	3.9%	-0.5%

Sutton & Cheam

CON HOLD
Majority: 12,698, 24.4% | Turnout: 51,970, 73.8% | Electorate: 70,404 | EU Ref: 51.3% Leave

PARTY	CANDIDATE	VOTES	SHARE	CHANGE 2015
Conservative	Paul Scully	26,567	51.1%	9.6%
Liberal Democrat	Amna Ahmad	13,869	26.7%	-7.0%
Labour	Bonnie Craven	10,663	20.5%	9.4%
Green	Claire Jackson-Prior	871	1.7%	-0.4%

Sutton Coldfield

CON HOLD
Majority: 15,339, 29.1% | Turnout: 52,858, 69.9% | Electorate: 75,652 | EU Ref: 51.7% Leave

PARTY	CANDIDATE	VOTES	SHARE	CHANGE 2015
Conservative	Andrew Mitchell	32,224	61.0%	6.3%
Labour	Rob Pocock	16,885	31.9%	9.6%
Liberal Democrat	Jennifer Wilkinson	2,302	4.4%	-0.8%
Green	David Ratcliff	965	1.8%	-1.0%
Independent	Hannah Sophia	482	0.9%	0.9%

Swansea East

LAB HOLD

Majority: 13,168, 37.4% | Turnout: 35,159, 60.1% | Electorate: 58,521 | EU Ref: 62.1% Leave

PARTY	CANDIDATE	VOTES	SHARE	CHANGE 2015
Labour	Carolyn Harris	22,307	63.4%	10.5%
Conservative	Dan Boucher	9,139	26.0%	10.7%
Plaid Cymru	Steffan Phillips	1,689	4.8%	-5.6%
UK Independence Party	Clifford Johnson	1,040	3.0%	-14.2%
Liberal Democrat	Charley Hasted	625	1.8%	-2.4%
Green	Chris Evans	359	1.0%	1.0%

Swansea West

LAB HOLD

Majority: 10,598, 28.5% | Turnout: 37,282, 65.5% | Electorate: 56,892 | EU Ref: 42.7% Leave

PARTY	CANDIDATE	VOTES	SHARE	CHANGE 2015
Labour	Geraint Davies	22,278	59.8%	17.2%
Conservative	Craig Lawton	11,680	31.3%	8.8%
Plaid Cymru	Rhydian Fitter	1,529	4.1%	-2.3%
Liberal Democrat	Michael O'Carroll	1,269	3.4%	-5.6%
Green	Mike Whittall	434	1.2%	-3.9%
Socialist Party GB	Brian Johnson	92	0.2%	0.1%

Tamworth

CON HOLD

Majority: 12,347, 26.2% | Turnout: 47,110, 66.1% | Electorate: 71,308 | EU Ref: 66.0% Leave

PARTY	CANDIDATE	VOTES	SHARE	CHANGE 2015
Conservative	Christopher Pincher	28,748	61.0%	11.0%
Labour	Andrew Hammond	16,401	34.8%	8.7%
Liberal Democrat	Jenny Pinkett	1,961	4.2%	1.1%

Tatton

CON HOLD

Majority: 14,787, 30.1% | Turnout: 49,116, 72.4% | Electorate: 67,874 | EU Ref: 45.8% Leave

PARTY	CANDIDATE	VOTES	SHARE	CHANGE 2015
Conservative	Esther McVey	28,764	58.6%	-0.1%
Labour	Sam Rushworth	13,977	28.5%	10.1%
Liberal Democrat	Gareth Wilson	4,431	9.0%	0.5%
Green	Nigel Hennerley	1,024	2.1%	-1.7%
Independent	Quentin Abel	920	1.9%	1.9%

Taunton Deane

CON HOLD

Majority: 15,887, 25.2% | Turnout: 63,053, 73.8% | Electorate: 85,457 | EU Ref: 52.9% Leave

PARTY	CANDIDATE	VOTES	SHARE	CHANGE 2015
Conservative	Rebecca Pow	33,333	52.9%	4.8%
Liberal Democrat	Gideon Amos	17,446	27.7%	6.3%
Labour	Martin Jevon	9,689	15.4%	6.1%
UK Independence Party	Alan Dimmick	1,434	2.3%	-9.7%
Green	Clive Martin	1,151	1.8%	-2.7%

Telford

CON HOLD

Majority: 720, 1.6% | Turnout: 44,686, 66.3% | Electorate: 68,106 | EU Ref: 67.1% Leave

PARTY	CANDIDATE	VOTES	SHARE	CHANGE 2015
Conservative	Lucy Allan	21,777	48.7%	9.1%
Labour	Kuldip Sahota	21,057	47.1%	9.3%
Liberal Democrat	Susan King	954	2.1%	-0.1%
Green	Luke Shirley	898	2.0%	-0.3%

Tewkesbury

CON HOLD

Majority: 22,574, 38.2% | Turnout: 59,084, 72.5% | Electorate: 81,440 | EU Ref: 53.8% Leave

PARTY	CANDIDATE	VOTES	SHARE	CHANGE 2015
Conservative	Laurence Robertson	35,448	60.0%	5.5%
Labour	Manjinder Kang	12,874	21.8%	7.0%
Liberal Democrat	Cait Clucas	7,981	13.5%	-0.3%
Green	Cate Cody	1,576	2.7%	-1.3%
UK Independence Party	Simon Collins	1,205	2.0%	-10.8%

The Cotswolds

CON HOLD

Majority: 25,499, 42.7% | Turnout: 59,702, 74.2% | Electorate: 80,449 | EU Ref: 47.8% Leave

PARTY	CANDIDATE	VOTES	SHARE	CHANGE 2015
Conservative	Geoffrey Clifton-Brown	36,201	60.6%	4.1%
Labour	Mark Huband	10,702	17.9%	8.7%
Liberal Democrat	Andrew Gant	9,748	16.3%	-2.3%
Green	Sabrina Poole	1,747	2.9%	-1.7%
UK Independence Party	Chris Harlow	1,197	2.0%	-8.9%
Independent	Sandy Steel	107	0.2%	0.2%

The Wrekin

CON HOLD

Majority: 9,564, 19.3% | Turnout: 49,523, 72.1% | Electorate: 68,604 | EU Ref: 58.2% Leave

PARTY	CANDIDATE	VOTES	SHARE	CHANGE 2015
Conservative	Mark Pritchard	27,451	55.4%	5.7%
Labour	Dylan Harrison	17,887	36.1%	10.1%
UK Independence Party	Denis Allen	1,656	3.3%	-13.4%
Liberal Democrat	Rod Keyes	1,345	2.7%	-1.6%
Green	Pat McCarthy	804	1.6%	-1.6%
Independent	Fay Easton	380	0.8%	0.8%

Thirsk & Malton

CON HOLD

Majority: 19,001, 33.9% | Turnout: 55,929, 71.1% | Electorate: 78,670 | EU Ref: 56.4% Leave

PARTY	CANDIDATE	VOTES	SHARE	CHANGE 2015
Conservative	Kevin Hollinrake	33,572	60.0%	7.4%
Labour	Alan Avery	14,571	26.1%	10.6%
Liberal Democrat	Dinah Keal	3,859	6.9%	-2.1%
UK Independence Party	Toby Horton	1,532	2.7%	-12.2%
Green	Martin Brampton	1,100	2.0%	-2.6%
Liberal	John Clark	753	1.3%	-0.8%
Independent	Philip Tate	542	1.0%	-0.4%

Thornbury & Yate

CON HOLD

Majority: 12,071, 23.9% | Turnout: 50,690, 74.6% | Electorate: 67,892 | EU Ref: 53.3% Leave

PARTY	CANDIDATE	VOTES	SHARE	CHANGE 2015
Conservative	Luke Hall	28,008	55.3%	14.2%
Liberal Democrat	Claire Young	15,937	31.4%	-6.5%
Labour	Brian Mead	6,112	12.1%	4.3%
Green	Iain Hamilton	633	1.2%	-1.5%

Thurrock

CON HOLD

Majority: 345, 0.7% | Turnout: 50,325, 64.4% | Electorate: 78,154 | EU Ref: 70.3% Leave

PARTY	CANDIDATE	VOTES	SHARE	CHANGE 2015
Conservative	Jackie Doyle-Price	19,880	39.5%	5.8%
Labour	John Kent	19,535	38.8%	6.2%
UK Independence Party	Tim Aker	10,112	20.1%	-11.6%
Liberal Democrat	Kevin McNamara	798	1.6%	0.3%

Tiverton & Honiton

CON HOLD

Majority: 19,801, 34.3% | Turnout: 57,815, 71.5% | Electorate: 80,731 | EU Ref: 57.6% Leave

PARTY	CANDIDATE	VOTES	SHARE	CHANGE 2015
Conservative	Neil Parish	35,471	61.4%	7.4%
Labour	Caroline Kolek	15,670	27.1%	14.4%
Liberal Democrat	Matthew Wilson	4,639	8.0%	-2.4%
Green	Gill Westcott	2,035	3.5%	-2.8%

Tonbridge & Malling

CON HOLD

Majority: 23,508, 41.3% | Turnout: 56,907, 73.7% | Electorate: 77,417 | EU Ref: 52.6% Leave

PARTY	CANDIDATE	VOTES	SHARE	CHANGE 2015
Conservative	Thomas Tugendhat	36,218	63.6%	4.2%
Labour	Dylan Jones	12,710	22.3%	8.2%
Liberal Democrat	Keith Miller	3,787	6.7%	-0.2%
Green	April Clark	2,335	4.1%	-0.3%
UK Independence Party	Colin Bullen	1,857	3.3%	-11.9%

Tooting

LAB HOLD

Majority: 15,458, 26.5% | Turnout: 58,171, 74.7% | Electorate: 77,971 | EU Ref: 25.3% Leave

PARTY	CANDIDATE	VOTES	SHARE	CHANGE 2015
Labour	Rosena Allin-Khan	34,694	59.6%	12.4%
Conservative	Dan Watkins	19,236	33.1%	-8.8%
Liberal Democrat	Alexander Glassbrook	3,057	5.3%	1.3%
Green	Esther Obiri-Darko	845	1.5%	-2.7%
UK Independence Party	Ryan Coshall	339	0.6%	-2.3%

Torbay

CON HOLD
Majority: 14,283, 27.9% | Turnout: 51,174, 67.4% | Electorate: 75,931 | EU Ref: 62.7% Leave

PARTY	CANDIDATE	VOTES	SHARE	CHANGE 2015
Conservative	Kevin Foster	27,141	53.0%	12.4%
Liberal Democrat	Deborah Brewer	12,858	25.1%	-8.7%
Labour	Paul Raybould	9,310	18.2%	9.5%
UK Independence Party	Tony McIntyre	1,213	2.4%	-11.2%
Green	Sam Moss	652	1.3%	-2.0%

Torfaen

LAB HOLD
Majority: 10,240, 26.6% | Turnout: 38,429, 62.2% | Electorate: 61,839 | EU Ref: 60.9% Leave

PARTY	CANDIDATE	VOTES	SHARE	CHANGE 2015
Labour	Nick Thomas-Symonds	22,134	57.6%	12.9%
Conservative	Graham Smith	11,894	31.0%	7.8%
Plaid Cymru	Jeff Rees	2,059	5.4%	-0.4%
UK Independence Party	Ian Williams	1,490	3.9%	-15.1%
Liberal Democrat	Andrew Best	852	2.2%	-1.1%

Torridge & West Devon

CON HOLD
Majority: 20,686, 34.8% | Turnout: 59,480, 73.9% | Electorate: 80,524 | EU Ref: 57.1% Leave

PARTY	CANDIDATE	VOTES	SHARE	CHANGE 2015
Conservative	Geoffrey Cox	33,612	56.5%	5.7%
Labour	Vince Barry	12,926	21.7%	11.1%
Liberal Democrat	David Chalmers	10,526	17.7%	4.5%
Green	Chris Jordan	1,622	2.7%	-4.2%
Independent	Robin Julian	794	1.3%	1.3%

Totnes

CON HOLD
Majority: 13,477, 26.9% | Turnout: 50,270, 73.4% | Electorate: 68,914 | EU Ref: 54.1% Leave

PARTY	CANDIDATE	VOTES	SHARE	CHANGE 2015
Conservative	Sarah Wollaston	26,972	53.7%	0.7%
Labour	Gerrie Messer	13,495	26.8%	14.1%
Liberal Democrat	Julian Brazil	6,466	12.9%	3.0%
Green	Jacqi Hodgson	2,097	4.2%	-6.1%
UK Independence Party	Steven Harvey	1,240	2.5%	-11.7%

Tottenham

LAB HOLD
Majority: 34,584, 70.1% | Turnout: 49,339, 67.7% | Electorate: 72,884 | EU Ref: 33.4% Leave

PARTY	CANDIDATE	VOTES	SHARE	CHANGE 2015
Labour	David Lammy	40,249	81.6%	14.2%
Conservative	Myles Stacey	5,665	11.5%	-0.5%
Liberal Democrat	Brian Haley	1,687	3.4%	-0.7%
Green	Jarelle Francis	1,276	2.6%	-6.7%
UK Independence Party	Patricia Rumble	462	0.9%	-2.6%

Truro & Falmouth

CON HOLD
Majority: 3,792, 6.7% | Turnout: 56,647, 75.8% | Electorate: 74,683 | EU Ref: 46.2% Leave

PARTY	CANDIDATE	VOTES	SHARE	CHANGE 2015
Conservative	Sarah Newton	25,123	44.4%	0.3%
Labour	Jayne Kirkham	21,331	37.7%	22.5%
Liberal Democrat	Rob Nolan	8,465	14.9%	-1.9%
UK Independence Party	Duncan Odgers	897	1.6%	-10.0%
Green	Amanda Pennington	831	1.5%	-7.2%

Tunbridge Wells

CON HOLD

Majority: 16,465, 30.4% | Turnout: 54,209, 72.1% | Electorate: 74,782 | EU Ref: 44.7% Leave

PARTY	CANDIDATE	VOTES	SHARE	CHANGE 2015
Conservative	Greg Clark	30,856	56.9%	-1.8%
Labour	Charles Woodgate	14,391	26.5%	12.3%
Liberal Democrat	Rachel Sadler	5,355	9.9%	1.4%
UK Independence Party	Chris Hoare	1,464	2.7%	-9.9%
Green	Trevor Bisdee	1,441	2.7%	-2.5%
Women's Equality Party	Celine Thomas	702	1.3%	1.3%

Twickenham

LIB DEM GAIN FROM CON

Majority: 9,762, 14.8% | Turnout: 66,290, 79.5% | Electorate: 83,362 | EU Ref: 33.7% Leave

PARTY	CANDIDATE	VOTES	SHARE	CHANGE 2015
Liberal Democrat	Vince Cable	34,969	52.8%	14.7%
Conservative	Tania Mathias	25,207	38.0%	-3.2%
Labour	Katherine Dunne	6,114	9.2%	-2.3%

Tynemouth

LAB HOLD

Majority: 11,666, 20.5% | Turnout: 56,858, 73.4% | Electorate: 77,434 | EU Ref: 47.8% Leave

PARTY	CANDIDATE	VOTES	SHARE	CHANGE 2015
Labour	Alan Campbell	32,395	57.0%	8.8%
Conservative	Nick Varley	20,729	36.5%	3.6%
Liberal Democrat	John Appleby	1,724	3.0%	0.1%
UK Independence Party	Stuart Houghton	1,257	2.2%	-10.0%
Green	Julia Erskine	629	1.1%	-2.7%
Independent	Anthony The Durham Cobbler	124	0.2%	0.2%

Upper Bann

DUP HOLD

Majority: 7,992, 15.6% | Turnout: 51,258, 63.9% | Electorate: 80,168 | EU Ref: Not available

PARTY	CANDIDATE	VOTES	SHARE	CHANGE 2015
Democratic Unionist Party	David Simpson	22,317	43.5%	10.9%
Sinn Fein	John O Dowd	14,325	27.9%	3.4%
Ulster Unionist Party	Doug Beattie	7,900	15.4%	-12.5%
Social Democratic & Labour Party	Declan McAlinden	4,397	8.6%	-0.4%
Alliance Party	Tara Doyle	2,319	4.5%	0.8%

Uxbridge & South Ruislip

CON HOLD

Majority: 5,034, 10.8% | Turnout: 46,694, 66.8% | Electorate: 69,936 | EU Ref: 56.4% Leave

PARTY	CANDIDATE	VOTES	SHARE	CHANGE 2015
Conservative	Boris Johnson	23,716	50.8%	0.6%
Labour	Vincent Lo	18,682	40.0%	13.6%
Liberal Democrat	Rosina Robson	1,835	3.9%	-1.0%
UK Independence Party	Elizabeth Kemp	1,577	3.4%	-10.8%
Green	Mark Keir	884	1.9%	-1.3%

Vale of Clwyd

LAB GAIN FROM CON

Majority: 2,379, 6.1% | Turnout: 38,684, 68.0% | Electorate: 56,890 | EU Ref: 55.9% Leave

PARTY	CANDIDATE	VOTES	SHARE	CHANGE 2015
Labour	Chris Ruane	19,423	50.2%	11.9%
Conservative	James Davies	17,044	44.1%	5.0%
Plaid Cymru	David Wyatt	1,551	4.0%	-3.0%
Liberal Democrat	Gwyn Williams	666	1.7%	-0.9%

Vale of Glamorgan

CON HOLD
Majority: 2,190, 4.1% | Turnout: 53,718, 72.6% | Electorate: 73,959 | EU Ref: 52.3% Leave

PARTY	CANDIDATE	VOTES	SHARE	CHANGE 2015
Conservative	Alun Cairns	25,501	47.5%	1.4%
Labour	Camilla Beaven	23,311	43.4%	10.8%
Plaid Cymru	Ian Johnson	2,295	4.3%	-1.3%
Liberal Democrat	Jennifer Geroni	1,020	1.9%	-0.7%
UK Independence Party	Melanie Hunter-Clarke	868	1.6%	-9.1%
Green	Stephen Davis-Barker	419	0.8%	-1.3%
Women's Equality Party	Sharon Lovell	177	0.3%	0.3%
Pirate Party	David Elston	127	0.2%	0.2%

Vauxhall

LAB HOLD
Majority: 20,250, 36.8% | Turnout: 55,042, 67.3% | Electorate: 82,055 | EU Ref: 22.4% Leave

PARTY	CANDIDATE	VOTES	SHARE	CHANGE 2015
Labour	Kate Hoey	31,576	57.4%	3.6%
Liberal Democrat	George Turner	11,326	20.6%	13.7%
Conservative	Dolly Theis	10,277	18.7%	-8.6%
Green	Gulnar Hasnain	1,152	2.1%	-5.5%
Women's Equality Party	Harini Iyengar	539	1.0%	1.0%
Pirate Party	Mark Chapman	172	0.3%	-0.1%

Wakefield

LAB HOLD
Majority: 2,176, 4.7% | Turnout: 46,284, 65.8% | Electorate: 70,340 | EU Ref: 62.0% Leave

PARTY	CANDIDATE	VOTES	SHARE	CHANGE 2015
Labour	Mary Creagh	22,987	49.7%	9.4%
Conservative	Antony Calvert	20,811	45.0%	10.8%
The Yorkshire Party	Lucy Brown	1,176	2.5%	2.5%
Liberal Democrat	Denis Cronin	943	2.0%	-1.4%
Independent	Waj Ali	367	0.8%	0.8%

Wallasey

LAB HOLD

Majority: 23,320, 48.3% | Turnout: 48,353, 71.7% | Electorate: 67,454 | EU Ref: 49.9% Leave

PARTY	CANDIDATE	VOTES	SHARE	CHANGE 2015
Labour	Angela Eagle	34,552	71.5%	11.1%
Conservative	Andy Livsey	11,232	23.2%	0.6%
UK Independence Party	Debbie Caplin	1,160	2.4%	-9.3%
Liberal Democrat	Paul Childs	772	1.6%	0.7%
Green	Lily Clough	637	1.3%	-1.7%

Walsall North

CON GAIN FROM LAB

Majority: 2,601, 6.8% | Turnout: 38,118, 57.3% | Electorate: 67,308 | EU Ref: 71.9% Leave

PARTY	CANDIDATE	VOTES	SHARE	CHANGE 2015
Conservative	Eddie Hughes	18,919	49.6%	15.9%
Labour	David Winnick	16,318	42.8%	3.8%
UK Independence Party	Liz Hazell	2,295	6.0%	-16.0%
Liberal Democrat	Isabelle Parasram	586	1.5%	0.7%

Walsall South

LAB HOLD

Majority: 8,892, 20.2% | Turnout: 44,072, 66.4% | Electorate: 67,417 | EU Ref: 63.6% Leave

PARTY	CANDIDATE	VOTES	SHARE	CHANGE 2015
Labour	Valerie Vaz	25,286	57.4%	10.2%
Conservative	James Bird	16,394	37.2%	4.4%
UK Independence Party	Derek Bennett	1,805	4.1%	-11.5%
Liberal Democrat	Anna Wellings Purvis	587	1.3%	-0.3%

Walthamstow

LAB HOLD

Majority: 32,017, 66.5% | Turnout: 48,143, 70.7% | Electorate: 67,957 | EU Ref: 36.4% Leave

PARTY	CANDIDATE	VOTES	SHARE	CHANGE 2015
Labour	Stella Creasy	38,793	80.6%	11.7%
Conservative	Molly Samuel	6,776	14.1%	0.7%
Liberal Democrat	Ukonu Obasi	1,384	2.9%	-1.1%
Green	Andrew Johns	1,190	2.5%	-3.9%

Wansbeck

LAB HOLD

Majority: 10,435, 24.6% | Turnout: 42,454, 68.4% | Electorate: 62,151 | EU Ref: 56.2% Leave

PARTY	CANDIDATE	VOTES	SHARE	CHANGE 2015
Labour	Ian Lavery	24,338	57.3%	7.3%
Conservative	Chris Galley	13,903	32.7%	11.0%
Liberal Democrat	Joan Tebbutt	2,015	4.7%	-1.5%
UK Independence Party	Melanie Hurst	1,483	3.5%	-14.7%
Green	Steven Leyland	715	1.7%	-2.1%

Wantage

CON HOLD

Majority: 17,380, 27.3% | Turnout: 63,602, 72.5% | Electorate: 85,786 | EU Ref: 46.4% Leave

PARTY	CANDIDATE	VOTES	SHARE	CHANGE 2015
Conservative	Ed Vaizey	34,459	54.2%	0.9%
Labour	Rachel Eden	17,079	26.9%	10.8%
Liberal Democrat	Chris Carrigan	9,234	14.5%	1.5%
Green	Sue Ap-Roberts	1,546	2.4%	-2.7%
UK Independence Party	David McLeod	1,284	2.0%	-10.5%

Warley

LAB HOLD
Majority: 16,483, 41.0% | Turnout: 40,206, 63.1% | Electorate: 63,739 | EU Ref: 61.8% Leave

PARTY	CANDIDATE	VOTES	SHARE	CHANGE 2015
Labour	John Spellar	27,004	67.2%	9.0%
Conservative	Anthony Mangnall	10,521	26.2%	6.8%
UK Independence Party	Darryl Magher	1,349	3.4%	-13.1%
Liberal Democrat	Bryan Manley-Green	777	1.9%	-0.2%
Green	Mark Redding	555	1.4%	-2.5%

Warrington North

LAB HOLD
Majority: 9,582, 19.8% | Turnout: 48,517, 67.4% | Electorate: 71,918 | EU Ref: 58.6% Leave

PARTY	CANDIDATE	VOTES	SHARE	CHANGE 2015
Labour	Helen Jones	27,356	56.4%	8.6%
Conservative	Val Allen	17,774	36.6%	8.5%
UK Independence Party	James Ashington	1,561	3.2%	-13.9%
Liberal Democrat	Stefan Krizanac	1,207	2.5%	-1.7%
Green	Lyndsay McAteer	619	1.3%	-1.5%

Warrington South

LAB GAIN FROM CON
Majority: 2,549, 4.1% | Turnout: 61,995, 72.4% | Electorate: 85,617 | EU Ref: 50.6% Leave

PARTY	CANDIDATE	VOTES	SHARE	CHANGE 2015
Labour	Faisal Rashid	29,994	48.4%	9.3%
Conservative	David Mowat	27,445	44.3%	0.6%
Liberal Democrat	Bob Barr	3,339	5.4%	-0.2%
Independent	John Boulton	1,217	2.0%	2.0%

Warwick & Leamington

LAB GAIN FROM CON
Majority: 1,206, 2.3% | Turnout: 54,055, 72.8% | Electorate: 74,237 | EU Ref: 41.1% Leave

PARTY	CANDIDATE	VOTES	SHARE	CHANGE 2015
Labour	Matt Western	25,227	46.7%	11.8%
Conservative	Chris White	24,021	44.4%	-3.5%
Liberal Democrat	Nick Solman	2,810	5.2%	0.2%
Green	Jonathan Chilvers	1,198	2.2%	-1.7%
UK Independence Party	Bob Dhillon	799	1.5%	-6.8%

Washington & Sunderland West

LAB HOLD
Majority: 12,940, 31.9% | Turnout: 40,574, 60.3% | Electorate: 67,280 | EU Ref: 65.1% Leave

PARTY	CANDIDATE	VOTES	SHARE	CHANGE 2015
Labour	Sharon Hodgson	24,639	60.7%	5.8%
Conservative	Jonathan Gullis	11,699	28.8%	10.0%
UK Independence Party	Bryan Foster	2,761	6.8%	-12.8%
Liberal Democrat	Tom Appleby	961	2.4%	-0.3%
Green	Michal Chantkowski	514	1.3%	-1.7%

Watford

CON HOLD
Majority: 2,092, 3.6% | Turnout: 58,610, 67.8% | Electorate: 86,507 | EU Ref: 51.2% Leave

PARTY	CANDIDATE	VOTES	SHARE	CHANGE 2015
Conservative	Richard Harrington	26,731	45.6%	2.2%
Labour	Chris Ostrowski	24,639	42.0%	16.0%
Liberal Democrat	Ian Stotesbury	5,335	9.1%	-9.0%
UK Independence Party	Ian Green	1,184	2.0%	-7.7%
Green	Alex Murray	721	1.2%	-1.1%

Waveney

CON HOLD
Majority: 9,215, 17.5% | Turnout: 52,674, 65.2% | Electorate: 80,763 | EU Ref: 63.2% Leave

PARTY	CANDIDATE	VOTES	SHARE	CHANGE 2015
Conservative	Peter Aldous	28,643	54.4%	12.0%
Labour	Sonia Barker	19,428	36.9%	-0.9%
UK Independence Party	Bert Poole	1,933	3.7%	-10.9%
Green	Elfreda Brambley-Crawshaw	1,332	2.5%	-0.8%
Liberal Democrat	Jacky Howe	1,012	1.9%	-0.1%
Independent	Allyson Barron	326	0.6%	0.6%

Wealden

CON HOLD
Majority: 23,628, 39.0% | Turnout: 60,464, 74.3% | Electorate: 81,425 | EU Ref: 52.5% Leave

PARTY	CANDIDATE	VOTES	SHARE	CHANGE 2015
Conservative	Nusrat Ghani	37,027	61.2%	4.2%
Labour	Angela Smith	13,399	22.2%	11.3%
Liberal Democrat	Chris Bowers	6,281	10.4%	1.3%
Green	Colin Stocks	1,959	3.2%	-3.1%
UK Independence Party	Nicola Burton	1,798	3.0%	-13.8%

Weaver Vale

LAB GAIN FROM CON
Majority: 3,928, 7.8% | Turnout: 50,613, 73.3% | Electorate: 69,016 | EU Ref: 50.2% Leave

PARTY	CANDIDATE	VOTES	SHARE	CHANGE 2015
Labour	Mike Amesbury	26,066	51.5%	10.1%
Conservative	Graham Evans	22,138	43.7%	0.6%
Liberal Democrat	Paul Roberts	1,623	3.2%	0.2%
Green	Christopher Copeman	786	1.6%	-1.0%

Wellingborough

CON HOLD
Majority: 12,460, 23.4% | Turnout: 53,240, 67.2% | Electorate: 79,254 | EU Ref: 62.9% Leave

PARTY	CANDIDATE	VOTES	SHARE	CHANGE 2015
Conservative	Peter Bone	30,579	57.4%	5.4%
Labour	Andrea Watts	18,119	34.0%	14.5%
UK Independence Party	Allan Shipman	1,804	3.4%	-16.2%
Liberal Democrat	Chris Nelson	1,782	3.3%	-1.1%
Green	Jonathan Hornett	956	1.8%	-2.6%

Wells

CON HOLD
Majority: 7,582, 12.5% | Turnout: 60,843, 73.8% | Electorate: 82,451 | EU Ref: 53.5% Leave

PARTY	CANDIDATE	VOTES	SHARE	CHANGE 2015
Conservative	James Heappey	30,488	50.1%	4.0%
Liberal Democrat	Tessa Munt	22,906	37.6%	4.9%
Labour	Andy Merryfield	7,129	11.7%	5.1%
Christian Peoples Alliance	Lorna Corke	320	0.5%	0.5%

Welwyn Hatfield

CON HOLD
Majority: 7,369, 14.2% | Turnout: 51,669, 70.9% | Electorate: 72,888 | EU Ref: 52.5% Leave

PARTY	CANDIDATE	VOTES	SHARE	CHANGE 2015
Conservative	Grant Shapps	26,374	51.0%	0.7%
Labour	Anawar Miah	19,005	36.8%	10.6%
Liberal Democrat	Nigel Quinton	3,836	7.4%	1.2%
UK Independence Party	Dean Milliken	1,441	2.8%	-10.3%
Green	Christianne Sayers	835	1.6%	-1.9%
Independent	Melvyn Jones	178	0.3%	0.3%

Wentworth & Dearne

LAB HOLD

Majority: 14,803, 33.7% | Turnout: 43,947, 58.7% | Electorate: 74,890 | EU Ref: 70.7% Leave

PARTY	CANDIDATE	VOTES	SHARE	CHANGE 2015
Labour	John Healey	28,547	65.0%	8.1%
Conservative	Steven Jackson	13,744	31.3%	16.4%
Liberal Democrat	Janice Middleton	1,656	3.8%	1.1%

West Aberdeenshire & Kincardine

CON GAIN FROM SNP

Majority: 7,950, 15.4% | Turnout: 51,625, 71.2% | Electorate: 72,477 | EU Ref: 38.6% Leave

PARTY	CANDIDATE	VOTES	SHARE	CHANGE 2015
Conservative	Andrew Bowie	24,704	47.9%	19.0%
Scottish National Party	Stuart Donaldson	16,754	32.5%	-9.1%
Labour	Barry Black	5,706	11.1%	6.5%
Liberal Democrat	John Waddell	4,461	8.6%	-12.8%

West Bromwich East

LAB HOLD

Majority: 7,713, 19.8% | Turnout: 39,098, 61.2% | Electorate: 63,846 | EU Ref: 67.6% Leave

PARTY	CANDIDATE	VOTES	SHARE	CHANGE 2015
Labour	Tom Watson	22,664	58.0%	7.8%
Conservative	Emma Crane	14,951	38.2%	13.3%
Liberal Democrat	Karen Trench	625	1.6%	-0.4%
Green	John Macefield	533	1.4%	-0.3%
Independent	Colin Rankine	325	0.8%	0.8%

West Bromwich West

LAB HOLD

Majority: 4,460, 12.4% | Turnout: 36,094, 54.7% | Electorate: 65,967 | EU Ref: 69.1% Leave

PARTY	CANDIDATE	VOTES	SHARE	CHANGE 2015
Labour	Adrian Bailey	18,789	52.1%	4.7%
Conservative	Andrew Hardie	14,329	39.7%	15.8%
UK Independence Party	Star Anderton	2,320	6.4%	-18.8%
Liberal Democrat	Flo Clucas	333	0.9%	-0.6%
Green	Robert Buckman	323	0.9%	-1.1%

West Dorset

CON HOLD

Majority: 19,091, 32.0% | Turnout: 59,598, 75.4% | Electorate: 82,277 | EU Ref: 51.0% Leave

PARTY	CANDIDATE	VOTES	SHARE	CHANGE 2015
Conservative	Oliver Letwin	33,081	55.5%	5.3%
Liberal Democrat	Andy Canning	13,990	23.5%	1.9%
Labour	Lee Rhodes	10,896	18.3%	8.3%
Green	Kelvin Clayton	1,631	2.7%	-3.0%

West Dunbartonshire

SNP HOLD

Majority: 2,288, 5.2% | Turnout: 44,083, 65.1% | Electorate: 67,602 | EU Ref: 38.0% Leave

PARTY	CANDIDATE	VOTES	SHARE	CHANGE 2015
Scottish National Party	Martin Docherty-Hughes	18,890	42.9%	-16.2%
Labour	Jean Anne Mitchell	16,602	37.7%	6.3%
Conservative	Penny Hutton	7,582	17.2%	10.2%
Liberal Democrat	Rebecca Plenderleith	1,009	2.3%	0.7%

West Ham

LAB HOLD
Majority: 36,754, 60.5% | Turnout: 60,708, 65.7% | Electorate: 92,418 | EU Ref: 47.4% Leave

PARTY	CANDIDATE	VOTES	SHARE	CHANGE 2015
Labour	Lyn Brown	46,591	76.7%	8.3%
Conservative	Patrick Spencer	9,837	16.2%	0.8%
Liberal Democrat	Paul Reynolds	1,836	3.0%	0.3%
UK Independence Party	Rosamund Beattie	1,134	1.9%	-5.6%
Green	Michael Spracklin	957	1.6%	-3.4%
Christian Peoples Alliance	Kayode Shedowo	353	0.6%	-0.1%

West Lancashire

LAB HOLD
Majority: 11,689, 21.5% | Turnout: 54,389, 74.2% | Electorate: 73,257 | EU Ref: 54.9% Leave

PARTY	CANDIDATE	VOTES	SHARE	CHANGE 2015
Labour	Rosie Cooper	32,030	58.9%	9.6%
Conservative	Sam Currie	20,341	37.4%	5.0%
Liberal Democrat	Jo Barton	1,069	2.0%	-0.6%
Green	Nate Higgins	680	1.3%	-1.9%
War Veteran's Pro-Traditional Family Party	David Braid	269	0.5%	0.2%

West Suffolk

CON HOLD
Majority: 17,063, 33.0% | Turnout: 51,746, 67.2% | Electorate: 77,348 | EU Ref: 63.3% Leave

PARTY	CANDIDATE	VOTES	SHARE	CHANGE 2015
Conservative	Matthew Hancock	31,649	61.2%	9.0%
Labour	Michael Jefferys	14,586	28.2%	10.7%
UK Independence Party	Julian Flood	2,396	4.6%	-17.1%
Liberal Democrat	Elfreda Tealby-Watson	2,180	4.2%	-0.8%
Green	Donald Allwright	935	1.8%	-1.8%

West Tyrone

SF HOLD
Majority: 10,342, 23.8% | Turnout: 43,486, 67.9% | Electorate: 64,009 | EU Ref: Not available

PARTY	CANDIDATE	VOTES	SHARE	CHANGE 2015
Sinn Féin	Barry McElduff	22,060	50.7%	7.2%
Democratic Unionist Party	Thomas Buchanan	11,718	26.9%	9.5%
Social Democratic & Labour Party	Daniel McCrossan	5,635	13.0%	-3.7%
Ulster Unionist Party	Alicia Clarke	2,253	5.2%	-10.7%
Alliance Party	Stephen Donnelly	1,000	2.3%	0.1%
Green	Ciaran McClean	427	1.0%	-1.0%
Citizens Indepement Social Thought Alliance	Barry Brown	393	0.9%	0.9%

West Worcestershire

CON HOLD
Majority: 21,328, 37.8% | Turnout: 56,471, 75.9% | Electorate: 74,375 | EU Ref: 52.6% Leave

PARTY	CANDIDATE	VOTES	SHARE	CHANGE 2015
Conservative	Harriett Baldwin	34,703	61.5%	5.4%
Labour	Samantha Charles	13,375	23.7%	10.3%
Liberal Democrat	Edward McMillan-Scott	5,307	9.4%	-0.3%
Green	Natalie McVey	1,605	2.8%	-3.6%
UK Independence Party	Mike Savage	1,481	2.6%	-11.7%

Westminster North

LAB HOLD
Majority: 11,512, 26.6% | Turnout: 43,295, 67.8% | Electorate: 63,846 | EU Ref: 33.0% Leave

PARTY	CANDIDATE	VOTES	SHARE	CHANGE 2015
Labour	Karen Buck	25,934	59.9%	13.1%
Conservative	Lindsey Hall	14,422	33.3%	-8.5%
Liberal Democrat	Alex Harding	2,253	5.2%	1.5%
Green	Emmanuelle Tandy	595	1.4%	-2.0%
Independent	Abby Dharamsey	91	0.2%	0.2%

Westmorland & Lonsdale

LIB DEM HOLD

Majority: 777, 1.5% | Turnout: 51,687, 77.9% | Electorate: 66,391 | EU Ref: 47.5% Leave

PARTY	CANDIDATE	VOTES	SHARE	CHANGE 2015
Liberal Democrat	Tim Farron	23,686	45.8%	-5.7%
Conservative	James Airey	22,909	44.3%	11.1%
Labour	Eli Aldridge	4,783	9.3%	3.8%
Independent	Mr Fishfinger	309	0.6%	0.6%

Weston-Super-Mare

CON HOLD

Majority: 11,544, 20.4% | Turnout: 56,415, 68.7% | Electorate: 82,136 | EU Ref: 56.7% Leave

PARTY	CANDIDATE	VOTES	SHARE	CHANGE 2015
Conservative	John Penrose	29,982	53.1%	5.2%
Labour	Timothy Taylor	18,438	32.7%	14.4%
Liberal Democrat	Mike Bell	5,175	9.2%	-1.3%
UK Independence Party	Helen Hims	1,932	3.4%	-14.4%
Green	Suneil Basu	888	1.6%	-3.4%

Wigan

LAB HOLD

Majority: 16,027, 33.7% | Turnout: 47,542, 63.1% | Electorate: 75,359 | EU Ref: 62.7% Leave

PARTY	CANDIDATE	VOTES	SHARE	CHANGE 2015
Labour	Lisa Nandy	29,575	62.2%	10.0%
Conservative	Alexander Williams	13,548	28.5%	7.8%
UK Independence Party	Nathan Ryding	2,750	5.8%	-13.7%
Liberal Democrat	Mark Clayton	916	1.9%	-0.8%
Green	William Patterson	753	1.6%	-1.2%

Wimbledon

CON HOLD

Majority: 5,622, 10.9% | Turnout: 51,526, 77.2% | Electorate: 66,780 | EU Ref: 27.0% Leave

PARTY	CANDIDATE	VOTES	SHARE	CHANGE 2015
Conservative	Stephen Hammond	23,946	46.5%	-5.6%
Labour	Imran Uddin	18,324	35.6%	9.5%
Liberal Democrat	Carl Quilliam	7,472	14.5%	1.8%
Green	Charles Barraball	1,231	2.4%	-1.7%
UK Independence Party	Strachan McDonald	553	1.1%	-4.0%

Winchester

CON HOLD

Majority: 9,999, 17.5% | Turnout: 57,156, 78.8% | Electorate: 72,497 | EU Ref: 39.7% Leave

PARTY	CANDIDATE	VOTES	SHARE	CHANGE 2015
Conservative	Steve Brine	29,729	52.0%	-3.0%
Liberal Democrat	Jackie Porter	19,730	34.5%	10.1%
Labour	Mark Chaloner	6,007	11.7%	3.4%
Green	Andrew Wainwright	846	1.5%	-3.3%
UK Independence Party	Martin Lyon	695	1.2%	-6.3%
Justice & Anti-Corruption Party	Teresa Skelton	149	0.3%	0.3%

Windsor

CON HOLD

Majority: 22,384, 41.5% | Turnout: 53,921, 73.3% | Electorate: 73,595 | EU Ref: 46.1% Leave

PARTY	CANDIDATE	VOTES	SHARE	CHANGE 2015
Conservative	Adam Afriyie	34,718	64.4%	1.0%
Labour	Peter Shearman	12,334	22.9%	9.5%
Liberal Democrat	Julian Tisi	5,434	10.1%	1.5%
Green	Fintan McKeown	1,435	2.7%	-1.0%

Wirral South

LAB HOLD

Majority: 8,323, 18.4% | Turnout: 45,195, 78.4% | Electorate: 57,670 | EU Ref: 45.6% Leave

PARTY	CANDIDATE	VOTES	SHARE	CHANGE 2015
Labour	Alison McGovern	25,871	57.2%	9.0%
Conservative	Adam Sykes	17,548	38.8%	1.6%
Liberal Democrat	Chris Carubia	1,322	2.9%	-0.6%
Green	Mandi Roberts	454	1.0%	-1.1%

Wirral West

LAB HOLD

Majority: 5,365, 12.2% | Turnout: 43,951, 78.5% | Electorate: 55,995 | EU Ref: 42.8% Leave

PARTY	CANDIDATE	VOTES	SHARE	CHANGE 2015
Labour	Margaret Greenwood	23,866	54.3%	9.2%
Conservative	Tony Caldeira	18,501	42.1%	-2.1%
Liberal Democrat	Peter Reisdorf	1,155	2.6%	-0.8%
Green	John Coyne	429	1.0%	1.0%

Witham

CON HOLD

Majority: 18,646, 37.9% | Turnout: 49,241, 71.2% | Electorate: 69,137 | EU Ref: 60.8% Leave

PARTY	CANDIDATE	VOTES	SHARE	CHANGE 2015
Conservative	Priti Patel	31,670	64.3%	6.8%
Labour	Phil Barlow	13,024	26.4%	10.6%
Liberal Democrat	Jo Hayes	2,715	5.5%	-0.6%
Green	James Abbott	1,832	3.7%	-0.6%

Witney

CON HOLD

Majority: 21,241, 34.8% | Turnout: 60,927, 73.6% | Electorate: 82,727 | EU Ref: 46.3% Leave

PARTY	CANDIDATE	VOTES	SHARE	CHANGE 2015
Conservative	Robert Courts	33,839	55.5%	-4.7%
Labour	Laetisia Carter	12,598	20.7%	3.5%
Liberal Democrat	Liz Leffman	12,457	20.4%	13.7%
Green	Claire Lasko	1,053	1.7%	-3.4%
UK Independence Party	Alexander Craig	980	1.6%	-7.5%

Woking

CON HOLD

Majority: 16,724, 30.2% | Turnout: 55,246, 72.5% | Electorate: 76,170 | EU Ref: 44.1% Leave

PARTY	CANDIDATE	VOTES	SHARE	CHANGE 2015
Conservative	Jonathan Lord	29,903	54.1%	-2.1%
Labour	Fiona Colley	13,179	23.9%	7.7%
Liberal Democrat	Will Forster	9,711	17.6%	5.9%
UK Independence Party	Troy De Leon	1,161	2.1%	-9.2%
Green	James Brierley	1,092	2.0%	-2.1%
Independent	Hassan Akberali	200	0.4%	40.0%

Wokingham

CON HOLD

Majority: 18,798, 31.5% | Turnout: 59,690, 75.1% | Electorate: 79,111 | EU Ref: 42.5% Leave

PARTY	CANDIDATE	VOTES	SHARE	CHANGE 2015
Conservative	John Redwood	33,806	56.6%	-1.1%
Labour	Andy Croy	15,008	25.1%	10.6%
Liberal Democrat	Clive Jones	9,512	15.9%	2.4%
Green	Russell Seymour	1,364	2.3%	-1.5%

Wolverhampton North East

LAB HOLD

Majority: 4,587, 12.5% | Turnout: 36,508, 60.0% | Electorate: 60,770 | EU Ref: 67.9% Leave

PARTY	CANDIDATE	VOTES	SHARE	CHANGE 2015
Labour	Emma Reynolds	19,282	52.8%	6.7%
Conservative	Sarah Macken	14,695	40.3%	10.3%
UK Independence Party	Graham Eardley	1,479	4.1%	-15.1%
Liberal Democrat	Ian Jenkins	570	1.6%	-1.2%
Green	Clive Wood	482	1.3%	-0.7%

Wolverhampton South East

LAB HOLD

Majority: 8,514, 23.4% | Turnout: 36,304, 60.2% | Electorate: 60,301 | EU Ref: 68.8% Leave

PARTY	CANDIDATE	VOTES	SHARE	CHANGE 2015
Labour	Pat McFadden	21,137	58.2%	4.9%
Conservative	Kieran Mullan	12,623	34.8%	12.4%
UK Independence Party	Barry Hodgson	1,675	4.6%	-15.7%
Liberal Democrat	Ben Mathis	448	1.2%	-1.1%
Green	Amy Bertaut	421	1.2%	-0.6%

Wolverhampton South West

LAB HOLD

Majority: 2,185, 5.2% | Turnout: 42,346, 70.6% | Electorate: 59,971 | EU Ref: 53.6% Leave

PARTY	CANDIDATE	VOTES	SHARE	CHANGE 2015
Labour	Eleanor Smith	20,899	49.4%	6.1%
Conservative	Paul Uppal	18,714	44.2%	3.0%
UK Independence Party	Rob Jones	1,012	2.4%	-8.3%
Liberal Democrat	Sarah Quarmby	784	1.9%	-0.3%
Green	Andrea Cantrill	579	1.4%	-1.3%
Independent	Jagmeet Singh	358	0.8%	0.8%

Worcester

CON HOLD

Majority: 2,508, 4.9% | Turnout: 51,423, 69.6% | Electorate: 73,893 | EU Ref: 53.7% Leave

PARTY	CANDIDATE	VOTES	SHARE	CHANGE 2015
Conservative	Robin Walker	24,731	48.1%	2.8%
Labour	Joy Squires	22,223	43.2%	9.3%
Liberal Democrat	Stephen Kearney	1,757	3.4%	0.0%
UK Independence Party	Paul Hickling	1,354	2.6%	-10.2%
Green	Louis Stephen	1,211	2.4%	-1.7%
Independent	Alex Rugg	109	0.2%	0.2%
Compass Party	Mark Shuker	38	0.1%	0.1%

Workington

LAB HOLD

Majority: 3,925, 9.4% | Turnout: 41,676, 69.2% | Electorate: 60,265 | EU Ref: 60.3% Leave

PARTY	CANDIDATE	VOTES	SHARE	CHANGE 2015
Labour	Sue Hayman	21,317	51.1%	8.8%
Conservative	Clark Vasey	17,392	41.7%	11.6%
UK Independence Party	George Kemp	1,556	3.7%	-15.9%
Liberal Democrat	Phill Roberts	1,133	2.7%	-1.7%
Independent	Roy Ivinson	278	0.7%	0.2%

Worsley & Eccles South

LAB HOLD

Majority: 8,379, 18.4% | Turnout: 45,642, 61.9% | Electorate: 73,689 | EU Ref: 61.4% Leave

PARTY	CANDIDATE	VOTES	SHARE	CHANGE 2015
Labour	Barbara Keeley	26,046	57.1%	12.8%
Conservative	Iain Lindley	17,667	38.7%	8.6%
Liberal Democrat	Kate Clarkson	1,087	2.4%	-0.2%
Green	Tom Dylan	842	1.8%	-1.1%

Worthing West

CON HOLD

Majority: 12,090, 22.2% | Turnout: 54,503, 70.7% | Electorate: 77,757 | EU Ref: 56.1% Leave

PARTY	CANDIDATE	VOTES	SHARE	CHANGE 2015
Conservative	Peter Bottomley	30,181	55.4%	3.9%
Labour	Beccy Cooper	18,091	33.2%	17.5%
Liberal Democrat	Hazel Thorpe	2,982	5.5%	-3.3%
UK Independence Party	Mark Withers	1,635	3.0%	-15.3%
Green	Benjamin Cornish	1,614	3.0%	-2.8%

Wrexham

LAB HOLD

Majority: 1,832, 5.2% | Turnout: 35,092, 69.6% | Electorate: 49,881 | EU Ref: 57.3% Leave

PARTY	CANDIDATE	VOTES	SHARE	CHANGE 2015
Labour	Ian Lucas	17,153	48.9%	11.7%
Conservative	Andrew Atkinson	15,321	43.7%	12.0%
Plaid Cymru	Carrie Harper	1,753	5.0%	-2.6%
Liberal Democrat	Carole O'Toole	865	2.5%	-2.8%

Wycombe

CON HOLD

Majority: 6,578, 12.3% | Turnout: 53,493, 69.4% | Electorate: 77,087 | EU Ref: 48.0% Leave

PARTY	CANDIDATE	VOTES	SHARE	CHANGE 2015
Conservative	Steve Baker	26,766	50.0%	-1.4%
Labour	Rafiq Raja	20,188	37.7%	15.2%
Liberal Democrat	Steve Guy	4,147	7.8%	-1.1%
UK Independence Party	Richard Phoenix	1,210	2.3%	-7.8%
Green	Peter Sims	1,182	2.2%	-3.8%

Wyre & Preston North

CON HOLD
Majority: 12,246, 23.3% | Turnout: 52,646, 72.8% | Electorate: 72,319 | EU Ref: 54.0% Leave

PARTY	CANDIDATE	VOTES	SHARE	CHANGE 2015
Conservative	Ben Wallace	30,684	58.3%	5.1%
Labour	Michelle Heaton-Bentley	18,438	35.0%	10.2%
Liberal Democrat	John Potter	2,551	4.8%	-0.6%
Green	Ruth Norbury	973	1.8%	-1.6%

Wyre Forest

CON HOLD
Majority: 13,334, 26.1% | Turnout: 51,129, 65.8% | Electorate: 77,758 | EU Ref: 63.1% Leave

PARTY	CANDIDATE	VOTES	SHARE	CHANGE 2015
Conservative	Mark Garnier	29,859	58.4%	13.1%
Labour	Matthew Lamb	16,525	32.3%	13.1%
Liberal Democrat	Shazu Miah	1,943	3.8%	1.3%
UK Independence Party	George Connolly	1,777	3.5%	-12.6%
Green	Brett Caulfield	1,025	2.0%	-0.3%

Wythenshawe & Sale East

LAB HOLD
Majority: 14,944, 32.6% | Turnout: 45,846, 60.0% | Electorate: 76,361 | EU Ref: 49.9% Leave

PARTY	CANDIDATE	VOTES	SHARE	CHANGE 2015
Labour	Mike Kane	28,525	62.2%	12.1%
Conservative	Fiona Green	13,581	29.6%	3.9%
Liberal Democrat	William Jones	1,504	3.3%	-1.2%
UK Independence Party	Mike Bayley-Sanderson	1,475	3.2%	-11.5%
Green	Dan Jerrome	576	1.3%	-2.6%
Independent	Luckson Francis-Augustine	185	0.4%	0.4%

Yeovil

CON HOLD
Majority: 14,723, 24.8% | Turnout: 59,404, 71.6% | Electorate: 82,916 | EU Ref: 59.3% Leave

PARTY	CANDIDATE	VOTES	SHARE	CHANGE 2015
Conservative	Marcus Fysh	32,369	54.5%	12.0%
Liberal Democrat	Jo Roundell Greene	17,646	29.7%	-3.4%
Labour	Ian Martin	7,418	12.5%	5.4%
Green	Robert Wood	1,052	1.8%	-2.1%
Independent	Katy Pritchard	919	1.5%	1.5%

Ynys Môn

LAB HOLD
Majority: 5,259, 14.1% | Turnout: 37,367, 70.6% | Electorate: 52,921 | EU Ref: 50.9% Leave

PARTY	CANDIDATE	VOTES	SHARE	CHANGE 2015
Labour	Albert Owen	15,643	41.9%	10.7%
Conservative	Tomos Davies	10,384	27.8%	6.6%
Plaid Cymru	Ieuan Wyn Jones	10,237	27.4%	-3.1%
UK Independence Party	James Turner	624	1.7%	-13.0%
Liberal Democrat	Sarah Jackson	479	1.3%	-0.9%

York Central

LAB HOLD
Majority: 18,575, 35.0% | Turnout: 53,088, 68.7% | Electorate: 77,315 | EU Ref: 38.5% Leave

PARTY	CANDIDATE	VOTES	SHARE	CHANGE 2015
Labour	Rachael Maskell	34,594	65.2%	22.8%
Conservative	Ed Young	16,019	30.2%	1.9%
Liberal Democrat	Nick Love	2,475	4.7%	-3.3%

York Outer

CON HOLD

Majority: 8,289, 14.4% | Turnout: 57,427, 75.7% | Electorate: 75,835 | EU Ref: 44.9% Leave

PARTY	CANDIDATE	VOTES	SHARE	CHANGE 2015
Conservative	Julian Sturdy	29,356	51.1%	2.0%
Labour	Luke Charters-Reid	21,067	36.7%	11.9%
Liberal Democrat	James Blanchard	5,910	10.3%	-1.3%
Green	Bethan Vincent	1,094	1.9%	-2.8%